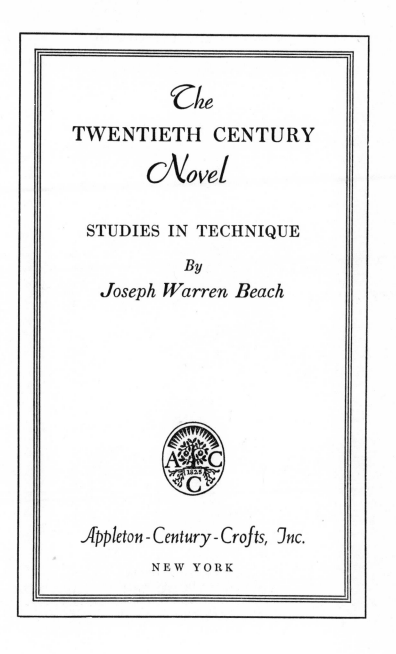

The TWENTIETH CENTURY *Novel*

STUDIES IN TECHNIQUE

By

Joseph Warren Beach

Appleton-Century-Crofts, Inc.

NEW YORK

628-16

PRINTED IN U. S. A.

E-07301

"There's no such thing!" Alice was beginning very angrily, but the Hatter and the March Hare went "Sh! sh!" and the Dormouse sulkily remarked, "If you can't be civil, you'd better finish the story for yourself."

—Lewis Caroll: Alice's Adventures in Wonderland

CONTENTS

PART ONE: PRELIMINARIES

PART TWO: THE DRAMATIC IDEAL

PART THREE: THE WELL-MADE NOVEL

PART ONE: PRELIMINARIES

Je commis ce que toujours je considérai comme une inconvenance: dès le potage, je m'exprimai en termes abstraits.

—MAURICE BARRÈS: "Le Jardin de Bérénice"

Wagner discovered that an opera had much better be melody from end to end, and the realistic school following on Wagner's footsteps discovered that a novel had much better be all narrative—an uninterrupted flow of narrative.

—GEORGE MOORE: "Confessions of a Young Man"

I

PROGRAM

It is my purpose in this book to trace certain outstanding features of form in the twentieth-century novel in English. The reader will understand from the start that this is not a general critical study of the twentieth-century novel. It is meant for a study in the evolution of novelistic technique.

It is of course impossible to discuss novelistic technique without some regard for the subject-matter, the intentions, of the writers considered. For obviously the object of technique is to help realize the artistic intention, and we shall see over and over again how the specific effect sought by the artist determines the technical methods consciously or unconsciously chosen. But there is a tendency in all the arts for craftsmen of a given period to show a preference for such and such subject-matter, to share such and such artistic aims, and to choose their methods accordingly. And while it is all-important for a novelist to have fine intentions and to realize them adequately, and while the ultimate business of criticism is to appreciate the author's intentions and determine how far he has realized them, the fact remains that his technique is the means by which he does realize them, and that the study of technique is a useful preparation for the business of criticism, as well as an interesting thing in itself. It is a preparation for their business which has been much neglected by critics, with the result that not merely does great confusion prevail in the criticism of novels—which is more or less the normal condition of criticism in all the arts—but we do not even have available for the description of novelistic technique terms approximately precise and generally understood.

This is not a state of things peculiar to contemporary criticism. Indeed, there has never been a time in the history of the novel when so much attention has been paid as at present to matters of technique, and the prospect is that they will be much better understood in the future than they have been in the past. We might almost say that the only English writer in the past who has given extended and detailed consideration to questions of technique is Henry James. What Fielding was most often occupied with in the critical essays prefixed to each book of "Tom Jones" was truth to nature, and that was the virtually exclusive concern of Thackeray, of George Eliot, of Meredith, in the frequent critical apologies thrust into the text of their novels. Strange to say, the novelists most interested in technique—that is, in the way the story was told—before the time of James, were probably Dickens and Wilkie Collins, novelists whose regard for truth to nature was so slight that we might not suppose they were concerned with anything so serious-sounding as technique. As a matter of fact, as I shall try to show farther on, their very want of concern for truth to nature—their want of realism—was one reason for their taking technique seriously.

As for the French naturalists, whose influence began to be so strongly felt in England in the eighteen-nineties, while they were no doubt great technicians, and had significant things to say here and there on the subject of structural technique (see Chapter XII below), what they most frequently discussed was either the "human document" (Zola, the Goncourt brothers), or the precise, the unique word (Flaubert, Maupassant)—the one a matter of "scientific" truth and the other, as I should classify it, a matter of style. And these, I imagine, were the great preoccupations of George Moore in his novels written under the influence of the French school.

Since 1920, the situation has radically changed. There have appeared three remarkably fine books specially devoted to the study of technique in the novel, Percy Lubbock's "The Craft of Fiction" (1921), Carl H. Grabo's "The Technique of the Novel" (1928), and Edwin Muir's "The Structure of the Novel" (1929). And besides these there is considerable incidental reference to technique in studies of a broader scope, such as "The Writing of Fiction," by Edith Wharton (1925), "Aspects of the Novel," by E. M. Forster (1927), "The History of the Novel in England," by Robert Morss Lovett and Helen Sard Hughes (1932), and, naturally, in nearly everything that has been written about James Joyce since the appearance of "Ulysses" (1922). Many other important books on the novel, on both the technical and the historical side, I have listed in a bibliographical note at the end of this study.

It is impossible to discuss the subject of technique at the present day without making acknowledgments in particular to Mr. Percy Lubbock. No one has written so beautifully on this special subject as he, and no one has given so complete an outline of what falls within its scope, nor so well-balanced, nor so critically sober. But, as Mr. Lubbock in several places lets us know, he has not undertaken to work out the details of the subject which he has so masterfully outlined, but has left untouched many important aspects of the craft of fiction. And that is one thing I propose for myself—to fill in some of the details, to go more minutely into what we may call the mechanics of the art. And then, Mr. Lubbock's is a general study of the craft of fiction without regard to particular periods and countries, and the latest of the novels discussed by him, James's "Ambassadors," was published in 1903. Whereas what I propose is a study of the novel in English in the twentieth century, with earlier periods and foreign fiction used for background and terms of comparison; and it is the later novels of James, and more particularly "The Ambassadors," which form my point of departure, as they formed the goal, the limit, of the evolution traced by Mr. Lubbock.

The whole of Mr. Lubbock's book is concerned, in the last analysis, with the balance and interplay of what he calls the pictorial (roughly, the expository, descriptive, discursive) and the dramatic (scenical) elements of the novel. And, having set forth the method by which James, in "The Ambassadors," turns pictorial matter into drama by straining it through the consciousness of the leading character, he concludes that here "the art of dramatizing the picture of somebody's experience . . . touches its limit. There is indeed no further for it to go." On the very next page, however, he guards against the possible notion that James, by touching the limit in this direction, has exhausted the possibilities of technical evolution. Through the work of the various men he has been discussing, "the range of method," he says, "is permanently enlarged; it is proved, once for all, that the craft of fiction has larger resources than might have been suspected before." And he ventures the guess that

> the novel may now be starting upon a fresh life, after the tremendous career it has had already. The discovery of the degree to which it may be enhanced dramatically—this may be a point of departure from which it will set out with vigour renewed; perhaps it has done so by this time. [He was writing the year before *Ulysses,* and he ignores Conrad.] Anyhow it is clear that an immense variety of modulations, mixtures, harmonies of method yet untried, are open to it if it chooses to avail itself. . . . There is still so much to be done, after a couple of centuries of novel-writing without a pause; there are unheard-of experiments to be made. A novel such as *The Ambassadors* may give no more than a hint of the rich and profound effects waiting to be achieved by the laying of method upon method, and criticism may presently be called on to

analyze the delicate process much more closely than I now attempt; it is to be hoped so indeed.

There are, says Mr. Lubbock, unheard-of experiments to be made. . . . They have already been made, some of them, by Joseph Conrad, D. H. Lawrence, Dorothy Richardson, James Joyce, Virginia Woolf, John Dos Passos, to name a few of the experimenters. And already criticism is called on to analyze the delicate process. But curiously enough, many of these unheard-of experiments have taken their start just from that paradoxical art, exemplified by James, of "dramatizing the picture of somebody's experience" by straining it through the consciousness of the character himself. They have taken their start at the point where James left off, and they have carried the process further. At least, they have invented such novel means of picturing the consciousness of the character that it amounts to a further extension of the method. And so it turns out that, in a sense, the method does not "touch its limit" in James. There actually was further for it to go.

But if the new experimenters have carried further this special technical feature of James (and his school), which evidently they found to their taste, there are other features of the school which they quite as evidently did not like. And the experimental type of novel represents in about equal proportions an intensification of James's methods and a reaction against them. So that on the whole, the novel since, say, 1920 has an aspect as distinct from that of James and his school as the novels of that school have from those of Dickens and Thackeray.

Now, the novels of James which represent the culmination of his method are products of the twentieth century. Still more obviously of our century are the novels of his leading disciples: Edith Wharton's "Age of Innocence," for example, dating from as late as 1920, and Joseph Hergesheimer's "Cytherea" and "The Bright Shawl" from 1922.

So that the school from which the newer experimenters have reacted falls well within the scope of our inquiry. And as there are many aspects of this general school of writing which Mr. Lubbock has left out of consideration, I have no hesitation in beginning with an extensive account of this type of novel—which I call the well-made novel.

"The well-made novel" is a term I have invented for my own convenience. It is obviously modeled on the familiar term "the well-made play." "The well-made play" is a term applied especially to certain French dramatic contraptions of the nineteenth century notable not so much for their seriousness as for the perfection with which they were constructed for their dramatic ends. They were perhaps called well-made plays because that was about all that could be said in their favor. So that the term carries with it a slight sense of disparagement. But that is not the sense which I wish to convey by the term "well-made novel": I should like to have it free from either disparagement or approval, except in so far as it does lay stress on careful fashioning in a strictly formal way. I use this term to indicate certain tendencies in form well exemplified, for example, in "The Ambassadors" and "The Age of Innocence."

In the same way I shall use the term "expressionistic" to apply to the tendencies in general which mark a reaction against the well-made novel, a going beyond it, at least such of them as can be associated more or less with Joyce's "Ulysses." It will be understood that I am not using the term "expressionistic" in a precise scientific and historical sense. Even in Germany, where it was definitely applied to a school of writing which flourished approximately between 1913 and 1925, it is impossible to give a definition of the term which will cover all the manifestations of the impulse in question. German expressionistic poetry is a different thing from expressionistic drama, and the drama quite different from the prose fiction. The novels in English which I discuss under this heading have probably a closer kinship to the German poetry and drama of expressionism than to the typical fiction of that school. In general the English novels have a more realistic cast than the German, and they are very seldom characterized by the strong religious and emotional tone of the German writers.

The term was derived from painting and then applied by analogy to the allied arts of sculpture, music, and literature. In origin it referred to those various movements in painting, French, Italian, Russian, German, which constituted a reaction against impressionism. They were all characterized by the desire not to be bound to the literal rendering of outward appearances in nature, but to make art a vehicle of the artist's personal reaction—an expression, as the Germans say, of his own spiritual life. And so, as the Germans go on to say in their metaphysical manner, they wish to subordinate the merely superficial and accidental aspect of things to the absolute, the essential, the inner reality. The movement begins with painters like Cézanne, Gauguin, and Van Gogh, with their freer handling of forms and colors, organized according to a rhythm which is more personal to the artist than imposed by the subject. It passes into the more arbitrary futurism of painters like Kandinsky, in which it is vain to seek for any precise subject taken from nature. And it reaches its extreme logical development in the cubists, who deny the validity of sensuous appearances as a subject for art, but aim to make an artistic abstraction of the essential forms found in nature.

In applying terms like "expressionism" and "impressionism" to works of fiction, I wish to suggest the roughly parallel development in our time of the several arts, being as they are but varied manifestations of the same spiritual life, the same cultural evolution. In using the term "expressionistic," or sometimes "post-impressionistic," I have particularly in mind the notion of abstract composition derived from painting. And since my subject is technique, I am more especially concerned with departures from the conventional type of novel on the side of form. I call certain writers expressionistic by way of indicating the extreme freedom and unconventionality with which they handle and reorganize the subject-matter offered them by life, transcending by methods primarily technical the more or less realistic stuff in which they work.

2

Once again I must remind the reader that this does not pretend to be a comprehensive history of fiction in the period covered. Of necessity I have been obliged to omit detailed consideration of many writers of distinction, such as Somerset Maugham, E. M. Forster, Frances Newman, and Pearl Buck, either because the writer in question does not stand for anything specially distinctive in the evolution of technique, or because what he stands for is sufficiently exemplified in other novelists discussed.

In general I have left out of account novelists of a strongly romantic cast, like W. H. Hudson, and in particular writers of historical romance, because they would too greatly complicate the subject. The air of reality sought by romancers may often mean a high effort of the imagination, and it has its bearing, in books like "Green Mansions," on certain questions of technique like that of the limited point of view. But it is, after all, a very different matter from the reality sought by writers who are dealing with contemporary and familiar things. Conrad is a special case, since his personal experience brought him into such close contact with picturesque and exotic material, and his passion to get to the bottom of human motives gives a depth and seriousness to subjects which, with most writers, could be classified as simply romantic. But it does not follow that we need clutter up our discussion with references to writers like H. M. Tomlinson, F. Brett Young, and William McFee, however good they may be in their way, and however much they may remind us of technical procedures of Conrad.

What I propose to do, then, is to trace first the tendencies culminating in the well-made novel, and then the reaction—the tendencies culminating in the expressionistic novel. Among the forces of reaction against the well-made novel, I include such disparate figures as Dreiser, whose impatient naturalism brings him back to an earlier, less rigidly formal composition, and Conrad, tireless experimenter, for whom the novel is a plastic form to be constantly reshaped in accordance with his ever changing intention and design.

In thus tracing an evolution, I wish to avoid the implication, so likely to creep into criticism of any of the arts, that what we are observing is an advance in the sense of an improvement on what went before. Let no one suppose I am wishing to imply that the novels of the 1920's are better work than the novels of the 1900's because they come later, or that the novels of the 1900's are better than those of the 1850's or the 1750's. Altogether apart from technique, one must take into account the stature of the man, and we do not meet every day a man of the stature of Fielding or Hardy. I do not even mean that the later work is better technically. For technique must be judged by reference to intention, and the intention of a Fielding or a Hardy is a very different thing from that of a Galsworthy or a Dos Passos. And most often, where there is a positive gain in technique, there may be some loss to match it, even a loss in technique. The discovery of a new device does not necessarily mean a technical improvement, since it is possible for the discoverer, and still more his imitators, to overdo it, to exaggerate it, to misapply it, and to produce an ingenious technical monstrosity rather than a work of art.

Still, it is obvious that, with the passing of time, new technical devices are discovered and tried out, and that he who comes later has at least the advantage of the experimentation of his predecessors. He is free to profit, if he can, by their successes and mistakes; and among the various procedures of the art, to choose those which best suit his particular needs. He may, if it suits his need, make use of procedures unknown to Dickens or Meredith, and so produce a better novel than he at least could have produced in 1850 or 1870. For him, at any rate, the passing of time involves progress, an evolution for the better.

There is one circumstance that tends to create the dubious impression that what we are following is a progressive improvement in the art of the novel. In tracing the tendencies that produced the work of the 1900's, or again the reaction of the 1920's, we are obliged to put ourselves at the point of view of the writers concerned. We have to consider what it was that they found unsatisfactory in their predecessors, what changes they wished to bring about, what particular improvements they were making. So that the emphasis, at least in the beginning, is all on the side of progress made rather than of ground lost. This is particularly true for the men of the 1920's. In the case of the well-made novel, we have at least the reaction of the 1920's to serve as "control." In the very act of tracing this movement, we make necessarily the critique of the well-made novel. But in the case of the expressionistic novel there is no later reaction to serve as control; at any rate, none sufficiently well defined, vigorous, and long-standing, to amount to much for this purpose. There we have nothing to fall back upon but our knowledge of the classics and our native critical sense.

But native critical sense is notoriously inadequate to deal with strictly contemporary work. We breathe the same air as these men. We are part and parcel of the social, the philosophical, the esthetic complex out of which they have taken shape. We cannot see them in perspective. Their triumphs are our triumphs. Their novelty is still novelty for us. Their experiments—it is as if we were in the laboratory with them, waiting on the result of their still uncompleted experiments. We are too busy making out what they are after to be able to judge of their success. And we are accessory to their crimes. If, at times, measuring them by the standards of Fielding or Hardy, we are inclined to wonder if they are decadent artists, we know that in that case we are decadents with them. And we have the pride of what we are. We had rather be damned with our own people than be saved with the dead.

On the whole, we shall do better to abjure the attempt at absolute criticism, at least for the time being. We shall be quite well enough occupied with a less ambitious program. What we want to study is certain procedures in the making of fiction, and the kinds of effect associated with those procedures. We shall not for a moment suppose that technique covers the whole ground, but we shall try to see how much ground it does cover, how far we can say, of such and such an artistic intention, it is best served by such and such a procedure. Necessarily we shall at times be obliged to consider the philosophical background, the temper of the age, since that has so much to do with the intention, and the intention determines the technique. The work of Joyce implies a different psychology from that of Edith Wharton; the work of Dos Passos a different social slant from that of George Eliot. But such considerations will be quite incidental to our main object. Our main object will be, over a limited field, to get at the effects intended and the technical means by which these effects are secured.

II

EXIT AUTHOR

In a bird's-eye view of the English novel from Fielding to Ford, the one thing that will impress you more than any other is the disappearance of the author. In Fielding and Scott, in Thackeray and George Eliot, the author is everywhere present in person to see that you are properly informed on all the circumstances of the action, to explain the characters to you and insure your forming the right opinion of them, to scatter nuggets of wisdom and good feeling along the course of the story, and to point out how, from the failures and successes of the characters, you may form a sane and right philosophy of conduct.

When he had finished "The Heart of Midlothian," Sir Walter was evidently worried over his having featured the unhallowed love-affair of Effie Deans and her bandit lover, and especially having got his frivolous lassie legally married and brought into high society. This happy outcome of her affair was demanded to fill up the cup of happiness of her virtuous sister Jeanie and to shed a rosy light over the concluding pages of the romance. The good baronet had taken pains to point out that even marriage and social exaltation did not make a happy couple of these sinners; but even so, he was afraid that a careless reader, some heedless girl, might be more dazzled by the melancholy great lady than by her contented sister married to the Scotch minister, and he felt obliged to add, in large capitals, an admonition to the Reader:

This tale will not be told in vain, if it shall be found to illustrate the great truth, that guilt, though it may attain temporal splendor, can never confer real happiness; that the evil consequences of our crimes long survive their commission, and, like the ghosts of the murdered, forever haunt the steps of the malefactor; and that the paths of virtue, though seldom those of worldly greatness, are always those of pleasantness and peace.

This tradition has survived even in the work of a novelist so thoroughly of our time as Mr. Ford Madox Ford. At least, in his dedicatory epistles, Mr. Ford does not hesitate to explain what it is he has been attempting to say, as for example in "A Man Could Stand Up":

> This is what the late war was like: this is how modern fighting of the organized, scientific type affects the mind. If, for reasons of gain or, as is still more likely, out of dislike for collective types other than your own, you choose to permit your rulers to embark on another war, this–or something very accentuated along similar lines–is what you will have to put up with!

But the resemblance here is superficial. It is only in his comment on the book that Mr. Ford permits himself to point out the moral of the thing. It is only there that he is the philosopher. Within the limits of his story, in his striking series of war novels, he does not appear at all. The story tells itself; the story speaks for itself. The author does not apologize for his characters; he does not give an account of them; he does not describe them; he does not even tell us what they do, but has them tell us, themselves. Above all, he has them tell us what they think, what they feel, what impressions beat in on their minds from the situations in which they find themselves. "To this determination—to use my friend's eyes as a medium [he is speaking of his central character, Tietjens]—I am adhering in this series of books." "And you have here his mental reactions and his reflections—which are not, *not*, NOT presented as those of the author."

This is a great outstanding feature of technique since

the time of Henry James, that the story shall tell itself, being conducted through the impressions of the characters. It is this which finally differentiates fiction from history and philosophy and science. For the most part in the old masters English fiction, and French fiction too for that matter, is a branch of philosophy or history. It is, to be sure, constantly tending to escape into the state of pure fiction, which is a moving picture of life itself, and the vivid imaginations of the great novelists are forever making us forget that it is anything but fiction pure and simple. But the intellectual and moral seriousness of the authors is working in the opposite direction—their responsibility, their sense of what they owe to the high calling of letters, not to mention the desire to make a display of their own excellent qualities: good sense, refined sentiment, humor, and a subtle understanding of the springs of human nature. It was an excellent device of Fielding to collect his sundry reflections and speculations into the introductory essays of each book, thus leaving the narrative portions of the story relatively unencumbered with this irrelevant material. Irrelevant, that is, from the point of view of story, of the illusion of life; relevant enough from the point of view of moral philosophy. With Scott and Thackeray, with Trollope and Meredith, this essay matter is scattered through the narrative, where it tends to reduce greatly the dramatic tension, the illusion of life. That is the point of objection. We cannot be the worse for the wisdom of these big men, these large souls. But, for better for worse, the fashion has changed; we like fiction unadulterated; we like the sense of taking part in an actual, a present experience, without the interference of an authorial guide.

In that series of chapters which constitutes the dramatic climax of "The Heart of Midlothian," Scott presents the meeting of Effie and Jeanie Deans in the Tolbooth prison, and the trial of Effie for child-murder. It is within the power of Jeanie to secure the acquittal of her sister if she will but swear to an untruth—if she will testify that Effie confessed to her before the birth of her child. Effie cannot understand why her sister will not do so little as that to save her life. And during the trial, through all the legal expositions of the counsel, we wait in suspense to see if Jeanie cannot overcome this fatal scruple of conscience. This is the stuff of drama; emotional stuff of the highest power; and these scenes can hardly be read even by a fastidious reader brought up on Conrad or Stevenson without some sense of their force. But their force is many degrees less than it might be had Scott been content to let the story tell itself—simply to present, for example, the impressions of Jeanie, or those of Effie, or those of the pious father who feels so profoundly the disgrace to his name. Instead of this, with the ranging view of the historian who is equally well at home everywhere, he tells us something of how each character appeared, something of how each felt, something of how the audience were impressed in the trial scene, and the judge, and the lawyers—dispersing our interest over too many different people for it to maintain any intensity.

But worst of all, he indulges freely throughout in those elegantly patronizing terms of conventional pity for the characters that render not the agony and tenseness of the situation to those taking part so much as the good heart and correct sentiments of the author. Effie is not Effie but the prisoner, or the unhappy prisoner; she and her sister are not Effie and Jeanie but the mourners; the gaoler is the hard-hearted turnkey. Especially is the trial scene decorated with such easy phrases of sentiment. Scott talks about the awful scene; he commends the judge for sharing in the general sympathy. On Jeanie's truthful declaration which means the condemnation of her sister, "A deep groan passed through the Court. It was echoed by one deeper and more agonized from *the unfortunate father*. The hope to which unconsciously and in spite of himself, he had recently clung, had now dissolved, and *the venerable old man* fell forward senseless on the floor of the Court-house, with his head at the foot of *his terrified daughter. The unfortunate prisoner,* with impotent passion, strove with the guards betwixt whom she was placed." [1]

There are two great offenses here against narrative art. In the first place, the scene is presented in tabloid. There has been no proper focusing of attention on either the old man or his daughter, no preparation of the reader by those little forward-looking references that arouse suspense. And when the bit of physical action comes, as, presumably, the climax of the scene, it is so briefly and conventionally disposed of that it sounds like a mere stage direction. You have but to compare this with some of the critical moments in Hardy or Moore to realize how completely Scott here neglected his opportunity, failed to meet the challenge of a scene to be presented. And his phrases of sympathetic description, which are the merest apology for neglecting his duty as a story-teller, are in themselves another offense to the present-day reader, with his notions of how a story should be told. For the author, instead of making us feel the poignancy and dramatic power of the scene, instead of making the action carry its own emotion, must needs tell us, himself, how we are to feel about it.

This manner of writing continues right down through the masters of the novel in the nineteenth century. Among the worst offenders are several of the greatest novelists. They seem to think it more elegant to refer at regular intervals not to Jeanie Deans or Eleanor Bold or Isabel Archer, but to "our heroine." And they do love to spill the phials of their pity over the gentle victims of their sympathy. Thackeray's Amelia is "our gentle Amelia." Trollope's Mr. Arabin is "poor Mr. Arabin"! George Eliot, in particular, makes lavish use of this ingredient of expressed

[1] In this passage, as in a number of others quoted throughout the book, I have italicized certain words which I wish to call particularly to the reader's attention.

pity in the sauce with which she smothers and serves up her excellent and erring people. Dorothea Brooke is the poor child; Rosamond Vincy is poor thing; there is poor Lydgate and poor Mrs. Bulstrode, and God knows how many other suffering bundles of protoplasm. Maggie Tulli ver in "The Mill on the Floss" is poor Maggie, by natural right as misunderstood and persecuted woman. In "Adam Bede," there is of course poor Seth, and (for the drunkard who was so providentially taken off) poor wandering father; and Arthur Donnithorne and Hetty, on the point of succumbing to sin—"Poor things! It was a pity they were not in that golden age of childhood when they would have stood face to face, eyeing each other with timid liking, then given each other a little butterfly kiss, and toddled off to play together." Above all is Hetty always and everywhere "poor little Hetty," "poor wandering Hetty," etc.

In the case of Hetty Sorrel, George Eliot's sympathy is by no means unmixed. This great bluestocking, this Victorian philosopher and companion of philosophers, this scholar with a face like a horse, could not regard with unqualified sympathy a creature so frivolous, so shallow, so brainless, and—let us not forget—so pretty as Hetty Sorrel. And Mary Ann Evans, living nobly and conscientiously in a state of sin, pioneer as she was of a responsible and rational attitude toward the relation between man and woman, could not but stiffen, with irony and scorn, the sympathy she felt for this rudderless little craft. One of the most remarkable instances of the Victorian passion for the edifying is that chapter entitled "The Two Bed-Chambers," in which George Eliot takes occasion to bring in vivid contrast the weak and selfish girl putting on her glass earrings before her mirror and the pious and beautiful soul, Dinah Morris, lost in silent prayer and troubling herself over the state of her erring sister. This is likewise an instance of the disposition to stack the cards against the one of whom we are not to approve.

> How pretty *the little puss* looks in that odd dress! [exclaims the author with the face of a horse.] It would be the easiest folly in the world to fall in love with her: there is such a sweet baby-like roundness about her face and figure; the delicate dark rings of hair lie so charmingly about her ears and neck . . . Ah, what a prize the man gets who wins a sweet bride like Hetty!

And there follows a long page of such ironic commendations; for it is thus that Adam Bede was taken in. And then the author makes her apology for Adam.

> Before you despise Adam as deficient in penetration, pray ask yourself if you were ever predisposed to believe evil of any pretty woman—if you ever *could,* without hard, head-breaking demonstration, believe evil of the *one* supremely pretty woman who has bewitched you. No: people who love downy peaches are apt not to think of the stone, and sometimes jar their teeth terribly against it.

There are three things to be noted in such passages of George Eliot—three major tendencies of the Victorian novel which have, for good or ill, gone largely out of fashion in the twentieth century. There is the disposition to be edifying in a moral way. There is the fondness for talking the characters over with the reader, taking sides, and letting the reader know what attitude he should take. And there is the scientific passion for explaining the character, making us understand how the particular phenomenon before us illustrates the laws of human nature in general. These three tendencies are closely related and they are generally found together. Thackeray wishes to make us realize the sufferings of Amelia when she is neglected by George Osborne, and at the same time he points out how her predicament is typical of that to which women are reduced by our social ordinances:

> To whom could the poor little martyr tell these daily struggles and tortures? Her hero himself only half understood

her. She did not dare to own that the man she loved was her inferior, or to feel that she had given away her heart too soon. Given once, the pure, bashful maiden was too modest, too tender, too trustful, too weak, too much woman, to recall it. We are Turks with the affections of our women, and have made them subscribe to our doctrine too. We let their bodies go abroad liberally enough, with smiles and ringlets and pink bonnets to disguise them, instead of veils and yakmaks. But their souls must be seen by only one man, and they obey not unwillingly, and consent to remain at home as our slaves —ministering to us and doing drudgery for us.

It is in a similar vein that all these Victorians are prone to apologize for their characters' conduct, to defend them to us and put us in a better humor with them. George Eliot thinks it necessary to make a plea for the clergyman Mr. Irwine, because, though a man of pure Christian feeling, he had no theological enthusiasms. Trollope in the same way begs his reader not to be too hard on the Rev. Mr. Arabin. And when his heroine has been so impulsive as to box the ear of the odious Mr. Slope, he thinks it a proper occasion to devote a long page to her defense.

To the reader fresh from the novels of the year, or, let us say, from those of Conrad or James, of George Moore or Arnold Bennett, there is something quaint about this Victorian manner. And he is often apt to forget that he is dealing here with masterpieces of fictional art perhaps greater than any that have since been produced. It is so hard to maintain one's perspective, one's historical sense, one's sense of the relativity of values, in dealing with a school of art that has gone out of fashion. I am not at all certain that the development I am tracing may not even be a kind of degeneration—accompanying the gradual decline in vigor and spontaneity. We are doubtless incapable of rightly appraising the art of our own day, an art which is expressive of our own state of mind. The best we can do is to make out what is the artistic principle involved in our preference for a different method of story-telling.

What bothers us in the Victorian treatment of character is that it is a talking about the characters instead of a presentation of them; or that if they are presented, it is from without instead of from within. The author tells us as much as we need to know of the thoughts or motives of his people in order to understand their conduct; but he does not tell us, he does not make us feel, how the situation presents itself to these people themselves. Trollope, for example, is fond of telling us that such and such a character, at such a moment, is or is not in love with some one. He assures us, at a certain point in the story, that Eleanor Bold is not in love with the odious Mr. Slope. He tells us that Mr. Arabin is not in love with Eleanor, and then, in due course, that Mr. Arabin *is* in love with her but doesn't know it. On several occasions he feels it incumbent on him to analyze the feelings of Mr. Arabin. Thus we read:

> Mr. Arabin had heard from his friend of the probability of Eleanor's marriage with Mr. Slope with amazement, but not with incredulity. It has been said that he was not in love with Eleanor, and up to this period this certainly had been true. But as soon as he heard that she loved some one else, he began to be very fond of her himself. He did not make up his mind that he wished to have her for his wife; he had never thought of her, and did not now think of her, in connection with himself; but he experienced an inward indefinable feeling of deep regret, a gnawing sorrow, an unconquerable depression of spirits, and also a species of self-abasement, that he—he Mr. Arabin—had not done something to prevent that other he, that vile he, whom he so thoroughly despised, from carrying off this sweet prize.

Well, you say, this is all very good—precise, succinct, orderly, complete. It is a perfectly satisfactory general statement of the situation as it is known to the logical faculty. But it is in no sense an imaginative presentation of the facts; and to the imagination, to that faculty demanding that the story shall be *told,* it seems an empty and perfunctory substitute for the real thing. It is as arid and superficial as an algebraic formula. You cannot make us feel that your characters are heart-whole or that they are in love, by telling us that one or the other is true. And if you do make us feel that it is true, there is no need at all for telling us so in these prim and conventional words.

D. H. Lawrence has, first and last, I suppose, had as many men and women subject to the attraction of sex as any other English writer; and he generally satisfies his readers of the reality of the experience in question, however the readers may like it or dislike it. But I fancy that he has had very little to say about people's being in love. He does not tell us that people are in love, but he describes their sensations.

> A daze had come over his mind, he had another centre of consciousness. In his breast, or in his bowels, somewhere in his body, there had started another activity. It was as if a strong light were burning there, and he was blind within it, unable to know anything, except that this transfiguration burned between him and her, connecting them, like a secret power.

Now, there are no doubt features of this writing which will some day seem quite as quaint as the writing of George Eliot, and perhaps much less sane and wholesome, into the bargain. With the vanishing of the author, there has vanished humor, irony, the prophylactic salt of common sense. And yet Mr. Lawrence is, in his own way, characteristic of our time; and he has made here a sincere and not unskilful effort to present a phase of truth in which the Victorians did not interest themselves—to render the very feel and texture of an erotic experience; not to tell about it in intellectual generalizations but to give the items of which it is composed. And this is the constant occupation of our cleverer writers of fiction: to render the very feel and texture of experience, not merely erotic, but of all experience that comes within the compass of the author's subject.

III

PSYCHOLOGY: FIELDING, ELIOT

One principal way in which the author may intrude himself between the reader and the story is by what we call psychology. Psychology in some form is essential to any but the simplest type of story. To begin with, a story is a series of acts or events. It is a series of events involving people or acts performed by people, and in any narrative that pretends to anything more than the most elementary form of interest, we are concerned in the acts of people as characteristic. We accordingly wish to know what the people are like: what their past history has been (exposition), what they look like (description), what sort of people they are (characterization). The means by which the author presents his exposition, his description, and his characterization of people, are important differentiæ of varying techniques, and will all be referred to later on.

But ordinary exposition, description, and characterization are not generally sufficient for the purposes of the serious writer of fiction, especially in our day, or indeed at any time since 1850. The reader wishes to know from time to time more particularly how the character feels in a given situation, how he reacts to a particular predicament, what conflicts arise in him with regard to his course of action, what are his motives for acting as he does—and so in general how his feelings and mental processes in a given situation reflect the general character of him which has been rendered in the characterization. This detailed presentation of his feelings and mental processes is what in fiction is called psychology. It may be a very different thing from psychology as understood by the professors of the science. But the origin of the word is clear, and its application in fiction is legitimate enough if we do not try to relate it too closely to the scientific use of the word. Psychology is that element in the narrative art that concerns the *psyche*—that is, the subjective aspect of experience.

The disposition to concern oneself with the subjective aspect of experience has been growing more and more dominant in fiction, at least in English fiction, since about the middle of the nineteenth century. It reached a peak in the novels of Henry James, but it did not there reach its extreme limit. And Joyce and Virginia Woolf and their school are even more extensively and intensively concerned with psychology than James and his school. To such a degree that critics right and left are bewailing the complete disappearance in such work of plot—that is, of the objective element in fiction, of the series of events and acts which makes the story to begin with. And yet, curiously enough, there are certain of the devices and procedures of nineteenth-century psychology which were almost altogether abandoned by James and his following, and which have not been taken up to any extent by Joyce and his school.

One of these procedures is what is called psychological analysis. This consists in the author's explaining what, in general or at a given juncture, were the motives determining the person's action, especially when the motives are complicated or obscure and require some ingenuity to disentangle or bring to light. This procedure did not originate in the nineteenth century, but may be found from time to time in eighteenth-century novelists and especially in that great philosophical and satirical writer Fielding. In "Tom Jones," for example, he wishes us to understand why that mean fellow Blifil, knowing that Sophia Western disliked him, and not being properly in love with her himself, still insisted on paying court to her.

To say the truth, Blifil had passed sentence against Sophia; for, however pleased he had declared himself to Western with his reception, he was by no means satisfied, unless it was that he was convinced of the hatred and scorn of his mistress: and this had produced no less reciprocal hatred and scorn in him. It may, perhaps, be asked, Why then did he not put an immediate end to all further courtship? I answer, for that very reason, as well as for several others equally good, which we shall now proceed to open to the reader.

Though Mr. Blifil was not of the complexion of Jones, nor ready to eat every woman he saw; yet he was far from being destitute of that appetite which is said to be the common property of all animals. With this, he had likewise that distinguishing taste, which serves to direct men in their choice of the object or food of their several appetites; and this taught him to consider Sophia as a most delicious morsel, indeed to regard her with the same desires which an ortolan inspires into the soul of an epicure. Now the agonies which affected the mind of Sophia, rather augmented than impaired her beauty; for her tears added brightness to her eyes, and her breasts rose higher with her sighs. Indeed, no one hath seen beauty in its highest lustre who hath never seen it in distress. Blifil therefore looked on this human ortolan with greater desire than when he viewed her last; nor was his desire at all lessened by the aversion which he discovered in her to himself. On the contrary, this served rather to heighten the pleasure he proposed in rifling her charms, as it added triumph to lust; nay, he had some further views, from obtaining the absolute possession of her person, which we detest too much even to mention; and revenge itself was not without its share in the gratifications which he promised himself. The rivalling poor Jones, and supplanting him in her affections, added another spur to his pursuit, and promised another additional rapture to his enjoyment.

Besides all these views, which to some scrupulous persons may seem to savour too much of malevolence, he had one prospect, which few readers will regard with any great abhorrence. And this was the estate of Mr. Western; which was all to be settled on his daughter and her issue; for so extravagant was the affection of that fond parent, that, provided his child would but consent to be miserable with the husband he chose, he cared not at what price he purchased him.

For these reasons Mr. Blifil was so desirous of the match that he intended to deceive Sophia, by pretending to love her; and to deceive her father and his own uncle, by pretending he was beloved by her. In doing this he availed himself of the piety of Thwackum, who held, that if the end proposed was religious (as surely matrimony is), it mattered not how wicked were the means. As to other occasions, he used to apply the philosophy of Square, which taught, that the end was immaterial, so that the means were fair and consistent with moral rectitude. To say truth, there were few occurrences in life on which he could not draw advantage from the precepts of one or other of those great masters.

There are many significant points to be observed in this early example of psychological analysis, all of them illustrating the sort of thing which does *not* greatly characterize either the well-made novel nor the expressionistic novel, but which grows out of the conception of the novel as a philosophical essay. It is clearly the author here who is talking about his character; there is no attempt to identify himself with the character nor in any way to "dramatize" his feelings or mentality. There is that reference to the reader which indicates that the author is addressing himself directly to him as one philosopher to another. The author is dealing with an unsympathetic character; he is frankly outside of him, explaining him to the reader with a tone of scornful irony. The psychology of the character is generalized so that the reader may see how his reactions to the present situation fall in with his general moral make-up. "Though Mr. Blifil was not of the complexion of Jones . . . yet he was far from being destitute of that appetite . . ."

His psychology is analyzed; that is, in this case, the author enumerates the several motives involved, and further distinguishes for us certain subtleties, or refinements, in his reactions. There were two seeming paradoxes in the way in which Blifil meets the situation. He finds Sophia all the more attractive because of her distress; and he desires her all the more ardently because of her aversion to him, so that there is a complication or multiplication of his pleasure.

Besides all this, the author refers the motives and reactions of his character to the general laws of psychology which they exemplify. Blifil was not "destitute of that appetite which is said to be the common property of all animals." It was natural for him to find Sophia more attractive in her present state of mind, since "no one hath seen beauty in its highest lustre who hath never seen it in distress."

And then also, the author will not let pass the opportunity to give an incidental thrust at certain vicious philosophies which he has more elaborately exposed in an earlier part of the book.

This philosophical tone is one of the things for which we prize Fielding; the soundness and humanness of his characterization are among the chief reasons for placing him so very high in our pantheon. There is no doubt that he himself regarded his philosophy as what gave weight to a literary form which was generally so frivolous and negligible. In one place he describes his introductory essays as a "kind of mark or stamp, which may hereafter enable a very indifferent reader to distinguish what is true and genuine in this historic kind of writing, from what is false and counterfeit." The point is that the ordinary light-weight novelist is incapable of producing a serious essay, as incapable as the ordinary essayist is of prefacing his compositions with a Greek or Latin motto, like "the ingenious author of the Spectator."

2

Fielding was distinctly the most philosophical of eighteenth-century novelists, and we do not again encounter anything comparable to his psychological analysis until we come to those highly philosophical novelists of the nineteenth century George Eliot and George Meredith. These writers are indeed infinitely more given to psychology than Fielding, who makes by comparison the impression of being a bold and simple narrator of action. These Victorians are so anxious about the morals of their people; there is a more romantic cast to their sentiment; and in many ways their general complexion is such as to distinguish them sharply from any eighteenth-century writer. There is something in their tone which is indeed irritating to readers to-day where Fielding is not irritating; there is something in their manner of analyzing psychology which interferes more with the flow and naturalness of the story, and which inevitably produced the reaction toward a more "dramatic" technique. And yet, when they are examined closely, we distinguish the same features of psychological analysis as we have found in the passage about Blifil.

George Eliot often goes behind the apparent motive to something lying deeper in the consciousness which is the main determinant of conduct. Thus in the reflections of Arthur Donnithorne in "Adam Bede" she points out how behind such an explicit resolution lay an implicit one of which Arthur was hardly aware, or how, still deeper down, "there was a motive at work" under such and such an attitude, "which had a sort of backstairs influence not admitted to himself."

But it was in "Middlemarch" that George Eliot did her most remarkable work in this line. She had evidently been studying the science of psychology as it then existed, and was not unaware of the light to be thrown on psychological processes from the study of physiology. Most interesting is her analysis of the mental processes of Mr. Bulstrode. He is a wealthy banker of a deep and sincere religious faith, whose fortune was founded in a dishonest line of business and diverted to him from the person who should rightly have inherited it. He is not a plain hypocrite, but at all stages of his career has been obliged to persuade himself that what he was doing was really to the glory of God. This process of "rationalizing," as we should now call it, is carefully analyzed in Chapter LXI, for example.

Then at a certain point in the story there turns up a drunken character named Raffles. He is the only one who knows of Bulstrode's wrong-doing, and is capable of exposing him to his wife and the whole country-side. Bulstrode is compelled to tell some lies to prevent his wife's learning the facts from Raffles, and this is a cause of great distress to him.

> For Bulstrode shrank from a direct lie with an intensity disproportionate to the number of his more indirect misdeeds. But many of these misdeeds were like *the subtle muscular movements which are not taken account of in the consciousness,* though they bring about the end that we fix our mind on and desire. And it is only what we are vividly conscious of that we can vividly imagine to be seen by Omniscience.

Here is a notion, wherever George Eliot picked it up, strongly suggestive, not merely of a psychology well aware of the physiological bases of behavior, but also of the Freudian theory of the Unconscious. This notion is more or less carried through in the account of the spiritual predicament in which Bulstrode now finds himself. It would be greatly to his interest if Raffles were dead. And Raffles is now in Bulstrode's house critically ill. Dr. Lydgate has specially warned against his being given any alcoholic stimulant. And Bulstrode cannot help thinking how fortunate it would be if Raffles were given something to drink and put out of the way. It is now that the doctor makes a visit, and

Bulstrode has an opportunity to make a favorable impression on him by agreeing to assist in a hospital project which Lydgate has much at heart.

> He did not measure the quantity of diseased motive which had made him wish for Lydgate's good-will, but the quantity was none the less actively there, like an irritating agent in his blood. A man vows, and yet will not cast away the means of breaking his vow. Is it that he distinctly means to break it? Not at all; but *the desires which tend to break it are at work in him dimly, and make their way into his imagination, and relax his muscles in the very moments when he is telling himself* over again the reasons for his vow. Raffles, recovering quickly, returning to the free use of his odious powers—how could Bulstrode wish for that? Raffles dead was the image that brought release, and indirectly he prayed for that way of release, beseeching that, if it were possible, the rest of his days here below might be freed from the threat of an ignominy which would break him utterly as an instrument of God's service.

And so in the end it is the image of Raffles dead that wins out over the intention to do right, and Bulstrode connives at the carelessness of the nurse who does give Raffles his much desired alcoholic stimulant.

"The desires which tend to break [his vow] are at work in him dimly." Here again is an expression that suggests the modern theory of the Unconscious. Similar suggestions are sometimes found in Meredith and Butler. The mechanism made use of by the unconscious will for securing results not approved of by our conscious self is exhibited in a remarkable passage in "The Way of All Flesh." It will be recalled that Ernest Pontifex, by a long process of grilling on the part of his parents, was induced to let them know many facts about his fellow-pupils at school which he felt bound in honor not to reveal. His father was determined to turn over all this information to the school authorities. He had got hold of a school list, and he copied out the names of the boys, on a card arranged in tabular form so that he could mark in little squares after the name of each boy whether he was guilty of smoking, of drinking beer, or of swearing and using obscene language. But even this was not enough to satisfy the inquisitorial passion of Ernest's father and mother.

> No matter how awful was the depravity revealed to them, the pair never flinched, but probed and probed, till they were on the point of reaching subjects more delicate than they had yet touched upon. Here Ernest's unconscious self took the matter up and made a resistance to which his conscious self was unequal, by tumbling him off his chair in a fit of fainting.

3

"The Way of All Flesh" (1902) is a delightful and highly significant book, but it is hardly a novel at all in the ordinary sense. It is autobiography thinly disguised, and it is written in the historical manner, with a maximum of generalized narrative, here and there sprinkled with brief and vivid anecdotes and episodes. Besides, it is too frankly and baldly philosophical to conform to the customary formula of fiction. Butler dumped so much of his note-books into each chapter that little room was left for the development of story or drama.

The want of all pretensions to novelistic technique is one reason why we so readily swallow Butler's psychology along with the other philosophical elements. Another reason is Butler's tone, which is the dry tone of the rationalistic eighteenth century, and not the romantic tone of the Victorians.

In the Victorians what often irritates us is the strange mixture of the rational and the sentimental. In George Eliot, the psychology itself is highly interesting and illuminating. What bothers us is the sense we have of her being there, outside the characters, examining them for our benefit. It is the moralistic, often tearful tone in which the whole investigation is conducted. It is her attitude toward the characters and toward us. Toward us she has so much the air of teacher, pointer in hand. Toward the characters she has the air of an anxious motherly hen, concerned about the safety of her chicks.

IV

PSYCHOLOGY: MEREDITH

One of the peculiarities of George Eliot as a psychologist is that she was concerned with the physiological mechanism of the processes which she was exhibiting. Meredith was not, so far as I know, concerned with this technical aspect of psychology. But he was even more given than George Eliot to tracing the subtle "twists of the heart" wherein lies the comedy of the sentiments. His analysis is more difficult to follow and much more difficult to describe.

With Eliot, the thing desired by the character, the ultimate goal of the process, is some selfish gratification, some familiar and tangible good, easily definable in the ordinary terms of plot. In Meredith the psychological process is a much more sophisticated affair, involving what he calls highly "civilized" people, that is, people more than ordinarily concerned with purely subjective values. What they are after is not so much a definite and tangible worldly good, in the interests of which they are willing for the moment to hush up their consciences. The ultimate aim of their endeavor is something subjective; it is the satisfaction of their own moral vanity. They are sentimentalists. What they seek more than all else is to feel good about themselves, and they do not depend on the ordinary objective standards for measuring their own worth—they are past masters in the art of manipulating their sentiments so as to give them the appearance of the utmost elevation and refinement.

Sir Austin Feverel, for example, is never really so much

concerned to take the course which will be best for his son Richard as to persuade himself that he has taken that course. His famous System is a means not so much for turning out a perfect human product as for flattering the moral and intellectual vanity of Sir Austin. When he learns of Richard's infatuation for Lucy, he is obliged to take an attitude of severity toward the young people in order to think well of himself and his System.

The same situation repeats itself in aggravated form after the unauthorized marriage of Richard and Lucy. And Meredith devotes an entire chapter, entitled "Nursing the Devil," to a study of Sir Austin's reactions to this second and irreparable intrusion on his experiment, following round and round the "twists of the heart" by which he maneuvers himself into the position that is most comfortable for himself, at the same time that it makes him responsible for the tragic outcome of the story.

"The Egoist" is not a tragedy. But here we have the same processes of sentimental sophistication. It is necessary for the moral comfort of Sir Willoughby to persuade himself and the world that he can be content with nothing but the best. And so, when he finds that he cannot have Clara, he is obliged to make himself think that Lætitia is the woman to be preferred; and, moreover, that it would be a generous act to hand over Clara—very fine woman but not the paragon—to his cousin Vernon.

Forthwith he set about painting Lætitia in delectable human colours, like a miniature of the past century, reserving her ideal figure for his private satisfaction. The world was to bow to her visible beauty, and he gave her enamel and glow, a taller stature, a swimming air, a transcendency that exorcised the image of the old witch who had driven him to this [the fear of being known to have been a second time jilted?]. The result in him was, that Lætitia became humanly and avowedly beautiful. Her dark eyelashes on the pallor of her cheeks lent their aid to the transformation, which was a necessity to him, so it was performed . . .

But already [some pages later] he had begun to regard the deed as his executioner. He dreaded meeting Clara. The folly of having retained her stood before him. How now to look on her and keep a sane resolution unwavering? She tempted to the insane. Had she been away, he could have walked through the performance composed by the sense of doing a duty to himself: perhaps faintly hating the poor wretch he made happy at last, kind to her in a manner, polite. Clara's presence in the house previous to the deed, and oh, heaven! after it, threatened his wits. Pride? He had none; he cast it down for her to trample it; he caught it back ere it was trodden on. Yes, he had pride: he had it as a dagger in his breast: his pride was his misery. But he was too proud to submit to misery. "What I do is right." He said the words, and rectitude smoothed his path, till the question clamoured for an answer: Would the world countenance and endorse his pride in Lætitia? At one time, yes. And now? Clara's beauty ascended, laid a beam on him.

We are on board the labouring vessel of humanity in a storm, when cries and countercries ring out, disorderliness mixes the crew, and the fury of self-preservation divides: this one is for the ship, that one for his life. Clara was the former to him, Lætitia the latter. But what if there might not be greater safety in holding tenaciously to Clara than in casting her off for Lætitia? No, she had done things to set his pride throbbing in the quick. . . . He might hold to her for vengeance; but that appetite was short-lived in him if it ministered nothing to his purposes. "I discard all vengeance," he said, and thrilled burningly to a smart in his admiration of the man who could be so magnanimous under mortal injury: for the more admirable he, the more pitiable. He drank a drop or two of self-pity like a poison, repelling the assaults of public pity. Clara must be given up. It must be seen by the world that, as he felt, the thing he did was right. Laocoon of his own serpents, he struggled to a certain magnificence of attitude in the muscular net of constrictions he flung around himself. Clara must be given up. O bright Abominable! She must be given up: but not to one whose touch of her would be darts in the blood of the yielder, snakes in his bed: she must be given up to an extinguisher; to be the second wife of an old-fashioned semi-recluse, disgraced in his first . . . As the instinct of self-preservation whispered to Willoughby, the world, were it requisite, might be taught to think what it assuredly would not think if she should be seen tripping to the altar with Horace De Craye. Self-preservation, not vengeance, breathed that whisper. He glanced at her iniquity for a justification of it, without any desire to do her a permanent hurt: he was highly civilized: but with a strong intention to give her all the benefit of the scandal, supposing a scandal, or ordinary tattle.

"And so he handed her to his cousin and secretary, Vernon Whitford, who opened his mouth and shut his eyes."

I have transcribed only a very small portion of this chapter, which is almost entirely given over to Meredith's variety of psychological analysis.

Meredith's variety includes all the features of Fielding's and George Eliot's, with certain specialties of his own. Some of his specialties tend in the direction of "dramatization," but the philosophical and authorial features are so much more marked than even in George Eliot that Meredith must have been still more the despair of novelists who held the ideal of distinguishing the art of fiction from that of history, philosophy, the essay, or any other form of exposition. The author is there with a vengeance, generalizing the psychology of his character and analyzing his feelings, distinguishing what he thought he felt from what he really felt. He stands to a large extent outside the mind of the character, looking in; he may not be scornful in his irony, but he joins with the comic spirit in watching the fun of a fine mind gone wrong. "His retinue of imps had a revel." More extensively than George Eliot he refers the reader to the general laws of human nature which are exemplified by the antics of his character. He is never through telling us about Sentimentalism in the abstract or quoting from the Book of Egoism. He does not hesitate any more than another Victorian to address the reader directly, and not seldom in the vein of exhortation, in the prophetic vein of a Carlyle.

2

The mention of Carlyle brings over one with a rush the realization of everything in Meredith that leads one at times to assert that he is not properly a novelist at all. Of course the novel is a form of infinite plasticity, and one that can be put to the greatest variety of uses. A genre which can be allowed to include "The Three Musketeers" and "Remembrance of Things Past," need surely not hesitate to extend its hospitality to "Richard Feverel" and "Diana of the Crossways." And with a writer as brilliant and as wise as Meredith we are obliged of course, in the end, to take him as he is, and, for his shortcomings, to regard them simply as the *défauts de ses qualités*.

Still, there is nothing to prevent us from noting the features of even a great writer which irritate us. In approaching any writer your satisfaction or disappointment depend on what you are looking for. In the case of Meredith, there was a time when I came to him looking for wisdom, and was completely satisfied. He gave me wisdom, and he gave it in a form that stimulated me by its originality and its gnomic subtlety. His cleverness I loved, his pyrotechnic display of verbal ingenuity. When people spoke of the faults of his style I would not listen.

In recent years I have returned to Meredith looking not for wisdom but for story, for that modest and self-effacing record of the ways of men which I had found in Maupassant and Sigrid Undset, in Jane Austen and Thomas Hardy. And this I did not find, or I found it so involved with intellectual gymnastics, with didactic intention, that

I had not the patience to disentangle it. I had been spoiled for Meredith by writers more humble in the presence of words and in the presence of facts.

The style of a novelist is always a technical consideration, since it determines the emotional tone of the story, and so the feeling with which one regards the characters. It becomes a particularly urgent problem of technique wherever it interferes with the right approach to the characters. "The lady gathered her mouth" may fairly well suit Lady Blandish, though I believe Meredith meant us to take her more seriously than that, in spite of her ill-chosen name. But certainly we do not approach the love-making of Lucy and Richard with the right feeling when we are asked to think of a kiss as a seal closing a rosy gate. And it does not help us to understand the psychology of Sir Willoughby to read that he was the "Laocoon of his own serpents" and that, in general, "the Egoist is the son of himself."

One of the peculiarities of Meredith, as compared with George Eliot, is his penchant for parable and symbolic abstraction. He began with sheer fantastic allegory in "The Shaving of Shagpat." His first novel was "The Ordeal of Richard Feverel," and it is perhaps there that the disease is most virulent and does the most harm to a story of tragic human interest. It begins with the burlesque elaboration of Sir Austin's System of education, with its great Shaddock Dogma, its anticipated Ordeal, and its ample provision of periods in a boy's development fancifully named, the "Blossoming Season," the "Magnetic Age," and so on. But that is only a beginning. In this story, nothing goes under its own name, and no one under his. A mute misunderstanding between Sir Austin and Richard is a dialogue between Cold Blood and Hot Blood. Richard humiliated is the Foolish Young Fellow; in action he is the True Hero. Richard and Lucy in love are Prince Ferdinand and Miranda; they are also Adam and the First Woman. Sir Austin is generally referred to as the Scientific Humanist; Lady Blandish is the Autumn Primrose; Adrian is the Wise Youth; Mrs. Mount is the Enchantress.

The symbol is a means of giving concreteness to abstractions, but when it comes to concrete things and to persons, the symbol is a dubious help to the imagination. It is likely to remove the subject one degree farther from reality, to put one veil more between us and the breathing world. It often seems as if Meredith wanted faith in things, in the eloquent appearances of life, as if he could not trust them, like other writers, to speak for themselves. It was, I take it, the aim of the French naturalists to render things so perfectly in themselves that they were their own sufficient commentary. They aimed to give a speaking likeness of their subject. But Meredith, somehow, does not rely on the speaking likeness. He does not take the *pains* to make it speaking, to render things so well that no commentary is necessary. He likes to furnish the commentary himself. In short, he is forever *interfering* with the subject.

One of the distracting features of Meredith is his uncertainty of tone. This is felt in all his work, but in "Richard Feverel," where it is particularly unfortunate, we can trace its very origin. "Richard Feverel" obviously started on a burlesque tone. The early chapters, so much cut down in the second edition (now the current version), present a purely ridiculous Scientific Humanist, surrounded by a court of farcical female idolaters. But the subject was too serious for the tone on which he started. Sir Austin and Lady Blandish, his "crucible woman," refuse to be creatures in a farce, and the reader feels throughout the incompatibility of the name "Blandish," modeled on the names of the cruder Restoration comedy, with her essential dignity and the serious part she has to play. Then come Richard and Lucy, so much more human and so much more tragic than the burlesque subject calls for, and quite upset the scheme. But still Meredith has begun with a burlesque treatment of Sir Austin and the momentum of this start carries him more or less through the book.

The trouble with this method, apart from the mere tiresomeness of the artificial style, is that it surrounds with its poisonous sophisticated air characters whom it is important that we should approach in all simplicity—not merely Sir Austin and Lady Blandish but Richard and Lucy themselves. The burlesque comedian never gets over the irony of the fact that these healthy young souls are accomplishing so much better by mere instinct what Sir Austin is laboriously working out with his System. And the whole love-making of Richard and Lucy is served up to us in an odious sauce curiously compounded of tender sentiment, whimsical patronage, enthusiastic nature-description, sententious philosophy—and burlesque humor! It is worth while quoting a rather long passage, that describing the first meeting of the young lovers, to show how a superbly conceived scene and the finest sensitiveness to beauty may be almost altogether spoiled by the intrusion of philosophic humor à la Carlyle. And note that I have chosen here not the extremest example of this phenomenon, but rather the passage in which Meredith comes nearest to simplicity in the presentment of human beings. The passage is introduced by the chilling philosophic generality, "When nature has made us ripe for love, it seldom occurs that the Fates are behind-hand in furnishing a temple for the flame." And then comes the set piece:

Above green-flashing plunges of a weir, and shaken by the thunder below, lilies, golden and white, were swaying at anchor among the reeds. Meadow-sweet hung from the banks thick with weed and trailing bramble, and there also hung *a daughter of earth.* Her face was shaded by a broad straw hat with a flexible brim that left her lips and chin in the sun, and sometimes nodding, sent forth a light of promising eyes. Across her shoulders, and behind, flowed large loose curls, brown in shadow, almost golden where the ray touched them. She was simply dressed, befitting decency and the season. On a closer inspection you might see that her lips were stained. *This blooming young person* was regaling on dewberries. They grew between the bank and the water. Apparently she found the fruit abundant, for her hand *was making pretty progress to her mouth. Fastidious youth, which revolts at woman plumping her exquisite proportions on bread-and-butter,* and would (we must suppose) joyfully have her scraggy to have her poetical, can hardly object to dewberries. Indeed the act of eating them is dainty and induces musing. The dewberry is a sister to the lotus and an innocent sister. You eat: mouth, eye, and hand are occupied, and the undrugged mind free to roam. And so it was with *the damsel* who knelt there. The little skylark went up above her, all song, to the smooth southern cloud lying along the blue; from a dewy copse dark over her nodding hat the blackbird fluted, calling to her with thrice mellow note: the kingfisher flashed emerald out of green osiers: a bow-winged heron travelled aloft, seeking solitude: a boat slipped toward her containing a *dreamy youth;* and still she plucked the fruit, and ate, as if no *fairy prince were invading her territories,* and as if she wished not for one, or knew not her wishes. Surrounded by the green shaven meadows, the pastoral summer buzz, the weir-fall's thundering white, amid the breath and beauty of wild flowers, she was *a bit of lovely human* life in a fair setting; *a terrible attraction* [an allusion to the Magnetic Age]. *The Magnetic Youth* leaned round to note his proximity to the weir-piles, and beheld *the sweet vision.*

I cannot think this is great art, though there are great elements of art brought together to the making of it. The natural description is at points unsurpassed: there is an outdoor freshness and magic to the atmosphere which only Meredith could evoke. But every time he has begun to cast his spell over one he breaks it up with some unhandy and self-conscious move. It is largely the System that is to blame. It is the System which requires that the girl should be a daughter of earth and a sweet vision and a terrible attraction, and that the boy should be the Magnetic Youth.

It is the System which reduces him from Richard Feverel, a boy whom we know and are interested in, to the inferior rank of "fastidious youth, which revolts at woman plumping her exquisite proportions." Here enters with a vengeance the burlesque style taken over from Sir Austin. "The damsel" is pre-Raphaelitism out of place. "Making pretty progress to her mouth" is mere Victorian self-consciousness and bad taste. But "this blooming young person" is Victorian bad taste "wedded to the System" and begetting a progeny of intolerable burlesque.

Meredith always has some system or other with which he is playing, and it generally results in a dubious complication of tone. It is this very feature which gives his work so much more "modern" an air than, say, that of George Eliot or Anthony Trollope. It is partly this, too, which gives so much sparkle and variety to his effects, saves them from "flatness" and monotony. There are many pages in which this mixed tone is handled with perfect tact and results in a peculiar beauty. But his tact is anything but sure, and he is apt at any moment to break out in that falsetto that is so fatal to the illusion.

3

The case in which his complication of tone is most relevant to the present discussion is that of his psychological analysis. For here we find him passing from the outside point of view of an author explaining the motives of the character to the inside point of view of a character thinking his thoughts in terms natural to his own mentality. So we have reached the border line between psychological analysis proper and the "dramatization" of consciousness which is the aim of the well-made novel. For Meredith does do a good deal of such dramatizing, and it is this which marks his advance over George Eliot as well as renders him more difficult to follow.

In the long passage about Sir Willoughby, for example, there is an insensible transition from the author's statement about the character to the direct rendering, without comment, of the thoughts and imaginings of Sir Willoughby:

> He dreaded meeting Clara. The folly of having retained her stood before him. How now to look on her and keep a sane resolution unwavering? She tempted to the insane. Had she been away, he could have walked through the performance composed by the sense of doing a duty to himself: perhaps faintly hating the poor wretch he made happy at last, kind to her in a manner, polite. Clara's presence in the house previous to the deed, and oh, heaven! after it, threatened his wits. Pride? He had none; he cast it down for her to trample it; he caught it back ere it was trodden on. Yes, he had pride: he had it as a dagger in his breast; his pride was his misery.

And so forth, to the end of the paragraph. Note that it is Sir Willoughby himself, not Meredith, who says (to himself) that he has no pride, and then takes it back. Yes, he says, he has pride; it is a dagger in his breast.

Meredith has for a moment allowed Sir Willoughby to do his own thinking without any explanations by the author, but now, in beginning the next paragraph, he feels impelled to explain the situation to us. "We are on board the labouring vessel of humanity in a storm," etc. After this philosophical reminder he is soon again inside the consciousness of Sir Willoughby. "But what if there might not be greater safety in holding tenaciously to Clara than in casting her off for Lætitia. No, she had done things to set his pride throbbing in the quick." And so he goes on, page after page, half the time in the mind of Willoughby, half the time hovering above it with his philosophical ironic comment. And then there are times when the reader is not sure whether it is the author or the character whose view is given. "Self-preservation, not vengeance, breathed that whisper. He glanced at her iniquity for a justification of it, without any desire to do her a permanent hurt." Is it the author making a distinction, or Willoughby defending himself in the court of his conscience?

This is one of the reasons for the relative ineffectiveness of the method. So strong is Meredith's dramatic instinct that his own statements of the character's reactions must be colored by the mentality of the character; so inveterate is his philosophical bias that the inner picture of the character's consciousness must be colored by the author's irony, the author's didacticism. The inner and the outer view continually penetrate each other in a subtle, sometimes fascinating, often bewildering manner. There is much in Meredith's way of turning to the light the consciousness of the characters that reminds one of his contemporary Browning; but there is seldom that purity of dramatic presentment that one has in poems like "My Last Duchess" or "Caliban upon Setebos." He shares all the obscurity of Browning—the obscurity which derives from the dramatic manner of projecting psychological processes. And he has the added obscurity that comes of mixing the dramatic with the philosophical, of passing back and forth constantly and without warning between those different planes of vision, planes which it is so hard to get into the same picture.

But the main reason for objection to Meredith's method is not the obscurity. The main objection is that the intrusion of the philosopher in Meredith so constantly destroys the illusion created by the dramatizing of consciousness. He is forever worrying and badgering the creatures of his imagination. He takes away with one hand what he gives with the other. With one hand he creates a living being and with the other he deals the mortal blow of indiscreet dissection. So that we might say that his analysis almost cancels the effect of his imagination. That is what we might say, if it were not for the characters, like Richard Feverel and Clara Middleton, whom he so largely exempts from the operation of his analysis, and for the excellent stories in which he generally involves the whole of his dramatis personæ. It is perhaps the moving stories which save the people of Meredith from being what he tries so hard to make them, psychological specimens.

V

PSYCHOLOGY: PROUST

THERE is one great work of fiction of the twentieth century, universally judged the French masterpiece of its time, which is very hard to classify, or to fit into any account of the evolution of the novel. This is Marcel Proust's series of books going under the general title, "A la Recherche du temps perdu," 1913–26 (in English, "Remembrance of Things Past"). It seems to stand there as a perpetual warning against generalization. For, to begin with its outward form, it is not, properly speaking, a novel at all, but a collection of *mémoires*. Only these are the *mémoires* of a person possessed of all the gifts of a novelist, a man with extraordinary powers of observation, extraordinarily sensitive to esthetic impressions, apt for the registration of social niceties, and given to acute analysis of psychology and to wise dissertation upon it.

Never was writer of fiction—unless it be Laurence Sterne—who was less in a hurry to get somewhere, more given to digression. He will begin with some historical circumstance. This suggests a reflection on the general principles of human nature involved, and leads to a comparison with analogous circumstances, which lead perhaps in turn to further reflection, and so back at last to the point of departure. Each one of these features is developed at great length, and the whole evolution occupies many pages—sometimes, one might almost say, a whole volume. Thus the impression given is that of a series of digressions, one digression sprouting another, until at last the final one of the series brings the reader back to the point from which the first one started.

It is not exact to speak of digressions where all is digression. But I use the term as it would apply if the object were to arrive somewhere in a story. Everything is digression which does not contribute to an understanding, or to the movement, of the action. But with Proust the object is to recapture the whole of experience, including any circumstances brought to mind in the course of the narrative, and all the reflections which at the time of writing he is moved to make on the past from the accumulated wisdom of the present. There is, to be sure, a main thread of interest, constituted by the sentimental relations of the supposed writer to Gilberte, the Duchess de Guermantes, and Albertine. But Gilberte is the daughter of Swann's wife; and belonging to the family of the Duchess de Guermantes are the Marquis de Saint-Loup and the Comte de Charlus. So that, before we can have the history of Gilberte, we must have that of Swann and the woman of the demi-monde whom he married; and the interest in Madame de Guermantes brings in the sentimental history of Saint-Loup and the erotic history of Monsieur de Charlus. And all these side issues consume volume after volume of this multi-voluminous chronicle. It is true that there is a sort of thematic relation between the case of Swann and that of the narrator, as there is between the perversions of Charlus and Albertine. So that perhaps the key to the composition is to be found in an elaborate contrapuntal development of themes; and this way of regarding it would enable us to associate the art of Proust with the work of such diverse novelists of our time as Huxley, Gide, Wassermann, and Dos Passos.

But at least in exterior semblance, the work of Proust is a rambling autobiographical chronicle, which acknowledges no obligation to the "economies" and adjustments of fiction. He has time for anything he wishes to include;

and one thing which he particularly likes is dissertating upon psychology. Sometimes it is psychology in the strict sense of the word. There is, for example, a delightful four-page excursus on the sense of hearing. It begins with a description of the sounds made by a grate fire heard through a closed door. Not knowing what they were, the character concerned did not associate them with a fire.

Something was being moved about, something else was being let fall; I had the impression that the room was not vacant but that there was some one there. In reality it was simply the fire burning. It couldn't keep quiet, it kept moving the sticks around, and that most clumsily. I went in: the fire let one stick roll over, and another one smoke. And even when it didn't keep making movements like ill-bred people, it kept emitting sounds which, from the moment that I saw the flame, appeared to me indeed the sounds made by a fire, but which, if I had been on the other side of the wall, I should have attributed to some one blowing his nose or walking back and forth.

He now sits down and looks around him.

I heard the tick-tock of Saint-Loup's watch, which couldn't be far from where I was sitting. This tick-tock kept coming from different directions, since I couldn't see the watch; it seemed to come from behind me, from in front, from the right, from the left; and sometimes it would grow faint as if a long way off. Suddenly I discovered the watch on the table. Then I heard the tick-tock in that one place, from which it did not budge. At least I thought I heard it in that place; I really didn't hear it there, I saw it there; for sounds have no location.

Beginning so, the discussion passes to the sensations of a sick person temporarily deafened, to the psychology of love, and finally arrives at the sound-world of the deaf, or, rather, the silent world of fairy-like manifestations which stand to the deaf in place of sounds.

Here is a pleasant kind of musing, and the reader may

enjoy himself a good deal wandering down these flowery lanes, provided he has a long evening before him and is not in haste to get on with the story. Observe that what we have here is the psychology of sensations, which is on the other side of Pater from Meredith and Fielding. Pater deals mostly in the analysis of esthetic impressions, which stands midway between the analysis of sensations on the one side and, on the other side, that of the sentiments, including the moral sentiments. Proust deals extensively with esthetic impressions too. And, moreover, he has a good deal to say of the psychology of the snob, of the motives that govern people in the game of "society."

But commonest of all in Proust, no doubt, is the analysis of the sentiments, particularly the sentiments involved in love. Here as elsewhere he indulges his penchant for referring the particular case to the general law. Love, he never tires of telling us, is a creation of the imagination, and often has little to do with the qualities actually present in the beloved object. The love of his hero for Madame de Guermantes is a case in point. It is a by-product of the glamour taken on in his childish imagination by the name Guermantes. Thus we come to the general subject of the prestige of names.

At the age when Names, in presenting us the image of the unknowable which we have poured into them, at the same time that they also denote for us an actual place, force us by that fact to identify the one with the other to such an extent that we start out to find in a certain city the soul which it cannot possess but which we no longer have the power to expel from its name, it is not simply to towns and to rivers that they give an individuality, as allegorical paintings do, it is not simply the physical world which they tint with various color and people with marvels, it is likewise the social world: so then every famous hôtel or château has its lady, or its fairy, as the forests their genii, and the waters their divinities. Sometimes, hidden in the depths of her name, the fairy transforms herself in accordance with our imagination which nourishes her; it is so that the atmosphere in which Mme. de Guermantes existed in me, after having been for years nothing but the reflection of a magic lantern slide and a church window, began to lose its colors, when altogether different dreams came to impregnate it with the misty dampness of torrents.

However, the fairy dies out if we approach the real person to whom her name corresponds, for the name then begins to reflect this person and she contains nothing of the fairy; the fairy may be born again if we go to a distance from the real person; but if we stay near her the fairy dies once for all and with her the name, as with that family of Lusignan which had to come to an end on the day when the fairy Mélusine disappeared. And so the Name, under the successive retintings of which we might end by finding, below all, the fine portrait of a stranger whom we have never known, is no more than the photographic identification card to which we refer to see whether we know, whether or not we ought to recognize, a person who is going by. But let a sensation from some former time—as with those recording musical instruments which keep the sound and the style of different artists who have played on them—let this sensation cause our memory to make us hear this name with the special timbre which it then held for our ear, and this name seemingly unchanged, we feel the distance which separates from one another the dreams which its identical syllables signified successively for us.

This is but a beginning of the dissertation on the psychology of names and the degrees by which, with personal acquaintance, the name of Guermantes gradually lost its original coloring for the young man in question. It is of course impossible to do justice in my translation to the rare quality of the original, which is more like that of Pater than of any other English writer. Only the nicest adjustment of the two idioms will prevent these interminable involved sentences from seeming ridiculous or from breaking down altogether, in spite of the suppleness and sureness of balance which, in the original, keep them floating so securely.

It will be obvious that Proust goes much farther afield than Meredith into the realm of general psychological reflection, and the question will be asked: why are we not irritated with Proust as we are with Meredith? Why do we not find it in his case a well-nigh fatal fault in method?

And the answer is, I think, mainly this. In Proust there is no effort to construct a dramatic story. There are no moments of rapid action, in which the issues are urgent; no tightness of suspense to be relaxed, nor tenseness of feeling to be interrupted. There is, compared with Meredith, no immediate dramatizing of the consciousness of the actors with which the author may interfere by his philosophical indiscretions. Proust's work is frankly reminiscent, leisurely, and reflective. The general reflections are of its essence. If they bore us, we are not obliged to go on reading. But if we do go on reading, it is because this is what we expect and what, in this work, we are seeking. This time we have set our hearts on something in the vein of Hazlitt or Pater, or something in the vein of Saint-Simon. It is precisely because Meredith is giving us something so much more like fiction that we object to the intrusions of the philosopher.

And besides, there is such a world-wide difference in tone. Not that Proust's tone is absolutely preferable to Meredith's; that would seem to put the disillusioned worldling above the hopeful "humanist." But the hopeful humanist is so much more liable to faults of manner than the sensitive worldling. And it happens in this case that the worldling—the scientific determinist and hedonist—maintains a certain serious gravity of approach to his human subject which contrasts favorably with the frequently forced note, the jocularity and facetiousness, of the romantic moralist. Meredith is a magnificent example of the viciousness of the romantic prose manner pushed to extremes—the want of simplicity, the passion for expressiveness, the disposition to be forever in costume and on parade.

French writers of fiction have in general a certain advantage for art over the English of the Victorian period by virtue of their bias in favor of determinism and scientific objectivity. Writers like Eliot and Meredith hold so strongly the Saxon faith in the power of the will to direct behavior and control the conditions of life that they cannot leave their characters alone. They are forever cheering them on in the good life, admonishing them, warning them, pointing out their mistakes, and telling them how different things might have been if only . . . etc. We are inclined to resent this know-it-all attitude on behalf of both the characters and ourselves; and we begin to doubt even the truth to human nature of showmen so anxious to be edifying.

It is true that these English authors are more bracing in their moral tone; they do not discourage us with their fatalism, nor make us feel that good and bad are indifferent in a world over which we have no control. And there must be some esthetic gain involved in this stronger moral tone. But there is also a great loss esthetically. We so often lose the drama in the doctrine, and the very illusion of truth is in danger of going by the board. That is one reason why the psychologizing of a Marcel Proust is for some readers more acceptable than that of a Meredith.

VI

PHILOSOPHY: VICTOR HUGO

THERE have always been novelists who were not satisfied to leave their work a dramatic picture of human nature, but have felt impelled to make it the obvious vehicle of their general philosophy of life. Such was Victor Hugo in his time, and such in our time are Romain Rolland and H. G. Wells. I do not include novelists like Dr. Johnson and Voltaire, whose philosophic studies are so abstract and unrealistic that they belong obviously in a class related as much to the allegory as to the novel. It is worth having in mind, however, that the eighteenth century was particularly rich in philosophic novels—witness Goethe and Rousseau—as if, in its origins, the novel were not well differentiated from philosophy nor constituted a literary form in its own right.

Let us consider for the moment only writers like Hugo and Wells, who have taken the novel as it came to them from the hands of Scott and Richardson, Dickens and Eliot, and made it bear a greater weight of reflective wisdom than even those serious writers. These philosophic novelists are often extremely able story-tellers. But it is evident that it is not to the story that they attach most importance, but to the social, the economic, the political lesson which is to be derived from it. Generally speaking, these novelists, in spite of their often extraordinary talents and qualities of mind, do not occupy a very high place in the estimation of literary critics, although they may be very widely read and are likely to be better known abroad than more highly esteemed contemporaries. And it is worth considering why such popular writers, who have so much to offer by way of "criticism of life," are relegated by fastidious critics to the limbo occupied by such as Alexander Dumas.

Let us take the case of Hugo's "Les Misérables" (1862). This is a combination of exciting story with social and political philosophy in liberal proportions. It is the history of Jean Valjean, an escaped convict. In origin an ignorant country fellow, he was condemned to the galleys for stealing a loaf of bread in order to feed his sister's starving children. He was not by nature bad, but the galleys have gone a long way to make him so. What proves stronger than the corrupting influence among criminals is the Christ-like treatment of him by the good bishop, Monseigneur Bienvenu, soon after his escape from Toulon. Even after the convict has rewarded his hospitality by stealing his silver plate, the bishop continues to have faith in him. He tells him to take the candlesticks too, bidding him use this silver to become an honest man. "Jean Valjean, my brother, you belong no more to evil but to good. It is your soul that I have bought from you; I take it away from black thoughts and the spirit of perdition, and I give it to God."

Some years later this same Jean Valjean turns up as "le père Madeleine," wealthy mayor of Montreuil, who has proved the benefactor of the whole district by the introduction of new methods in manufacturing. He becomes the protector of a poor girl, whom he saves from a life of prostitution and enables to bring up her daughter Cosette in the country. But in order to save the life of a man who has been identified as the escaped convict Jean Valjean, the real Valjean has to give himself up to justice; and then, escaped from prison, he loses himself in Paris. There he is old Monsieur Leblanc. He has with him Cosette, who passes for his granddaughter. Her mother is dead, and he has come to love her as his own child. But there is a certain bloodhound of a police officer, Javert, who gets on his track.

Jean Valjean is pursued through the streets of Paris and has to take refuge in a convent. The convent gardener turns out to be a man whom he has befriended in earlier days, and helps him to make his escape.

It is now necessary to introduce the *jeune premier,* the estimable young man who is destined in the end to marry the heroine, Cosette. But I cannot follow the many turns of the plot which lead to the marriage of Marius and Cosette. Jean Valjean cannot bear to give up Cosette to her young lover, and he dies of a broken heart. And yet he dies happy, realizing that he has expiated his crime, and he is recognized by Marius as the very image of the Savior.

In this outline I have enormously simplified the story and omitted all mention of some of the major incidents and characters. This is, as everybody knows, a formidable book. There are five parts, 48 books, 321 chapters, in my edition more than 2,000 pages. And first it must be said that, so far as story goes, it is very well done. In a narrative involving many characters drawn from the most diverse *milieux,* the author follows the excellent method of establishing one group of characters very solidly before introducing another group which is eventually to be closely linked with them. It is a well-ordered story, free from the innumerable fussy little interruptions and changes of center that spoil so much of Balzac's story-telling. Hugo has many high qualities in the *manner* of doing it. Such is the excellent objectivity with which, at one point and another, he shows us a character in action, especially Jean Valjean. In general the story is notable for its bold modeling, its dramatic intensity. I know nothing in the whole range of fiction which goes faster where it does go, which holds the reader in a tighter grip of suspense. Is there anything more exciting than Jean Valjean's flight through Paris that ends with his scaling the convent wall, or his adventure in the underground labyrinth of sewers?

It is true that this fine story-telling is the good side of

a vicious method, since it is made possible, for one thing, by the author's election to narrate only the most exciting moments of the history, to "hit" only the "high spots." The moments of ordinary life are neglected altogether or treated in hasty survey. There is none of the patient following of small incidents such as make up the staple of most lives and such as Thackeray and the French realists excel in. In other words, this is, on the side of action, a pure adventure story. It is one long tissue of coincidences, of extraordinary and well-nigh incredible happenings, of impudent clever *coups de théâtre,* which, taken all together, amount to simple melodrama. Everywhere the author depends for effect on surprise and on the "noble gesture."

Jean Valjean is invariably, after his conversion, as noble in soul and action as he is physically strong and quick of wit. He is always taking the high line of magnanimity, and without the least regard for his own safety. More than once he gets himself into new and frightful difficulties by his indiscreet generosity, his rôle of "the beggar who gives." Perhaps the most grandiose of all his gestures is that at the tenement of the Thénardiers when they have laid an ambush for him and are about to put an end to him with a flaming hot iron. They have bound him hand and foot, but he has succeeded with a sharpened coin in freeing himself all but one foot, and then by a trick he gets possession of the red-hot iron. So then he has them in his power, and he has the means of escape from their ruthless and cruel hands. But instead of using it against them, even to make his escape, he turns it on himself and deliberately burns his own flesh. This is to show that he will not betray them, since he has power over his own will and never tells anything that he does not wish to tell.

With great and high natures, the rebellion of the flesh and the senses in the pinch of pain merely serves to bring out the soul and make it show upon their foreheads, just as the mutinies of soldiers force the captain to show his mettle.

"Wretched ones!" cries Jean Valjean, "fear not me any more than I fear you."

And tearing the iron from his wounded flesh, he flung it out of the open window. The horrible implement disappeared whirling in the night, fell to the ground far away, and was extinguished in the snow.

Such bombastic scenes may hold the reader for the moment, but they will not bear the weight of thoughtful consideration. When examined closely, few scenes are found to be well done save on the side of suspense and drama, and where the theatrical element is not strongly present it is hard to realize the situations imaginatively. Compared with the work of the really serious artists, this is simply chromo, and in his story Hugo may be said to have altogether neglected what the novelist proper—whether of the rank of Tolstoy and Flaubert, or that of George Moore or George Gissing—regards as of the essence of his craft.

2

But then, it may be said, it is not in the story proper that one should look for the serious significance of Victor Hugo; it is in the political history with which the private chronicle is so richly interlarded, it is in the social comment, the philosophy. And indeed no good story-teller ever took out so much time to work up a background of general historical and social interest. Whole books, many chapters long, are devoted solely to this background material: one entire book to the battle of Waterloo, another to a sociological study of the Paris street urchin, another to the history and description of the sewers of Paris. Two books are devoted to an account of a convent of the Bernadines and to the general theory of convent life. There are entire books in which there is nothing but general discussion, and during which the story simply waits. And there are scattered through the novel many more chapters wholly devoted to general background and theorizing, not to speak of the incidental passages in the course of the action in which the author instructs the reader what to think about it all.

As for the background material, it is brilliantly served up, and tends, in the long run, to give the book in review a sort of monumental solidity and grandeur. But in so far as it is a substitute for the serious close-up presentation of human nature—the ordinary business of good fiction—it serves simply to deceive both author and reader into supposing that the book is on a higher intellectual level than it really is. As a study of human nature it is not at all on a high level intellectually. The historical and philosophical digressions are for the most part a turning aside from the particular case at issue, an evasion of the problem of fiction. And while they are interesting enough in their own right, and full of information, they are, after all, only a kind of high-class journalism.

The style of Hugo is the style of high-class journalism, or more exactly that of the clever parliamentarian of the romantic period. It is self-conscious and complacent. It is sentimentally effusive where the occasion calls for pathos. It is given to rhetorical repetition in the manner of Dickens and rhetorical question in the manner of De Quincey. It is witty, antithetical, bombastic, pathetic, figurative, grandiloquent, and makes an English reader think of Macaulay and Carlyle and De Quincey and Frank Crane and Fra Elbertus all rolled into one. And it is that kind of style which has the effect, very often, of diverting attention from the characters, the subject, on to the author himself.

One trick will serve to illustrate the general quality. In his concern for dramatic effect, Hugo indulges freely in the penchant for making his paragraphs very short, like the successive utterances of an actor who wants to be sure that each effect shall sink in. The indentations of the successive paragraphs are equivalent to the pauses by which the actor gives the impression of an emotion too strong for continuous utterance. This mannerism has been adopted in America by cheap publicists for spicing up the editorial page of their yellow journals. It is often used by Hugo at exciting points of the narrative to increase the theatricality of effect. Or it is used in passages of philosophical speculation, often in combination with rhetorical questions. The following is taken from a brilliant and bombastic discussion of the causes of Napoleon's defeat at Waterloo.

> Still other fatalities were destined to arise.
>
> Is it possible for Napoleon to win this battle? We answer, no. And why? On account of Wellington? On account of Blücher? No. On account of God.
>
> Bonaparte victor at Waterloo, this was not within the law of the nineteenth century. Another series of facts was preparing, in which Napoleon had no longer any place. The evil will of events had long ago announced itself.
>
> It was time for this vast man to fall.
>
> The excessive weight of this man in human destiny disturbed the balance . . . [Here I omit several sentences of this paragraph.]
>
> Napoleon had been denounced in the infinite, and his fall was decided on.
>
> He was in God's way. [*Il gênait Dieu.*]
>
> Waterloo is not a battle; it is the change of direction of the universe.

So then we have, in "Les Misérables," on the one side an exciting story, and on the other a series of dissertations on history, sociology, psychology, etc. But that would seem to imply that there was no relation between Hugo's story and his philosophy. Whereas it is clear that the whole story was constructed with a view to proving a thesis. Hugo tells us most explicitly what was his thesis in "Les Misérables":

> The book which the reader has under his eyes at this moment, is nothing, from one end to the other, in the whole and in the details, whatever may be the interruptions, the exceptions and the failures, but the march forward from evil to good, from the unjust to the just, the false to the true, from night to day, from appetite to conscience, from decay to life, from bestiality to the sense of duty, from hell to heaven, from nothingness to God. Point of departure: matter. Goal: the spirit. A hydra at the beginning, an angel at the end.

This evolution from evil to good, social, moral, religious, is to be seen in operation, according to his design, not merely in the individual characters—the bishop, the convict, the street urchin, the political revolutionary—but likewise in the whole state and body politic. What the "socialists" of Hugo's time were seeking, he says, is "the end of oppression . . . the end of the sword, work for man, instruction for the child, social sweetness for woman, liberty, equality, fraternity, bread for all, ideas for all, the Edenizing of the world—in short, Progress."

This social progress it was the political mission of the republic to bring about; hence the opposition of the republican and virtuous Marius to his frivolous monarchist grandfather. The republic had been ushered in by the Revolution and had been defended by Napoleon. Hence the devotion of Hugo and of Marius to the first emperor. But Napoleon had proved unworthy of his trust; he had substituted the empire for the republic. Hence the statement of Hugo that Napoleon was "in God's way," and the conversion of Marius to pure republicanism. The festering submerged tenth was the result of social conditions for which the monarchy was partly responsible. Hugo points out that the abandonment of little children was not discouraged by the old monarchy. A bit of Bohemia in the lower classes was an accommodation to those in the higher spheres. They were against educating the people. Particularly was there need of galley-slaves to maintain a fleet of boats not subject to the caprices of the wind. And galley-slaves were recruited in part from men like Jean Valjean, who were not criminals at all. Not every starving man who steals a crust of bread is a criminal. But it is very easy to turn him into one if you treat him like one. Every man has a soul of goodness which can be drawn out if he is treated right. The right way is to trust him, to assume that he is good, to make your appeal to his better nature. This is the Christian way, and the way most in harmony with the ideals of the Revolution.

It is clear that Hugo is a romantic humanitarian. And one may not be so down on romanticism and humanitarianism as Professor Babbitt to realize that Hugo's humanitarianism is rather sentimental, exaggerated, and naïve. But as an artist, what is the matter with him is not merely that he has a sentimental philosophy, but that he has constructed his fable to be a simple vehicle for this philosophy, and that human nature is considered exclusively as a means of proving a theory. The good bishop is in every respect an ideal figure of Christian virtue. Long before one has finished the fourteen chapters which make up the first book, and which are entirely given over to an account of the character of Monseigneur Bienvenu, one realizes that one has to do here not with that art whose aim is to present human nature as the author knows it from experience. Each of the characters is a type and little more: Jean Valjean, though he adds some of the qualities of a Douglas Fairbanks creation to those already exemplified by the bishop; Fantine, the loving, loyal woman, turned into a prostitute by unjust social conditions; Javert, the incarnation of human justice in its blind official phase; the Thénardiers, incarnation of *le mauvais pauvre;* Marius, incarnation of the political spirit of the republic, etc.

Here again we are reminded of the chromo, so crudely simple is the coloring, so glaring the contrasts of good and evil. The fault of "Les Misérables" is not that a philosophy of life is implied in the action, and is breathed forth by the characters—that is sometimes true of novels of a finer grain, like "Anna Karenina," "Vanity Fair," Kristin Lavransdatter," or "Manhattan Transfer"—it is that in "Les Misérables" the fable is artificially constructed, the philosophy is forced, and the characters are but puppets in a pantomime.

And this is probably the principal reason why Victor Hugo, as a novelist, does not occupy a very high place in the estimation of serious critics. There is, however, one notable dissenter. I feel bound in honor to mention that no less a critic than the poet Swinburne has pronounced "Les Misérables" "the greatest epic and dramatic work of fiction ever created or conceived." So long as such differences of opinion exist among critics, we can never expect their pleasant art to be erected into an exact science!

VII

PHILOSOPHY: H. G. WELLS

If Victor Hugo illustrates the difficulty of reconciling philosophy and fiction, a still more striking example is afforded by our contemporary H. G. Wells. And if the reputation of Hugo as a novelist has suffered something of a decline since his own day, may we not expect that the reputation of Mr. Wells will suffer a similar abatement with the lapse of time? For it must be obvious to a critical view unbiased by the interest of the contemporary that Victor Hugo is a much greater novelist than H. G. Wells.

These two men occupy a somewhat similar position in relation to the general trend of thought in their respective times. Much water, to be sure, has run under the bridge since the time of Hugo, and Wells's philosophy wears a very different dress from his. Science and industry have a much greater prominence in Wells, politics has fallen into the background, and especially the brand of Liberté-Egalité-Fraternité. And while Wells has had, in certain phases, his own brand of religiosity, he makes nothing at all of that moral and Christian spirit exemplified by Jean Valjean and the good bishop.

But both men are radicals, and Wells continues unabated into a disillusioned age Hugo's fervid faith in human and political progress, though he may not express himself in such rhetorical terms. So that it is not unnatural to bring them into comparison as novelists. And once they are brought into comparison, it is clear that Victor Hugo is not merely more interesting reading in his speculative phase, but that he is an infinitely better story-teller. This is most obvious if with Hugo's we compare novels of Mr. Wells's later period like "The New Machiavelli," "Mr. Britling Sees It Through," and "The World of William Clissold"—novels which combine a realistic presentation of contemporary life with extensive interlardings of social philosophy.

A brief review of "The World of William Clissold" (1926) will make clear what I mean. This book purports to be the life history of a British industrialist living in retirement in a Provençal farm-house, together with a sketch of the new world-order which he visions as coming into being. Each one of the six books recounts certain of the facts about William Clissold and his brother Richard. But in each book the author, in accordance with his design, slips over from the individual case to a consideration of the general social conditions; and the bulk of each is taken up with abstract theorizing. Thus in the first book William Clissold, at the age of fifty-nine, has been dining with a happy and devoted scientist. And this leads him into a discussion of the relations of science and religion, which occupies more than nine of the sixteen sections comprised in this book. The third book reviews the life of his brother "Dickon" as an advertising man with an imagination, touches briefly on the married life of the two brothers, and recounts their activities during the World War. But the real subject of the book is Dickon's ideas—on advertising as a means of publicity, on the war, the reconstruction period, and the period of debt-collecting—running over into William's ideas on the same subjects. The fifth book contains no private history, but is entirely occupied with an account of the new order which is coming into being under the auspices of science and industry, and of educational methods calculated to produce an "adult mentality" in citizens of the new order. The sixth book is virtually all devoted to a discussion of types of love and the right attitude to take toward sex and marriage.

This review of the matter of "William Clissold" will indicate the difference between Wells's method and Hugo's. In the first place there is much less story in proportion to philosophy, and what there is of it is almost entirely wanting in that direction upon special dramatic issues which makes a story enthralling, which gives it suspense and coherence and growing interest. There is perhaps about the same proportion of story to general speculation as in "Sartor Resartus," and the story elements are dispersed perhaps still more widely through the mass of speculation than in the history of Teufelsdröckh. In the second place, the theorizing in "William Clissold" is much more spread out, more rambling and abstract, than in "Les Misérables," where it has such a large stiffening of historical fact and the scholarly documentation gives a solid foothold for the mind in the bogs of speculation.

And then, finally, one feels even more acutely in Wells than in Hugo the forced association of fiction and philosophy, and all the more so, perhaps, because of Wells's effort to weave the two together. So much of Hugo's background material is relegated to special books entirely given over to it, while the story waits. You read these books if you care to, and you find them as fascinating as fiction. Then you return to the story, with this reinforcement of background material, and you move swiftly through a plot of absorbing interest. The story, in its place, is given the fullest swing, and you have no such feeling as in Wells that the story has been diluted by the philosophy.

Of "William Clissold" it is too much to say that the story has been diluted. There is not enough of it for that. There is really no one episode which is sufficiently well developed on its own account to constitute part of a story. The story is disposed of in the briefest possible space so as to make room for the abstract discussions; it appears to be introduced in perfunctory fashion merely to give a plausible starting-point for the general topics, and so that the book may be what the author asserts it to be in the preface, "a complete full-dress novel, that and nothing more."

As a matter of fact, it is a good deal more than a full-dress novel—and a good deal less. For, whatever else a full-dress novel may do, it does not entirely neglect to present the individual case, the private history, which gives it its character as a novel. The most distinctive feature of a novel is the concreteness of its picture of life, and the tendency of Wells, in his later period, is to give his story in sketchy outline, in general terms and not in the concrete. This sort of thing, for example, is what in the long run makes dull reading of so many of Wells's later novels:

> I suppose I did quite a lot of promiscuous love-making in those vacuous days. It is nothing to boast of and nothing to conceal. For a long time I found no one I could love very much, and I began to prefer women who plainly did not care for me very greatly to women who brought a personal passion, or the pretence of one, into the game. I was ready enough to admit they were charming and delightful creatures, but not that they were personally indispensable, and that I was tormented by yearnings, uncertainties and monstrous fidelities on their account. I began to feel a tolerance for meretricious love which I had once thought revolting. But I rarely came to absolutely meretricious love. If I had been a poor man and manifestly ungenerous I should have failed in some of these love affairs in which I did not fail, so much of paying was there in it, but that is not quite the same thing as meretriciousness.
>
> Such was the quality of my life in the middle forties. Cut down in this fashion to its heart, it was friendless, loveless and aimless. But that is not to say that there was not steady, extensive, interesting toil, much fellowship and kindly commerce with pleasant men and women, æsthetic gratifications, fun, excitements, a great deal of incidental happiness in it. But there was dissatisfaction waiting for me in the shadows and

the quiet moments. It was not good enough. Life was passing by. I was not being used to the full.

Here we have a blanket description, in general terms, of the quality of a man's life, and that not at one moment, or over a short period of time, but over a number of years. Summaries of this kind are of course necessary occasionally in any novel which undertakes to cover a considerable length of time and an action of some complexity. They help to secure perspective and save the author from the necessity of narrating in detail parts of the story which he regards as of secondary importance. They may accordingly subserve economy; they save time for those parts which are to be treated at length.

But in this case Wells takes but meager advantage ot such economies. For the saving he has made in summarizing the promiscuous and meretricious love-making of William Clissold is not matched by any adequate development of the serious sentimental affairs which are really important for his theme. Immediately after the passage quoted he goes on to an account of Clissold's affair with the actress Helen, who represents the free and independent female citizen so necessary to his new social order. This relation is one of considerable delicacy and requiring patient and ingenious development if it is to be convincing. It requires, if nothing else, a certain extension and bulk, so that it may register and leave a lasting impression. But Mr. Wells, at this period of his writing, has little patience left for the love-stories called for in the scheme of his novel; he is so much occupied with more important things that he is unequal to the effort of imagination necessary to give them reality.

For a form as indeterminate as that of the novel there are not many dogmatic rules that can be laid down. But if there is one such, it is this: if an episode is important enough to be chronicled, it is important enough to be chronicled adequately. This is a principle well known to Arnold Bennett, for example, and it is his observance of it which makes "The Old Wives' Tale" so much greater than any of the novels of Wells.

2

It may turn out that the best of Mr. Wells's books are not his realistic full-dress novels but some of his utopian romances and mechanical forecasts in the manner of Jules Verne. In such stories the private history of individuals is of little importance; there is no occasion for the development of sentimental episodes; the imagination of the author may expatiate without let and hindrance over matters of common interest. The trouble comes, in his realistic novels, with the attempt to tie up the private emotional histories with public movements and social theories. It is very difficult to do this tying up in a convincing manner. And then, moreover, in this association of private history with public movements, it is the public movements that are in danger of dominating the outlook, to the great detriment of what we call fiction.

With a writer like Mr. Wells, there is a constant disposition to substitute the general social theory for the story which is supposed to float it. And once he lets himself go, once he reconciles himself to the subordinate rôle of story, there is nothing to check him in his rambling. He has a naturally discursive mind, and in later years he has grown diffuse and repetitious. So that, if we agree to overlook the inadequacy of the story-telling and find his main interest in the incidental philosophy of the novels, there is still something left to be desired.

There is no doubt that Mr. Wells has been a pamphleteer of a very high order. He has stimulated many readers to think. He has been, in contemporary thought, what William Clissold called himself, "a ferment, a catalytic agent, a provocation." He has brought into circulation, or kept in circulation, more general ideas on the social order than any English writer since Arnold. But he is not so brilliant a pamphleteer as Voltaire or Swift or Anatole France, as Shaw or Chesterton or Mencken. He has not the wit of any of these, nor their power of concentration. He often falls into the abstract and arid manner of leading articles in newspapers and weekly reviews; and he has not the excuse of editorial writers, the need to boil down the argument. He does not seek with passion *le mot juste*. He is capable of writing banal sentences in that mood of absent-mindedness that overtakes all but the greatest writers. Here is description: "What a gracious and splendid vista is that of the Champs-Elysées, the finest, I think, in the world!" Here is characterization: "For me she was wonderful and mystical; she was beautiful and lovely for me as no human being has ever been; she had in my perception of her a distinctive personal splendour that was as entirely and inseparably her own as the line of her neck or the timbre of her voice."

But the worst is the long-windedness. One hundred pages at a stretch in "William Clissold" on the abstract outline of the World Republic! Carlyle was long-winded too, and Ruskin. But they were more picturesque, to say the least; and while they did not resort to the vehicle of fiction, they were never at a loss to give concreteness to their general discussions. Whereas Mr. Wells so often makes a feint of telling a story only to abandon it for interminable and tepid dissertation.

There was a period when he came very near making a really artistic synthesis of theory and fiction. It was the period of those entertaining character sketches, "Kipps" (1905), "Tono-Bungay" (1908), and "The History of Mr. Polly" (1910). "Tono-Bungay" in particular combines a most amusing story with many anticipations of the ideas of "William Clissold." Uncle Ponderevo, the manufacturer of an only slightly deleterious patent medicine, forger, bankrupt, and floater of dubious business enterprises, reminds one of the father of the Clissold brothers; only, instead of committing suicide in court, he is carried off in an airship to the south of France to die. He is also suggestive of Dickon in his enthusiastic faith in the power of publicity and the variety of articles that he advertised. He was a Babbitt, a boomer of towns and business. He was childishly vain and fond of spreading himself, like so many little big operators of his type. He was the incarnation of that prevalent modern notion that trade is good in itself, and the more of it the better. When his nephew George protested against his dosing the public with this "slightly harmful rubbish"—it was bad for the kidneys—the uncle declared, "It's as straight as—it's fair trading . . . It's the sort of thing everybody does."

Uncle Ponderevo, then, is a representative comic figure, standing, like Don Quixote or Sir Roger de Coverley, for significant social tendencies, for an age and a culture. And he enables his author to make his reflections on commerce, on our social order, without the necessity of indulging in dissertations. He is certainly a droll character, a comic figure like Tartarin or Micawber, though not so funny as either of these.

And the whole book is highly entertaining. At least I am sure it was so in the days before the World War. Mr. Wells has offered us a varied and spicy fare. There is, of course, the theme of casual marriage through mere sexual attraction, unhappy married life, and separation—a theme which recurs in "Mr. Polly" and "William Clissold" and so many of his novels. There is the more unusual notion, for 1908, of making his hero a flier of airplanes, who can carry off his defaulting uncle like a god in a machine. There is the still wilder adventure of the search for "quap." Mr. Wells could always be trusted to serve up an appetizing dish of novelties. And if it is a kind of Russian salad of ingredients not too well mingled, if it seems rather an agglomeration of themes loosely heaped together than the adequate development of a chosen theme, there can be no doubt, at any rate, that this is fiction in the obvious meaning of the term.

And this is true of books like "Kipps" and "Mr. Polly." They are clearly fiction, and they are entertaining narratives. "Mr. Polly" introduces the novelty of making indigestion a main motive in the history of a man's life. But it is not a book that we need take seriously. There is an amusing chapter in which one Parsons, salesman in a shop, is discharged because he insists on decorating the window with artistic "window tickets." It is reminiscent of the scene in "The Old Wives' Tale" in which Mr. Povey is offended by the lack of appreciation of window tickets on the part of Mrs. Baines and throws his latest creation into the fire. But the Parsons episode is not nearly so good as the other. Bennett's humor is more refined; and besides, his incident is not primarily humorous. It is an important item in the characterization of a person who is very important for the story as a whole. It is tense and dramatic. It is quiet and unobtrusive and at the same time structurally important. Mr. Povey is a much more real person than Parsons, or Mr. Polly, or Kipps, or even than Uncle Ponderevo.

For Arnold Bennett has a fundamental seriousness in approaching his art which is not shared by Mr. Wells. Wells is really not good in characterization except in a superficial way. He has a knack of hitting off types, no doubt of that. But he does not get *into* the characters. Indeed, he does not seem to realize the importance of getting into them. He does not seem to have envisaged this as something involved in his undertaking as a writer of fiction. He takes seriously his business of entertaining the reader, but he does not take seriously the art of characterization, which is three fourths of fiction. He takes his philosophy seriously, for he is primarily a thinker on social themes. And mainly he has conceived of the novel as a means by which people may be lured into swallowing his philosophy.

Now, I suppose it is legitimate to make the novel carry whatever you can make it carry; you are certainly free to make it serve your ends, whatever they are. But, in our survey of methods in the novel, it is proper to distinguish those which serve mainly the ends of philosophy and those which serve what we may call the ends of fiction. The primary end of fiction is the study of human nature in the concrete. This is true not merely of realism but of romantic and idealistic fiction, even of those types which Mr. Forster includes under the headings of Fantasy and Prophecy. But the primary ends of Mr. Wells are philosophical, and while he has written entertaining and thought-provoking books in the outward form of novels, we might as well be clear that they are in essence pamphlets, and that, in the history of literature, his place is among the pamphleteers rather than among the novelists.

VIII

HORS-D'ŒUVRES: BARRÈS, FRANCE

WHAT I have had to say of Hugo and Mr. Wells does not imply a prejudice against the novel of philosophical reference. It is a question of the method by which the philosophical element is related to the story-element and the terms on which they live together. It is also a question of style in both the narrower and the broader sense of the word.

Ever since the novel was constituted as a highly distinct form, there has been an almost constant succession of what we may call literary hors-d'œuvres in the form of novels—works lying outside the main stream of development. Here belong "Candide" and "Tristram Shandy"; the witty dialogues of Peacock, with their modern counterparts in "South Wind," "Crome Yellow," and "The Private Life of Helen of Troy"; and here belong the works of Anatole France, and the exquisite scholastic treatises of Maurice Barrès. These are among the most delicious of all works cast in the form of fiction, and certainly no disparagement is involved in putting them into a class by themselves. And the term "hors-d'œuvres" is not meant to imply that they are not often extremely meaty. They may contain more meat of thought than their often duller contemporaries in regular-line novels. The question is how far it may be regarded as the meat of fiction proper.

Consider, for example, "Le Jardin de Bérénice" (1891) by Barrès. The very simple story concerns a certain Philippe, candidate for membership in the Chamber of Deputies from Arles, and Bérénice, dreamy daughter of the Midi, who symbolizes for him the fascinating and backward country which he loves, as well as various unpractical and antique qualities of spirit. Being distressed by certain features of her erotic life, he persuades her to marry an excellent philistine. But this proves a mistake. Bérénice dies, and Philippe comes to the conclusion that he has misinterpreted the will of the Unconscious in reference to her.

The book ends with the appearance of her spirit to him one warm October night in her garden at Aigues-Mortes. She talks with him at some length, and sets him right in his thinking, pardoning him for having been "a trifle vulgar in wishing to substitute his notion of correctness for the urge of nature." He reminds her of their evenings together of old time in the garden. And she replies: "I was there; but I am everywhere. Recognize in me Petite-Secousse, the little push by which each least parcel of the universe makes manifest the secret impulse of the Unconscious. Where I am not, is death. . . . Think well, too, of the wretched ones: sometimes there is in them such an urge that from having aimed too high they fall into the depths. . . . In order to satisfy your need of spiritual unity, you must not fail to keep in touch with me, with me alone, Petite-Secousse, who animate indifferently all these moving forms, deemed by us wrong or right according to our short-sighted judgments."

I could not hope, even with a longer outline, to make the reader understand the complicated and elusive thought of this book, let alone the peculiar charm of the thing. It has more than a suggestion of Sterne's "Sentimental Journey," but is much too individual to be caught in any net of description or comparison. What I want is to make clear the extremely abstract nature of the story and the frankly symbolic function of Bérénice. This author has no intention of giving a presentation of manners in detail, à la Thackeray or Daudet, nor a detailed account of mental processes, nor even of offering us bits of dialogue which reproduce the way people talk. What Philippe says to Bérénice is not credible as actual speech but merely as a representation of his attitude toward her. The book is really, under a slight fictional form, the exposition of a philosophy of life, an attitude of mind, in somewhat the symbolical fashion of the "Vita Nuova."

So far from wishing to disguise the abstract character of the book, Barrès does his best to bring it to the fore. Many of the heads of sections are conceived in terms which underline this dialectical tendency. There is one chapter entitled "Bérénice's Pedagogy," and this is subdivided into sections bearing the captions "Bérénice's Method," "Bérénice's Pleasures," "Bérénice's Duties." And of all this part he says himself, "This teaching of the method, the pleasures and the duties of Bérénice, I give in arid outline (*je le dessèche*) in order to make an exposition of it according to the scholastic procedure." He insists on this scholastic method with the coquetry of a man of letters who is bored with the silly story-telling of his day. So that if "The World of William Clissold" is to be thought of as a treatise under the mask of a novel, "The Garden of Bérénice" is a novel under the mask of a treatise.

If it is not, properly speaking, a novel, it is at any rate a solid and rare imaginative creation. For all the scholastic dissection, for all the spareness of description, of psychology, of "scene" and action, Bérénice *exists*. She exists as an individual, and apart from the symbolism, as Beatrice exists in the "Vita Nuova." And Languedoc exists, Aigues-Mortes exists, and the dusty provincial museum of Joigne, with its tapestries and painted panels. From the whole work there emanates a subtle and pungent fragrance of old France, of the Midi. And over it all there is a play of sentimental nuances which you may hold suspect but which you cannot fail to find seductive.

"The Garden of Bérénice" has the quality of poetry, which we cannot say of "William Clissold"; and it has the quality of wit. Above all, comparing it with Wells, we are impressed with its brevity—that brevity which is the soul of wit. In this it is at one with the work of Anatole France. Like his work, it is not in line with the regular evolution of the novel. It has no pretensions to be regarded as naturalistic fiction.

2

And so with Anatole France. His spirit is too classical for the labored human document of naturalism. He is not interested in these exhaustive inquiries into the private lives of frequently dull people. The fact that they take themselves seriously is no reason why he should take them so, or the fact that if you cut them they will bleed. With the logic of will and fate he does not concern himself, and he has no ambition to show things human in their entirety, to build them up and finish them off.

In his choice of characters he is highly selective and in the aspects of his characters chosen for exhibition. He likes children and loves to dwell with tender sentiment on memories of his own boyhood. He is fond of old men, scholars, antiquaries, visionaries, absent-minded and eccentric dreamers. And he is fond of any one who can be the butt of his humor and provocative of his wit. His rationalism is of the type that revels in the superstitions of the Golden Legend; his irony goes hand in hand with his fantasy. He resents any standards of verisimilitude which rule out the unfettered play of the fancy, and he insists on salamanders and sylphides and on baptized penguins that raise a theological problem in the courts of heaven.

Everywhere in Anatole France the general idea dominates, as it dominates "Candide" and the "Tale of a Tub," and the story is so shaped as to bring into relief the attitudes of the author, to turn a point neatly and, as it were, demonstrate a theorem. Perhaps the thing which distinguishes this approach from that of the novelist proper is that the novelist is thinking of what people are like as individuals; he is thinking of their individual problems of conduct, and he wishes to make us reproduce in imagination the very state of mind with which they confront their problems, to make us follow through the whole agonizing process. Whereas the "classical" writer is thinking of what human nature is like in general, in its large lines, and is concerned with the individual only in so far as he will stand for the type.

Thus France conceives of human nature as superstitious, gullible, irrational, sensual, and egotistical, and his fables are mainly a series of witty anecdotes in illustration of these traits. But he holds likewise an ideal of reason and an ideal of humane society, never yet realized, and most likely never to be realized, but persisting in bookish tradition and in the dreams of a few "humanists," and he invents his professor Bergeret as mouthpiece of these ideals. Only he is wise enough to know that such men are seldom efficient characters, and Monsieur Bergeret appears accordingly as absent-minded, impractical, and a cuckold. And his beautiful socialistic dreams have an air of futility, overwhelmed as they are by wave on wave of vulgar animal behavior in the world about him.

Sometimes, when there is a favorable conjunction of theme and fable, a book of France has the shapeliness and symmetry of a demonstration in geometry. Such is the case in "Thaïs," with its neat reversal of rôles—the monk who would convert the courtezan falling convert to her transcendental doctrine of Love—with the incidental banquet of philosophers and the ironic dissection of Christian theology. Often, where the author has started too much game, there is not this appearance of formal shapeliness. Thus in "L'Ile des Pingouins" he begins with his rationalistic irony at the expense of religion and ends with a burlesque commentary on the Affaire Dreyfus. It is true that, in this history of humanity from primitive times, he is tracing throughout the same irrationality in human behavior. But one has the impression that the subject-matter is too heterogeneous to be successfully reduced to form.

This is the case in "Monsieur Bergeret à Paris" (1901), which has the interest, moreover, of bearing a closer resemblance to the ordinary novel than many of his books. Treating contemporary matter, it enlarges on the domestic life of a character as well realized in the manner of fiction as my Uncle Toby. When you begin the book you think that the main subject is Monsieur Bergeret, but before you are through you know that it is something much more public and general. The main subject is the Affaire Dreyfus. On review you find that Monsieur Bergeret occupies a little less than one half the volume which bears his name; the other half is a satire on the anti-Dreyfusards, the royalist-nationalist party. Looking still closer, you find that not more than half of the part devoted to Monsieur Bergeret is concerned with him personally; for in at least one half of his part, or one quarter of the whole book, he is simply a mouthpiece of the socialist ideal. Still less perhaps of the other part, dealing with the royalists, is personal history; it is simply dialogue, à la Peacock, intended to show up the absurdities of the nationalist position. And then, while the book begins with Monsieur Bergeret, it does not end with him at all. It ends with a series of fantastic scenes in a royalist salon.

Of course the case is not so bad as it seems. There is a principle of composition which partly justifies this seeming inconsequence. This is simply the contrast between the personality and opinions of Bergeret, who represents the ideal side of human aspiration, and the petty, selfish, and ridiculous views and gestures of the nationalists. But still there is this discrepancy between the two parts of the narrative: Bergeret and his friends have an infinitely greater reality than the people of the opposing camp. So that the two parts are not merely contrasted in theme, they are in sharp contrast as to style of presentation. And so it is as if we had two different kinds of art in the same book, loosely associated by the underlying theme but never really reconciled esthetically.

The art of fiction is best shown in the domestic life of Monsieur Bergeret, and it is here that we have the most charming passages and those most likely to live. Monsieur Bergeret is the academic and speculative type, given to neat little discourses on every subject. What he has to say is penetrating and just; but since he is concerned primarily with the theoretical aspect of things, he has an air of dreamy impracticality, which entitles us to laugh at him at the same time that we follow what he has to say with gratified interest. His Shandean character is heightened by the dry, taciturn practicality of his sister, who plays the Sancho Panza to his Don Quixote. This humor is of a radiant delicacy that could not live in the presence of an intrigue of gripping interest; the fine point of these little dialogues would be imperceptible amid the garish colors of drama and passion.

Wherever the members of one family are gathered together, there will be some differences of opinion and some ignoring of those conversational amenities which we so carefully observe with strangers. The tone of familiar conversation, with its unanswered questions, its discontinuity of subject-matter arising from the diversity of interests, its funny little ellipses, is well rendered in various slight skirmishes between Bergeret and his daughter Pauline or his sister Zoé.

"You have a dog, papa?" said Pauline.

"You were not to have come till Saturday," said Monsieur Bergeret.

"You got my letter?" said Zoé.

"Yes," said Monsieur Bergeret.

"No, the other one."
"I've only received one."
"There's no understanding one another."

The one thing that is most delicious in the book is the dog Riquet. On him the author has lavished his powers of observation, his love, his philosophy, all of which appear together in the radiant synthesis of his humor. There are here no invidious distinctions between man and the lower animal world. Everything in the conduct and psychology of this dog is described in strictly human terms. For it seems that the author agrees with Monsieur Bergeret in considering that Riquet is an intelligent being. "It is true that he doesn't understand all of our ideas; but then we don't understand all of his." I do not feel certain that, at bottom, Anatole France is not in agreement with the Behaviorists. And the consistency with which he attributes to his dog intellectual motives such as men claim for themselves may simply be his subtle way of throwing doubt on the pretensions of men.

Monsieur Bergeret finds in Riquet the rudiments of religious sentiment. When his master offers him a bit of chicken, Riquet declines.

> The majesty of the place overawed him. And perhaps he had received, in his earlier days, lessons which had taught him to respect the food of the master. And so he regards Monsieur Bergeret with humble and reproachful eyes, as much as to say, "Master, why do you tempt me?" And, with lowered tail, with loose paws, dragging his belly in sign of humility, he went off to seat himself sadly on his backside, over by the door. And there he stayed during the whole meal.

Riquet takes very seriously his duty of protecting his master against any invasion of the premises by strangers, who are necessarily enemies. For Monsieur Bergeret, Riquet is a symbol of the primitive mind of man, blindly conservative—the creature of instinct and of ingrained habits of truculence derived from a savage state of being. He believes that, in mankind, this primitive mind is capable of evolution and of being raised into something more reasonable and more suited to the civil condition. He believes that Riquet has a good heart, and so he can love and tolerate in the dog instinctive reactions which in humans serve only to arouse his satirical spirit. Him he can treat with humor. Monsieur Bergeret himself has not merely a good heart but a civilized, reasonable mind; he too is a subject of humor and sympathetic admiration instead of satire. And it is the chapters dealing with him which we may characterize as fiction.

Still, essentially, in method and manner, this is a classical piece of writing, typical of the period antedating the novel, and having in view rather different ends. It is a commentary on human nature rather than a presentation of it. The author's concern is ever for the idea rather than for the substance of its incarnation. Such slight narrative as there is, is little more than a device for getting the characters talking, a starting-point for philosophy. This is hardly more of a novel than Lucian, Erasmus, Rabelais. There is no effort at that dramatic and close-range study of human lives in their particularity, with the strain and stress of passionately sought personal interests, which does so much to give life to the characters of fiction proper.

Once allow that this is not meant for a novel, and we need not worry about these matters. Here, by rare good luck, is an author really witty, and even, within marked limitations, wise. This is a rarer phenomenon than a good story-teller, a dramatic projector of human beings. There is probably no greater proportion of fictional matter here than in the essays of Lamb or Hazlitt. Why not accept such a writer on the same terms as we accept these wise and witty essayists?

And no one need complain that there is no blood in the veins of these characters. It is good for once, in a book about men and women, to have a writer whose style is dry and free from hysterics, who does not give us that feeling of heat and sweat and messiness that we have in reading so many novels. When one reads Paul Bourget or Dorothy Canfield one says to oneself, "Here is more heat than light, the sticky heat of a steam laundry." When one reads Hardy, one says, "Here is the sun's heat, and some of the light of the sun." Of Tolstoy at his best one says, "Here is the heat and light of the sun, pure and full." Of Anatole France one says: "There is little heat here; it is all light. There is little passion, but there is much gaiety. The light may not be the full burning light of the sun, but it is a pure white light, the light of a cultivated intellect."

Only, we must distinguish. The peculiarity of fiction is its heat. For fiction is a reproduction of life rather than a commentary on it: and of life the specific character is heat more than light. In Fielding and Thackeray there is more light than heat; but there is heat enough to make them novelists. This is hardly the case with Anatole France.

IX

HORS-D'ŒUVRES: CABELL

LIGHT, again, rather than heat, is the distinguishing quality of our American James Branch Cabell, who stands in so like a relation to the traditional novel with France and Barrès, and who shares with them so many traits of form and manner. France he brings to mind not merely by his irony and grace, and by his general persuasion, in regard to human aims and business, that they are matters of little importance. He even suggests him at times by the quality of his humor and the sort of persons on whom he turns the light of his amused affection. Is it too fanciful to see in Colonel Musgrave a kinsman of Sylvestre Bonnard and Monsieur Bergeret? There is at least a similarity of antiquarian tastes, of old-fashioned genteel virtues. And the wry tenderness of the relation between Musgrave and his sister Agatha makes one think of that between Bergeret and Zoé.

But still more like is the fondness these writers have for embroidering their narratives with episodes of amorous gallantry and for exposing human folly, and the delight they take, by some witty turn, to lay bare those paradoxes which inhere in the nature of human effort and circumstance. Such were the ironies turned up by Kennaston, in "The Cream of the Jest," while exploring history in his dreams. There was Cristoforo Colombo. "He had doubled the world's size and resources, in his attempts to find some defenceless nation which could be plundered with impunity; and he was dying in ignorance of what his endeavors had achieved." And there was the alchemist who, "seeking to find the means of making life perpetual, had accidentally discovered gunpowder."

Similarities I could also point out between Cabell and Barrès, but to labor the point of similarity might seem to suggest a want of originality in the American writer. And we have few writers more original than Cabell. His prose style is in itself a creation highly individual and of the utmost suppleness and charm. Of that I have treated at length in "The Outlook for American Prose." Again, he has shown the greatest inventiveness in adapting to his use the matter of medieval romance. Never does he take a plot or an incident ready-made. Never can one trace the original of an episode. But, deeply impregnated as he is with romance and folklore, he has always ready to hand some incident of necromancy, some typical notion of the folk-mind as to the working of fetish and talisman, which will perfectly symbolize the spiritual transaction called for by his theme. Thus he has invented two entire cycles of imaginary adventure, the cycles of Jurgen and Manuel, completely furnished with kings and queens, with wizards and champions, monstrous creatures, speaking birds, invisible cloaks, and magic transformations. And literal-minded persons he has the pleasure of mystifying with learned reference to text and source.

The invention itself is fun, but what is important is the meaning underlying each event, the systematic development of a theme; and, above all, the perfection with which the author has compounded his diverse elements—romance and rationality, irony and idealism—reducing them to one consistent elixir, of characteristic flavor and virtue.

I am speaking now more particularly of his legendary tales like "Jurgen" (1919) and "Figures of Earth" (1921). He has stories, too, dealing with "real" people, who take part in credible action in the contemporary setting of old Virginia towns. Such are "The Cords of Vanity" (1909) and "The Rivet in Grandfather's Neck" (1915). But in many ways these stories are all of a piece with the pure romances. You are likely to hear, at any time, that a citizen of Lichfield is a great-grandson of the mythical Jurgen, and that, through the favor of Ole-Luk-Oie, he has been permitted to meet—in the glaze of a mustard jar!—the dead woman he loved. The most realistic of all the novels is "The Rivet in Grandfather's Neck." But even this story begins with an anecdote out of Andersen, about a china shepherdess and a chimney-sweep, who once went up the chimney to take a look at the wide world and then came back frightened at the world's great size, and content to stay cozily at home in the cupboard. And the story, having begun with this pretty fable, to which, moreover, allusion is made from time to time throughout the narrative, there clings to it all some scent of apologue and allegory.

In "The Cream of the Jest" (1917) the two types are deliberately blent. And this curious performance illustrates how in all Cabell's work, implicitly or explicitly, the natural and the magical, the ideal and the dreary matter-of-fact, interpenetrate one another in a sort of "misty mid-region" or borderland of real and imaginary. This book begins with an introduction by a Mr. Harrowby, who has made his fortune in cold-cream, and who gives an air of pedestrian authenticity to Felix Kennaston, the deceased author. Then we pass directly to mythical Storisende, where we meet the subtle clerk Horvendile and Ettarre, the lady of dreams. From thence we return again to Lichfield and the commonplace world of Felix Kennaston. Like other commonplace people, Kennaston marries and goes to whist parties and takes little satisfaction in "the world of use and wont." But he has an artist's imagination, and has brought with him from Storisende the magic sigil of Scoteia, with which he can induce dreams. With the aid of this he returns at will to the dream world and communes with the immortal Ettarre. And not merely this, but he finds himself in the most delightful variety of places and times, making acquaintance with the greatest and most picturesque figures in history. He appears himself under many names and qualities, but always at an agreeable age, anticipating so the system of Virginia Woolf's "Orlando."

Thus, he was in Jerusalem on the day of the Crucifixion and was aged about twenty-three; yet in another dream he was at Capreæ when Tiberius died there, seven years afterwards, and Kennaston was still in the early twenties: and, again, he was in London, at Whitehall, in 1649, and at Vaux-le-Vicomte near Fontainebleau in 1661, being on each occasion twenty-three or -four.

Thus Kennaston receives his education in history, and before we know it the story takes on the aspect of a treatise on creative writing (like "Beyond Life"), and—what comes to the same thing—a treatise on religion, on the relation between dream and actuality, on the esthetic way of life (which is Pater's).

We come down to earth with a bang when we learn that the magic sigil of Scoteia was, in literal truth, the metal top of a cold-cream jar, and Mr. Harrowby makes us understand that the dreamer Kennaston was but a sorry fellow in the practical relations of everyday life. But in this he was a type of humanity. And while it was a sad thing to view the contrast between his dreams and what he was, there was at the same time something not altogether hopeless in it.

The man could create beauty, to outlive him; but in his own appearance he combined grossness with insignificance, and he added thereto a variety of ugly senseless little mannerisms. . . . Again, he could aspire toward chivalric love, that passion which sees in womankind High God made manifest in the loveliest and most perfect of His creations; but in the quest he had succeeded merely in utilizing womenfolk either as toys to play with and put by or as drudges to wait on him; yet, with all this, he could retain unshaken his faith in and his worship of that ideal woman. He could face no decision without dodging; no temptation without compromise; and he lied, as if by instinct, at the threatened approach of discomfort or of his fellows' disapproval; yet devils, men and seraphim would conspire in vain to dissuade him from his self-elected purpose. . . .

[And] it occurred to me that his history was, in essentials, the history of our race, thus far. . . . For it is in this inadequate flesh that each of us must serve his dream; and so, must fail in the dream's service, and must parody that which he holds dearest. To this we seem condemned, being what we are. Thus, one and all, we play false to the dream, and it evades us, and we dwindle into responsible citizens. And yet always thereafter —because of many abiding memories—we know, assuredly, that the way of flesh is not a futile scurrying through dining-rooms and offices and shops and parlors, and thronged streets and restaurants, "and so to bed." . . .

It was in appropriate silence, therefore, that I regarded Felix Kennaston, as a parable. The man was not merely very human; he was humanity. And I reflected that it is only by preserving faith in human dreams that we may, after all, perhaps some day make them come true.

Thus through all the work of Cabell we feel the alternating pulse of dream and disillusion. The pendulum swings back and forth perpetually between the visioned ideal and the realized futility—actual dissonance mocking the imagined harmony, and intended harmony making us indulgent with the fatal dissonance. The incidents and figures of every day are forever dissolving like mist, to show us fleeting glimpses of the faëry landscape behind. And the shadowy heroes of romance are forever taking on the grotesque substance of common burghers. Jurgen turns back weary from gallant adventure to his shop and spouse. Dom Manuel sets forth bravely to follow after his own thinking and his own desire. But soon he finds himself caught in the net of success, making endurable terms with the world, experiencing only the correct emotions, and in all things doing that which was expected of him. Thus even the figures of romance are like broken mirrors giving us back the dusty world of matter-of-fact.

2

Of the more realistic novels the one which has the greatest consistency of texture is perhaps "The Rivet in Grandfather's Neck." The theme objectified in the character of Colonel Musgrave is the old South surviving precariously in times with which it is out of keeping. This gentleman preserves the pride of family without the material prosperity which once gave it support. He preserves the old honor and the old gallantry and the old refinements, without usefulness or accomplishment. He is married to a girl who represents the new blood, the new wealth and energy; and she, with all her admiration for his fineness, cannot be content with his futility.

It is a significant theme, and the flesh in which it is clothed has just sufficient color of naturalness to give it plausibility and charm. It is not sufficient to give it a strong effect of actuality. The figures are outlined suggestively; the drawing is delicate and artful. But the people have an air as if they had just stepped out of a canvas by Boucher, Watteau, or Fragonard. We should not be surprised to see them in flounced skirts gracefully balanced in a swing, or taking boat for the isle of Cythera.

The plot, too, is ingenious rather than natural. Things come about not as in ordinary life so much as in a comedy of Beaumarchais or Marivaux. Everything is arranged so that Colonel Musgrave may make invariably the gesture appropriate for a gentleman of the old school; and one has a feeling that it is all very much arranged. To begin with, Musgrave has taken on himself the blame for the adulteries of his friend Charteris, in order to keep Charteris's wife from knowing of her husband's infidelity. For Musgrave loved Anne Charteris, and wished to see her happy. Gesture number one. . . . Then, in middle age, Musgrave falls in love with ravishing young Patricia Stapylton, and becomes engaged to marry her. But a young man intervenes, capturing the imagination of Patricia; and on the evening when Musgrave's engagement to Patricia is to be made public, the Colonel anticipates by announcing magnanimously the engagement of Patricia to her young man. Gesture number two. Tableau. . . . But the noble gesture proves the best strategy, and Patricia marries not the young man but the Colonel. The years pass by, and who but John Charteris is making love to Musgrave's wife Patricia in Musgrave's own garden? For life has grown dull, and Patricia has fallen in love with the brilliant, unscrupulous writer. . . .

What shall Musgrave do? He will fight to keep his wife —yes, but not for her sake or his own. He will fight to prevent her eloping with his friend—in order to spare his friend's wife. For he has loved Anne Charteris and is determined, at all costs, to leave her undisturbed in her fool's paradise. Fine attitude, and fine distinction of motive! . . . But how prevent the elopement, seeing that Charteris is such a cynic? There is nothing for it but to reveal to him that he is the Colonel's own half-brother, illicit scion of the Musgraves! Tableau. *Coup de théâtre.*

I do not mean to suggest for a moment that Mr. Cabell is theatrical in his handling of this plot. Every point is made with the cool precision of a player who detests mouthing and panache. But the pattern of action itself is such as suggests the make-up and artificial lighting of the stage more than the crude or sober colors of common life. Even more ingenious in "The Cords of Vanity" is the arrangement of ironies in a sardonic "comedy of shirking." It is amusing enough when the writer Townsend, requiring for his next novel just the right tone of ingenuousness in love, spends the summer taking notes on his tender passages with an ingénue . . . only to find that his ingénue is herself a novelist, and an old hand, at that, and that she has taken notes as industriously as he and has already brought out her book before he has his ready for the printer. But one such contretemps is not enough. The comedy becomes positively hilarious when Townsend, needing a rich wife, discovers that he has wooed and won the poor cousin of the heiress instead of the heiress herself . . . and then discovers that the poor cousin has accepted him because she took him for a wealthy friend, a man whose one passion in life is to be loved for himself and not his wealth. It is clear that Mr. Cabell is much more concerned with pattern than with plausibility.

Of course we should not undertake to judge him by a standard of realism to which he does not subscribe. He has recently told us, in "These Restless Heads" (1932), how different were his own artistic aims from those of his contemporaries. There is no doubt that he is in pursuit of truth as well as beauty. Only, the truth he seeks is not the truth of "life" so much as the essential truth of human nature. It is representative or "general" truth, as Aristotle calls it, the truth of poetry, which is "a more philosophical and a more serious thing than history, for poetry is chiefly conversant about general truth, history about particular." In this contrast of functions, fiction has mostly ranged itself along with history, since it has gone in for the particular, the documentary. But Mr. Cabell has thrown in his lot with poetry, which goes in for the general, the spiritual. It is this difference of aim that Mr. Burton Rascoe has in mind when he says, in his introduction to the revised edition of "Chivalry": "We must accept the truth that Mr. Cabell is not a novelist in the common acceptance of the term, but a historian of the human soul."

3

In the matter of form, Mr. Cabell leaves little to be desired. Form is what one is aware of in him before all else, though not apart from substance. The form of his books is the form of his thought, which, however diversified it may be, and subtly shaded even at times to elusiveness, follows still a simple and unbroken line. Mr. Cabell has somewhere said that every man's story takes naturally the form of a journey. And that is generally the shape of his stories. Only, the journey is not into material space but into the ideal realm of Poictesme, and it follows ever the same invariable cycle, back and forth between the visioned ideal and the disillusioning compromise. "For it is in this inadequate flesh that each of us must serve his dream; and so, must fail in the dream's service, and must parody that which he holds dearest."

There is never any question with Cabell of unassimilated philosophy. For the poet's faculty never fails him of creating myths and symbols to body forth his thought. Such are the persons and events of his dream world. And while these may not have the material substance of a Michael Henchard in the corn market, they do have the poetic substance of an Endymion upon Latmos, ever pursuing a supernal Cynthia only to fall back humanly on his Indian Maid. Thus we have in him, as I say, more light than heat. And this light is not the light of the sun, but the pale diffused illumination of the moon. Through every figure in his garden shines the pearly radiance of his moon of dreams.

X

PHILOSOPHY: DOSTOEVSKI

FOR dramatizing in the novel form a systematized moral philosophy, the palm must be given to Dostoevski. In many respects I do not think him as great a novelist as Tolstoy or Turgenev. He is a specialist in morbid psychology, and there is about all his books a sort of lurid nightmare atmosphere which, like that of Poe's tales, is no doubt a fine artistic creation, but which corresponds only partially to the common daylight atmosphere of our general experience. He is not capable, like Tolstoy, of varying the tone of "Macbeth" with that of "Twelfth Night" or "Henry the Fourth." He has none of that command of the comedy of manners which in Tolstoy makes us think of Thackeray or Trollope. I think I have an inkling of what it was in Dostoevski which made Conrad so rabid against him. If Conrad did not like the fanaticism of Tolstoy, how much less would he have liked the strange mystical transvaluation of normal human values which so often is felt in Dostoesvki.

Like Tolstoy's, his moral philosophy is at root religious. It is infidelity that is at the bottom of the murders about which are woven the stories of "Crime and Punishment" (1866) and "The Brothers Karamazov" (1881). Both Raskolnikov and Ivan Karamazov have been infected with that atheism which, coming from western Europe, seems to have taken so much more virulently in holy Russia. They have fallen victim to the scientific materialism described by Father Païssy.

"Remember, young man, unceasingly, that the science of this world, which has become a great power, has, especially in the last century, analyzed everything divine handed down to us in the holy books. After this cruel analysis the learned of this world have nothing left of all that was sacred of old. But they have only analyzed the parts and overlooked the whole, and indeed their blindness is marvellous."

With these young students their atheism is associated with a want of faith in human nature, which they believe to be radically cruel, scoundrelly, and corrupt. Dostoevski goes to great pains to make clear the actual cruelties and miseries existing in the world which have proved too much for the faith of these sensitive souls. And having lost their faith in God and the order of things, they arrive by logical deduction at the conclusion that for the infidel all things are lawful.

In accordance with this logic, both Raskolnikov and Ivan Karamazov have erected for themselves a Nietzschean ideal of the overman. Raskolnikov, in "Crime and Punishment," believes that, in order to prove himself such a man-god, he must commit a murder. Only by shedding blood in all coolness and deliberation can he rise from the class of ordinary slavish humans into that of the great free spirits like Napoleon. Incidentally he has many incitements to the crime. He is in extreme poverty, so that he cannot even pursue his university studies. He has only to put out of the way a mean and scoundrelly old woman—a good act in itself—and he will be able to save his sister from a degrading marriage, and in general to indulge his natural generosity.

His crime is a great experiment in the new morality. Unfortunately, it does not succeed. He does not do it coolly; he is overcome with nervousness and confusion of mind, and fails to secure his victim's money; he finds himself obliged to murder the old woman's sister, an excellent person, who does not deserve to be put out of the way. After the murder he is perpetually tortured by the fear of discovery. But worst of all, he is overcome with an intolerable sense of his isolation. He will never again be able to speak freely and naturally to any human being. He finds he has a loathing for every one. His beloved mother and sister come to Petersburg, but he can no longer take any pleasure in their society. Much as he loves them, he is obliged to torture them with his savage unsociability. He falls into a state of permanent hopelessness and despair. His spiritual isolation becomes intolerable.

There is one beautiful and wretched soul to whom he is strangely attracted. This is Sonia, a poor girl who has been supporting her miserable family by the sole means open to her, prostitution. To her he confesses his crime, and that is already a great relief to him. But Sonia is a profoundly religious soul, and she believes that his only salvation is in confessing to the police and expiating his crime. His heart is hard; he does not yet believe that it is really a crime that he has committed; he holds out as long as possible against the suggestions of Sonia. But in the end he is driven to following them. He confesses to the police and is sent to Siberia for eight years.

This is virtually the end of the story, but the sequel is briefly adumbrated in the Epilogue. Here we find Raskolnikov in the penal colony a year and a half later. His heart is still hard. But his good angel has followed him to Siberia, where she gives up her life to charitable works. Occasionally Sonia and Raskolnikov see each other, and the love that springs up between them is a good augury for the future. This was the beginning of a new life for Raskolnikov—a life which "would not be given him for nothing," but "would cost him great striving, great suffering."

"That," says Dostoevski, "might be the subject of a new story, but our present story is ended." He did not undertake to tell that infinitely more difficult story. But what he did undertake, that he accomplished—the record of how a man found it impossible to bear the spiritual isolation of crime, and how, accordingly, he was brought to the point where his spiritual regeneration might begin.

I cannot imagine how a psychological experience of this magnitude could be more satisfactorily worked out in dramatic form. The whole affair up to the Epilogue involves but nine days, if we count out the half a dozen days of the mere obliviousness of sickness and exhaustion: two days of preparation for the crime, the day of the crime, and six days leading up to the confession and surrender. Each of these days is crowded with the experiences of a soul, expressed in the form of sensations, incidents, acts, and dramatic confrontations.

What we are everywhere concerned with is the states of mind of Raskolnikov. But they are never states of mind presented abstractly. They are almost always those of a man confronted with a present urgent problem; they are almost always provoked by and embodied in a dramatic situation. During the three days leading to the crime, we are being prepared for this act by many specific incidents. The cruelty and scoundrelism of human nature is not for Raskolnikov the platonic abstraction of a disillusioned young man. It is pictorially forced upon him by the family life of drunken Marmeladov and, in particular, by the case of Marmeladov's daughter Sonia. The reverberation of these things in his unconscious mind is vividly objectified in his terrible dream of the peasant who beats his mare to death. The need to save his sister from a degrading marriage is not something that he conceives in the abstract. It is urgently forced upon him by the immediate situation revealed in his mother's letter. After his crime, the fear of discovery is rendered in scene after scene of desperate fencing with the officers of justice. Above all, the effects of his crime in cutting him off from the sweet intercourse of humanity are developed in great detail in the many scenes with his sister, his mother, and his friend Razumihin. It would take much too long to set forth all the turns of the plot. The point is that we have here a highly complicated and at the same time close-knit plot, all devised for displaying the predicament of this lost soul, and that every incident does but give a further turn of the screw to his desperation.

One feature only I will mention, and that is the character of Svidrigaïlov. It illustrates so well Dostoevski's unfailing instinct, whenever he has an abstract principle to develop, for inventing a real character to be its embodiment. Raskolnikov, his leading character, he wishes to be on the whole sympathetic to the reader. His very sensitiveness of nature makes him all the more liable to an unfaith which is the measure of his sympathy for miserable humanity. The same thing is true of Ivan Karamazov. But in both cases Dostoevski wishes us to understand the profound moral ugliness implied in the man's religious position; he wishes the man to understand it himself. And in each case he has used the same device for shadowing forth this necessary truth. For each of these men he has provided a kind of obscene double or shadow. For Ivan Karamazov it is Smerdyakov; for Raskolnikov it is Svidrigaïlov.

Raskolnikov is a noble soul corrupted by a false philosophy. He has committed murder and theft, but there is nothing mean or sensual about him. Svidrigaïlov is, on the side of sensuality, what Raskolnikov is on the side of pride. He comes into Raskolnikov's story because he has been the cause of great trouble to Raskolnikov's sister, and now wishes to marry her. But the main purpose that he serves in developing the theme is to present to Raskolnikov a picture of what his theories might involve in a person whose weakness is for women. Raskolnikov abhors Svidrigaïlov; he thinks him the vilest of the vile. But Svidrigaïlov knows that Raskolnikov is a murderer, and has therefore a certain moral advantage over him. And he seems always to be in his path. It is not an agreeable situation for Raskolnikov. It is as if another self, a viler self, were perpetually there to remind him how vile he is.

The best of it is that Svidrigaïlov is a complete and independent character, with his own history and his own way of solving his problem—in his case, as in that of Smerdyakov, it is by suicide. And, moreover, it is not Dostoevski who tells us that he has this kind of symbolical relation to Raskolnikov. We draw that conclusion without the least prompting by the author. So that if Svidrigaïlov is an important factor in driving Raskolnikov to confession and expiation, this is but another reminder of how completely the philosophical theme is in this novel dramatized in the story.

2

The theme of "The Brothers Karamazov" is very similar to that of "Crime and Punishment." Only, it is developed on more sides than in the other book. Instead of the one leading character, Raskolnikov, we have three brothers, each typifying a different attitude toward the fundamental spiritual question, a different state of grace. There is first Ivan, who has been so impressed with the senselessness and cruelty of human life that he rejects the God who has so ordered things. There is, at the other extreme, the true and simple believer, Alyosha, whose mind and life are penetrated with the good in which he trusts. And between the two is Dmitri, at heart a believer but one in whom, almost without his knowing it, the doubt which is in the air he breathes has been working to corrupt him, making him unsure of himself, and turning him into an even wilder and more unbridled sensualist than he is by nature.

Dmitri is really the central figure in the composition, and the climax comes with his arrest for the murder of his father. He knows he is not actually guilty of this crime; but he realizes that in his heart he did wish his father's death; he regards himself as a thief and a despicable worm. What pride he had is completely broken down by the grilling he is put through by the police officers. And he begins to feel that it does not matter if he is condemned. Like so many of Dostoevski's characters, he is persuaded of the salutary power of suffering, and he begins to look forward, as the means of his salvation, to the expiation of a crime he did not commit.

I have given no indication of the complicated events which make up the plot of this book. Dostoevski here shows himself one of the great masters in the art of arousing curiosity and maintaining suspense. He knows how to keep back his main facts and "release" them at just the right moment. Among other things, "The Brothers Karamazov" is a "murder mystery" so expertly conducted that by comparison the contraptions of Messrs. Van Dyne and Wallace pale into insignificance.

But, some one will say, the book is fundamentally sentimental in its assumptions. The psychology may be consistent, but it is not true, it is mythical. What we have to do with is not intellectual or religious wrong-headedness but simply mania, simply this and that form of psychological perversion. On this point I am not able to judge. It is a question for the experts. What concerns me here is Dostoevski's art as a novelist. He has, at any rate, a philosophical system which he holds in all sincerity in common with a good many people. And the important thing for us is that he has succeeded in bodying it forth magnificently in terms of individual character, speech, and action.

Alyosha alone is a great dramatic creation, a personality of radiant beauty whom he has succeeded in making thoroughly plausible, and whose simple goings back and forth among the hideous circumstances of this story constitute a way of life worthy of our most serious thought. He is one who understands the human heart without despising it. He knows how to deal with the disease known as an "inferiority complex," which in Russia seems to have raged with particular virulence—witness Gorki's recent novel, "Bystander." He has a genius for getting along with children, whom he always treats precisely as if they were grown-ups, and thereby wins their confidence. It would be worth while studying in great detail Dostoevski's handling of this character. For in it he has accomplished that well-nigh impossible feat of making goodness as real and as interesting as evil.

But it is the story of Dmitri that gives the best illustration of how Dostoevski objectifies a thesis in moral philosophy. It is he who is driven by his undisciplined passions, his self-contempt, and his unsettlement of spirit, to a series of rash and scandalous acts which culminate in his being convicted of murder. It is he who, under the grilling of the police officers, has his pride so broken down that he is brought at length to a penitent and spiritually serious state of mind. It is he who, through the love and faith of Alyosha and Grushenka, is supported in his self-respect and his determination to maintain himself in a state of grace.

His case is very similar to that of Raskolnikov. The difference is that Dmitri, never having been so thoroughly corrupted by false doctrines as Raskolnikov, is more readily restored to his right mind. So that his spiritual history is carried much farther than that of Raskolnikov—and always in the objective manner of fiction. And then, if we include the variant cases of Alyosha and Ivan, each at his own different point in the road of grace, we see that "The Brothers Karamazov" is a still more remarkable illustration of the possibility of dramatizing philosophy.

Of course, I might have chosen Tolstoy to illustrate this possibility. Or I might have chosen Turgenev or Gorki, writers whom many connoisseurs regard more highly than Dostoevski. It is certain that they are plainer realists than he, more simply presenting life under its familiar aspects, less given to warping it in the direction of their moral predilections. My reason for choosing Dostoevski is twofold.

In the first place he gives better examples of a positive philosophical system worked out in the form of fiction. And then he is much more dramatic a writer, in several senses of the word "dramatic." In any case he is the great builder of plots. And plot is one of the most obvious means of objectifying theme. He is the most remarkable of Russian story-tellers, in the plain and simple sense of that word. And this being so, he is the best one to choose for showing how philosophy and story may go hand in hand.

XI

PHILOSOPHY: ZOLA, THOMAS MANN

BEFORE leaving the subject of the philosophical novel, I wish to mention two other men, outside of Russia, who have undertaken large things in this line. And first Zola, who stands in such marked contrast to Dostoevski in his fundamental assumptions. It is to science that Zola looks as the hope of mankind, and the whole purport of his writing is to make prevail a materialistic interpretation of social phenomena.

His "Lourdes" (1894) is a study of a prodigious manifestation which he had witnessed within his own lifetime, the return of the supernatural to the modern world. This was a challenge to Zola's rationalism. And in his novel he undertakes to give a detailed account of one of the typical cures wrought by Our Lady of Lourdes, while at the same time bringing in a history of the city of pilgrimage, with especial emphasis on the simple sheep-girl to whom the Virgin made her first appearance in the year 1858. Along with all this, he wishes to work in a mass-view of the sufferings, horrors, heroisms, pieties, enthusiasms, and hypocrisies which are associated with such pilgrimages. He has chosen for his central character a young woman, Marie de Guersaint, who has been a helpless cripple from girlhood, though the most modern physicians regard her as essentially a "nervous case."

But for his register of impressions he has chosen a skeptic, the young Abbé Pierre, who has long been in love with Marie. Pierre has ceased to be a believer, but he goes to

Lourdes with Marie in hopes of seeing her cured and regaining his faith. Unfortunately, her cure does not convert him, for he does not regard it as a miracle. Nor does it restore to him the object of his love; for Marie has made a vow to the Virgin that if she is cured she will never marry. So that Marie is a second time and doubly lost to Pierre. He can only console himself with the hope of a new religion that shall not be opposed to the natural life.

This study of Lourdes is made in all seriousness, and with great sympathy even for opinions which Zola regards as mistaken. And the novel is constructed with a high degree of formal skill. The whole action covers but five days, the first day occupied with the journey to Lourdes in the *train blanc,* the second, third, and fourth days with events at Lourdes, and the fifth with the return to Paris. To each day Zola gives a book. Each book is divided into five chapters, and in each case the fifth chapter is devoted to the history of Bernadette and Lourdes. An enormous amount of typical incident and character is massed around the central story of Marie and Pierre, and one cannot imagine more material concerning the pilgrimage, and more poignantly human material, collected within the compass of a story which is a story. The intense personal interest of Pierre in the question of miraculous cures makes him an ideal emotional vehicle, and his special materialistic bias, along with his craving to believe in the supernatural, naturally makes him serve the purpose of Zola with the utmost nicety. And the case of Marie, still a young girl, and naturally so beautiful, hopelessly crippled and yet full of faith, is again ideally chosen to objectify the problem in the form of fiction.

But for all this, I do not regard "Lourdes" as one of the best of Zola's novels. In spite of the emotions aroused by both Marie and Pierre they somehow fail to register thoroughly as individuals. They cannot compare, as living characters, with Nana, Gervaise, Coupeau, le père Bazouge, or dozens of other creations of Zola in novels less ambitiously conceived.

Of course I do not mean to suggest that the Rougon-Macquart series was not ambitiously conceived, and that, taken as a whole, it is not an impressive monument of social philosophy. Many of the individual novels of the series have their themes, or subjects, like other novels, and develop them with art and imagination. "L'Assommoir" and "Nana" are certainly among the most skilful and moving pieces of fiction I have ever read. Only I do not regard them as philosophical novels. The subject of "L'Assommoir" (1878) is clearly stated in Zola's preface:

> I have wished to paint the fatal decline of a working-class family in the poisoned atmosphere of our faubourgs. In the wake of drunkenness and idleness follow a relaxing of family ties, the obscenities of promiscuity, the progressive loss of honest feelings, and then, for dénouement, shame and death. It is simply moral causes in action.

The subject of "Nana" (1880) is another aspect of the same theme. In each case, there is in the background the implication that society as a whole is to blame for the conditions that make possible creatures like Coupeau and Nana. But Zola is too wise an artist to suppose that he can develop these implications within the limits of a single novel; and what we have is in one case simply the degradation following in the wake of alcoholism and idleness, in the other the ruin and dissipation of fortunes attending on lust. These subjects are boldly conceived, conscientiously studied, and most humanly presented. The greatest structural skill is shown in organizing the material around a series of occasions which follow out a plan of scenical narrative. Considered purely as novels, they are much better work than books like "Lourdes" and "Vérité" (1902). And one reason for this may be that they are so much more purely works of the imagination, that they undertake to carry a much smaller load of social theory. The others make by comparison the impression of being doctrinaire, and fail to rise into the class of masterpieces. So that, on the whole, Zola serves to show us once again the difficulties of making fiction the vehicle of philosophy.

2

My final example of the use of the novel as a vehicle for theory is the work of a contemporary author, Thomas Mann, and even a product of this-side-the-war, "The Magic Mountain" ("Der Zauberberg," 1925). To this book I came with every prepossession in favor of its author. Books like "Buddenbrooks," "Death in Venice," "Tristan" had made me think that he was perhaps that one of living novelists who most perfectly suited my personal taste in quality and method. Above all, "Buddenbrooks" (1903), with its epic sweep in the representation of life through several generations, its authoritative treatment of family life among the wealthy "bourgeoisie," so parallel to the work of Mr. Galsworthy, but having to my seeming so much more depth and mass and resonance.

It was of Thomas Mann I thought when I wished to represent to myself what it was that seemed to me lacking in contemporary American fiction, and for which I can find no word but that one of strictly European connotations, "soul" (*âme, Seele*). I do not refer to that entity which it is the function of religion to save immortally, and I am far from meaning sentimentality. Thomas Mann is not a writer who specializes in sentimental characters, and still less does he interpret them in a sentimental way. What I have in mind may perhaps be denominated simply quality in personal experience, the sense on the part of the author of value in personality itself. It is this which gives what I have called resonance, which gives depth and a kind of bloom to the work of Continental writers such as do not often characterize present-day novelists in England, and still less in America.

This quality I find in almost any French writer of distinction, whatever his rank in the scale of "greatness." I find it in Colette, in Mauriac, in André Gide. I find it in Russian writers of the Soviet age, in Gladkov, author of "Cement." In Italy I find it in highest degree in Pirandello (for example in "Il fu Mattia Pascal" and "Si Gira"). Almost invariably I find it in Scandinavian writers, in Hamsun, in Lagerlöf, in Sigrid Undset.

I do not find it in Aldous Huxley or in Sinclair Lewis. And in writers like Maurice Baring, Charles Morgan, and Hugh Walpole what I find is a sentimental substitute for it. The American writers who interest me most are sometimes those who have the least suggestion of it. They are clever and smart and inventive no end, sophisticated as the devil, but they do not seem to invest the human personality with that sense of value in and for itself which comes so natural to any European writer. Of course there are exceptions. There is Sherwood Anderson in "Winesburg Ohio" and "Poor White."

I do not know how to account for this lack in our contemporary fiction of a quality which was formerly there in plenty (witness Hawthorne, Melville, Howells, James), unless that somehow, for the moment, we are younger and cruder than we were; or else that we have been too strongly infected with English utilitarianism. However that may be, Thomas Mann is the author who most stands in my mind for the possession of this quality. Tragic and cruel as his picture of life may be, there is always in his treatment of character a sensitiveness, a *feeling* quality, as of one who realizes that he has to do with living creatures. And what could be a better equipment for the art of making characters *live?*

In "Buddenbrooks" that is all he undertakes to do. There is no philosophy to be found there, at least on the surface. The book may imply some theory of cyclical rise and fall in the social organism. At any rate, there is no overt philosophical speculation. But "The Magic Mountain" is as full of philosophy as it can hold. There is page on page of exposition of scientific matters—physiology, embryology. There are hundreds of pages of overt discussion of matters political, religious, social. And there is, not quite so much on the surface, a subtle and elusive theme involving a philosophy of personal conduct.

The central theme of the book, if I rightly understand it, is that sickly disposition to turn one's back on reality and retreat into some ivory tower of speculation, or, otherwise phrased, that will to death, which the author must have found to be a dominant feature of pre-war mentality.

The leading character is a certain Hans Castorp, a young engineer from Hamburg. Before starting out on his professional career, he will make a three weeks' visit with a cousin who is taking a temporary cure at a famous hospital for consumptives at Davos Platz. So great is the power of suggestion, that Hans Castorp has not even stayed out his three weeks before he comes down with a bad cold, and before long he has been found to have certain rough spots (*feuchte Stellen*) in his lungs. He is condemned to a several months' stay at the sanatorium.

The thing drags along, and the months extend themselves to years. He gets the habit of this invalid life; he loses touch with the world down below; he gets absorbed in the endless business of "balancing his accounts" intellectually and spiritually; and it comes to pass that he loses track entirely of that time by which ordinary mortals measure their experiences. As a matter of fact, he has been there seven years at the outbreak of the World War. This event it is that wakens him from his long sleep. He is one of the seven sleepers in the Magic Mountain roused at last by the thunder-stroke.

And what was he doing all those years in the Magic

Mountain? He was taking the rest-cure on his airy balcony, comfortably installed in a reclining-chair and wrapped up in excellent blankets which he had learned to wind about himself with expert skill. He was eating five hearty meals a day at the well-provided table, and recording his temperature seven times a day. He was nursing his love for a married lady with Asiatic eyes and cheek-bones, with ill-kept finger-nails and a beautiful skin, who had the habit of slamming the glass door every time she came into the dining-room.

But above all, he was "balancing his accounts." In this he was helped by several interesting men—three men of striking personalities and decided opinions, who alternately swayed his mind.

The first of these is Lodovico Settembrini, an Italian suffering from tuberculosis, a Freemason, a humanist, the descendant of patriots and rebels, a believer in the Reason of the eighteenth-century Enlightenment, member of an "International League for Organizing Progress." Another is Herr Naphta. He is by origin a Jew, a Catholic and Jesuit by conversion and education. He believes in the dictatorship of the proletariat as the best means in our time for bringing about the salvation of men's souls. He has a great theoretical contempt for the body, and is inclined to defend the methods of torture of the Inquisition as a means of purifying the spirit. He too is suffering from tuberculosis.

Herr Naphta is a subtle and persuasive reasoner, and, like Herr Settembrini, is fond of arguing and making converts. And they often engage in passionate and interminable debates. Thomas Mann refrains conscientiously from intervening in these combats, and the reader is left to infer for himself how far he agrees with this or that one of the disputants. But in one matter he seems to weight the balance in favor of the Italian humanist. Herr Settembrini is very much opposed to what he considers Naphta's cult of suffering and death. He is for life and action; and if he were consulted, Castorp would long ago have given up his idle, self-indulgent ways. He seems to think Castorp's illness is self-induced, and that he would do much better to return to the lower world.

Neither Settembrini nor Naphta, however, quite has the secret of the riddle. In both of them there is lacking something essential to a true philosophy of life. And this, I take it, is what the author undertook to supply in the person of Mynheer Peeperkorn. He is a Dutchman from Java, who has come to Davos badly attainted with tuberculosis and alcoholism. He is an elderly man of great stature, with face deeply and nobly lined and a beard to match. Every one instinctively feels him to be a great, a royal personality. And that in spite of his want of practical prudence, and the almost complete incoherence of his speech. In the end he commits suicide, in order to make way for Castorp with the woman he loves. Thus he puts an end to that Life of which he has been the prophet and devotee, and gives a demonstration, perhaps of cowardice and morbidity, perhaps of the Love which he is evidently meant to symbolize.

3

The above outline will serve to show what an enormous freight of abstract thought is carried by this novel. But the beautiful thing is the high degree to which the thought is objectified in the story. Not story in the sense of incident and intrigue, for there is very little of these, infinitely less than in Dostoevski, less even than in Zola's "Lourdes" or "Vérité." The principal action of the story is simply the battle over the soul of Hans Castorp. But this is sufficient, and the reason why it is sufficient is that Thomas Mann has such a prodigious, such an exhaustless faculty for giving life to the creatures of his imagination. He is simply incapable of inventing a character who shall be the mere mouthpiece of an idea—as we may say of Marie de Guersaint and the Abbé Pierre. There is not a single one of the major or minor characters of "The Magic Mountain" who has not his own unmistakable and unforgettable personality.

To begin with, he has imagined them to the least detail in their looks and dress, their several habitats, as we may say, their idiosyncrasies of speech. There is the crisp and alarming manner of Fräulein von Mylendonk, the ugly head nurse, with the enormous sty, who is called in to see Hans Castorp because he has "caught cold." Catching cold is something not in favor at this sanatorium. Nothing short of a rough spot in the lungs is worth the attention either of patient or doctor, and they all look with the same air of mingled suspicion, indignation, and superiority on any one who announces he has a cold—that air of suggesting that he must be out of his mind if he thinks there can be such a thing as a mere cold in a tuberculosis sanatorium. So when Fräulein von Mylendonk comes to see Hans Castorp, and he says he has a cold, she soon puts him in his place, if only by her way of asking, "What sort of a cold is that?" and by her further questions.

"Do you often have colds? Didn't your cousin also often have such colds? How old are you then? Twenty-four. It goes with your age. And now you come up here and catch cold . . . ? We have no call to speak here of a cold, honored manchild; that is simply some of the nonsense of the people down there (*das ist so ein Schnickschnack von unten*)." She had a formidable, a frightening way of uttering this word *Schnickschnack*. "You have the most beautiful case of laryngitis, I agree to that; that is perfectly clear to the naked eye. . . . But laryngitis doesn't come from a chill; it comes from an infection to which one is susceptible; and the only question is whether we have before us a benign infection or a somewhat malign one—everything else is *Schnickschnack*. . . . It is possible indeed that your susceptibility leans more towards the benign," she said, and looked at him close with her ugly sty, he knew not how.

"Here you have a harmless antiseptic. May possibly do you good." And she drew a little parcel out of the black leather bag that hung at her girdle, and laid it on the table. It was formamint. "Besides, you look excited, as if you had a temperature." And she did not cease looking him hard in the face, but ever somewhat askance. "Have you taken your temperature?"

He said no.

"Why not?" she asked, and left her underlip shoved out on a slant. . . .

He couldn't say a word. The good fellow was still so young he had kept the dumbness of a schoolboy, who stands beside his seat, knows nothing, and keeps still.

"Don't you ever take your temperature then?"

"Why yes, Frau Oberin. When I have a fever."

"My dear man, one first takes one's temperature to find out whether one *has* fever. And at present, in your opinion, you have none?"

"I don't know, Frau Oberin; I can't be sure. Ever since I came up here I have been a bit hot and shivery."

"Aha! And where do you keep your thermometer?"

"I haven't any with me, Frau Oberin. I just came here on a visit; I'm perfectly well."

"Schnickschnack! Did you send for me because you were perfectly well?"

"Well no," he laughed politely, "but because I had taken a slight—"

"A slight cold. Such colds have frequently come to our notice. Here!" she said, and fished again in her bag, bringing to light two longish leather boxes, a black one and a red one, which she likewise laid on the table. "This one here costs three-francs-fifty, and this one five francs. Naturally you would do better to take the one at five francs. That will last you all your life if you take proper care of it."

The clinical side of sanatorium life is handled, my professional friends assure me, with competence and thoroughness. What a layman can answer for is the visibility, as I may call it, the complete realizing for the imagination of the details of the history. There are certain features of person and object which are notable instances of the writer's power of giving human significance to physical detail. Much has been made by critics of Charles Bovary's hat so meticulously described by Flaubert as rendering objectively the character of that school-boy. Quite in a class with this are the descriptions of Frau Chauchat as seen by Hans Castorp during Dr. Krokowski's Freudian lecture. As it chanced, he sat directly behind her. She "sat slouching and hunched up; her back was round, she let her shoulders slump forward; and more than that, her head was shoved forward, so that her vertebræ stuck out above the neck of her white blouse." As the lecture goes on Castorp is greatly distracted by her hand and arm as she fusses with her back hair.

It was oppressive to have that hand so close to one's eyes—one must look at it whether or not one wanted to, and study it in all its human defects, as if one had them under a magnifying glass. No, there was certainly nothing aristocratic about it, this pudgy schoolgirl's hand, with the finger-nails cut off anyhow—one could not even be sure whether her knuckles were perfectly clean, and the skin around the nails was gnawed close, there could be no doubt about that. Hans Castorp made a wry mouth, but his eyes stayed riveted to Madame Chauchat's hand, and an indefinite half-thought went through his head about what Dr. Krokowski had said of the bourgeois resistances which opposed themselves to the working of love. . . . More beautiful was the arm, this soft arm bent round behind her head, and which was scarcely clothed, for the stuff of her sleeves was thinner than that of the blouse—the lightest gauze it was, so that the arm thereby took on a certain misty luminosity, and would clearly have been less attractive if it had been entirely without covering. It was at the same time tender and plump—and cool too, so far as one could judge. Where that arm was concerned, there could certainly be no question of bourgeois resistances.

Hans Castorp went on dreaming, with his gaze fixed on Frau Chauchat's arm. How women dressed! They displayed this and that part of neck and bosom, they brightened their arms with transparent gauze . . . And that they did all over the world, in order to arouse our passionate desire. Good God, but life was beautiful. It was beautiful precisely because of that deliberateness with which women made themselves desirable by their way of dressing—for deliberate it was, and so generally understood and above-board that you hardly even thought about it, and let it please you unconsciously and without any fuss. But one *ought* to think about it, said Hans Castorp to himself, in order rightly to enjoy life and realise that it was a blessed and at bottom almost fairy-like contrivance. To be sure, it was for a definite purpose that women might dress in such a fairy-like and blessed way, without violating propriety; it was a question of the next generation, of the reproduction of the race of men. Oh yes! But what if the lady had some organic disease, so that she was not capable of motherhood—what then? Was there any sense in wearing sleeves to make men desirous of their bodies—their diseased bodies? That obviously made *no* sense, and ought to be considered indecent and be forbidden by law.

4

The most minute material documentation is consistent in Mann with our confident assurance that we are never stopping on the surface of things. In this respect I find him superior to Zola—not to speak of Zola's American counterpart, Mr. Dreiser—and that without yielding to any one in my admiration for performances like "L'Assommoir." I am speaking now of that art by which infallibly the objective detail is made to render the individual quality of scene or character, and translates itself directly into what we may call spiritual values. It is in this art that Thomas Mann is such an unusual figure.

He is a writer, for one thing, who takes his time. The passage I have just cited is an example of his use of the "close-up." The classic French naturalist would consider that too much was made of Frau Chauchat's hand and arm, that they should have been left to speak for themselves in their own hard, sharp, objective manner. But, then, it would scarcely occur to a French naturalist to handle a subject so simple, shy, and elusive as the mind of Hans Castorp. The hand and arm of Frau Chauchat—typical of everything at variance with his German and Occidental notions of a civilized and orderly life, and yet so strangely fascinating to him—these physical details are part and parcel of Castorp's moral problem and the "balancing of accounts" in which he is occupied at Davos Platz. And the tempo in their description is made to correspond to that of his spiritual process.

Mann is one of those rare writers who can afford to take his time and to make much of apparently small details. That is because he is so substantial, and in two directions—in that of objective detail and in that of subjective discrimination. He is so much of a scientist, and he is so much of a philosopher. He is a profound and humane writer because he reveals beneath every external appearance that animating essence which makes of each human being something so much more than a differentiated mass of protoplasm. It is almost as if he did this in spite of himself. His characters are representative types—they all stand for something in his philosophical scheme. But he cannot leave them there. Once he sets them on their feet as persons, they begin to act like persons, and he could not stop them if he would.

All this means creative imagination in a high degree. And it means something more, and something perhaps even rarer. What it comes down to in the last analysis is the extraordinary humaneness of the man. This writer has wisdom and ripeness of understanding far beyond those of the average successful novelist. And that brings me to his personal style, which is the intimate language of his wisdom.

Perhaps the outstanding feature of his style is its simplicity. He has none of the smartness that characterizes so much of the most interesting contemporary fiction in the

English language. He seems to have more faith in his subject, more confidence in his power to get his effects without facetiousness or straining at cleverness. He takes his characters seriously. It is true that he sees all round them. But he also sees deeply enough into them to know they are more than Babbitts, more than musical motifs in a philosophical counterpoint.

He has that supersophistication which brings the wisest men back to the conception of value. Thomas Mann is perhaps in our day the novelist most conscious of those spiritual essences which our mathematicians and physicists are laboring to bring back to a mechanical and materialistic world. He knows as well as any one what frail wisps and motes we are on the shoreless tides of destiny. But he thinks no less of us for that. He is "humanist" enough to realize that values are ideal entities, and that the human mind is all there is to furnish a gage of human values.

Hans Castorp he means for a type of the ordinary serious, bewildered intellectual dilettante of the pre-war period. A German of course. The German author is fully conscious of the Teutonic mentality of his hero, and goes to some lengths to bring his German quality into relief. None but a German could have been so grave and thorough in his researches, so easily impressed with learning, and so inveterately metaphysical. There is nothing extraordinary about him except his seriousness and tenacity. He means infinitely well and goes far astray. He loses touch with reality and with humanity. But his heart is sound, and the author brings him back in the end to those contacts through which he may be fulfilled. He is a most amusing character, and more likable than he is amusing. It is with a mild, enveloping, insinuating, and ever discreet humor that the author unfolds his somewhat pathetic story.

If there is one thing more beautifully "done" than another in the book, it is those earlier chapters in which he shows him falling into the trap of invalidism and the sanatorium mentality; growing hourly more nervous under the polite insinuations of the doctors and nurses; alarmed by the nosebleed that comes upon him in his mountain walk; taking the rest-cure on his balcony and falling under the spell of reclining-chairs and peaceful hours, wrapped up in woolen blankets. The first serious intimation that all was not going well with him was the loss of his power of enjoying tobacco.

Nothing could be more delicious than Hans Castorp's eloquent connoisseurship on the subject of cigars and his bewildered reflections over the fact that he can no longer take a real pleasure in his favorite Maria Mancini. It is one of those material details that in the hands of a master serve to render the very idiosyncrasy of a man. And it brings us back to the moral of our discussion, which is this: what an enormous amount of discursive philosophy can be conveyed in the form of fiction if the writer has the genius of Thomas Mann for "dramatizing" it, for rendering it in the proper terms of story.

PART TWO: THE DRAMATIC IDEAL

When any extraordinary scene presents itself (as we trust will often be the case), we shall spare no pains nor paper to open it at large to our reader; but if whole years should pass without producing anything worthy his notice, we shall not be afraid of a chasm in our history: but shall hasten on to matters of consequence, and leave such periods of time totally unobserved.

—HENRY FIELDING: "The History of Tom Jones, a Foundling"

XII

TOWARD THE WELL-MADE NOVEL

In the writing of fiction, particularly since about 1885, there has been a growing preoccupation with form. It began perhaps with the short story, but it soon spread to the novel, and it is this movement which gave rise to what I call the well-made novel—the novel that prides itself upon its neatness of construction. The well-made novel need not be the great novel, any more than the well-dressed man need be the great man; nor need the great novel be the well-made novel. Many of the novels that best deserve the adjective "well-made" are the products of weak imaginations or flimsy brains; and it may turn out that extreme preoccupation with technique has been the accompaniment of a decadent tendency in art. The emphasis on form may be exaggerated, with a corresponding loss in vitality. Nevertheless the considerations which have produced the well-made novel are real artistic considerations; the preoccupation with form will certainly tend to good art, provided it is not allowed to occupy the whole field. It is not the cause of decadence, nor is it even the symptom of decadence, except in so far as it is exaggerated and exclusive.

Romance and realism have both made their contributions to the ideal of the well-made novel, though neither romancer nor realist is necessarily bound to that ideal. The realist is concerned to give a serious picture of life; he is the scientist in fiction; and he may be so dominated by his love of detail or by the disposition to ride his hobbies, that he may largely neglect to make his story shapely or even telling. The romancer may lose himself in mysteries, in exciting adventure, in the complications of plot, and leave the design to take care of itself and the situations to make themselves interesting by their own inherent force. But when the romancer begins to consider nicely the means by which he can produce illusion, maintain suspense, and lead the reader on by due degrees from one level of curiosity to another; when he begins to ask himself how an improbable story can be made to seem as real as everyday life, he has started in the path of the well-made novel. And when the realist is concerned more for the choice and relevance of details than for the mere assembling of them; when he begins to consider his story in the light of a subject which gives pattern and significance to his material—then he is moving in the direction of the well-made novel.

The nineteenth-century realist, under the influence of his scientific ideal, may wish to give a full and comprehensive view of human society, like Balzac in his Comédie Humaine, or to bring the greatest possible amount of evidence to establish some social theory, like Zola in his Rougon-Macquart series. But it is equally a scientific ideal which leads him, in any one book, to limit his matter so as to give a thorough study to the particular subject treated. It is here that the scientific and esthetic ideals are identical, both making for unity, simplicity, precision of outline.

Among the theorists of realism, the one who has probably given the best account of how the realistic ideal affects the organization of matter in a novel, is Guy de Maupassant, in his famous preface to "Pierre et Jean" (1887). He is really grounding his apology for the realists in fundamental principles of art in general. Seldom or never, in a discussion of the novel, had any English critic employed terms which so brought this bourgeois form of writing into relation to other forms of art.

Life [he says, for example] leaves everything on the same scale; it crowds facts together or drags them out indefinitely.

Art, on the contrary, consists in using precautions and making preparations, in contriving artful and imperceptible transitions, in bringing the essential events into full light, by simple ingenuity of composition, and giving to all others the degree of relief suited to their importance, so as to produce a profound sense of the special truth which one wishes to exhibit.

Thus Maupassant insists that the principles of selection and arrangement apply to the realistic novel as well as to any other form of art. But he has also a good deal to say of the features which distinguish the serious, the realistic work from ordinary fiction, which has no other object than to help pass the time agreeably. For example:

The novelist who professes to give us an exact representation of life ought to avoid with care any linking together of events which might appear exceptional. His aim is not to tell a story, to entertain us or touch our hearts, but to force us to think and understand the deep and hidden significance of events. . . . Instead of contriving an adventure and unfolding it in such a way as to keep up the interest to the end, he will take his character or characters at a certain period of their lives and conduct them, by natural transitions, to the following period. In this way he will show us, it may be, how character is influenced and altered by surrounding circumstances; it may be, how the sentiments and passions develop, how people love, how they hate, what struggles are going on in all social conditions . . .

The artfulness of his plan is not to be found, then, in emotional effects or charm of writing, in an attractive beginning or a moving catastrophe, but in the skilful massing of little insistent details which will serve to bring out the essential meaning of his work. If in three hundred pages he compasses ten years of a life, in order to show what, in the midst of all the beings who surround it, has been its special and characteristic significance, he must know how to eliminate, out of the innumerable little daily events, such as do not subserve his intention, and to show in high relief, in a special way, all those which might pass unnoticed by less acute observers, and which give to the book its importance and its effect as a whole.

It is easy to see that such a method of composition, so different from the old, obvious procedure, often baffles the critics, who cannot discern all the fine, secret, almost invisible threads employed by certain modern artists in place of the single larger thread called the Plot.

So writes the author of "Une Vie" (1883) and "Fort Comme la Mort" (1889). So one *would* write *en plein Paris,* in the age of Manet, Renoir, Cézanne, when it came perfectly natural to treat the novel as an art form like any other. In much the same spirit, and out of the same artistic background, George Moore wrote in English his "Confessions of a Young Man" (1886)—a much neglected book which had in Walter Pater at least one distinguished and admiring reader. Meantime, we must bear in mind that to most readers and to most writers it does not occur to take this severe esthetic view of what they regard as simply a superior form of amusement.

2

The novelist as novelist is concerned chiefly to provide as much entertainment as possible, and is pledged to every device for procuring variety, surprise, and sentimental gratification to the reader. The greatest of all masters in this art is Dickens. No one has ever brought together in one story so much of the interest of plot, character, and setting, together with the sentimental interest of the love-story. And in all these elements the concern is not that of the realist, to study and understand, but that of the storyteller pure and simple, to strike the imagination, to hold the attention, to entertain. The plot is conceived of not as a representative sequence of events throwing light on character and guided by the logic of cause and effect in human conduct, though all due attention is given to making things reasonably plausible. The plot is a tissue of mysteries and complications, in which the largest possible number of persons are implicated.

The plot of "Bleak House" (1852–53), concerning the relationship of Esther Summerson and Lady Dedlock, and the identity of the copying-clerk who died in Mr. Krook's rag-and-bottle shop—which might well have been unraveled by the lawyer, Mr. Tulkinghorn, with a minimum use of minor characters—is most ingeniously handled so as to bring in group after group of persons, who serve to heighten the sense of mystery and the delicious sense of complication. There is Mr. Guppy of Kenge and Carboy, who observes the striking resemblance of Lady Dedlock in her portrait to Esther Summerson, who plans to marry Esther on guessing of her high connections, who brings in his friend Jobling to watch old Krook and try to get possession of the lost letters, and is brought into connection with Tulkinghorn, with the Smallweeds, with Jo the crossing-sweeper, etc. There is Jo the crossing-sweeper, who guided the veiled lady to the burying-ground of the dead clerk, who brings in the brickmakers' wives, the Snagsbys, the Chadbands, Mr. George of the shooting-gallery, and several other groups, as well as connecting up with Esther and her guardian.

There are a score or more little worlds of people like wheels in a watch, each one interlocking more or less with every other one. This is of the very essence of a romantic plot, and the fact of these varied and surprising relations of people apparently so alien to one another makes its own strong appeal to the imagination. Turning the rich morsel under his tongue, the author says:

> What connexion can there be between the place in Lincolnshire, the house in town, the Mercury in powder, and the whereabouts of Jo the outlaw with the broom, who had that distant ray of light upon him when he swept the churchyard-step? What connexion can there have been between many people in the innumerable histories of this world, who, from

opposite sides of great gulfs, have, nevertheless, been very curiously brought together!

The sentimental interest I have listed separately. The clearing up of the mysteries is one thing. The love-story is another. Here all that is required is that we should be fond of the heroine, and should maintain undisturbed our confidence in the rightness of her emotions. The love-story is, in Dickens, as in his master Smollett, the merest tribute to the taste of the reader. The story of the chancery wards is mainly the means of bringing in a large number of characters that are picturesque and amusing on their own account. They are plausibly enough brought in, but they have no real function to serve, and once they appear on the scene they proceed to occupy the center of the stage. They are not drawn to scale; there is no principle of perspective; the aim is to fill up all the available space.

Each type is more eccentric than the last; and the reader, while he cannot deny that people as droll as these may be met with any day, knows that so many droll people never came within any one's normal experience. The items may be taken from life, but life is not made up of any such assemblage of items. And, above all, the droll and jolly items do not bulk so large in the perspective of anybody's life. This is, together with the sheer genius of Dickens as a draftsman, the reason why his books are such a refreshment to the tired mind, why we lose ourselves as delightfully in them as in records of travels among cannibals and coral isles. They are fairy-stories for grown-up children.

But, some one will say, why do you leave out of account the serious purpose of Dickens? Did he not set out to correct abuses? And are not Dotheboys Hall, the poorhouse system, the prisons, the Court of Chancery, subjects for the study of the realist?

Well, I have no doubt that Dickens was glad enough to influence public opinion in regard to certain social sores;

and certainly the showing up of these abuses must have given him and his reader the sense that they were serious people combining artistic gratification with the betterment of the world, and not mere children at a puppet show. It is also true, in the case of the Chancery Court, that Dickens has used this sinister and half-mythological entity as a sort of sun around which revolve the myriad planets with their satellites that make up the dramatis personæ of "Bleak House," and so has given to the complicated story a design other than that of the plot itself. This is certainly a device making for artistic effect. Crazy little Miss Flite, with her caged symbolic birds, which she intends to free when her judgment is finally given; old drunken Krook, the "Lord Chancellor," who dies, again symbolically, of spontaneous combustion; the dark places, the fog, the mud, Tom-all-Alone's, disease and death—all these are fine themes for the grotesque poetry and theatrical chiaroscuro of which Dickens is such a master. But it is obviously the grotesque poetry and theatrical chiaroscuro that are the aim of Dickens, and not either that semblance of truth or that inner coherence of truth which we name realism.

The great principle of composition with Dickens is that of alternation. We have in "Bleak House" Esther Summerson's story giving place, every two or three chapters, to those parts of the action that go on outside the knowledge of Esther. And within each of these main movements, there is a constant change of scene and world, with ever varying color and tone. We pass from the life of the cousins at Bleak House to the fantastic ménage of the Jellybys or the Turveydrops, and then to the sinister glooms and madness of the rag-and-bottle shop, and back to pleasant Bleak House, and childish Skimpole, and thence to the pious ministrations of Mr. Chadband at the Snagsbys, or the picturesque interior of George's shooting-gallery. Each group of characters, and each peculiar setting, comes back again and again with its familiar features, following immediately upon the contrasted familiar features of some other group and setting.

To the author each scene is worth exactly as much as he can get out of it, without reference to any value it may have for the development of a theme. The only theme one can discover running through these myriad changes of scene is that of the odd contrasts and piquant variety of human experience. There is not much more here in the way of an artistic principle than in the vaudeville show, or the moving picture, in which we pass swiftly and frequently from one aspect of a situation to another. Every shift is a fillip to the sluggish imagination.

Dickens, then, is the classic example of the novelist pure and simple, and unaffected by the preoccupations of realism. The preoccupations of realism often show themselves in the reduction of plot to a minimum and the substitution of an interest in character for the mere exploitation of characters. And these changes follow naturally from the realist's aim of making a serious study of a subject—human nature in some limited phase. The realist is interested not in the odd and thrilling situations arising from the discovery of lost wills, disguised relationships and identities, or from a tissue of coincidences beyond all normal likelihood. He is interested in the typical reactions of human nature in typical circumstances, in the logical sequence of moral conduct, in the way in which human beings meet the test of life.

Nor is the realist concerned to bring upon the scene a large number of characters interesting for their peculiarities and work them for all they are worth. His business is to present as many characters as naturally belong to the human experience he has chosen for his subject, and to develop each character just so far as necessary to illustrate fully the significant elements of that experience. He may have a very large number of characters, but their relative importance is thoughtfully gaged and each one allotted the proper space and emphasis. And, generally speaking, his subject does not require anything like the enormous number of people presented by Dickens, whose motto is "Plenty."

3

George Eliot was a very serious realist in her intention; and while, in "Felix Holt" and "Middlemarch," for example, she yields somewhat to the Victorian taste for mysteries in the background, this element is considerably reduced in amount and importance, even in those books, while in "Adam Bede" and "The Mill on the Floss" the plot depends on no such artificial and mechanical devices. The plot in those best of her novels, and almost altogether in "Middlemarch" too, for that matter, consists of a working out of the reactions of the characters to situations which are largely of their own creation. The question for the characters is not, as it so often is in Dickens, what is going to happen next? or what is the meaning of this mysterious circumstance? but—how shall we meet the challenge of this situation?

So that one feels strongly in her books that moral tension which is so large a part of the experience of any conscientious person, and which in a work of fiction does so much to give us the impression of reality. The author makes a serious attempt to show how this tension brings out the characteristic strength and weakness of each person. And the most striking characters are those which carry the major rôles, the Maggie Tullivers and Dorothea Brookes and Adam Bedes and Philip Wakems—not, as in Dickens, the Sairey Gamps, the Pecksniffs, the Sammie Wellers.

It is true that the second-line characters in George Eliot are often very delightful creations, and Mrs. Poyser, Caleb Garth, old Tulliver, and the Dodsons make a considerable showing in her landscape. But these figures have a very important function to play in the study of character which is the aim of George Eliot. They represent the solid structure of society, and first of all the family, which is so constant an element in the problem of the major characters—the mothers and fathers, the aunts and uncles, who are a responsibility, a steadying influence, the perpetual reminder of a common interest which must be taken into account by the young man or woman seeking his own good.

None of these characters occupies an appreciably larger place in the novels than he does occupy in the social scheme of George Eliot. And it is to be specially observed that, while they are developed at considerable length in the opening parts of the story, they do not continue to make those regular appearances and to hold the center of the stage when the main action is well under way, like many characters in Dickens who have nothing more to justify their return than that we already know them well and look forward to the same droll antics and remarks in which they have all along indulged. And so we have much more the impression in George Eliot of an action and a world of people limited by the subject chosen, with each detail given a stress proportionate to its significance in relation to the subject.

This is much more striking in some of the French realists, who owed no allegiance to the English ideals of plot and humor, and who, by long national traditions, were more inclined to simplification of theme in any work of art. Thus in Flaubert's "Madame Bovary" (1857), there is a still greater reduction in the number of characters, and especially of such as are presented in any detail. There are no secondary groups of characters with plots interlocking with the main one. The theme is the tragic love-life of a woman who has grown up on a diet of sentimental dreams all out of relation to the actualities and obligations of life. The center of interest is Emma Bovary, and her desperate attempt to find in love-affairs that life of passion and sentiment which she does not know how to find in her own home. The bulk of the story then is concerned with her love-affairs with Rodolphe and Léon. The only other persons who are given any prominence in the story are her father, in whose farm-house the young girl dwells as an alien, her imagination all occupied with her factitious dream world; Monsieur Homais, the enterprising and unscrupulous apothecary, who serves for the chief representative of provincial life and a foil for the simple virtues of Emma's husband; and the husband himself, Charles Bovary, the country doctor, who has not the remotest notion of the romantic world in which his wife's soul moves, who goes about his business conscientiously, who does his best to provide his dearly loved Emma with comforts and luxuries and to make her happy, but who can do nothing that will please her.

The story begins with Charles Bovary, and it ends with him; for we are to be shown the misery and ruin caused by her selfish sentimentalism and the tragic devotion of real love in a person who lives in the world of realities. But this is merely the framework of the picture; the picture itself is the portrait of the sentimental woman. The story of her romantic infatuation, and the resultant financial entanglements, which drive her to shame, despair, and suicide, moves with a steady and terrible movement never equaled in English fiction of that day, which would not give itself up to the simple and tragical logic of its theme.

4

Closely associated in Paris with Flaubert and the other giants of French naturalism—Zola, Daudet, and Edmond de Goncourt—was the Russian, Turgenev. His work furnishes many examples of the simplification of form produced by the realist ideal, and was greatly admired by English and American writers, among them Howells and James. What James admired in Turgenev was his emphasis on character rather than plot, his choice of characters who were "morally interesting," and, in the planning of his work, his way of proceeding from character to action. James wrote in 1884:

> The germ of a story with him was never an affair of plot—that was the last thing he thought of; it was the representation of certain persons. The first form in which a tale appeared to him was as the figure of one individual, or a combination of individuals, whom he wished to see in action, being sure that such people must do something very special and interesting. . . . With this material in his hand he was able to proceed; the story all lay in the question, What shall I make them do?

Perhaps James did not sufficiently take into account what lay back of Turgenev's choice of characters and may be said to have preceded it in the evolution of his work. Generally speaking, in his best novels, it was a broad social theme to which the charaters were pertinent, and it is this which gives form to his work. For example, in "Fathers and Sons" (1862), the general theme is a contrast between the temper and outlook of two successive generations of Russians. On the one hand were the older men, liberal and well-meaning, but dominated by genteel and sentimental considerations. On the other hand was the rising generation of intellectuals, hard-boiled and ruthless in their attitude toward all that their elders held precious, not to be taken in by phrases and romantic ideals, and dominated by the positivist notions of physical science in their interpretation of social problems.

Turgenev is said to have been the first to use, in this novel, the term "nihilist" in reference to these precursors of modern socialism. Until he brought it to their attention, Russian readers were not aware of the tremendously significant movement which was getting under way. In the light of recent history, "Fathers and Sons" is positively prophetic, and is perhaps the most significant of Russian novels in point of broad social reference. But, however much his sympathies were on the side of the young intellectuals, Turgenev was not a propagandist writer. He was a most fastidious artist, a conscientious realist; and on the side of form the book is as remarkable as on the side of thought.

He took his departure from the vivid impression made on him by a real person, a provincial doctor whom he knew. This was the model for his Bazarov. His problem was to arrange a story in which this central character should be brought into opposition to representatives of the romantic generation. And this he does very simply. He makes him a young man returning home from his scientific and medical studies, with a still younger friend and disciple, and he follows these two persons through a few weeks of their summer vacation.

They first visit the home of the younger man, Arkady. There we make the acquaintance of Arkady's father, Nikolai Petrovich, a liberal landowner, who has done his best by his peasants, but who is a sentimental potterer, an inefficient manager, and the father's brother, Pavel Petrovich, a society man, who has retired to the country to nurse a broken heart, and who continues there to dress like a dandy and maintain the aristocratic and chivalrous notions of his world. The rudeness and intransigence of Bazarov hurt the feelings and offend the sensibilities of the older men, and especially of Pavel Petrovich. But it is a more personal emotion which comes in to provoke Pavel to action, leading him to challenge Bazarov to a duel, in which he is wounded, and which puts an end to Bazarov's stay at Maryino.

In the meantime, Bazarov and Arkady have been staying for some time at the country place of an attractive and wealthy widow, and it is here that Bazarov's nihilist principles are put to a severe test. In spite of all his theoretical hatred of romantic sentiment, he himself becomes the victim of love. Both he and Arkady fall in love with their hostess, Anna Sergyevna; but Arkady's love is the indeterminate sentiment of youth and soon gives way before a more real, though gentle, passion for Anna's younger sister Katya.

Before the conclusion of these episodes, the young men have paid a visit to Bazarov's parents. Bazarov's father is of lower social standing than Arkady's, a retired army surgeon now engaged in farming. His mother is an old-fashioned woman, absorbed in the cares of housekeeping, extremely religious and given over to every conceivable superstitious belief. They are both inordinately proud of their son and inclined to smother him with affection. But he hates every manifestation of feeling, finds his parents fussy and ridiculous, and is terribly bored at home; and he deeply grieves the old people by leaving them after a stay of several days. Later on he comes back to them, and gratifies his father by helping him in his charity practice of medicine. He is infected with typhus while conducting a post-mortem dissection. In this backwoods place he cannot find a means of sterilizing his cut in time. And he dies in the flower of his youth and promise.

Of the characterization I cannot take time to speak, though it is one of the main artistic merits of this book. For humanness, for honesty, and for economy of means by which the effect is secured, the character of Bazarov is one of the greatest triumphs of fiction. I have given a detailed account of the plot in order to bring out two features: the way in which he and all the other characters are related to the general subject of the book; and the extreme simplicity and naturalness of the action by which the subject is dramatized, without intrigue, without melodrama, and with the barest minimum of elaboration. I am not acquainted with any work of fiction in which types of so wide a variety, and each one so significant, are brought together in a story of this compass for the illustration of a social theme. In the simple record of a few summer weeks are concentrated all the elements of the Russian revolution.

5

Other examples of the simplification produced by the realist ideal are the novels of the Goncourts, such as "Madame Gervaisais" (1865) and "Germinie Lacerteux" (1869). Here, indeed, the studious confinement of subject is so severe and determined that most readers can hardly breathe in such an atmosphere—or is it perhaps not so much the confinement of the subject that oppresses us as the simple want of animation and largeness of soul of the authors?

Much more to the average taste of the serious cultivated reader is the treatment of similar themes by George Moore. "Esther Waters" (1894) reminds one of "Germinie Lacerteux" in having for its theme the difficult life of a servant-girl, and it is equally serious in its realism; only the English writer has chosen a heroine who will appeal not merely by her pathos but by the strength of her character. Esther Waters is such a sturdy, obstinate soul, with so much fight in her; she is so well-meaning and religious, so devoted to her child and so loyal to her husband; so beautiful is her relation to the suffering lady who shares her faith of the Plymouth Brethren and her strong maternal instinct: that the hardness of life as she experiences it is mitigated for the reader by a sense of the essential fineness of human nature. "Evelyn Innes" (1898) reminds one similarly of "Madame Gervaisais" in its theme of religious conversion. But it is what Evelyn gives up for religion—love and the career of an artist—which lends its high dramatic interest to the English novel.

In both cases, as well as in "Sister Teresa" (1901), the sequel to "Evelyn Innes," the important matter for technique is the centering of interest in the one woman whose typical experience is the subject of the study, with the consequent great simplification of story. There is no chapter in the whole of "Esther Waters" that is not mainly devoted to Esther, and very little information is given by the author with regard to any circumstances that are not before her eyes. The longest part of the book is that in which she appears as the wife of William, tavern-keeper and book-maker for the races. Here the interweaving of the two cultural motives of race-track gambling and Esther's religion makes a strong background for the picture of her domestic life. She believes gambling to be wicked, but still more deeply she believes in her duty to her husband. His book-making is illegal and threatens to make him an outlaw. He is converted to her view of gambling; but he must make on the races enough money to enable him to give up book-making; and when it appears that he is consumptive, and that his very life depends on his going to Egypt, the outcome of the great race becomes a matter of tragic importance for Esther.

The simplification of form is but one of many features that constitute the greatness of this book as a work of art. The fine humaneness of the author's conception, the simple gravity of his tone, the purity of style, the self-restraint of a writer who will not yield to the temptations of artificial pathos, melodrama, facetious humor; the thorough and honest realism; the objectivity of treatment; the careful selection of details for rendering the physical effect of things seen and felt—all count for much in producing the effect of solid truthfulness and beauty.

But it is the simplification of form that is our present concern, the organization of material in reference to the central subject of the picture. Our interest in the life of this woman of the servant class is not diverted and dissipated by the mysteries of plot, by constant excursions into the realm of the eccentric and grotesque. The steady preoccupation with Esther's problems produces a growing tension, a broadening and deepening of the emotional stream. The story may be much less easy reading for tired minds, less lively and diverting, than the typical Victorian novel, but it takes deeper hold on the mind and feelings, and gives much more the impression of being first of all a work of art.

The same considerations hold for "Evelyn Innes." The problem of Evelyn is much less on the plane of primitive needs and difficulties; and the author has somewhat over-documented, in the naturalist manner, the subject of styles in music. But the sharp opposition in Evelyn's spirit between the life of an opera singer and the demands of her faith gives a strong emotional tension to the period during which she is approaching a decision. The bulk of the novel is taken up with this period, and half of it is at the height of her struggle. The uninterrupted pressure of her agonizing problem gives to this book a highly dramatic character. It goes along with the limitation of the number of persons, the steadiness with which the center of interest is maintained, and the concentration of action within a limited period of time, which are characteristic features of the well-made novel.

In "Sister Teresa" all the action takes place in the convent, and thus we have the narrow limitation of place which represents another characteristic tendency of the well-made novel. "The Lake" is another of George Moore's novels with a religious theme; it is virtually the same theme as in "Evelyn Innes," with the outcome reversed. "The Lake" is the story of Father Gogarty, an Irish priest in a remote country parish, who, under the influence of love, gradually loses his religious faith, and in the end gives it up and disappears. The striking technical feature of the book is the handling of the point of view. Not merely is the center of interest Father Gogarty; but the whole action is presented from his point of view.

It is probably not without significance that "The Lake" (1905) dates from eleven years later than "Esther Waters," nine years later than "Evelyn Innes." It illustrates the growing vogue of the well-made novel. "The Lake" follows immediately after the most notable productions of Henry James in his later technique. The restricted point of view I shall leave for discussion later when I speak of the contributions of romance to the ideal of the well-made novel.

6

With regard to the limitation of subject-matter, which represents one phase of realism, it is observable that this is likely to make its appearance sporadically in the work of novelists who are not so much concerned with technique as George Moore, and who in general represent the old Victorian traditions. And the limitation of subject-matter in these writers generally results in a neatness of form and a general artistic effectiveness which are not always characteristic of their work.

Meredith is in many ways a typical Victorian novelist. He has the Victorian passion for intruding his philosophical reflections and explaining his characters to the reader. He loves to create and exploit at length humorous and eccentric characters in the manner of Dickens and Thackeray. He likes to crowd his pages with people who succeed one another in holding the reader's interest and often break up the continuity of the story and dissipate the dramatic tensions. Some of his stories, like "Harry Richmond," are built on the autobiographical model which Dickens inherited from Smollett.

His notion of comedy is, on the other hand, an essentially formative ideal, leading to the presentation of types à la Molière in a relatively simple plot. It is true that certain elements of emotional appeal are lacking in the stories that conform closest to the comic formula, and many readers will prefer "Richard Feverel" to "Evan Harrington," and "Diana of the Crossways" to "The Egoist." But the book in which unquestionably the most is made of the materials chosen, in which the action is most fully put before the reader in dramatic scenes, is "The Egoist" (1879). And this is made possible, for one thing, by the simplicity of the plot, which is concerned from beginning to end with the attempt of young Clara Middleton to get free from her engagement to the complacent and selfish Sir Willoughby. Crossjay Patterne, Lætitia Dale, Vernon Whitford and Horace De Craye all have their parts determined by reference to this simple drama. As for Dr. Middleton, his fondness for old port and old books, together with his strict sense of honor, serve to add much to the urgency and misery of Clara's predicament.

This simple, uncomplicated drama, without the ghost of a sub-plot, plays itself out altogether in one spot, at Patterne Hall and its immediate neighborhood, so that there is no waste of energy in the adjustment to new settings. And it is all confined, after four brief introductory chapters, to a few summer weeks; indeed, the bulk of the book occupies but two or three days, following close on one another's heels. I can think of no English novel of that century in which a single limited situation is played up for so many pages, through so many close-knit scenes. The emotional interest of the reader is held by Clara's predicament; his intellectual interest, by the vanity and selfishness of Sir Willoughby; and the two interests are constantly fed by the one continuous action. Ample time is given for the full development and realization of each aspect; and the slight objective occurrences are so timed as to give new interest and animation to the story when it is needed. The chapter headings, so often consisting of the names of persons in the scene, suggest the kinship to drama; and the immediate sequence of one scene upon another involving always some of the same characters suggests the *liaison-des-scènes* within the act of a French play.

Meredith was no doubt much influenced in this story by the ideals of drama; and it shows the advantage which the novel may derive from an observance of something like the three classical unities. There is of course a corresponding sacrifice of that variety which is so much more possible to the novel than the play, and which is more called for by the great length of the novel. Many readers, who demand the stimulus of frequent change of scene and subject, will doubtless find "The Egoist" tedious, the strain of continuous attention too great, especially considering the character of the dialogue, which is so much more clever and allusive than that of everyday life. One must acknowledge that Meredith is hard reading; but for this his amazing style, his intrusive cleverness, is very largely to blame. It is also quite possible to conceive that "The Egoist" would benefit by a good deal of cutting.

Beyond this it is impossible to arbitrate between those readers who find "The Egoist" more tedious than his other books and those who find it more fascinating. One can only say that it has the defects of its qualities, and that its qualities are those of a subject strictly limited and fully developed on the lines of the classic drama.

7

In some respects Hardy is even more Victorian than Meredith. He is entirely free from Meredith's elephantine playfulness. And he is infinitely more inclined to let the story speak for itself. But in plot he often out-Herods Herod in his Victorian fondness for mystery and complications. He is inordinately fond of coincidence and the crisscross of circumstance that comes to upset the plans and betray the best intentions of the characters. This is Hardy's dark angel; it gives a quaint and almost ridiculous air to such books as "Two on a Tower," and even bothers the fastidious reader in much nobler work, such as "The Mayor of Casterbridge." For, apart from the strain on our sense of probability, so much complication of plot requires a deal of explaining; and the impatient author quite often contents himself with telling us what happened instead of showing it to us; so that large portions of Hardy's weaker novels affect one like the scenario for a work of fiction rather than the developed work itself.

Hardy's greatness lies, more than anything else, in the association of events with the setting in which they occur. There has never been a novelist so sensitive to impressions of sight and hearing, one who renders them with so much precision and at the same time with such regard for the total esthetic effect of the scene or object rendered, its harmonious relation to the emotions involved. The appeal is threefold: to our sense of reality, to our sense of beauty, and to our sympathetic emotions; and such a combination, so rare, if not unique in fiction, is what gives Hardy his superiority over many a novelist with greater endowments in other directions.

This order of appeal is strongest in those novels in which the setting is his native "Wessex," and is either the out-of-doors, under the full dominance of nature and the weather, or such interiors as most suggest the molding of life through countless generations by this particular rural environment. "Far from the Madding Crowd" is only in the second place a drama of love, jealousy, betrayal, and loyalty; it is first of all a portfolio of exquisite pictures of pastoral and farm life, in which the passions of the heart take their tone and color, their vividness and actuality, from the rural occupations with which they are associated.

In most novels the characters are photographed against a conventional background which is kept ready for all occasions; and we have no sense of the oneness of the picture, of there being any essential relation of the figures to the background. Hardy has a constant realization, both esthetic and philosophical, of the inseparableness of people from the natural setting in which they appear. They are growths of the soil, creatures of weather and circumstance, seen as objects in a landscape, the meaning of which is conveyed to us, like that of other objects, by their mass and shape and movement.

Hardy is predominantly an objective writer, taking his position and directing his observation upon his characters like some one placing a camera, and then proceeding to interpret in terms of human feeling the objects and movements he observes. This at least is his method in many passages where he has the most uncanny effect of focusing our attention with great intensity on certain characters that interest us. This is his method in the chapter in which Fanny Robin makes her way so painfully from milestone to milestone along the Casterbridge highway. She is Fanny Robin, a character in the story in whom we are interested; but she is more than that. She is a kind of portentous figure in a symbolic landscape, and she takes on the tragic dignity of a symbol—suggesting far more of human suffering, loneliness, and bewilderment, than mere Fanny Robin betrayed and dying.

The most famous example of the association of story and setting in Hardy is also that one of his novels which is most remarkable for unity and simplicity of design, "The Return of the Native" (1878). And it is the association of story and setting which, more than anything else, determine this structural beauty. Enough has been written about Egdon Heath since Lionel Johnson's fine appreciation in "The Art of Thomas Hardy." And I wish to dismiss this subject with as few words as possible, since I have written of it so extensively elsewhere. I shall therefore say nothing of the special imaginative appeal of "The Return of the Native," the power and subtlety with which Hardy has made us see the characters in their savage, mournful setting.

What I must not fail to mention is the importance of Egdon Heath in the motivation of the characters, its philosophical significance in the very design of the story. Each one of the major characters—and especially Eustacia Vye and Clym Yeobright—is determined by his attitude toward Egdon Heath. For Eustacia it means stagnation, exile from all that she loves, from the pomps and vanities of the great world. For Clym—who has returned from the great world, disgusted with its pomps and vanities—it means much what Wordsworth's mountains meant to him; the simple, natural life of labor and usefulness. When Clym loses the use of his eyes for reading and is obliged to earn his living in the humble occupation of a furze-cutter, it is no hardship for him, but for his young wife, as well as for his mother, it is nothing short of tragedy. And actual tragedy is the outcome in the plot.

The view of him as discovered by Mrs. Yeobright moving like an insect in the vast barren landscape of the heath, a drab inhuman figure clothed in leather—this scene alone is sufficient to establish Hardy as one of the greatest of English writers. But its peculiar greatness lies in the perfect appropriateness of the setting, its absolute identification with the story, the fact that philosophically it is *indispensable.*

Something similar is true for "The Woodlanders," for "Tess of the D'Urbervilles," for "Jude the Obscure." And in the two last mentioned, the effect of design is heightened by their being built about a single center of interest, a single character. But in none of these novels is the unity of place so remarkable nor so organic as in the story laid in Egdon Heath. And in none of them does the same structural instinct lead to such an effective composition as regards the element of time. I leave out of account the sixth book, entitled "Aftercourses," which was Hardy's concession to the magazine editor's demand for a happy ending and was not included in his original design. The story then is all included in one year's time, beginning and ending with long scenes at night centering around the Guy Fawkes celebrations of the fifth of November. Each one of the five books is like a single act of tragedy, with the subject-matter strongly massed about certain events and issues which give it a distinct unity of effect.

There is no English novel of the nineteenth century better suited than "The Return of the Native" to delight the connoisseur with sheer beauty of form. And this, for one thing, derives from the fact that beauty of form here grows so inevitably out of beauty of conception that we are justified in speaking of their being identical. That is, of course, the ideal for all works of art.

8

Thus we have traced in some of the masterpieces of the Victorian novel the tendency toward that simplicity of form which is the ideal of the well-made novel. We have noted it in "Adam Bede," "Esther Waters," "The Egoist," "The Return of the Native." In the foreign field, we have found this tendency still more marked in "Madame Bovary" and "Fathers and Sons," and have seen how the scientific ideal of the French naturalists tended to reinforce it. If I had begun my survey at an earlier period, I should of course have included some one of Jane Austen's stories, say "Mansfield Park" or "Pride and Prejudice." If no one of these great books is a perfect example of the well-made novel, that will serve to remind us that the well-made novel is not a synonym for greatness. It is a convenient term for indicating a tendency which has been more or less present all along, but which became dominant in the period between 1895 and 1925.

XIII

DRAMATIC PRESENT

As one surveys the whole field of the novel, one becomes aware of the existence of a certain type which for convenience we may briefly call dramatic. Or it would be more exact to refer to a tendency toward the dramatic. This is not a type that knows itself and can infallibly be distinguished by the presence of all the characterizing features like, say, some breed of dog or variety of goldenrod. It is a tendency showing itself in greater or less degree in a large number of novelists, and standing, broadly, in contrast to the opposed and on the whole commoner tendency. A classic example of the dramatic novel is very hard to name, so many different features are involved in the perfect expression of it, and so seldom are they all found present at the same time in a single work. The completest example of a dramatic novel with which I am acquainted is Schnitzler's novelette "Fräulein Else" (1923).

The dramatic tendency has been on the whole a growing one, and is strongly present in what I have called the well-made novel. But there are certain features of the well-made novel which constitute a special contribution, and which give a point to our feeling that the well-made novel should be separately classified, especially since some of these features, while logically involved in the complete formula of the dramatic novel, actually lead away from it into a quite distinguishable type.

The essential differences between the novel and the play grow out of the fact that the novel is to be read and the play is to be presented on the stage. In the novel the action is described; in the play it is performed before our eyes. The limitations of stage presentation enormously reduce the amount of action that can be shown in the play. Practically speaking, the play consists entirely of dialogue with the accompanying gestures. The stage directions, though they tend in modern plays to bulk large on the printed page, are not, properly speaking, a part of the play, since the play has no real existence except on the stage. There the stage directions are translated directly into painted scenes and gesture or stage business. The thoughts of the characters, the whole subjective accompaniment of the action, is excluded from the matter of the play, except in the dubious and unplausible form of soliloquy and aside. Moreover, it is impossible for the play to explain the circumstances which have given rise to the present action, except as this may be accomplished in the dialogue. The play cannot explain the characters and make it clear to the spectator what they are really like behind the masks which they wear for one another. The playwright has to provide his characters with masks which are transparent to the spectator.

So that, at every point, the play is distinguished from the novel by its greater limitations, by all it has to go without. It has to go without exposition, description, characterization, without "psychology," and almost entirely without action.

And so at first thought, the novel appears to have all the advantages and the play all the limitations involved in their essential difference of function. But one has only to be present at a play, even a third-rate play, to become aware of an advantage this form possesses over its rival which more than makes up for all its limitations. The story of the novel is passed on to us second hand, through the relatively dull medium of the imagination. That of the play is given direct; we are present in person, we see with our own eyes, we hear with our own ears. And while, in human beings, the imagination is a highly developed and powerful faculty, it is, after all, derivative, secondary; it cannot at all compare in intensity with the immediate impact of things upon the senses. Intellectually the novel has all the advantage; emotionally it is the play. And we are, first of all, creatures of emotion. So that to have the appeal of a play of a given caliber a novel must be ten times as powerful in its kind.

All along novelists have been more or less obscurely conscious of the disadvantage under which they labored in comparison with playwrights, and have been seeking to supply the elements wanting to their form of writing. What the stage has is directness, immediacy. This derives from the fact that the story is enacted, is put on before the eyes of the spectator. It is not something in the past, but something going on now, in the immediate present. And this is where the "dramatic" novelist takes his cue from the drama. Even in novels there is something that is felt as the dramatic present. It is distinguished from all that generalized narrative of antecedent circumstances which goes by the name of exposition, characterization, etc. We feel that now at last, on such and such a day, in such and such a place, events are actually moving to their climax; we are done with explanations and are present at the scene for which the author has been preparing us.

Balzac is famous for the elaborateness with which he lays down the antecedent circumstances of his stories; and he is clearly aware of the point where he passes from that part of his material lying in the past to the scenes that are felt to constitute the present of the story. In Balzac this point is sometimes actually more than half-way through the book. Thus in "Ursule Mirouet" it is at the end of the first part, which is rather longer than the second and concluding part, that he informs us that his story proper is about to begin. "If one should apply to the narrative the laws of the stage, the arrival of Savinien, in introducing to Nemours the only personage who was still lacking of those who should be present at this little drama, here brings the exposition to an end." In "Le Père Goriot," again, Balzac indicates for us the point—here a little less than one third through the book—at which he turns from the exposition to the dramatic present. "This information was all that was known to a M. Muret in regard to old Goriot, whose securities he had purchased. Here ends the exposition of this obscure but fearful Parisian tragedy."

But since, in the narrative, everything is really in the past, and nothing more present than anything else except by a trivial approximation in time, what is it gives us, in a story, this sense of the dramatic present? On the stage everything is present because everything is enacted directly for our eyes and ears. In a story, we have the psychological equivalent of the dramatic present whenever we have a vividly "constituted scene," as Henry James calls it, a selected, a "discriminated occasion." When the author is done with explaining the circumstances that led to the present situation, he arrives at the situation itself in its concrete immediacy. The persons are confronted in some particular place, at some particular hour of the day; they begin to act, they begin to talk, they are actually in the process of working out the issue. It is an issue which may have existed historically for a long time, and various operations may have been going on "behind the scenes." But now it becomes an immediate issue; it is brought upon the stage; the opposed forces are engaged; the battle is on; there must be some decision—some solution must be found, and that here and now.

It is this urgency of an immediate issue which does the most to give a dramatic character to certain portions of a story—it is this which cheats the imagination, and persuades the reader that he is actually present, as a spectator, nay perhaps as an actor in the drama.

But even without the presence of a clearly defined issue, without a sharp opposition of forces, the effect of the dramatic present is secured by the skilful writer of fiction every time he shows us his characters in action on a particular occasion. Our mere interest in human character, our mere curiosity as to what these people will say next, will fire our imagination to the point of forgetting that it is merely imagination, will beguile us into thinking we are there in person.

There are long stretches in Dickens where we are not concerned with the dramatic issues of the story. We are being introduced to people so droll, so peculiar, so enchanting—to households so deliciously impossible—that we are perforce transported to the scene and give ourselves up for hours at a time to "listening in" on the talk of Mr. and Mrs. Micawber, say, or of Sairey Gamp, pouring out strong liquor from her tea-pot and spinning the myth of her friend Mrs. Harris.

It has always been a favorite occupation of critics to contrast the art of Dickens and Thackeray, so very like in many points, so very unlike in general effect. There is much involved in this difference of effect—matters of temperament, philosophy, style, social level presented. But not all these together are enough to explain the decidedly greater popularity of Dickens, a popularity which persists in spite of the coldness of many critics toward him. I suspect that the most important single factor involved is the much greater generosity of Dickens in the matter of the discriminated occasion. The proportion of pages in which we feel ourselves to be actually "there" is enormously greater in Dickens than in Thackeray. And that is enough to make up, with the general reader, for the more genteel style of Thackeray, his more conscientious realism, his more intellectual approach to his subject. And it doesn't necessarily mean that Dickens has been guilty of working the emotional stops; it means in part that he is, in this particular matter, a better technician, a more skilful, and probably a more conscious, artist than his rival.

The scenes of Dickens are, on the average, many times longer than those of Thackeray. This may seem a merely mechanical feature; but it has a powerful effect on the reader's psychology, and makes strongly for the sense of the dramatic present. Scenes on the stage are very long; in the modern drama, they occupy an entire act, and take on the average about forty-five minutes to perform. If at the start the spectator finds it a bit difficult to adjust his mind to an occasion so foreign to his own experience, by the time the act is a third-way through he will be thoroughly "en rapport"; by the time it is half-way through his interest will be profoundly engaged by the dramatic issue; and before he knows it he will have forgotten that he is sitting in his seat in a theater—he will be completely absorbed in the scene in which he is taking part. If the mere passage of time has this effect in a play, where the spectator has the powerful evidence of eye and ear to the present reality of the action, how much more must it be so in a story, where he has the feebler testimony of mere imagination.

It takes a certain length of time for a scene to work up sufficient momentum to carry the reader along with it in complete obliviousness of its being fiction, and to give him a sense of being there with the characters in an unquestioned Now. Suppose we have a chapter of generalized narrative, covering the developments of a month or a year. Bits of anecdote may be introduced to illustrate the doings of the characters. They may even involve an exchange of remarks on some particular occasion. They may be very well told, very well chosen for their illustrative ends. But they are over in less than a page, before we have had a chance to take hold upon that particular occasion with any vivid sense of present reality. And the whole chapter impresses us in retrospect as so much history—interesting enough as history, it may be, but without that raising of the temperature, or acceleration of the pulse, that goes with scenes at which we are personally present.

Other things being equal, the longer the scene the stronger the hold on the reader's imagination. Much is involved, to be sure, in that plausible phrase, "other things being equal." It is necessary, of course, that the characters and the situation should be sufficiently interesting to hold our attention, and this implies great imaginative power on the part of the author. Or else it implies a dramatic issue so strong, and capable of such extensive development, that the reader will follow the scene with growing suspense. And this is the point at which some abatement should be made of the praise given to Dickens as an artist in comparison with Thackeray. Sometimes he presumes on his power of animating puppets, and is inclined to make them go through their amusing antics once, twice, half a dozen times too often. Tastes change with the age, and we to-day demand that an author get his effects more swiftly. We are sometimes inclined to prefer the brief anecdotal manner of Thackeray's scenes to the elaborated fullness of Dickens's.

And in the one case and the other, we are inclined to complain that their scenes often fail in power for want of a sharply defined dramatic issue. It is the issue which creates suspense and enables us to keep our attention fixed for a considerable period on the same situation without feeling the strain. It is the issue more than anything else that makes us forget the lapse of time and maintain ourselves in one tremendous and continuous Now. And it is the issue alone that enables the skilful author to bridge the gap between scene and scene and keep up for hundreds of pages the emotional tension which is of the essence of drama.

One reason why a long scene means ordinarily a strong appeal is that a long scene means an uninterrupted maintenance of the dramatic present. When one scene is over, another must be prepared for. And that means a slackening of the tension, a lowering of the temperature. The mere phrase, "in the meantime," or "during the next few weeks," implies a drop back into the narrative past. And while this may be altogether necessary to a right understanding of the story, while it may even be psychologically desirable in order to relieve the strain upon the reader's feelings and attention, there is inevitably some loss of momentum. And the writer who has an instinct for drama is inclined to make as little as possible of the passages that lead from one scene to another.

In the modern play there is a disposition to make one scene follow very soon after another in story-time as it does actually follow close upon it in time of presentation. There is a general feeling that something is gained if the action of the whole play is included within twenty-four hours, so that the three acts may be headed Morning, Afternoon, and Night of the same day. In any case it is held desirable that, however much time may intervene between the occurrences of one act and the next, very little shall have happened in the interval, so that one may take up the action at approximately the point at which it was dropped. This dispenses with the necessity of explanations, which are difficult to make without slowing up the play, and which in any case reduce the emotional momentum. The three acts of a play are thought of as ideally three successive waves, each higher than the other, the one mounting as it were on the back of the other, with only a slight subsidence of the level before the later wave starts rising to its crest. The instinct of the modern playwright is to arrange that the several acts of the play shall be virtually continuous. And this end is secured by taking an issue which, while it may be divisible into several minor issues, each susceptible of working out in a single act, yet remains one close-knit theme running without interruption through the whole drama. A rigorous selection and simplification of subject-matter is called for, a concentration of all forces upon the single dramatic line on which the playwright depends for his effect.

I have spoken of this as the ideal of the modern playwright, in order to distinguish it from the way of Shakspere and most of the great Elizabethan dramatists. But it was likewise the academic ideal of the "classic" French and English playwrights of the seventeenth and eighteenth centuries, following the practice of the ancients. It had its theoretical expression in the critical dogma of the three unities. It was the common strategy of successful French playwrights of the nineteenth century, like Augier and Dumas *fils*. It was the natural way of Ibsen, the most influential of all playwrights since Shakspere. And it is, on the whole, the dominant procedure with contemporary playwrights everywhere in Europe, so much so that brilliant exceptions stand out by the daring and originality displayed in their departure from traditional stagecraft.

In origin this way of writing plays is based in a very simple fact of psychology. It is dictated by the desire to secure the strongest emotional appeal possible within the limits of an evening's performance. But that which had its origin in such a practical consideration, in the shrewd calculating of emotional economies, comes to have an attraction of a more purely esthetic character. That simplicity of line which is prescribed by the exigencies of dramatic appeal comes to be prized for itself as an element of formal beauty, a mark of elegance and grace. The process is similar to that which goes on in the world of morals and manners, where courage and honesty and politeness come to be admired in themselves and without regard to the useful purposes they have served in social organization. So the three unities are regarded as classic features of the dramatic form, giving a touch of distinction to the play to which they are applied. And it may even be that the play in question is not otherwise particularly effective as drama.

I fancy that this purely esthetic consideration has been present in the consciousness of certain novelists who, in our own day, have emulated the formal simplicity of the drama, without, in many cases, producing an effect which is felt by their readers as "dramatic." But the more striking instances of this tendency in the nineteenth-century novel seem to me to be largely motived by the practical consideration, by the instinct for emotional appeal. Thus in novelists who show a disposition to develop their scenes at considerable length, to subordinate the passages linking scene to scene, and to make the successive scenes follow upon one another with an almost uninterrupted continuity of effect, it is, I fancy, the sheer genius for storytelling rather than any theoretical preoccupation with form that has determined their method.

XIV

DRAMATIC PRESENT: DOSTOEVSKI

Of all serious nineteenth-century novelists, the one who has given the most striking examples of the dramatic tendency is Dostoevski. And it is for this reason that I am led once more to a special examination of his work. In making clear the unusual lengths to which he has pushed the dramatic ideal, it will be most convenient to consider a number of distinct features involved in that ideal when carried to its logical limits.

To begin with, it will be obvious that the naturally dramatic author makes as little as he can of himself as showman and commentator. This theme I have sufficiently labored in earlier chapters, and it will necessarily come in for incidental mention more than once in the chapters which are to follow. And I shall be as brief as possible in discussing Dostoevski's practice. In "Crime and Punishment" the author is so little in evidence that the ordinary reader is not conscious of his presence.

Where it is necessary to begin the story with a certain amount of exposition, as in "The Possessed" and "The Brothers Karamazov," Dostoevski has very ingeniously put these introductory chapters, as well as certain later passages of exposition, into the hands of an imaginary narrator—an anonymous gentleman of "our town" whose relation to the author is not unlike that of Captain Marlow, Captain Mitchell, and Captain Davidson to Joseph Conrad. He is, in a way, a character in the story, being acquainted with the other persons, having been present (in "The Possessed") on many of the occasions recorded. Where he has not been present personally, he has his information from reliable sources, or else he has pieced it together from common rumor, using his judgment and his knowledge of human nature to arrive at a version of what happened which shall be least remote from probability. He is constantly distinguishing between what is known to be true, what is probably true, and what "people say." His narrative is lively, picturesque, and such as to give a faint suggestion of complacent egoism on the part of the writer. It is—if one can trust the translation—the style of an elderly clubman with a genius for gossip. It is full of phrases like: "I know for a fact," "I must frankly own," "I may add here for myself personally," "I only learned the other day to my intense amazement, though on the most unimpeachable authority . . ." It often reminds one of the style of Defoe in his incomparable "Apparition of Mrs. Veal." In short, where he could not get rid of him, Dostoevski has made of his expositor a dramatic creation on his own account.

Another element predisposing to drama is a theme single, clear-cut, and calling for a close continuous treatment. That this element is notably present in Dostoevski I have shown in Chapter VIII. A recurring theme with him is the effect of crime on the spiritual state of his characters. This is likely to be most marked during the period just preceding and just following the crime, and is so powerful and relentless that it will not let its victim go for an instant until he has somehow met its terrible challenge. It is obvious how this makes for the sense of the dramatic present.

Coming now to the specific mechanical features of the dramatic method, I shall list them under five headings. I do not, however, attach any magical significance to that number, which might readily be enlarged or decreased by some other method of classification. And it will be observed that these five separate features have a way of being involved with one another, and that they combine in many ways to bring about the same result.

First then, as to the *center of interest.* The longer the author keeps to a single center of interest, the more it makes for drama. In "Crime and Punishment" the story follows Raskolnikov virtually without interruption through the first 200 out of 550 pages; or still farther, as far as page 363, if we include a scene of 23 pages between his friend Razumihin and his mother and sister at which he is not present. He is the main subject of their discussion, so that we may say that he is still the center of interest. In the later part of the book, there are scenes involving Luzhin, Sonia, and Katerina Ivanovna (20 pages), and others involving Sonia and Svidrigaïlov (25 pages). The first of these passages is in preparation for a scene in which Raskolnikov plays the principal rôle; in the second we leave Raskolnikov, only to follow his spiritual shadow, Svidrigaïlov. To all intents and purposes Raskolnikov is the center of interest throughout the story; and he is actually present in nearly seven eighths of the narrative.

In "The Idiot" Prince Myshkin is the center of interest throughout. And he is personally present almost continuously during the first 460 (out of 588) pages. In "The Brothers Karamazov" the interest is divided among the three main characters. But there are long scenes in which they are present together: for example, the scene at the Elder Zossima's (70 pages) and that of the trial (120 pages). And still more, there are extremely long suites of scenes in which one or other of them is continuously present and the center of interest. Mitya holds the stage during the whole of Book VIII (100 pages), and then, after a brief interruption to explain how the police got on his trail, through the whole of the next book (69 pages more). Alyosha, in addition to being present through the scene at Father Zossima's, is the center of interest throughout most of the following books III, IV, and V (in all about 264 pages, allowing for 10 pages of exposition on the subject of Smerdyakov).

These novels of Dostoevski belong neither to the autobiographical nor to the biographical genre. Outside of those genres, it would be hard to find novels in the nineteenth century that keep single individuals on the stage so continuously as Dostoevski's. But the full significance of this does not appear until it is considered along with the accompanying features of dramatic structure.

My second point is a sort of corollary of the first, the *limited point of view* which tends to go along with the limited center of interest. This is a matter which Dostoevski seems not to have considered, and I shall put off discussion of it to a later chapter.

My third point is the *limitation of place.* In "Crime and Punishment" the action is limited to the city of Petersburg; in "The Brothers Karamazov" it is limited to the provincial city of Skotoprigonyevsk and the neighboring village of Mokroe; in "The Possessed" to "our town" in the provinces. In "The Idiot," it is distributed between Petersburg, Moscow, and the summer resort of Pavlovsk. In each of these novels there is a considerable number of settings within the particular town.

This is particularly true of "Crime and Punishment." There are Raskolnikov's house, that of the old woman whom he murders, Marmeladov's, Porfiry's, Sonia's, that where Dounia and her mother stay; not to speak of several taverns and places on the streets. The nature of the action is such that Raskolnikov is perpetually going from one house to another, and—in his distraction of mind—wandering about in the streets. So that while in the large there is unity of place, in detail, within that frame, there is very frequent change of place, perhaps as frequent as in the average novel.

In this respect the other novels of Dostoevski are more dramatically arranged. In all of them there are extremely long scenes played out continuously in a single room. Such is the scene at General Epanchin's in "The Idiot" (Part I, Chapters II to VII, 72 pages); the scene at the convent, the long suite of scenes at Mokroe and the trial scene in "The Brothers Karamazov" (the last one occupying the whole of Book XII, 14 chapters, 120 pages).

Altogether, Dostoevski is sufficiently remarkable for the length of scenes laid in a single place. And, even taken by itself, this feature shows him to be a novelist of strongly dramatic bent. But its significance, again, becomes much greater when it is taken along with other features which accompany it.

My fourth point is the *amount of time covered* in the aggregate. In "Crime and Punishment," leaving out of account the brief Epilogue, which is professedly a mere looking forward to the theme of a separate book, the entire time of the action is limited to some fifteen or sixteen days, a little more than a fortnight. This is an exceptionally short period of time—especially in the older novel—for a book of over five hundred pages. And the limitation of time is more notable still if we take into account only those days whose events are actually presented. Between the days of presented action there are two intervals of unconsciousness and clouded mind on the part of Raskolnikov which are very briefly summarized. Of days actually presented there are but nine.

In "The Brothers Karamazov," the entire period of the action, exclusive of the introductory exposition, is less than three months. But here again there are two intervals which the author passes over, a period from the end of August, time of the murder, to the beginning of November, time of the trial; and a five days' interval between the day of the trial and that of the Epilogue. Of days actually presented there are but seven—and this in a book of nearly a thousand pages. "The Idiot" opens in November; then, after an interval briefly summarized, it begins again with the following Easter and continues into July. In all, then, it covers about eight months. Of days actually presented there are about nine. "The Possessed" covers something like six weeks' time, exclusive of the epilogue-like Conclusion, which brings us down to a period three months later to clear up a few points in the sequel. Fourteen days are actually presented, apart from the summarized intervals.

These are all books very much longer than the average for English novels, even in the nineteenth century, when novels ran long. The aggregate time covered is very much less than that of the average novel anywhere. Inevitably this results in such a concentration of the action in time as to give much more than usually the sense of our being without interruption in the dramatic present.

This effect of concentration is even more evident when we consider my final point, the *length of development of the events of a single day,* or *of suites of days following one another* without interval. In this respect Dostoevski has, I think, no parallel before the time of James Joyce. In "Crime and Punishment" there are three separate days developed to occupy 92, 121, and 104 pages respectively. More than that, there is a suite of four days occupying 119 pages, and another suite of three days occupying 319 pages. In "The Possessed" there is a suite of five days occupying 269 somewhat larger pages. In "The Idiot" there is one single day treated to the length of 176 pages. In "The Brothers Karamazov" there is one suite of four days extending to 644 pages, much longer than a good-sized novel in our time.

When I speak of days following one another without interval, I mean without the intervention of other calendar days. I have allowed for the night as a period of sleep and oblivion. But the people of Dostoevski hardly have time or inclination for sleep. They are so relentlessly hounded by the furies of fear, shame, passion, remorse, indecision—the pressure is so strong upon them to do something, to reach some decision, to come to a settlement of all that is at issue—that they cannot take time for sleep or food. They seem to live on tea and champagne, which can be consumed while they go on talking and thinking. From time to time they fall into the fitful sleep of nervous exhaustion, only to be haunted by dreams which bring back the preoccupations of their waking hours. Very often they keep going all night, like eight-day clocks, so that the second day is literally continuous with the first. In "The Possessed" there are four successive days thus linked by all-night sessions. And no matter how often they change their location in space, these people carry with them the same fevers, the same unsolved and urgent problems.

One who has not read Dostoevski might easily derive from this description a quite false notion of what he is like. It does not allow for the large diversification of interest he is able to introduce while keeping his characters thus upon the strain, for the strong appeal of mystery and strangeness, for the manifold objectification which he knows how to give to a theme so simplified. His work is neither so monotonous nor so melodramatic as my account might suggest. It is his inexhaustible imagination which enables him thus to expand the occurrences of one day so as to fill an ordinary person's quota of drama for a lifetime.

What I am trying to indicate is the extraordinary emotional tension which goes along with his packing so much experience into the limits of a few days, and those days crowding upon one another without pause or respite. And since my subject is technique, I am trying to show how the very physical conditions of his narrative lend themselves to the creation of such emotional tension.

The reader will have observed how the several features of this method work together to make the drama more and more concentrated. In "Crime and Punishment" it is not merely that the same person is the center of interest through the greater part of 550 pages, but that the action in which he takes part almost continuously is confined to nine days' time. In "The Idiot" it is not merely that the same person is the center through a narrative of still greater length, but that one single day of action in which he is continuously present occupies 176 close-printed pages, that the setting is but three times changed within that period, and that one single scene in one place is 72 pages long. In "The Brothers Karamazov," where there are three main centers of interest, each one in turn is followed through passages of great length: Mitya occupying the center of the stage, during two successive days and the intervening night, to the tune of 169 pages; Alyosha being present and, for the most part the center of interest, through 260 pages devoted to two successive days. Sometimes all the leading characters are assembled in a single scene, on a single day and in one place, running up in one case to 70 pages, in another to 120. And the action of this prodigious drama is crowded into the limits of seven days, of which the first four are absolutely continuous.

To the end that the reader may have strongly the sense of the dramatic present in a story, it is a good thing to have a single person for center of interest. It is still better that this person shall play out his part in close limitations of place so as to guard against too frequent change of scene. It is still better that his action, so limited in place, shall be narrowly limited in time so as to provide continuity of effect. And the better to secure such continuity, it is well that the story should be limited to a small number of days whose action is presented, and that the whole period covered, including intervals not presented, should be as short as possible.

Naturally, there are many considerations which make it impossible to carry out this scheme with any rigor of logic, so that we must add, to each one of these statements, the saving phrase, "other things being equal." The novel has plenty to offer besides drama. But drama is a good thing too. No serious novelist has gone so far to meet the conditions of dramatic fiction as Dostoevski. And among the many reasons for his effectiveness this is one of the most important.

XV

DRAMATIC PRESENT: THACKERAY, TOLSTOY

IT WOULD be hard to find a writer whose methods of composition are more in contrast with Dostoevski's than Thackeray's. And it is worth while—leaving out of account the shining merits of Thackeray in other directions—to consider some of the disadvantages under which he labors from his neglect of the dramatic principle. The method of Tolstoy in "Anna Karenina" (1875–76) is midway between Dostoevski's and Thackeray's, and a comparison of that novel with "Vanity Fair" (1847–48) in certain points of structure will serve to bring out in higher relief the peculiarity of Thackeray's system.

It is significant that Tolstoy divides his novel into parts, thus showing a consciousness of larger groupings of material than is indicated by the chapter division. The principle is—given his three main centers of interest (Anna, Vronsky, Levin), or his six main characters, one of whom is always present throughout and dominant—to carry them forward chronologically through eight main periods, or phases, massing the experiences of each group or center during a limited period of time. Generally each part will be confined to the events of three months—summer, winter, or spring.

If we attempted a similar division for "Vanity Fair," we could not reduce the parts to fewer than eleven. And this in itself, considering that the English novel is appreciably shorter than "Anna Karenina," is an indication of the more dispersed character of the material. This becomes still more evident when we consider that the number of years covered in the aggregate is something like three and a half for "Anna" and not fewer than fourteen for "Vanity Fair." There is a much greater average lapse of time within each division in the English novel. This becomes more significant when we ask how much time is given to the doings of one day or succession of days.

In Tolstoy, we find, there is an approach to the practice of Dostoevski, of developing extensively the doings of individual days and groups of days that follow closely on one another in dramatic sequence. Thus the first part is confined to the events of four days, all in Moscow, so that we have the impression of uninterrupted action during 34 chapters, 136 pages. In II and III we have a group of 96 pages devoted to the horse-race and the days immediately following. In general it is probably true that in each part there will be two groups, of one or several days, each of which occupy from 75 to 90 per cent of the entire division.

With Thackeray the case is quite the contrary. In the whole book I find only three occasions on which he remotely approaches the grouping of Tolstoy, let alone Dostoevski. The first group comprises the first six chapters, beginning with the day when Amelia and Becky leave Miss Pinkerton's school and covering the two weeks in which Becky makes her first unsuccessful assault on the heart of Jos Sedley. This is with Thackeray a very exceptional case of the development of a group of scenes. And here we may reckon that Thackeray gives about one seventh as much space as Tolstoy to each day's occurrences.

There are several other circumstances that reduce the dramatic character of those rare occasions in Thackeray where the occurrences of several days are developed at some length. In Tolstoy the presence of one major character throughout gives continuity to passages of considerable length, even when the setting is several times changed. In Thackeray there is no such thing as dramatic continuity;

we are perpetually passing from one place to another, from one character to another. Thus in the culminating scenes of "Vanity Fair," the most dramatic in the book—beginning with Becky's triumph at Lord Steyne's party, and ending with the break-up of her ménage with Rawdon—we are part of the time with Rawdon, part with Becky, part with Rawdon again; we pass continually from one place to another; there is a whole chapter inserted at the height of the action which goes back to an earlier period and brings the story up to the time of the party. Altogether this climax of the book is handled in as undramatic a manner as possible.

The want of a steady center of interest is naturally still more to be felt in those passages—the staple of the book—in which there is no development of any scene or group of scenes beyond a very few pages. In order to get the greatest effect from a steady center of interest, more is necessary than to refrain from shifting from one person to another. It is necessary to have characters strong enough so that we recognize them as constituting centers of interest, persons who take strong hold on our feelings or imagination, and whose rôle is important enough to make them major characters. Of such there are in "Vanity Fair" but two, Becky Sharp and Amelia, with the possible addition of Major Dobbin and Rawdon Crawley, admitted to the rank of major characters more on account of their rôle in the story than because of their intrinsic interest.

If, then, these four persons were followed steadily through the story, if some one or other of them were invariably present, so that the action came to us as part and parcel of their personal experience, "Vanity Fair" would more nearly meet the conditions of dramatic narrative. But this is very far from being the case. There is a large number of minor characters, less important in the plot, to whom the author gives his attention from time to time. They are more or less interesting in one way or another, but not interesting enough to stand by themselves, and yet their histories are given in fairly regular alternation with that of principals. Such are the Osbornes—the old man, Captain George, who married Amelia, and their son Georgie, together with Maria and Fred Bullock; such are the Crawleys of Queen's Crawley; the Bute Crawleys, rivals of the others for the favor of the wealthy Miss Crawley; the old Sedleys and Jos; Lord Steyne and the Gaunts.

Toward all these characters Thackeray seems to feel an equal responsibility; since they are in his chronicle, he will tell us what there is to be told of them; and he will tell it at the point where it comes in most naturally, which is generally in the midst of what he is saying about his major characters. We find them amusing; we recognize their importance as social exhibits; we regard them as acquaintances and are glad to know what happens to them. But there is nothing important about them, nothing that we cannot wait until to-morrow to learn. And it is figures such as these, who interest us as gossip interests, for whom the principals are constantly being asked to give way.

Not that there is anything so very urgent about the principals. These are not figures of tragedy, creatures of destiny. Their story flows on with the slow, equable movement of everyday events. It hangs upon no thread and is not going to be decided by the fatal choices of a night. It is not packed into the confines of a breathless week, but strings itself along diffusely through many years of minor happenings. There is no mystery to be solved, but merely the mild question of what next. So that the reader suffers no great hardship when he is asked to postpone his interest in Becky or Amelia in favor of Mrs. Bute Crawley or old Mr. Osborne.

In Tolstoy each one of the leading characters takes such hold upon us that we cannot bear to leave him except for another whose case is equally urgent. In "Anna Karenina" in addition to the three characters of major interest there are three others who, at certain points, are shown in predicaments tight enough to make us follow them for a space with considerable suspense—Karenina, Kitty, and Stepan Oblonsky. I believe there is no entire chapter in the whole novel in which one or more of these six persons is not actually present. And in the great bulk of the story it is one of the leading three—Anna, Vronsky, Levin—who is invariably there.

So that Tolstoy displays a distinct sense for composition which is lacking in Thackeray. Thackeray's novel gives, by comparison, the impression of a mere series of sketches loosely strung along on a tenuous thread of plot. And we are reminded that Thackeray started as an essayist and illustrator, and was a long time coming to the novel form.

2

That the essayist was still dominant in Thackeray's technique is indicated by the very large proportion in his novels of summary narrative where the born story-teller (say Dickens) would have given us drama. Here again he is in startling contrast to Tolstoy. In "Anna Karenina" the amount of formal exposition is very slight, considering the length of the book and the number of characters involved. I reckon it would not come to more than 20 or 30 pages in all, scattered through a volume of 950 pages. As to formal characterization, distinct from exposition, there is extremely little. Here is an author, famous for the vivid reality of his characters, who very seldom thinks it necessary to halt his story for two minutes in order to tell us what these people are like.

The proportion of exposition and formal characterization is very much greater in "Vanity Fair." There is, for example, one long chapter (IX) given to the account of the Crawleys of Queen's Crawley, and another still longer (XLVII) to the Gaunts, with all the ramifications of family history detailed and all the family skeletons dragged to light. It should be conceded that Thackeray is in his element in this kind of thing, which favors his gift for social satire. The subject-matter is more highly colored than that in Tolstoy's expository passages, and finely flavored with Thackeray's irony. There is superb writing in these parts of "Vanity Fair," but it is none the less true that we are reminded more of the essayist than the writer of fiction.

But the method of generalization is not by any means confined to those passages in which is explained what needs to be understood before the story can begin. It is extensively used as a means of bridging the gulf between one main scene and another, giving an idea of developments which do not lend themselves to dramatic presentation. And it is just here that the writer with a penchant for drama is distinguished from the undramatic writer.

The dramatic writer makes the least possible use of generalized narrative. He passes from one scene to another, from one period to another, with the slightest reference to what was going on in the interval. This is the instinct of Tolstoy. Each new part begins at a period considerably later than the one preceding, and almost invariably without preliminaries, in the midst of a scene. "At the end of the winter, in the Schcherbatsky's house, a consultation was being held." "Princess Schcherbatsky considered that it was out of the question for the wedding to take place before Lent." "Vronsky and Anna had been travelling for three months together in Europe." "Levin had been married three months. He was happy, but not at all in the way he had expected to be." We find ourselves planted solidly in the midst of the new scene, in the mind perhaps of one of the characters.

The reason why Tolstoy has so little occasion to summarize events is that he manages to make the large single dramatic occasions stand for the mass of minor events. We might put it this way—that he chooses to represent only those major occasions that have dramatic significance; as if he could pay always in large bills and let the small change go. And then, comparing his procedure with that of Dickens and Thackeray, we might say that Dickens deals largely in small change, which he treats as if it were large bills—that is, he erects each minor event into a major dramatic occasion. Thackeray too deals largely in what for Tolstoy would be small change, but he does not treat it as large bills—neglecting to erect it into major dramatic occasions or scenes.

There is in Thackeray an enormous amount of small change. His "Vanity Fair" is an entire composition of little happenings illustrative of greed, snobbishness, social climbing. There are so many of these little happenings that not a quarter of them could be properly presented scenically, and Thackeray does not seem willing to leave any of them out. But if they are all to be included, a large number of them must necessarily be presented in sketchy summary.

These two young couples had plenty of tales to relate to one another. The marriages of either were discussed, and their prospects in life canvassed with the greatest frankness and interest on both sides. George's marriage was to be made known to his father by his friend Captain Dobbin; and young Osborne trembled rather for the result of that communication. Miss Crawley, on whom all Rawdon's hopes depended, still held out. Unable to make an entry into her house in Park Lane her affectionate nephew and niece had followed her to Brighton. . . . The two wedding parties met constantly in each other's apartments. After two or three nights the gentlemen of an evening had a little piquet, as their wives sat and chatted apart. This pastime, and the arrival of Jos Sedley, who made his appearance in his grand open carriage, and who played a few games at billiards with Captain Crawley, replenished Rawdon's purse somewhat, and gave him the benefit of that ready money for which the greatest spirits are sometimes at a standstill.

It often seems as if Thackeray were overwhelmed by the sheer bulk of the multiple history about which he feels called on to keep us informed. He loses himself in the items without making anything of them as story. He can neither reconcile himself to leaving them out, nor find the energy or time to show them to us properly. It is as if his spirit flagged, as if he were overcome with sheer laziness. He must let us know of the bankruptcy of John Sedley. He says he is "not going to follow the worthy old stock-broker through those last pangs and agonies of ruin through which he passed." And yet he cannot refrain from naming the several steps of the process:

> They declared him at the Stock-Exchange; he was absent from his house of business; his bills were protested; his act of bankruptcy formal. The house and furniture of Russell Square were seized and sold up, and he and his family were thrust away, as we have seen, to hide their heads where they might.

It is Osborne's attitude toward the bankrupt and toward his daughter which makes the climax of this whole affair. Here if anywhere, the author of fiction is called on to give us the situation in the form of scenes. But all we have is the barest statement of the facts:

> At the meetings of creditors [Osborne] comported himself with a savageness and scorn toward Sedley which almost succeeded in breaking the heart of that ruined, bankrupt man . . . When the great crash came—the announcement of ruin, and the departure from Russell Square and the declaration that all was over between her and George—all over between her and love, her and happiness, her and faith in the world—a brutal letter from John Osborne told her in a few curt lines that her father's conduct had been of such a nature that all engagements between the families were at an end—when the final award came, it did not shock her so much as her parents, as her mother rather, expected. . . . Amelia took the news very palely and calmly. It was only the confirmation of the dark presages which had long gone before.

It is all perfectly general. There is no pretense of showing Amelia on the occasion when she received old Osborne's letter; not even the letter is offered in evidence. The author is lavish of phrases of condolence for the Sedleys in their tragic fall and disillusion; but he does not take the trouble to show us the scenes which would so much more impress us with the reality of their case.

At times we feel as if Thackeray were simply incapable of selection. He follows his characters from day to day as if he felt it necessary to account for every moment of their time. In Chapter LVII he gives us a sort of diary of the ocean voyage of Dobbin and Jos Sedley on their return from India. Not that anything happens that is worth recording. The next chapter gives us a diary of Dobbin's activities on his first day in London, and in the following chapter the same thing is done for Jos. When Thackeray has, for some good purpose, brought a group of people together, he feels he has them on his hands; and he cannot get them off his hands without disposing of each one in turn. Each minor division of the story must be concluded, like the whole story at the end, by telling what happened to everybody.

This author seems at times to be carried along on the stream of his story instead of himself directing the story in a carefully marked channel. He is like a traveler conscientiously recording from day to day the progress of the journey and the occupations of his fellow-voyagers. The story carries his characters to Belgium. But you can't get to Belgium without crossing the Channel, and you can't cross the Channel without going down the river, and you can't go down the river without first embarking on transports. So Thackeray embarks you, and takes you down the river and then across the Channel, duly recording the degree of your sea-sickness. In Belgium you are in a city suitable to sight-seeing and the pursuit of pleasure. And so Thackeray proceeds to record the fact that his characters engage in sight-seeing and the pursuit of pleasure. This is what makes slow reading of so much of Thackeray.

It is true that, even in such generalized narrative, Thackeray can sometimes be entertaining. This applies particularly, in "Vanity Fair," to whatever concerns Becky Sharp. He is so genuinely interested in this plucky and unscrupulous adventuress, and in the means by which she manages to make her way in the world, that even an outline statement of her methods has its savor. One of the longest chapters in the book is entirely taken up with a historical sketch of her vagabond life after the break-up of her marriage with Rawdon Crawley. It shows the most competent acquaintance with Bohemian life in various European towns and of the shifts by which a woman of tainted reputation manages to cling to the skirts of good society. Above all the irony of Thackeray is forever vividly aware of the slight and as it were merely technical differences between the ways of good society and of Bohemia, and the most cursory statement of some of Becky's experiences is pleasantly spiced with this irony.

Much of this is highly amusing in its way—in somewhat the way of an essay by Addison or Goldsmith. But even so, it is questionable strategy in a novel to give more than seven thousand words to this kind of history. And when it comes to old Mr. Sedley in his decline, and to his worthy spouse, to the various landlords and landladies who were fond of Amelia, and the children of said landladies, and to Major Dobbin and Glorvina O'Dowd and Maria Osborne and Fred Bullock, the interest is certainly much too mild —at least for the present-day reader—to sustain the tiresome mass of trifling detail offered us in the non-dramatic form. "Vanity Fair" is like a great sheet of drawing-paper filled from rim to rim, from corner to corner, with charcoal sketches of human figures, crowded close together for economy of space. They are exercises in drawing and have this much in common that they are all in illustration of a common theme. But the lover of pictures cries out for spacing, for grouping, for subordination and perspective, for some organic principle of composition.

3

It is worth while in this connection to consider what Thackeray does with his chapter divisions, and here again to compare his practice with Tolstoy's. Thackeray's chapters are on the average three or four or five times as long as Tolstoy's. Tolstoy's chapters are almost invariably confined to one occasion; and very frequently several chapters will be given to the development of successive phases of the same occasion. Thackeray's chapters, on the other hand, are almost always omnibus affairs, in which many separate occasions are briefly disposed of.

It is difficult indeed to be sure which portion of the narrative should be defined as constituting an occasion, where so much is told in summary implying many occasions, and where the actual bits of scene are so deeply embedded in this viscous mass of generalized narrative. But suppose we take chapters like XXIV and XXV, in which we do have the impression of being present now and then at some particular scene, and try to count the number of such occasions, at least in their rudiments: we find that in these two chapters alone there are approximately thirty of them, though many of them are but sketchily suggested. In XXIV there is one well-developed and really dramatic scene between Captain Dobbin and Mr. Osborne, in which the Captain defends Amelia against the aspersions of the old snob and announces her marriage to George. But then the narrative loses itself in a series of no-account fragments of scene with Mr. Chopper, Osborne's clerk, with Ensign Stubble, together with various items of Osborne history too minute to be listed. In short, it is a chapter made up of odds and ends, including one or two good scenes, which might have stood out as important, but which are crowded together in one chapter with a heap of less impressive matter and smothered with trifling detail.

The following chapter is longer and more confused. There are two main groups of scenes, those clustered about a dinner at Brighton with all our principal characters present (the young Osbornes, the young Crawleys, Dobbin, and Jos), and those clustered about the rivalry of the Rawdon Crawleys and the Bute Crawleys for the favor of the wealthy Miss Crawley. Each cluster of scenes is broken up into a confusing jumble of bits of "occasion" embedded in summarized narrative. And there is nothing to connect the two groups of scenes but chronology and the fact that they all take place at Brighton. By all natural principles of artistic arrangement they belong in separate chapters.

There appears to be no planning at all in Thackeray's writing of his chapters. He does not seem to consider in advance what scene is to be the culminating point and just what is necessary in preparation for this scene; which details are to be subordinated and which may be eliminated altogether. He does not seem to be concerned to bring down the curtain effectively at the end of the act. He has so much material to cover, or so much copy to turn out, for this instalment. He seems to live from hand to mouth. He ambles along pleasantly, taking his time, plucking here a flower and there a wholesome herb.

One thing leads to another. If a character is mentioned, he stops to tell you about him. If he finds that something has not been explained, he stops to explain. Once in a while his conscience troubles him. "Our history is destined in this chapter to go backward and forward in a very irresolute manner seemingly, and having conducted our story to tomorrow presently, we shall immediately again have occasion to step back to yesterday, *so that the whole of the tale may get a hearing*." I have italicized the final phrase. Thackeray is much too concerned that the whole of the tale may get a hearing, by which he means that everything shall be told about everybody and all at the same time.

All that I have had to say of Thackeray in this chapter has reference to his manner of telling the story when he is actually engaged in telling it. I have left out of account the innumerable digressions—passages of comment on human nature in general, often of considerable length, which are simply essays in the manner of Addison or Goldsmith, and which occupy anywhere from three to eight per cent of the entire bulk of his novels (in "Vanity Fair" about six per cent). These digressions are so notorious a feature in Thackeray as scarcely to need mentioning. In spite of their satirical humor and worldly wisdom, they are frequently tedious and platitudinous in a high degree to a present-day reader, and it goes without saying that they are a wearisome interruption to the story.

The net result of his method is that we have in Thackeray a minimum sense of that dramatic present that makes the reading of a novel swift and exciting.

The dramatic novelist, whose concern is for the scenes where we have this sense of the here and now, wishes to reduce so far as possible the element of exposition. With him the exposition is the irreducible minimum of generalized narrative necessary as an introduction to the scenical element. With the non-dramatic writer, the exposition is the very body of the story, which is one long tissue of summary chronicle. The scenes give the impression of being anecdotes illustrative of the chronicle. They may be, and in Thackeray they frequently are, the cream of the book, but they give the impression of being merely incidental. In the dramatic novel they are the be-all and the end-all.

XVI

SUBJECTIVE DRAMA: JAMES

It must have occurred to some readers that I am using the words "drama" and "dramatic" in senses that ignore or leave out of account certain dominant connotations of those words as they are commonly used. For the primary definition of "drama" we may for the moment be content with its synonym "play." A drama is a play, that is, a story presented in the form of dialogue and action. The connotations that are likely to confuse the issue come out more strikingly in the adjective, "dramatic." "Dramatic" means, of course, "of or pertaining to the drama; appropriate to, or having the qualities of, a drama."

So far everything is simple, free from confusion. But the dictionaries add a word or two in further explanation of what is appropriate to the drama, "having the qualities of a drama; vivid; expressed with or as if with action." "Vivid" means for most people full of action, movement, the excitement of incident, suspense, surprise. If we look further we find under the account of synonyms for "dramatic," "That is dramatic which is appropriate to the drama, esp. as suggesting vividly expressive action or gesture, unexpected conjunctions, or a striking dénouement."

In all this one notes the emphasis laid on features of plot, that is, the external events whose complication and resolution make the objective framework of the story; also on action; that is, the movements or gestures by means of which states of mind are objectified. Now, there is in Dostoevski and Tolstoy a sufficient provision of plot for the ordinary serious reader; enough happens, and enough remains in suspense, to hold the attention of readers who are primarily interested in story, provided they are not positively childish in their mentality. But the dominant interest of these Russians is not in the objective drama of plot and gesture so much as in the subjective drama of spiritual states.

The subjective and objective aspects of the story cannot well be separated; one is the necessary complement of the other. But the primacy of the subjective in these Russian novelists will be vividly realized if we bring them into comparison with Smollett or Scott, or even with Balzac, Zola, or Hardy, in all of whom motivation seems of such slight importance relatively to the hard facts, the irreducible objective circumstances, which make the substance of the narrative.

And yet it is Dostoevski whom I choose to illustrate the "dramatic" ideal in the novel rather than any of these French or English writers. And this because of his superior command of the technique of dramatic concentration. There is plenty of action in Smollett, but it is rambling and dispersed, too much broken up into strings of mere episodes, to give the effect of drama. There is in Scott plenty of heroic action, plenty of noble and histrionic gesture, and in some rare cases, such as "Ivanhoe," it is all grouped and centered in such a way as to give the compactness and cumulative power of drama. But "Ivanhoe" is exceptional, and in general there is too little form and far too much history in Scott, to make his novels effectively dramatic. In Balzac, drama is an occasional happy accident in the vast expository sea of his Comédie Humaine. In Hardy the "unexpected conjunctions," the complicated entanglements and surprising resolutions of plot, too often defeat the dramatic purpose for which they were devised. So that our best example of the essentially dramatic ideal in the novel is found to be a writer who is more than ordinarily concerned with the spiritual states of his characters.

Another source of confusion lurks in the word "subjective." "Subjective" is often used to designate fiction which is highly colored by the sentiment and philosophy of the author directly expressed. Thus Fielding would be a subjective writer because he discusses with his readers the problems of conduct brought up by his story; and still more so Thackeray, Meredith, Wells. Richard Aldington's "Death of a Hero" would be in this sense a highly subjective novel because the author devotes whole pages to his satirical tirades against the Victorian way of life.

But, generally speaking, this kind of subjectivism, which consists in the intrusion of the author into the story, is distinctly opposed to the dramatic ideal in the novel. It is opposed to the ideal of objectivity cultivated by the French naturalists, and is in general much less prominent in French and Russian novelists than in English. It is almost completely wanting in "Anna Karenina," in spite of Tolstoy's philosophical penchant. It is quite opposed to the spirit of Turgenev, of Gorki, of Chekhov. It is not present in Dostoevski, for the simple reason that he has found means of presenting his philosophy dramatically.

"Subjective," then, be it understood, is here used in the sense of being concerned with the states of mind of the characters. Dostoevski is subjective because he is more concerned with motives of action than with the action itself.

But how can we talk of subjective drama? Stage drama is limited to the words and gestures of the characters. There is no author there to explain the mental processes lying back of these objective manifestations—that is the first condition of drama—and with the abandonment of soliloquy, the last vestige of subjectivity disappears. If we are to talk of dramatic novels at all, is it not necessary to concede that a novel is dramatic just in proportion to its objectivity? But is it not the prime distinguishing feature of the novel that the author is there to explain? And might not one conclude that the proper line of the novel would be in its sharp differentiation from the objective technique of drama?

There can be no doubt that the presence of the author—the narrator—determines certain fundamental differences between the play and the novel. And it is obvious, on a general survey of its evolution, that the novel has tended to grow more and more subjective, that a larger and larger proportion of space has come to be devoted to the mental states of the characters, and proportionately less to their words and gestures.

But here a most important distinction must be drawn between what we may call the dramatic and the undramatic methods of presenting mental states. Whenever the author in his own person expatiates upon his characters' states of mind, he is following an undramatic method, since we are then conscious of the author standing beside his characters on the stage, and our attention is divided between them and him. The dramatic method is simply to present, to project the characters' states of mind, without comment or explanation. It is of course the author who is choosing the words which describe the state of mind in question, but his effort is, in so far as he follows the dramatic ideal, to make his words the mere uncolored medium for rendering the mental process. He does not characterize it—that would be undramatic, and authorial—he reproduces it.

But he is none the less the author, an indispensable agent in the rendering of his subject. Being the author, he is capable of visioning his character's mind with a clearness and wholeness of which the character is himself incapable. He is even capable, like Dostoevski or Thomas Mann, of presenting a large part of his own philosophy of life, simply by an arrangement of the states of mind of a certain number of characters reacting to a certain set of circumstances. The author is author, again, by virtue of his power over words. He is capable of rendering the mental processes of his characters with a precision and nicety, with a subtlety and warmth of coloring of which they themselves are incapable.

But granting the special ability of the author for conceiving and putting into words the mental states of his characters, his great ambition is, in so far as he is dominated by the dramatic ideal, to obliterate any distinction between author and character which might lead to a division of interest between them. He does not wish to be caught standing apart from the character and saying clever things about him. He wishes instead to read himself right into the consciousness of the character, to identify himself with him in impression, feeling, outlook, to reproduce with absolute fidelity of tone the character's reaction to everything in his experience. He wishes to give, as consistently as possible, an inside rather than an outside view of things. And it will be realized that this is to make the narrative highly subjective.

It is to make the narrative subjective, and at the same time it is to make it, in a very significant sense, dramatic. The dramatic method is the method of direct presentation, and aims to give the reader the sense of being present, here and now, in the scene of action. That is why those elements are undramatic which make us aware of an author explaining things: exposition, description, and characterization by the author, psychological analysis, philosophizing and sentimentalizing about the characters and events.

But obviously a certain amount of exposition is necessary to any story: there are some things we must know in order to understand the scenes at which we are present. Some description and characterization are necessary: we want to be able to vizualize the setting and the characters and to know what they are like. Well, all these things are accomplished in the play without intervention on the part of the author. Description is dispensed with by the physical stage setting. Exposition and characterization are both conveyed through the dialogue and action of the characters.

There are, to be sure, distinct limits to what can be done through these objective means, and that is what makes the play, generally speaking, so much thinner and cruder a medium for the thoughtful delineation of life. Everything has to be so rigorously simplified and conventionalized. One word must stand in the play for the score of words which the novelist may wisely use for the same intention. And it must be a word as unmistakable in meaning and connotation as a silver dollar. The types presented must be such as can be at once recognized by every one in the theater, from the most thoughtful "highbrow" to the most unreflective groundling. It is true that such disadvantages are amply compensated for by the immediacy of appeal to eye and ear. It is, moreover, the supreme triumph of the literary artist, like Ibsen and Pirandello, to succeed, with such crude implements, in combining dramatic appeal with subtle intellectual effects. But after all has been said in favor of the drama it remains true that it is a comparatively thin medium by the mere fact of its complete and inveterate objectivity.

Thus we are brought back to our seeming paradox of subjective drama in the novel. The novel can never attain that immediacy of effect which derives from the direct appeal to eye and ear. It must be content with the fainter immediacy of appeal to the imagination. By way of compensation, it may cover infinitely more ground, may go in for comment and explanation which are not possible to the stage play. The novel has, accordingly, large means of intellectual appeal special to itself. It may have a richness and subtlety quite beyond the scope of drama.

Only, comment and explanation tend to weaken the imaginative appeal; they tend to remove the story one degree farther from direct experience. The novelist is thus landed in a dilemma. How can he keep his story "dramatic" without losing that intellectual appeal which is peculiar to his form?

There is one solution for this problem which has been more and more seized upon by novelists with the passing of the years. It is to use the consciousness of the characters as a medium for explanation and comment. What the author tells us *in propria persona* is formal and official. It is often necessary, and accepted by us like any other practical necessity. But it is not of a piece with the story. What goes on in the minds of the characters on a given occasion is another matter. That is of the essence of the story itself. And the aim of the author who has chosen this solution for the novelist's problem is so to present what is going on in the mind of his character at a given moment that we shall forget the author and ourselves and have a sense of being actually there. The scene of action has been transferred to the character's mind.

2

In the process of experimenting with this method, it has been found that much of the information which was formerly passed on by the author can be gathered directly by the reader from the character's thoughts, thus dispensing very largely with undramatic official explanations. What the author tells us, in a formal paragraph of characterization, is likely to be a lumpish mass of items. It is heavy and solid and authoritative, but hard to digest. What most helps us to form an idea of a character is of course what he says and does, the emotional situation in which he finds himself. Such things speak for themselves. What others say of the character is another powerful means of translating him to us. It fits in at once with the general dramatic situation, and is easily lodged in our imagination, especially if people disagree about him, confess their uncertainties, their partial knowledge, if they are prejudiced against him or infatuated with him. Our curiosity, our disposition to take sides, serve to fix our attention on the items presented and fit them into a system of impressions so that they are not readily lost.

This is what I mean by our digesting the facts. In the highly subjective type of fiction, people are likely to be characterized through the thoughts of some one else about them. In the subjective state of the person whose point of view is followed they find a sensitive plate prepared to take in as much of them as is relevant for the time being, and it is the interest of this reflecting subject that doubles the mere interest of the items and makes them so much more digestible.

Henry James came to have a great dislike for what he calls a "seated mass of information," and in his later novels and tales (say, from 1897 on) he virtually never ushers in a character with a formal introduction. One character is introduced by another. Thus in "The Wings of the Dove" (1902) we meet two ladies traveling together in Switzerland, a Mrs. Susan Stringham of Burlington, Vermont and a Miss Milly Theale of New York City. Milly Theale is to be the heroine of this story, and the author wishes to give us from the beginning a strong impression of her personality and circumstances. But he does not trust himself to do this in his own official capacity. He is not himself inside the story. Susan Stringham, on the other hand, is from the first moment well within the story. She is there for many good reasons, and the most important of these is the need for some one who can give the reader a more intimate view of Milly Theale than any mere omniscient author. Mrs. Stringham can throw upon her the light of a particular New England experience. And the author very promptly gives his heroine the benefit of Mrs. Stringham's view of her. Mrs. Stringham is represented as recalling in Switzerland the impression Milly Theale had made upon her at the time when she came up to Boston on a visit to friends.

Milly Theale had Boston friends, such as they were, and of recent making; and it was understood that her visit to them—a visit that was not to be meagre—had been undertaken, after a series of bereavements, in the interest of the particular peace that New York couldn't give. It was recognized, liberally enough, that there were many things—perhaps even too many—New York *could* give; but this was felt to make no difference in the important truth that what you had most to do, under the discipline of life, or of death, was really to feel your situation as grave. Boston could help you to that as nothing else could, and it had extended to Milly, by every presumption, some such measure of assistance. Mrs. Stringham was never to forget—for the moment had not faded, nor the infinitely fine vibration it set up in any degree ceased—her own first sight of the striking apparition, then unheralded and unexplained: the slim, constantly pale, delicately haggard, anomalously, agreeably angular young person, of not more than two-and-twenty summers, in spite of her marks, whose hair was somehow exceptionally red even for the real thing, which it innocently confessed to being, and whose clothes were remarkably black even for robes of mourning, which was the meaning they expressed. It was New York mourning, it was New York hair, it was a New York history, confused as yet, but multitudinous, of the loss of parents, brothers, sisters, almost every human appendage, all on a scale and with a sweep that had required the greater stage; it was a New York legend of affecting, of romantic isolation, and beyond everything, it was by most accounts, in respect to the mass of money so piled on the girl's back, a set of New York possibilities. She was alone, she was stricken, she was rich, and in particular was strange—a combination in itself of a nature to engage Mrs. Stringham's attention. . . . Susan privately settled it that Boston was not in the least seeing her, was only occupied with her seeing Boston . . . *She* was seeing her, and she had quite the finest moment of her life in now obeying the instinct to conceal the vision. She couldn't explain it—no one would understand.

Now, many readers will think that the necessary information in regard to Milly Theale might have been conveyed in a much shorter paragraph, or that in a paragraph of this length much more information might have been conveyed. And this is perhaps the place to state candidly that Henry James is not a popular writer, and that a large number even of the most intelligent and discriminating readers remain incurably impatient of his way of telling a story, and after a trial or two at his later novels, simply decline to give further time to him. They find him fussy and long-winded. And there is no use trying to convert them into devotees. Other readers, like myself, while extremely fond of Henry James, are equally fond of novelists who, like Hardy for example, proceed on lines almost diametrically opposed to those James follows, and we do not wish to set up either of them as exclusive models. We do not condemn one novelist because we admire another very unlike him, any more than we condemn the poetry of Baudelaire because we admire that of Lamartine.

The reason why I give so much more attention to the method of James than to that of Hardy is because he represents certain procedures which have been gaining ground during the last thirty-five or forty years, because he has had such an incalculable influence on other novelists in the matter of technique, so that he occupies more than any other a pivotal position in the development of the twentieth-century novel. And then, in spite of his eccentricities, his excesses, his mannerisms, he is a remarkable illustration of certain principles of esthetics which no one can afford altogether to ignore. Thomas Hardy may be in certain ways the finest English novelist of his time, but he might have learned a great deal from Henry James.

Returning to the characterization of Milly Theale, we note that James vouchsafes a relatively small number of concrete items of information about her. They could all be summed up in a sentence: she was pale and slim; she had striking red hair and strikingly black mourning clothes; she had lost all her relatives and was fabulously rich.

In one of his earlier stories James would have given us three times that number of facts about her, including perhaps a notation, à la Balzac, of the exact figure of her fortune. But in the meantime James has come to realize that it is more important to choose the facts than to assemble them in quantity. He knows that the mind of a reader has a limited capacity, a low saturation-point. After a certain point the facts cease to register. He knows that what is more important than the facts themselves—their number, their size and specific gravity—is the impression they make on the reader's imagination. What determines the impression for the reader is not merely the facts but the way they are lighted, the meaning they carry.

And James has discovered the enormous effectiveness of lighting them from within the story itself. Milly Theale is to be a romantic heroine not merely because of her loveliness, her loneliness, and her great wealth, but because of the extraordinary appeal she makes to a small number of discriminating persons. The first of these is Susan Stringham. Though a New Englander, Susan is not a Bostonian, and can see more in Milly Theale than the excellent people of Boston, who are capable of doing everything for the bereaved young woman except appreciate her special quality. It is only Susan Stringham in that city who has the kind of imaginative insight to take in the full "value" of Milly's personality, and give due place in the total effect to her New York mourning, her New York hair, and the legendary megalopolitan scale of her bereavement and material endowment. Thus the few expressive strokes of objective characterization are made significant and effective by the background of subjective coloring on which they stand out.

But note that in general James likes to leave much to the imagination of the reader, and that Milly in particular is a character about whom he wishes to trace a sort of glamorous margin of haziness. Moreover, it is one of the features of his method that certain things should always be left for clearing up at a later point in the story, if only to lure the reader on with the bait of curiosity.

And aside from all this, James has a fondness for slow and leisurely unfolding of facts, both in exposition and characterization. He does not wish us to gobble our food and risk an indigestion of mere knowledge. In this connection one is a little puzzled by his discipleship of many years to that most objectively factual of novelists, Balzac. One is even led to wonder whether it is not a case of the fascination of opposites. James was never in his best work particularly generous with objective detail. And throughout his later period he was remarkable for the small amount of "solid" fact which he made to serve. Every hard pellet of information is swimming in a bath of the digestive juices of reflection and appreciation.

It is the very opposite of the method of history, in which each page bristles with numerous and ponderable facts in serried phalanx. In history we feel that we can never have too much information. Our object is to know. In fiction, our object is to feel and appreciate, and what counts is not the number of facts but the degree to which we have been made to live with them. James believes in a slow tempo in the "release" of these facts, a tempo determined by that of the reflective process out of which from time to time emerges for the reader some item of objective information.

3

This principle holds for the general exposition as well as for characterization. James's method is to introduce a character, on a given occasion, brooding over the situation in which he finds himself. Whatever we learn about the antecedent circumstances comes out, in the beginning, as it were by accident. A given fact is referred to—or, better, alluded to—because it is there in the background of the person's thought. James's effort is to give it for the reader the same air of something known and implied in the mental process which it has for the character. Perhaps no better example of this can be found than the opening paragraph of "The Ambassadors" (1903).

Strether's first question, when he reached the hotel, was about his friend; yet on his learning that Waymarsh was apparently not to arrive till evening he was not wholly disconcerted. A telegram from him bespeaking a room "only if not noisy," reply paid, was produced for the inquirer at the office, so that the understanding they should meet at Chester rather than at Liverpool remained to that extent sound. The same secret principle, however, that had prompted Strether not absolutely to desire Waymarsh's presence at the dock, that had led him thus to postpone for a few hours his enjoyment of it, now operated to make him feel he could still wait without disappointment. They would dine together at the worst, and, with all respect to dear old Waymarsh—if not even, for that matter, to himself—there was little fear that in the sequel they shouldn't see enough of each other. The principle I have just mentioned as operating had been, with the most newly disembarked of the two men, wholly instinctive—the fruit of a sharp sense that, delightful as it would be to find himself looking, after so much separation, into his comrade's face, his business would be a trifle bungled should he simply arrange for this countenance to present itself to the nearing steamer as the first "note" of Europe. Mixed with everything was the apprehension, already, on Strether's part, that it would, at best, throughout, prove the note of Europe in quite a sufficient degree.

We begin with Strether himself, not with an account of who he was. We begin with the way he felt, when he first landed in England, at the thought of meeting his friend Waymarsh. We are not told in so many words that he landed in England, but we infer as much, since that was one of the things that determined his feeling. We are not told who this Waymarsh was; we simply infer from Strether's feeling that there was something about him which made it disagreeable to have one's first impression of the Old World spoiled by the sight of him. We are not told what sort of person Strether was, where he came from, what his life was like back there, nor why he had come abroad.

By the author himself we are never told much about any of these matters. But in due course of time we learn all that we need to know, mostly by process of inference from what Strether thinks and from what he has to say to other people. We gather that he has some "business" in the Old World. We learn something, a little later, of what he looked like to a lady whose acquaintance he picked up in the hotel lobby. We have intimations, from his own thoughts, of "a certain person" who might not have approved of the intimacy which so soon established itself between him and this Maria Gostrey. It is clear that Waymarsh does not much approve of "Europe," and in the second chapter we learn more about him by following Strether's impressions of him and cogitations about him as they talk together in the gas-light in Waymarsh's hotel room, Waymarsh sitting in trousers and shirt on the edge of his couch.

One thing to be observed in all this is how infallibly the general information has its pertinence in relation to the particular occasion which we have before us, and seems to justify its introduction only in so far as it has such relation. The reader learns what he needs to know not because the author knows it and is there to give it to him—as, let us say, in Walter Scott—but because a certain character in the story happens to be thinking about the matters in question.

This Lambert Strether whose view we are following in "The Ambassadors" is a magazine editor of Woollett, Massachusetts, who has come abroad on an errand in behalf of a certain wealthy lady of that town, a widow named Newsome. Her son Chad has long been living in Paris, and she thinks it time he was coming back to take charge of the large manufacturing business which he has inherited. He has shown no signs of interest in that business and seems to prefer the life of cultivated idleness offered by Paris. It looks as if there were a woman in the case, and to the imagination of Woollett it can be nothing but a person who is "no better than she should be." So that Strether's errand —his embassy—is to try to pry him loose from his vulgar liaison. If he is successful, the understanding is that Strether shall marry Mrs. Newsome.

Such are the facts to be set forth in the exposition. But to state them in these bald and abstract terms is entirely contrary to the system on which this sort of book is written. And for this reason: that these bald and abstract terms are not the terms in which they present themselves to the consciousness of Lambert Strether on any of the occasions on which it is opened up to us. They are all *implied* in his mental process all the time. In his thought he is forever alluding to them, but he cannot be imagined telling himself things which are the primary facts of his conscious life. And so the author, who does not consider his subject "done" at all unless it is done in the tone of the characters' own consciousness, must leave us to gather these primary facts either from Strether's "allusion" to them in his thoughts, or from what actually comes out in conversation between him and other people.

This is certainly a slow and inefficient method of exposition if exposition is taken to mean putting before the reader the ponderable facts. But it has its great advantages if what we are most concerned with is the so-called imponderables of the story—the quality of the character's feeling and approach to life, and the meaning and value he attaches to the given facts. In "The Ambassadors" the reason why so much attention is given to Waymarsh is that he stands for the "Woollett" reaction to life; whereas Maria Gostrey stands for a more subtle and more liberal way of taking things, and in particular "Europe." This whole story is one which is built up of imponderables—that is, of subjective attitudes and appraisals, of shades and discriminations in values. So that if there ever was a story naturally well adapted to the subjective method of narration it is this one.

Moreover, so far as slowness of exposition goes, the reader actually suffers no hardship on that score. For, while the exposition waits, the story itself moves on; and so insensibly are the items of the exposition insinuated into the course of the narrative that we never realize that this process has taken place. The story starts with the first sentence, with Strether's inquiry about his friend Waymarsh. For is not Strether's instinct to postpone a meeting with Waymarsh all of a piece with his instinct to postpone his problem in reference to Chad? The same underground reference to Chad and Strether's difficult errand is present in all his feeling toward Maria Gostrey. From the first moment of their encounter begins Strether's training in another way of viewing things; she is to serve as the main agent in his corruption or conversion, however we should phrase it. That is the subject of the story, and thus the story is well under way before we have finished the first chapter. Meantime the exposition is little by little being accomplished, always in the most intimate relation to the story in its immediate present phase.

And thus the antecedent facts are absorbed by the reader almost without his knowing it, which is always the easiest way of taking in facts of any kind. Facts are assimilated most readily where the attention is most vivid, and in fiction it is the here and now of the story, it is the character's immediate situation and predicament which give such vividness to the reader's attention. So that in this method the exposition is accomplished by a kind of painless operation as if the patient had been put under an anesthetic.

XVII

POINT OF VIEW: JAMES

IN AN earlier chapter the restricted point of view is listed among the elements that make for the realization of the dramatic ideal. It is time we were discussing why this is so. The fundamental impulsion to dramatic concentration in general is the desire to secure in the novel something equivalent to the dramatic present in the play. The limitation of time tends to produce the effect of the dramatic Now; the limitation of place, the dramatic Here; the "center of interest" concentrates the attention, as in the drama, upon these particular people or this particular person now present here. And, finally, the restriction of the point of view carries to its full logical outcome the esthetic idea of the limited center of interest.

In many cases the one idea implies the other and the two elements of technique cannot be distinguished. Thus in novels like "Henry Esmond," "Kidnapped," "Green Mansions," "The Arrow of Gold" the narrative, purporting to be composed by the central character of the story generally in the first person, must necessarily be restricted to the point of view of this central character. He writes as an eye-witness and participant in the action, he is the voucher for its truth and the interpreter of its meaning. If he relates anything that took place when he was not present, he lets us know just how it came to his knowledge, and this very process of coming to know things which he did not witness is incorporated as a part of the whole personal experience which he is engaged in setting forth.

Even when the narrative is given in the third person, if any one character holds the center of the stage for an appreciable length of time we have a strong tendency to identify ourselves with him, as children identify themselves with the hero of a fairy-story. We see things through his eyes, we share his point of view, and it is his point of view to which the story is more or less for the moment restricted. What happens he sees; and most of it in some sense happens to him; at any rate, he is interested in it by hope and fear, by curiosity and suspense; he approves or disapproves; he interprets for us.

Such is the case with "Crime and Punishment." We have the general impression, on putting down the book, not only that it is Raskolnikov's story but that it is told from his point of view. And yet there is a very considerable difference between his method and that of James in his later novels, where the matter of the point of view has evidently been the subject of much more careful attention.

The relation between center of interest and point of view is in "Crime and Punishment" about like that in James's early novel "The American" (1877). This is the story of one of our business men who wishes to marry a young Frenchwoman of rare personal distinction and social standing among the old noblesse, but finds himself engaged in a strange battle in the dark with her relations, who, though attracted by his great wealth, have an invincible repugnance to marrying into "business." It is an absorbing story, and at the same time a charming comedy of manners on that ever recurrent theme of James's—the contrast of American and European attitudes and styles of behavior. In general quality and effect there is nothing more unlike Dostoevski, and I have brought this novel into the discussion simply to illustrate a point of technical likeness more notable in this period of James's writing than later. The story is beautifully conducted through a series of well-developed "scenes," and almost invariably the central character is Christopher Newman. In this respect, then, "The American" is as good an example of dramatic concentration as "Crime and Punishment." But like Dostoevski, James here fails to show that meticulous concern for the restricted point of view which he does show in his later novels.

In each case the book begins by introducing the central character in the objective biographical manner. "On an exceptionally hot evening in July a young man came out of the garret in which he lodged in S. Place and walked slowly, as though in hesitation, towards K. bridge." "On a brilliant day in May, of the year 1868, a gentleman was reclining at his ease on the great circular divan which at that period occupied the centre of the Salon Carré, in the Museum of the Louvre." You have only to compare these statements with the opening sentence of "The Ambassadors," given in the last chapter, to see what a totally different system of communication of facts is implied. In the later novels we start immediately inside the particular situation, at a particular moment, as it presents itself to the person involved. In "Crime and Punishment" and "The American," the authors approach the situation with all the ceremony of the expository method, in which we are to be regularly informed by the narrator from without of the time and the place and the physical action or attitude of the as yet unnamed individual, whom it will then be the author's business to give us an account of.

In "The American" four solid pages are devoted to a general account of Christopher Newman, his physical appearance, his habits, the sort of man he was, including a good many things on which he had never himself reflected. And throughout the book there are scattered passages, from half a page to several pages long, devoted to descriptions of persons and places, to characterization of persons, and in general to blocks of information given in the lump, with little attempt to assimilate it to the special mental process of Newman. Dostoevski, in "Crime and Punishment," manages for the most part to avoid passages of this sort by certain expedients long known to the craft, though more often used by novelists dominated by the dramatic ideal. A large part of the necessary exposition of this sort is conveyed by means of letters received by Raskolnikov and by narratives made to him by some other character in the course of conversation. So that in this respect he manages to keep more strictly within the point of view of the central character.

When it comes to those passages necessarily occurring here and there through the book which are devoted to the reflections of the central character, we feel ourselves to be very closely identified with him. So contagious is the emotional excitement of the book that we have the impression of being shut up within the very soul of this man. As a matter of fact, the mental processes in question are not always presented strictly and rigorously from the point of view of Raskolnikov. On closer examination one is aware of the author behind his character, ready to explain things which the character does not understand. "It was not that he understood, but he felt clearly with all the intensity of sensation. . . ." The author makes a distinction. "If he had cared to think a little, he would have been amazed indeed. . . ." The author explains what the state of mind of his character would have been if his thinking faculties had been a little more alert. It is not a marked feature of Dostoevski—this disposition *to go behind* the mental process of his character—but it is a feature that shows itself frequently enough to distinguish him from those later writers who make a shibboleth of the consistent point of view.

Henry James had been writing novels for more than twenty years before he took this last step toward dramatic consistency. There are many partial anticipations, in "The American," of the uniform subjectivity of his later novels.

But there is also a much greater likelihood, at any point, that we shall become aware of the author's *going behind* the character; and this he often does in the openest manner, as one with a full license to disagree with his hero. "He flattered himself *he* had not fallen, and hadn't need to fall . . . in love, but *his biographer may be supposed to know better* what, as he would have said, was the matter with him." "He gave a groan as he remembered what he had meant to do; he was annoyed, and yet partly incredulous, at his having meant to do it: the bottom suddenly had fallen out of his revenge. Whether it was Christian charity or mere human weakness of will—what it was in the background of his spirit—I don't pretend to say; but Newman's last thought was that of course he would let the Bellegardes go. If he had spoken it aloud he would have said he didn't want to hurt them."

James here touches on one of the most interesting points of psychology—the difference between the feelings of which a man is conscious in taking a certain position and the fundamental motives, generally unknown to him, which lie behind the conscious feelings. James, however, was not prepared, in "The American," to do anything with this interesting consideration, and he did nothing more with it than to touch upon it in the passage quoted. It was not, it seems, within his province. It is interesting to be reminded, as in the passage quoted, that James was aware of the frequent contrast between what lies in the foreground and the background of the spirit. But it is significant that such reminders are confined to his earlier novels. By the time he came to write "The Spoils of Poynton" (1897) he had learned that his forte was not for psychological analysis, for the detection of what lies in the background of the human spirit, but rather for the dramatic presentation of mental states as the characters themselves are conscious of them. And his great concern came to be to maintain a beautiful consistency of point of view—not to allow the least scratch or stain of "undramatic" comment on the polished surface of the subjective mirror.

This must not be taken to be an absolute statement, admitting of no exceptions whatever. My point is that in his later novels, in third-person narrative, James carries the principle of the limited point of view farther than any writer had ever done. Even when, rarely, he feels it necessary to give an outside view of the central character of the moment, he has his ways of getting it done without seeming to tell you himself, as author, what it is he wants you to see.

The most obvious way in which the concern for point of view shows itself in the later novels is the length of time during which our observation of what is going on is confined to the view of a single person. Such limitation of view over a considerable stretch of time is a means of intensifying the effect analogous to the lengthy development of the events of a single day, the limitation of place, and the continuity of action. And it may be said broadly that this is the great distinctive feature of the novels of Henry James.

2

But even so, there is an obvious distinction between novels like "The Golden Bowl" (1904) and "The Wings of the Dove" (1902) on the one hand, and those like "The Spoils of Poynton," "What Maisie Knew" (1897), and "The Ambassadors" (1903) on the other. In the three last mentioned a single point of view is maintained virtually without interruption from beginning to end. In "The Golden Bowl" and "The Wings of the Dove" the story is built up of large blocks of narrative, each told from the point of view of a single character, but with these characters taken in alternation. In each of these books there are five different persons whose view is followed at one time or another. The reason for this is clear enough. The very point of these stories largely lies in a contrast of views. It does not have its existence absolutely and without reference to the various minds that mirror it. Its peculiarity is its chameleon-like character, as one color after another plays upon it and shows it in a different light; the succession of these colors is its spectrum.

But that is not the only way to consider the matter, and a different metaphor will better bring out the relevance of this method to the problem of *telling the story*. The different characters view the facts from a different angle of vision, an angle of vision which in each case shuts off from one of them much of what is seen by another. There *is* in each case a story—there are facts—something does happen. It is necessary for the story-teller to present at any given moment just those facts which he wishes the reader to know. The reader must be kept in the dark as to certain things; and, above all, he must be made curious about what he does not know. He must be kept in suspense as to how things are going, and his suspense must be directed skilfully, and centered on certain issues.

This was always a principle of James's story-telling, as it was of Dostoevski's, but now he brings the method of the restricted and alternating point of view to the support of his principle of directed suspense. At a given point in the story he views the situation through the eyes of a certain one of the characters. He sees what that person sees, and wonders about whatever he wonders about. His curiosity or suspense are thus directed upon certain points. Then he views the situation through the eyes of another; light is thrown on places formerly dark; but meantime the situation has developed, has altered; and there are new areas of darkness into which his vision cannot penetrate. When he has thoroughly familiarized himself with the ground as viewed from this angle, he moves to a new position and looks through the eyes of another character.

"The Golden Bowl" has for its subject a quadrangular

situation growing out of Maggie Verver's desire to provide companionship for her father after her own marriage to the Prince Amerigo. She provides for him by marrying him to her old friend Charlotte Stant—an old friend of Amerigo's, too, though this is unknown to Maggie. And then what comes about insensibly is that Maggie spends more and more time with her father and Charlotte spends more and more time with the Prince. The matter goes so far that even the innocent-minded Maggie begins to wonder how far it has gone. She and her husband are too "civilized" to talk these things over in plain terms, but Maggie makes a slight gesture which gives her husband to understand how she feels. He in turn makes a slight gesture which gives her to understand that it will be all right.

And now, with no words spoken, there comes about, here again, a kind of fierce struggle in the dark, in which Maggie's aim is to make herself the confederate of her father and her husband, to isolate Charlotte, and, in a perfectly civilized way, force her to retreat from her position as Amerigo's intimate.

One important character I have left out of this account, because her importance is, after all, not for the story itself but for the story-telling. This is Mrs. Assingham, the woman who had engineered the marriage of Maggie and the Prince and who is very much concerned that it should be a success. She is a characteristic Jamesian personage, whose sole purpose in the story is to offer an approach other than that of the characters of the drama—a sort of fourth dimension very useful in calculating from time to time the exact location of certain points involved in this mathematical problem.

Now for the distribution of the point of view. The almost invariable principle is to keep to that of one of the characters through several chapters at a time. In the first half of the book it is the Prince Amerigo and Charlotte Stant who are most often used as mirrors of the action, for this first half is mainly given to building up the quadrangular situation as it appears to one or the other of them. There is, however, one entire book of more than 100 pages devoted to the point of view of Maggie's father. And more than once the author finds it convenient to put us at the angle of vision of Mrs. Assingham. Only so can he develop the full implications of the situation without enlightening us more fully than he desires. Mrs. Assingham and her husband, with whom she discusses things, are persons with a legitimate concern for what is going on, and occupying a very favorable post of observation. But they are not actors in the drama, they are not "in the know." All they can do is watch and speculate, and they serve to help us watch and speculate, to define the conditions of the problem and direct our interest to the significant points.

They help also to delay the progress of the illumination. There is a very real and ugly fact at the core of things here. But it is a fact born of a phantom. And the phantom is one of those shadows projected from the minds of men. This apparition James wishes to conjure slowly with slow strange music, in some "misty mid-region" of shadowy adumbrations, letting it grow and swell by insensible degrees before our fascinated eyes. It is one of those things that would shrink up and slink away if full daylight were turned too rudely on it. And so, in addition to the views of the Prince and Charlotte and Mr. Verver—inside views but each one partial and shut in upon itself—we are given the relatively outside view of Fanny Assingham, who can do nothing but speculate and wonder.

But in the second half, it is Maggie's view of things which becomes most interesting to the author. It is the married woman and daughter, generous and candid soul, who has never in her life experienced the reality of Evil in the world, who gradually comes to realize that Evil itself is camped in her own household, that she is in danger of losing her husband, the man she adores, and that it is her father's wife who is the agent of this alienation. At first she does not know the facts, but only feels them in the air; it is a curious accident that brings them unmistakably to her attention, making her understand how great an intimacy had existed between Charlotte and Amerigo before her marriage. But she cannot speak to any of them, restrained by her pride, her notion of civilized behavior, and even by her instinct for strategy. She can only watch. She can watch the working on Amerigo of her little gesture of awareness; she can watch the growing restlessness and desperation of Charlotte, isolated even more than herself by the return of Amerigo to his loyalty; and she can watch the silent maneuvering of her father to sound her out and find a way to make things right for his daughter and at the same time save the faces of them all.

It is this tense and tireless watching, like the sleepless watching of an Indian in the forest, attention ceaselessly strained for the slightest rustle or snapping of a twig that may give evidence of danger—this perpetual living in the presence of issues that mean life and death—which gives its extraordinary and unique character to "The Golden Bowl," its atmosphere of breathless charged stillness, comparable only to certain effects in Conrad and Poe. And the main technical means by which the effect is secured is the limitating of observation over such long stretches to the consciousness of Maggie. There is in the second half one interruption to Maggie's view. James was no doubt aware that there is a limit to any reader's capacity to remain shut up within the narrow circle of one person's consciousness. He must have realized that our imaginations languish if confined too long to the flat two-dimensional plane of the subjective, that we crave from time to time the outside view of a character which serves to furnish the third dimension and give body to it. There is one passage of nearly sixty pages in which he shows us Maggie through the eyes of Fanny Assingham, so that her suffering, her perplexity, her final certainty may be bodied forth in speech and gesture. But then again we return to the mind of Maggie, and do not emerge again till the end of the book.

Altogether, in this half of the book, we have over 300 pages given to the point of view of Maggie. Moreover, with the exception of 15 pages, in which she is the subject of discussion between Mrs. Assingham and her husband, Maggie is always present, the center of interest, even when it is not her point of view that is followed. The likeness to Dostoevski's method will be at once apparent, with the special addition of James's featuring of the point of view.

XVIII

POINT OF VIEW: JAMES AND OTHERS

"The Ambassadors," as I have said, belongs in a distinct group among the novels of James in that the story is told from beginning to end (except for slight variations in the first chapter) from the point of view of the same person. It marks, therefore, the furthest point to which this method had been carried at the date of its publication (1903)—the extreme limit of the dramatic tendency so far as this device is concerned. "The Ambassadors" is a full-length, two-volume novel. Already, however, James had applied the same technique in shorter novels—"The Spoils of Poynton" and "What Maisie Knew." These are indeed very short novels, as novels go with James, only 265 and 363 pages, respectively, in the New York edition. "The Turn of the Screw," which no one thinks of calling a novel, is 162 pages long; it is a very long short story. "The Spoils of Poynton" and "What Maisie Knew" were long enough to be published in separate volumes immediately after their appearance serially in magazines. It is therefore convenient to call them novels. Moreover, they include more characters than "The Turn of the Screw"; they involve more plot; they cover more ground spatially and temporally. They are not mere anecdotes, like "The Turn of the Screw." So perhaps we may with a clear conscience call them novels.

The fact of the matter is they are transition pieces, on the borderland between the novel and the short story. We know, from James's preface, that "The Spoils of Poynton" started out to be a short story, and that the magazine editor was considerably embarrassed by its turning out so long. This story and "What Maisie Knew" are the products of a ten-year period (between "The Tragic Muse" and "The Awkward Age") during which James produced no novel on the grand scale, but in which he was as busy as ever turning out short stories. And it is a significant item of history that at least the first of these novels in which the single point of view was consistently maintained was originally intended to be a short story.

One is reminded that the single point of view is one of the commonest features of the short story; that, for example, every one of the more famous of the stories of Poe is strictly limited in this way (e. g., "MS Found in a Bottle," "Ligeia," "The Fall of the House of Usher," "The Murders in the Rue Morgue," "The Gold Bug," "The Black Cat," "The Cask of Amontillado"). And the same thing is true for many of the tales of other famous masters, like Maupassant and Kipling.

Note, however, that all the tales of Poe listed above are written in the first person; the author is incapable of interfering with the character's point of view simply because he is identical with the character. So that, so far as this matter of technique is concerned, these stories are on all fours with "Robinson Crusoe," "Kidnapped," and dozens of other romantic novels of adventure. The writer of romance has always fancied the first person narrative for the reason that it gives such an air of authenticity to his record. In romance the intellectual interest in character and society is relatively slight; what happens is often strange and hard to credit, and it is all the more important that attention should be given to whatever makes for verisimilitude. Since the author is dealing not in everyday truth, it is still more incumbent on him to cultivate the semblance of truth. And this is greatly helped by having the story told by an eye-witness, by one of those most concerned in it.

Sometimes the story is so complicated and involves so many people that it is impossible to make any one person witness of all that occurred. In such cases the writer of romance often resorts to the device of a series of documents, diaries, etc., by different people, which he, as editor, has brought together, having the story told by relays of witnesses. This method is used in "The Woman in White," in "The Master of Ballantrae" and "Dr. Jekyll and Mr. Hyde." And the authors of these stories have used the most cunning ingenuity in differentiating the manner of the several narrators, and of arranging them in that sequence which will best contribute to the gradual and timed "release" of the wonders and mysteries which are their subject-matter.

Stevenson seems to be laboring at present under an eclipse—the same eclipse that shadows Browning and other Victorian writers whose stock was at its peak during the first years of this century. In the case of both Browning and Stevenson, I suspect it is not real esthetic considerations which have led to their rejection by present-day critics, but something scarcely relevant to a judgment of their art. They were cheerful men, who believed in God, and our highbrow critics prefer a gloomy outlook and religious unbelief.

Stevenson is quite generally regarded as a writer of story-books for boys. And few critics stop to consider what extraordinary story-books they are. The mere style is an achievement so rare that this alone lifts the boyish tales of Stevenson into the rank of literary masterpieces. It is in one sense a literary style, for it is the result of wide reading and devoted care, and compounded of elements derived from many sources. But these elements have been so skilfully blent, and the product is so exactly suited in tone and spirit to the requirements of the story, that to say it is literary is to give it the highest praise.

Sometimes, in his essays, Stevenson is a bit self-conscious, a bit precious; he goes in for spots of archaic coloring and refinements of Latinism, for effects of archness and roguery which suggest the fooleries of Lamb without matching them. But in his stories he has too great regard for the "modesty of nature" to let himself go in such fanciful ways. The quaintness is the true quaintness of an eighteenth-century chronicle, the saltiness is that of men trained in the school of adventure, the elegant plainness is that of gentlemen of the old school. But above all, throughout these chronicles, the literary connoisseur is enchanted with the nervous idiomatic flavor, the true crisp vernacular in phrase and turn of expression, so completely in contrast to the prevailing manner of those eighties and nineties in English fiction—the smart, the turgid, the sentimental, or the simply vulgar and flabby—and is grateful to Stevenson for the long discipline of literary study which enabled him to restore to English prose some of the clear sparkle that it had before the romantic movement started it off in the direction of "sincerity" (Carlyle, Ruskin) and expressiveness (Meredith, Pater).

As for technique in the larger, structural sense, Stevenson was probably the English novelist of his time who had the most fastidious concern for those nice adjustments and economies which it gave James so much pleasure to contemplate and to practise. James's personal friendship with Stevenson began in 1885, and continued until Stevenson's death nine years later. He was an enthusiastic reader of Stevenson's stories, especially his novels, and his letters are full of praise for his achievements, for example in "The Master of Ballantrae" and "Catriona" ("David Balfour"). He was forever sending books to Stevenson in Samoa, including his own books, and it was to Stevenson that he confided in 1888 his intention, after completing "The Tragic Muse," to write nothing but short stories for some time. This was to prove the dividing line between his earlier and later period, the novels of the later manner being ushered in (in 1897) by the long short story or short novel "The Spoils of Poynton."

These facts are at least suggestive. I should hesitate to state baldly that James was strongly influenced by the technique of Stevenson; but it is true that the carefully considered point of view in writers like James and Conrad marks the application in "realistic" novels of a device that had long been of importance to the writer of romance. James and Conrad are indeed, on the whole, felt to be most closely allied to the realists, so much are they concerned with "psychology," which is human nature seen from the inside. But they were unwilling to dispense with those aids to illusion which, being more or less indifferent to realists like Balzac and Flaubert, were quite indispensable to the romancers.

But while the point of view is likely to be an important matter with the romancer, it is still more likely to be a mark of the short-story writer, and it is time to come back to my original suggestion that the single point of view in the later novels of James was a natural outgrowth of his preoccupation, during the ten-year period in question, with what he calls in his letter to Stevenson "short lengths." It was during this period that he turned out, for example, those remarkable tales "The Liar," "The Pupil," "The Private Life," "The Real Thing," "The Altar of the Dead," and "The Turn of the Screw." Some of these are in the third person and some in the first, but all show the most rigorous observance of the single point of view. The last-named is presented in the form of a document, the written statement of the woman concerned in the strange happenings, with an introductory scene accounting for this person, like the "framework" introduction of Turgenev's "A King Lear of the Steppes," Conrad's "Heart of Darkness," and certain anecdotes related by word of mouth in Maupassant.

"The Turn of the Screw" is a tale of supernatural mystery, of terror and suspense, like so many of the tales of Poe. And that brings to mind the statement made so often in regard to the short story (for example, by Clayton Hamilton), that one of the defining elements of the genre is singleness of impression. Poe had a highly romantic imagination. But he had likewise a sharply logical mind, trained by the disciplines of mathematics and the law, and he always set out with great deliberation to produce a particular effect. Every one is familiar with the thick and gruesome atmosphere of horror and mystery which he could build up step by step, by the selection of just those items best calculated to make their special assault upon the reader's sensibilities. And it is evident how important an element in securing this effect is the single point of view. He wishes never to blur the effect by a change of focus. He wishes to keep the reader's interest centered upon some particular point from which at any moment may spring the monster of his morbid imagining, to permit no moment's relaxation of his terrified concern, and so to hold the reader throughout in a state of quivering tension.

But this is not the only purpose served in Poe's tales by the single point of view. A considerable number of them belong to the genre of detective stories, for example, "The Gold Bug" and "The Murders in the Rue Morgue." In stories of this type it is very important that the solution of the mystery should be made by gradual degrees, and that the reader's knowledge should be limited at each stage of the narrative to just that which the author wishes him to know. It has always been a natural procedure to secure that limitation of knowledge by letting the reader follow the process of one given mind—the mind of the detective, or the mind of some companion of the detective, less clever than he, to whom the detective makes his revelations in the order that will best maintain the other's suspense.

Henry James, in his short stories and in those later novels which followed the middle period of short-story writing, is clearly aiming at a singleness of impression like that of Poe's tales. In general it is not an impression of physical fear and supernatural horror that he wishes to produce, but something much harder to define, which takes its quality from the mind of one or more of the characters.

Again, the stories of James (like those of Conrad) are mystery stories, almost we might say detective stories. The principle of their composition is to pose a question, or better, a series of questions, or problems for solution; by cunning suggestion to fix our attention on certain points of intenser interest and doubt; to hold us there watching those points until we have become thoroughly at home in the particular situation from which they are visible as "questionable" shapes; and then, by the proper illumination of those points, to create beyond them a new zone of obscurity.

Mystery stories, I call these fictions of James and Conrad. Only, the mysteries are for the most part psychological; the questions to be resolved are not so much matters of fact in the objective world as matters of interpretation, appreciation. Appreciation, not by a mere professional author—one who knows everything, has known everything from the beginning, and has nothing to learn—but by some one closer to the story, some one (in James) actually within the story, who can be shown in the very process of learning, of coming to understand little by little whatever it is that lies at the heart of the mystery. So that in this type of realistic, of psychological fiction, there is a double reason for cultivating a technique which has hitherto been the specialty of romance.

2

Thus in "The Ambassadors," the most remarkable of the full-length novels of James in which the single point of view is maintained, Lambert Strether has come abroad on an errand that calls for the subtlest exercise of his faculty for interpretation and appreciation. His task is to bring home Chad Newsome, but the first condition for success in this undertaking is that he shall make the acquaintance of the young man and get some understanding of the forces which have hitherto kept him so constant to Paris. When he first encounters Chad, in a box at the opera, he is at once struck by the fact that he is not the callow young thing he was when he left home, but rather a person of decided distinction; and Strether is at once conscious that he will find himself at a considerable disadvantage in dealing with a man so fine and so well armed in all worldly ways. And his task becomes still more difficult when he meets the woman who is holding Chad—a person of birth, breeding, sensibility. It is not a crude situation which can be met with crude measures.

In each one of the twelve books into which the novel is divided there is of course a provision of objective fact on which Strether is to exercise his faculty of appreciation. But the really important thing, to which the author gives the front of the stage, is not the facts but what he makes of them. There is, for example, the all-important fact—objectively considered—of the precise relation subsisting between Chad and Madame de Vionnet, whether or not it is a "guilty" one. The thing is never put explicitly into words; it would be characteristic of Lambert Strether to surround such a matter with the utmost discretion even in his own thoughts. When by accident he is presented with evidence which he cannot ignore that the relation is not "platonic," it is clearly a considerable shock to his New England prudery or idealism. But this merely confirms him in his conviction that Chad ought to stay. Strether has been too busy "appreciating" Madame de Vionnet and what she has done for Chad for this little discovery of fact to turn him against her.

"Nuns fret not at their convent's narrow room." It is the pleasure of the artist to choose the special conditions under which he is to present his subject and to work out all its richness within the limits of those conditions, whether they are constituted by the sonata form or by "the Sonnet's scanty plot of ground." In "The Ambassadors" it was not the story of Chad Newsome and Marie de Vionnet that James undertook to present, nor the relations between Lambert Strether and Mrs. Newsome, nor Franco-American society in Paris: it was just so much of all these as bore upon Strether's embassy, and just so much of these as came to him in the pursuit of that embassy; it was his "appreciation" of all these things in their relation to his undertaking. And the beauty of the performance lies in the justness with which he measures out the exact amount of each of these elements that is to enter into the composition, indicates the exact degree of their emergence in the consciousness of Strether, *controls* everything artist-wise in the interest of the effect he is after. And the effect he is after is the growing excitement of appreciation in the mind of Lambert Strether.

3

That is one sort of excitement, and sufficient for a certain kind of reader. It is not, however, the sort that for the most part readers of novels crave and demand. What they crave and demand is the emotional excitement aroused by situations involving extreme danger or suffering for at least the principal character, or predicaments putting a terrible strain upon him because of the urgent necessity of taking decisive action or making a choice between difficult alternatives.

Such emotional excitement is present in but slight degree in books like "The Ambassadors." And that is, I believe, even more than the over-elaboration of style, the reason for James's want of popularity. He deals very little in the crude obvious truth of the human passions and appetites. His is primarily a world of sentiments. Perhaps the best definition we can make of sentiment is intellectualized or idealized emotion. This intellectualization or idealization of the emotions implies a very great degree of abstraction; it means the ruling out, almost completely, of the mere appetites and undifferentiated passions. James rules them out of his world partly, no doubt, because of a certain over-fastidiousness of taste, a New England old-maidishness, which there is no point in trying to deny, and which accounts very largely for his rather exaggerated dislike for Flaubert, Zola, Maupassant, and other artists whom as artists he could not help but admire.

But that is not the whole story. Another powerful, and this time purely esthetic, reason for ruling out the cruder appetites and passions is simply that they tend to upset those finer equations of sentimental mathematics which it is his delight and specialty to work through to their conclusions. Mathematics is the art of abstraction from the tangible realities of tables and chairs. Numbers is, as I understand it, the art of considering things without relation to their individual qualities; and when we get to algebra, we have arrived at a still higher degree of abstraction, in which numbers themselves have been subsumed in a category to be designated by a, b, c, by x, y, z, by n and pi. And the thing goes on to higher and higher degrees of abstraction until it becomes necessary for Professor Whitehead to resort to the Deity as the Principle of Concretion without which we should have no actuality whatever.

James does not go so far with his sentimental mathematics; but he does like to conceive a world in which a certain number of people behave as if they were rational beings, without too much interference from the freakish cross-currents of casual appetite or subconscious infantile motivation which in everyday experience confuse and bewilder us. He is like a physicist who wishes to carry on his experiments free from electrical or magnetic disturbances. He makes, accordingly, a choice of passions which can be described in terms of intelligible and social motives—sentiments, that is to say—and brings them together in a field free from magnetic disturbances, where they can work out together the equation constituted by their opposing or collaborating forces.

Of course this is, in some degree, the procedure of all literary artists. The difference is in the degree of abstraction. It must be acknowledged that it is very high in James, and that in novels like "The Awkward Age" and "The Sacred Fount" it is so high that the interest of these books is almost exclusively intellectual. What keeps it from being such in books like "The Spoils of Poynton" and "The Golden Bowl" is the poignancy of the heroine's predicament and the intimacy with which we are made to realize it by the handling of the point of view.

In "The Spoils of Poynton" the heroine, Fleda Vetch, is a homeless girl of unusual taste and refinement, who falls in love with a young man already engaged to marry a rather common young woman, Mona Brigstock. Owen Gereth, the man, is heir to the beautiful country place of Poynton, which is particularly notable for the precious objects collected and housed there by his mother and his dead father. Mrs. Gereth highly approves of Fleda, but detests her prospective daughter-in-law and cannot bear to see her mistress of Poynton and its "spoils." And she secretly transfers the finest pieces to a more humble country-house of her own. There Fleda visits her, and finds herself in the extremely delicate position of go-between when Owen comes out to expostulate with his mother. She learns from Owen that his fiancée is highly indignant at Mrs. Gereth's "steal," and has indeed postponed the marriage until such time as the spoils are returned to Poynton. But, Owen warns her, she must not tell his mother that this is Mona's position, since that would only make her more determined to keep the things at Ricks. In the course of their conversation Owen manages to convey that he realizes the superiority of Fleda to his vulgar-minded fiancée, and that indeed, with encouragement, he might be induced to transfer his affections.

Fleda realizes that there is one way out: if Mrs. Gereth holds on long enough, Owen will cease to insist on the return of the spoils, and will simply give up Mona. This, Fleda feels, would be a beautiful solution of all their difficulties; it would dispose of Owen, of herself, and of Mrs. Gereth. Only, it would not provide for Mona, nor for Owen's obligation toward her, nor Fleda's obligation toward them both. So that Fleda Vetch finds herself in as tight a dilemma as any young woman ever found herself in, between the complicated and irreconcilable demands of honor on the one hand, and, on the other hand, the simple dictates of passion. If she had been a mite less clever an actor, or if the mere instinct of love had been given slightly more sway in her, the situation would have cleared up at once and the story been over.

But that is not the way with heroines of James. They are generally consummate masters of dissimulation (mostly in the good cause), and their emotions are so largely cast in the pattern of an ideal behavior, determined by conscience and a fabulously refined notion of honor, that they are incapable of acting directly upon instinct. They are obliged to think out the line of action demanded by their ideal sentiment; and they have to think it out, from moment to moment, in the very presence of the enemy. This is what gives the urgency and tension to predicaments like Fleda's. She feels impelled to give an instance of a manner of loving as different as possible from Mona Brigstock's. It is a tribute she owes to her pride, her self-respect, which is about all the poor girl possesses.

The line which Fleda takes at once leads her into a relation to Mrs. Gereth calling for a desperate display of strategy. She has three secrets which she is bound in honor to keep from Mrs. Gereth: her love for Owen, Owen's inclination for her, and Mona's ultimatum. Mrs. Gereth is a very keen woman and hard to hoodwink, and the tenth and eleventh chapters, in which the two women discuss Fleda's interview with Owen, are an example of breathless intellectual fencing, all on a level of the finest breeding. Fleda is driven back from one position to another; she has to give up the secret of her love for Owen, and she has to give up Mona's ultimatum. But she manages to preserve the secret of Owen's love for her, and she manages to stick to her view that, whatever happens, Mona will never give up Owen.

This is but the beginning of Fleda's battle, but will sufficiently illustrate what is a rather constant feature of James's fiction, especially in the later period. The principal characters are likely to be engaged most of the time in a sort of spiritual game which involves a sharp, continuous trial of wits at close range. This is doubtless one thing that alienates many readers, since it gives what they feel to be an unduly intellectual cast to the story.

It is probably less true of "The Spoils of Poynton" than of most of the later novels. Fleda shows herself, in the long run, human enough, and she is, in the whole view, a plucky, pathetic character, who makes a strong appeal to the reader's sympathy. There is in plenty the material of emotional appeal. Only it is James's way to throw the emphasis in another direction. More or less, he leaves the characters' emotions to be inferred from the tenseness of their effort to meet the trial of wits.

The emphasis falls accordingly not on the moral struggle, as in George Eliot or Mrs. Humphry Ward; not on the sentimental sufferings of the character, as in Hugh Walpole, in Dorothy Canfield, or (to go farther down the scale of art) in A. S. M. Hutchinson; nor on what we might call the sufferings of passion—though that is perhaps too fine a word for the occasion—as we have them in writers like Hergesheimer and Swinnerton. What is most prominent is the strain upon the character's wits. We are reminded of dramatic passages of romance, in Hugo, in Dumas, in Stevenson, Cooper, Scott, where the hero is called upon to show his resourcefulness on the spur of the moment in order to get himself out of a tight place.

There are passages in James that have the same quality, in the moral world, as that chapter in "Kidnapped" where David Balfour, being sent by his devilish uncle to climb the dark stairway in the ruined tower, gropes his way from step to step in the murk, vaguely conscious of perils which he cannot define, until a providential flash of lightning reveals the gap in the stairway through which, but for that accident, he was destined to fall to his death. There is in James the same breathless suspense for the character whose point of view we share; the same relentless strain upon his vigilance and ingenuity.

So that there is, after all, in work like "The Spoils of Poynton," an intensity analogous to that of well-written romance. And talk as we like of the intellectual cast of a story in which the stress is not laid directly on the sentimental factors, when we use the word "intensity" we are using a word which has some kind of emotional connotation. It is the intensity of such fiction which saves it from the reproach of being unemotional.

XIX

POINT OF VIEW: JAMES, STENDHAL

We have not yet done with the restricted point of view. This technique is made to serve purposes more narrowly esthetic than any discussed in the preceding chapters, and difficult to describe except with the help of those analogies which are the staple of art-criticism. The very assumption of a definite point of view implies an ideal of refinement in execution such as is prized in the arts of painting and engraving. It implies an author who is not content to dump his matter down in a heap. It is one pattern of arrangement; it implies a system of presentation. If the intention is successfully realized, that in itself is an artistic merit, like accurate drawing or observance of the laws of perspective.

In "The Spoils of Poynton" we derive our impressions of all the characters except Fleda from the way they strike her. It is through the medium of Fleda's finer spiritual perceptions that we are made to realize the grosser, though more robust, reactions of Mrs. Gereth to questions involving conscience and the sentiments. Mona Brigstock and her mother appear very little on the actual scene, and the vivid impression we have of their quality is derived almost altogether from the disgust aroused in Fleda and her friend by the crassness, the philistine commonness of taste and motive, the gross vitality of these people in the background. It is the great triumph of this method that characters who are seldom seen and heard take on nevertheless the actuality of persons present before our eyes, loom portentously as forces to be reckoned with.

Owen himself is a figure of the middle distance; and yet, thanks to Fleda's attentiveness to the least sign, we feel that he has been limned with all firmness and delicacy of stroke. He is to his mother's view a mere stupid fellow. But to Fleda his simplicity has from the beginning an engaging quality, associated with her sense of his helplessness, his good nature, his dyed-in-the-wool gentlemanliness. And she comes to realize, as time goes on, that the rightness of his feelings is capable of making of his simplicity a social instrument as fine as cleverness. It is very interesting to see how his character "comes out" in the course of these prolonged negotiations; and it is Fleda's powers of appreciation for this sort of thing that serves to bring it out.

Of course there are quite other ways for the author to accomplish these effects in characterization. But there is a distinct esthetic pleasure derived from this method of doing it through the consciousness of one of the characters. In what does this pleasure consist? Let us carry the question a little farther back, and inquire in what consists the pleasure derived from representation of any kind. Nature is in her own way so much more beautiful, so much more "stunning" than any picture can make her. And yet it is one of our most persistent urges to make representations, with every kind of artificial medium, of that Nature whose special beauty can never be approached. And there are moods in which we much prefer the artificial product to the natural thing.

The mere skill involved in that degree of accuracy which will serve to remind us strongly of the original is sufficient to arouse our admiration. But literalness of reproduction is but the beginning—or else the decadent end—of the matter. Critics of all schools agree that art involves a high degree of selection and elimination, of rearrangement of the elements of the subject, of composition within the limits of the square of canvas. One chief pleasure to be derived from painting is an understanding of what is done by interpretation, by positive modification of a given subject in the interest of some unifying and enriching idea. We like a picture for its expressiveness. And this expressiveness is traceable not merely to composition in the larger sense but to the details of technical procedure. We take the keenest pleasure in the mere brush stroke of a Van Gogh in painting in a sky, his manner of applying thick masses of oil which give sparkle and animation to the object presented. The painter has translated nature into the terms of art, and in translating has enriched it, has brought to it an increment of pleasure.

But, if our analogy is to be of any use in connection with the art of fiction, we must return to the primary fact of representation. In the freest of painting there must be some correspondence between the subject and the artistic product. Otherwise we should miss that pleasure of recognition; we should not appreciate the skill in selection and interpretation. It is this primary and mysterious correspondence between nature and art that lies at the heart of all our pleasure in technique. Our joy in the visible world is doubled by our joy in its reproduction through the medium of art. In art, we enjoy nature somehow for the very fact that it comes to us indirectly. It is at one remove from what we call reality, and this may be in itself a reason for the glamour which it holds for us.

This applies as well to the novel as to any form of art. It is obvious that the story which the author tells is at one remove from what we call reality, and gives us a different sort of pleasure from that which we derive from the direct observation of life. But if the author so arranges his story that it shall be told entirely from the point of view of one of his characters, he has made an extension of the principle involved in all artistic process. The special consciousness of the character constitutes an added principle of selection, of composition and interpretation. As in the author's statement of his subject we have the pleasure of recognizing the original reality enhanced by what the author reads into it or by the mere process of straining it through the medium of words; so, in the character's special view of the subject, we have the pleasure of recognizing the author's view of it enhanced by the contributions of the character's temperament. And if there is a glamour in the fact that all art is at one remove from what we call reality, there will be an intensification of that glamour in an art that is at two removes from it.

I say, what we call reality. But everybody knows what a tricky word has there entered into the discussion. Reality, we say naïvely, is constituted by the facts themselves, without regard to what we may think about them. But a brief initiation into metaphysics—or even, in these days, into physics—is sufficient to show us that of the primary facts themselves we know absolutely nothing. A physical scientist like Eddington will tell you that scientific knowledge consists of a series of formulas, all of them creations of the human mind, which serve very well the practical purpose of controlling certain processes of nature and predicting what will happen under certain circumstances, but that this series of formulas is a closed circle, entirely distinct from the presumable reality to which it corresponds, and never at any point bringing us actually in contact with that reality.

If this is true of the physical world, the one world which has long been regarded as the very type of hard reality, how much more true is it in the esthetic realm! In science, at least, there is a near approach to universal agreement on terms for describing the phenomena which form its subject-matter, and the effort is to make as little as possible of the temperaments of individual investigators. Whereas in art, while there have always been conventions of one kind or another, a premium has been put on the individual quality of the interpretation. In all art, the great thing is not accuracy so much as fullness or richness in the rendering of reality. In fiction, facts are made important by being set in such a light that they become not facts but meanings.

One way of doing this is to give the facts just that meaning which they have for some one of the characters. They are like so much lumpish matter which can be made available only by being dissolved. The consciousness of the character is a chemical fluid capable of dissolving the facts and making them available. And the important matter for art is that we should have a perfect solution. If there remains at the bottom a deep sediment of undissolved matter, so that it is necessary to shake the bottle hard before using, the artist has fallen short of his aim. This objective-subjective solution should be saturated but not over-saturated. The mixture of elements should be so perfect that we have a complete obliteration of the distinction between objective and subjective.

Of course, a similar result may be obtained by a process directly opposite to that of James. In James the objective is completely assimilated to the subjective, and the effect is best rendered by our analogy of the fluid solution. In Maupassant the subjective is for the most part completely assimilated to the objective; and a better analogy would be a boxful of perfectly formed crystals. These crystals have a glitter and weight which have their own appeal, and one may well prefer the method of Maupassant. In his tales the characters seem to have no existence except in the objective facts in which they are completely absorbed. It is the dominance of the objective.

So here we have two beautiful methods of representing human nature—two esthetic conventions, we may call them—beautiful in their simplicity, their richness, their artistic precision. Neither of them involves a complete description of human nature. Maupassant's system implies that men exist in the objective aims in which they are absorbed. James's system implies that men are creatures living mainly in reflection, perpetually conscious of their own reactions to the situations of which they form a part.

We are obliged, if we are to appreciate either of these kinds of art, to accept its conventions. We are obliged, in James, to grant the existence of people who live more constantly and consciously by reflection than our Aunt Dinah or our Cousin Ned. They are given in an unusual degree to brooding over the social situation, the relation in which they stand to the other characters, watching from moment to moment the subtle changes that come over this relation and affect, as it were, the balance of power in the sentimental world.

And if it so happens that we like this kind of thing, we may derive from such narratives that supreme pleasure offered by the arts, the sense of complete immersion in the medium chosen. We are plunged deep, deep in this richly flavored and tinctured fluid, and soak it in at every pore. We are confined so long and strictly within the character's range of vision that we grow to have an intimacy with its minutest features which becomes for us an imaginative possession never to be lost. We are absorbed, to the last inch of consciousness, in this special world of illusions, as we are absorbed in the world created by great actors, by George Arliss or Emil Jannings. And when we come out into the daylight, we rub our eyes almost in pain, and it takes a certain length of time to adjust ourselves uneasily to what we call "reality."

2

The world of reality is the world of newspapers and window displays, of self-starters and bumpy pavements, of telephone bills and telephone numbers scrawled on a pad. It is a world of irrelevant facts not yet got into order, unframed, unlighted, uninterpreted. And printed books are full of matter from the world of facts, big facts and little, important and trivial; and, above all, crude facts, facts not yet assimilated to any system of meanings, nor strained through any effective medium.

This is the way I feel about even so powerful a book as Henry Handel Richardson's "Ultima Thule" (1929). Here is in great plenty the stuff of human nature and emotion. Here is a tragic story if there ever was one, such a story as lurks behind many a cheerful façade of social appearances. It is certainly an unusual achievement for an author to have seen the importance and the possibilities of such a subject and to have got it set down in some kind of consecutive narrative. But somehow I feel that the higher processes of organizing art are largely absent, and that the thing remains an artless and irritating performance. Emotionally the author understands her characters, but esthetically she does not seem to appreciate them—as, for example, Julian Green appreciates his characters in "The Dark Journey" (1929).

Superficially her characters are commonplace people; the children are brats from a back street. Now, there are two ways of dealing with superficial commonplaceness. One is to recognize it and play it up, make it an element in the artistic effect. Another is to ignore it as unimportant in comparison with the tragic issues, considering that persons who suffer what this family suffers rise above all superficial commonplaceness, transcend it. The one method is George Eliot's, and the other is Balzac's. But the author of "Ultima Thule" seems to have chosen neither one nor the other, almost as if she did not realize the commonplaceness of her characters, or at any rate as if she did not appreciate it as a factor in her esthetic problem.

The bane of fiction is the unassimilated fact. The peculiar brilliance of Julian Green lies in his avoidance of this danger, the sureness and intensity with which in him all facts are lighted with the calcium glare of some artistic intention. Now, this is the great point about James's method, infinitely different as it is from Julian Green's. He never jars the reader with crude facts that give one that shivering sense of being outside the subject instead of inside. His intimacy is the quality which distinguishes him most from that giant among psychological novelists, Stendhal.

Such books as "La Charteuse de Parme" (1839) and "Le Rouge et le Noir" (1830) are perfect quarries of solid and precious facts of human nature. Poor low-born Julien Sorel, eaten up with Napoleonic ambition, and tortured not with his love for this or that woman but with the need to prove in love-affairs with aristocratic persons the prestige of his personality—there we have something of first-rate importance in normal psychology, almost altogether neglected in fiction, which prefers to indulge simpler views of amorous sentiment. And Stendhal has other matter too. He is a realist in a sense in which the term will not apply to James. He is, moreover, a great romantic personality, and he writes well—with gusto, wit, and force.

He may be in many ways a much greater writer than James, but he is not so fine an artist. Julien Sorel is like a convincing historical figure rather than an intimately known personage of fiction. We understand him perfectly, we know what he stands for and can give a satisfactory account of him; we know what he did and what happened to him. We even know what he thought. But him we do not seem to know; we do not feel that we have lived with him.

This may be due partly to his foreignness, the remoteness of those days, those types and issues. But it is also partly due to something in the technique that strikes the modern reader as quaint and old-fashioned. Stendhal is full of stuff. He is ready at any moment to give us all the facts, all at once, all in a heap. He is prodigal of psychology; in "Le Rouge et le Noir" he will spend whole chapters on the thoughts of a character. And yet he seems in a hurry, and is forever turning to mere analytical summaries to reinforce the effect of situations which have not been made sufficiently intimate. Speaking of Madame Rênal's conviction of sin, following the illness of her child, he says:

> This great moral crisis changed the nature of the sentiment which united Julien to his mistress. His love was no longer simply a matter of admiring her beauty and taking pride in possessing it. Their happiness was from now on of a greatly superior nature; the flame which devoured them was more intense. Their joy would have seemed greater in the eyes of the world. But they no longer found that delicious serenity, that unclouded felicity, that easy happiness of the first periods of their love, when the sole fear of Madame de Rênal was not to be loved enough by Julien. Their happiness had at times the air of a crime.

The author is more concerned to make us understand the psychology of his hero than to make us share it.

There are plenty of fine scenes which dramatize in vivi l fashion the psychology of Julien, but even here intrudes the habit of psychological analysis to spoil the intimacy of our contact with the character. On the night when he climbed into the window of Madame de Rênal, after a long period of separation when she had given him up for the good of her soul, there is a constant alternation between statements which *present* the state of mind of Julien and statements which *describe* and *explain* it. When Madame de Rênal urges him to take his departure before he has satisfied his pride, he realizes what a shame it would be for him to be sent away, enough to poison his whole life.

> From this moment all that there was of celestial in the position of Julien disappeared rapidly from his heart. Seated beside a woman whom he adored, almost straining her in his arms, perceiving in the deep obscurity that she had been weeping, feeling by the movement of her breast that she was sobbing, he had the misfortune to turn into a cold and calculating creature of policy.

There is in all this an air of the literary and theoretical quite hostile to the purposes of dramatic intimacy.

It goes without saying that Stendhal feels free to pass, without warning, from the point of view of one character into that of another. He is the omniscient historian, ready at any moment to give any piece of information which seems pertinent to his chronicle. There are no limits to his vision, even temporary, no unlighted places waiting for the due amount of illumination. Now, limitation of vision is one of the chief means of securing intimacy. It is like the window curtains by which you shut yourself in with the particular fireside where you choose to feel at home. One reason why Stendhal can pass so cavalierly from one consciousness to another is that he has never penetrated very deep, has never shut himself up very cozily, in any one of them.

In James it is not the mere strictness with which he limits the point of view that gives the effect of intimacy. It is the depth of penetration, the density of the medium, the degree of saturation of the facts. So complete is this saturation in James that the minutest grains of fact are given an effectiveness as great as that in Stendhal of actions on a sensational scale. In Stendhal, the hero must climb into the heroine's window by a ladder, and risk his life each time he visits her, in order to impress us. The lovers must be at every moment in a state of frenzied passion or of icy indifference. In James, situations of great quietness may be given a breathless importance by the fidelity with which he renders their significance to the persons involved.

There is the simple, unmelodramatic incident—and yet in the finest sense highly theatrical—by which Lambert Strether is made to realize finally the nature of the intimacy between Chad and Madame de Vionnet. Spending a quiet afternoon in the country, Strether discovers these two enigmatic persons together under circumstances which can bear but one interpretation. For Strether it is the resolution of doubts he has harbored and repressed during many months. The characters all behave beautifully, chatting together over their dinner to cover the embarrassment of this encounter. But there had been the moment when Strether knew that the others had seen him; there had been that instant of hesitation as to whether they should recognize him. And this, in the scale of values so carefully maintained by the author, takes on an importance nothing short of sensational.

Here again it is the subjective method that is largely responsible for the effect secured. It is like some amplifying process for reproducing the finest shades of expression and tone in music. Well, these finest shades are often, in life, what gives its peculiar point to any experience, and an art that can recover them for us is an art which gratifies us not merely by its fineness but by its truth. We do not know whether we are more grateful for the amount of human experience thus restored to us or for the delicate stroke by which the trick is turned.

PART THREE: THE WELL-MADE NOVEL

Little circumstances, which were perhaps accidental in a great author, were by these critics considered to constitute his chief merit, and transmitted as essentials to be observed by all his successors. To these encroachments, time and ignorance, the two great supporters of imposture, gave authority; and thus many rules for good writing have been established, which have not the least foundation in truth or nature; and which commonly serve for no other purpose than to curb and restrain genius, in the same manner as it would have restrained the dancing-master, had the most excellent treatises on that art laid it down as an essential rule that every man must dance in chains.

—Henry Fielding: "The History of Tom Jones, a Foundling"

XX

VARIATIONS: BENNETT

WHAT I call the well-made novel, with its "dramatic" tendencies, is merely, let the reader bear well in mind, a sort of ideal construction. It is perhaps never found in its absolute form, with every element perfectly represented, unless it be in some novelette of Schnitzler like "Fräulein Else" (1923). It is none the less the ideal toward which tended most of the characteristic work of, say, 1895–1925, in England and America, and is still strongly in evidence, in spite of the new tendencies epitomized in Joyce's "Ulysses." In one author the stress will be on certain factors, in another on certain others.

The author's disposition to keep himself out of the picture is almost universal, as one realizes the more strongly by considering the exceptions. A novelist like Arnold Bennett, whose work is the modern equivalent of the panoramic novel of Thackeray, is strikingly in contrast with Thackeray and all his contemporaries by virtue of the dryness of his tone. It is true that he does not hesitate, wherever he thinks fit, to observe his characters from the outside and interpret them to the reader, even to tell us how he feels toward them himself. After relating the death of Samuel Povey, the author remarks:

> He lacked individuality. He was little. I have often laughed at Samuel Povey. But I liked and respected him. He was a very honest man. I have always been glad to think that, at the end of his life, destiny took hold of him and displayed, to the observant, the vein of greatness which runs through every soul without exception. He embraced a cause, lost it, and died of it.

Again, Mr. Bennett does not scorn to enliven even his most serious novels with occasional facetious comments faintly suggestive of the humor of the great Victorians, as where he disposes of a certain charwoman by remarking that "she had caught smallpox and she died of it, thus losing a good situation."

But altogether passages of this sort are extremely rare in novels like "The Old Wives' Tale" (1908) and the Clayhanger series (1910–16). Mr. Bennett was writing too consciously under the inspiration of the French naturalists, with their ideal of dry objectivity in the treatment of character. His personal comments serve only to give a slightly ironic or slightly sympathetic coloring to the mainly unvarnished narrative.

And even so, Arnold Bennett seems a bit old-fashioned in this respect when brought into comparison with any number of typical novelists of the day like Margaret Kennedy, Willa Cather, Somerset Maugham, Ellen Glasgow, O. E. Rölvaag, or Julia Peterkin.

Consider, for example, how entirely free is Mrs. Peterkin's "Scarlet Sister Mary" (1928) from any flavoring of patronage, sentimentality, apology, defense. The author makes no effort to present her heroine "subjectively." She retains full privilege as author to explain, describe, narrate the life of this maternal dark Venus. But she never in the slightest degree presumes on these privileges. The facts are left to speak for themselves in all simplicity. The author presents the sorrows of Mary—she shows her flourishing with her children and her love-charm. She shows us the "meetings" of the religious party in the negro village and makes us feel the consolations of religion to these disinherited ones. But she does not give the impression of "telling us" about these things. She simply sets them before us. She makes no use of irony or scorn as a means of playing up one character against another, one philosophy against another.

Even more remarkable in this kind is the achievement of Pearl Buck in "The Good Earth" (1931). The biblical simplicity of her style corresponds to the grave matter-of-factness of her chronicle. Without censoriousness and without sentimentality, the Occidental Christian delineates the manners and morals of the Chinese peasant, following through the whole cycle of life from boyhood to old age, from indigence to wealth, keeping always strictly within the limits of a provincial Chinese mentality. So she builds up little by little the picture of an alien culture having its own weakness and strength, its own dignity and rightness, and its independent claim to consideration. It is all done in the open-minded scientific spirit of modern sociology. But it is also a notable effort of sympathetic imagination, and there is high art in the consistent maintenance of the tone. Never does the author indicate a moral. And if a moral arises from this deeply moving story, it is one so universally human that it transcends the bounds of race and creed.

These two distinguished books are the more representative of current tendencies in that there is nothing peculiar about them technically—nothing specially "modern" or experimental to set them off from the common run of novels.

2

The principle of selectiveness is again everywhere in evidence in the characteristic work of 1895–1925. It goes along with that complete alteration in the conception of plot as the basic element of form in the novel.

Even so late as 1905 academic critics were still talking of "Tom Jones" as the supreme model of formal composition by virtue of its well-nigh perfect plot. Dr. Maynadier tells us:

> "Tom Jones" is firmly composed,—so firmly that as it stands it is one of the best-constructed novels in our language, and,

with the omission of a few chapters, it might become the very best. . . . The mystery of Tom's birth, on which all the complications hinge, is put before us in the third chapter of the first book—that is, in the second chapter of the story—and it is not explained until the seventh chapter of the last book,—only six chapters from the end. Nor is this any too soon to divulge the secret, when we consider how much is to be cleared up before the last page. Moreover, various episodes of the story which do not seem pertinent as we begin to read them, always turn out somehow to help towards the end.

So then, it seems, the essence of good composition is to have a complicated tangle of mysteries to be "cleared up," with one central mystery which is propounded early and not disposed of till very near the end. Now, it has long been a puzzle to me why "Tom Jones" should so often be cited as the supreme example of this art when we have so many nineteenth-century novels which answer all the prescriptions, and which, in the matter of complication and suspense, go it decidedly one better. What about "Guy Mannering" and "Ivanhoe"? What about "The Woman in White," or "Dr. Jekyll and Mr. Hyde"? Could not something be said even for Hardy's "Desperate Remedies"?

Nothing ever is said for "Desperate Remedies," for the simple reason that, while it is "firmly composed," God knows, and, like all good stories of this kind, keeps its master-mystery unrevealed to the last chapter, it does not happen to display the special genius of Hardy even in the art of composition. Hardy's genius for composition is displayed in "The Return of the Native," in "Tess" and "Jude," and this without his being obliged to conceal the identity of any of the characters or, at the last moment, discover in an old cupboard the suppressed will which restores the rightful heir to his inheritance. Such tricks as these were the stock in trade of the nineteenth-century composer of plots, and I see no reason why Fielding should be preferred in this respect to the author of "Bleak House,"

"Great Expectations," and the "Tale of Two Cities."

We are not here concerned, be it noted, with the Edgar Wallaces and S. S. Van Dines of an earlier day. The men of our time who correspond to the serious novelists of the past are men like Galsworthy and Lawrence, and these men do not occupy themselves with the invention of plots which hang on the suppression throughout the major part of the story of the facts necessary to explain it and to bring about a suitable ending. If Arnold Bennett sometimes tries his hand at this sort of thing, it is with his tongue in his cheek and frankly to make the pot boil. When he writes seriously, he writes soberly—relying for his appeal not on the mysterious and sensational in event but on the interest we take in the normal daily lives of people like ourselves.

Now, the preoccupation with *intrigue* as the basis of story naturally tends toward complication and away from simplicity of line. The emphasis is thrown on surprising happenings rather than on the development of character and on the simple moral dilemmas that make the drama of character. And it is the ever increasing emphasis on psychology—that is, upon character intimately rendered—which, in the well-made novel, goes hand in hand with the elimination of intrigue.

There is one variety of intrigue which does not necessarily call for sensational mystery and yet implies a considerable complication of plot. It involves the assemblage within the covers of one book of a large number of characters whose fortunes are closely related, and so they belong together, but who take turns in holding the center of the stage, as the story of one or the other becomes the subject of the moment. Such is the type of story favored by Trollope, for example, in the famous cathedral series.

In "Barchester Towers" (1857), we begin with Archdeacon Grantly, the gentleman among clergymen. We turn next to Mr. Harding, his father-in-law, recently warden of Hiram's Hospital, and Harding's daughter, the widowed

Eleanor Bold; then to the newly appointed bishop, the evangelical Dr. Proudie, and his bossy wife; and then to the bishop's low-church chaplain Slope, who is Mrs. Proudie's great rival for power in the diocese. Enter next the family of the Stanhopes; the Thornes of Ullathorne; and the high-church Mr. Arabin. I have named only the principals in this drama, and have therefore left out of account the Quiverfuls and many other interesting figures.

The questions at issue are threefold: (1) Which one of several eligible men shall marry Eleanor Bold? (2) Who shall be appointed to the vacant wardenship? (3) Who shall be made dean? But the dramatic oppositions involved are much more numerous than is implied in this simplified statement of the issue. Taking into account only the ecclesiastical intrigue, there are (1) the opposition of the Grantlyites in general to the episcopal party; (2) the struggle for mastership between the bishop and his wife; (3) that between Mrs. Proudie and Slope. And when we add the complications of the love-story and the many ways in which it interlocks with the church plot, and attempt to estimate the number of minor dramatic situations resulting from all his, we get into the higher mathematics.

And note that the story is very well told, very well told indeed according to the principles of story-telling practised in this school. Trollope has much more sense than Thackeray for the dramatic handling of individual chapters and suites of chapters developing a single situation. The two chapters picturing Mrs. Proudie's reception, with the arrival of the Signora Neroni and the jealous rage of the bishop's wife, and several other chapters involving the struggle for power between Mrs. Proudie and the chaplain, or between Mrs. Proudie and the bishop, are equal in sheer comedy to anything in Thackeray and superior to anything in him for theatrical arrangement. As for firmness of composition, must one not pronounce "Barchester Towers" (or even "Framley Parsonage," for that matter) superior to

"Tom Jones," if we take into account the large number of threads of plot here interwoven and the extreme deftness of their interweaving, without any touch of sensationalism or mystery, but all within the "modesty of nature"?

But it is this very art of interweaving threads of plot—this cunning joiner's work—which came to seem antiquated in the period of the well-made novel. To writers like Galsworthy and Edith Wharton, like Ellen Glasgow and Somerset Maugham, it must seem that Trollope has laid his emphasis too much on plot for plot's sake, and too little on character, on the feeling of life itself which comes thicker and thicker with the emphasis on character. No one will question the brilliancy and glitter of Trollope's characterizations, nor his general observance of the truth of human nature. Only, it is character seen, for the most part, from the outside, and in its relation to the comparatively artificial mechanism of plot. And with the distribution of interest over so large a number of principal persons, it is virtually impossible to attain that emotional force and massiveness which is a great feature of Maugham's "Of Human Bondage," of Miss Sinclair's "Mary Olivier," or Rölvaag's "Giants in the Earth," not to mention "The Man of Property" or "Women in Love." Trollope does not force human nature into a mold; he does not misrepresent it. Neither does he render it with intensity, or penetrate to its secret places of agony, despair, and exultation. He gives life truthfully enough but ever on the surface level of social comedy.

For such purposes he does not feel the necessity for ranging all his material around one center of interest, and is in this respect in marked contrast to the great French naturalists, his contemporaries. These men, who took so much bolder a grasp on life and human nature in its most intense manifestations, have almost invariably that French sense for composition which is so very different a matter from the sense for composition seen in the plot of "Tom Jones." And it is not merely Flaubert and the Goncourts and Maupassant, with their narrow range of characters and relative thinness of action. Zola too, with his enormous crowded canvases, his titanic accumulation of detail, has an unfailing sense for building everything round one emotional center. Everything in "Nana" is made to circle round that magnificent courtezan, that nodus of corruption. The whole epic of "L'Assommoir" is felt as the story of the laundress Gervaise. The whole cycle of "Lourdes" is presented from the point of view of the Abbé Pierre and given a reference to his love for the crippled Marie de Guersaint.

The same principle prevails in Turgenev, the friend of Flaubert and Zola, and generally speaking in the Russian novel. Neither Tolstoy nor Dostoevski is concerned with the weaving of intrigue in the English manner. And it is against this background of the great French and Russian realists that the well-made novel shaped itself in England and America.

3

It is worth while giving some examples of how this new principle of composition works out in novelists who otherwise show a wide variation from the formula of the well-made novel. Arnold Bennett gives the best example in the period we are discussing of the "panoramic" method of Thackeray and Dickens. In his best-known novels, "The Old Wives' Tale" and the Clayhanger series, he covers a very long space of years, and gives us that sense of intimacy with the characters which results from our living through their whole lives with them.

They are not particularly eventful lives. The characters are absorbed for the most part in what are relatively little things. The married life of Constance Baines was one of infinite small besieging cares which never left her mind free for anything but a sort of profound contentment. Bennett allows Sophia a somewhat romantic experience when she runs away with Gerald Scales. And later there is something romantic, at least to the reader, in her being buried in such a strange foreign environment. But what the author features is her capacity as manager of a boarding-house.

He lays great stress in all his masterpieces on family life rather than erotic adventure. And this is in accordance with our normal experience. The average life in its bulk and in its obvious features consists of two stages: that in which we are growing up in the house with our mothers and fathers, and that in which we are bringing up our own children in our own house. Quarters are necessarily close for all but wealthy people, and we all have a tendency to get in one another's way. In some fashion it is likely to be with all of us as it was with the Clayhanger children, whose father was such an awkward obstruction to their own activities. Edwin bears a deep grudge against his father for his lifelong tyranny. The tables are turned inevitably when his father becomes a weak and helpless old man, who must give up his keys to his son and make over to him the power of signing checks. This part of the story occupies three fourths of "Clayhanger." It is only in the fourth part that a love-affair is introduced, and it is clear that the main theme of the book is the family life of the Clayhangers.

The second novel of the Clayhanger series is the somewhat more romantic story of "Hilda Lessways," but the third, "These Twain," deals with the unromantic relation of husband and wife. It is simply an account of the tug-of-war between two people who are genuinely fond of one another but each of whom wants to have his own way. It is a powerful and significant story, and it presents another aspect of that commonplace and pedestrian experience, family life.

But while Bennett is in these books a sober realist, without intrigue or melodrama, and without the poetic elements of Meredith, Hardy, or Conrad, we must not conclude that he represents life as being dull and placid. One of the most remarkable features of his work is the sense he gives us of the exciting character of experience to those who lead such commonplace lives. When Sophia looks back upon her life, at the bedside of her dead husband, she thinks: "I wish I was dead. I have been through too much."

That is the constant note of "The Old Wives' Tale"—how much the characters go through. Arnold Bennett has realized one of the capital truths of human existence—that our emotion is not commensurate with the material circumstances which call it forth; it is not the circumstances but our own hearts that make life exciting and significant. The values of life are subjective, and the prime value is the simple sensation of living. Of one of his heroines he says, "She began to perceive that this that she was living through was life."

This is a dominant note in the Clayhanger series. Edwin Clayhanger leads in the Five Towns a very humdrum life, but this does not prevent him from having moments of the highest excitement and satisfaction. It might be simply a quiet evening of good talk at a neighbor's house; it might be events of major importance that called for such moments of realization. After his father's death his sensations are a mingling of pity with a sort of exultant wonder. "Edwin's distress was shot through and enlightened by his solemn satisfaction at the fact that destiny had allotted to him, Edwin, an experience of such overwhelming grandeur." A little later we have a summary of his general situation and how he regarded himself. He hadn't accomplished much, that was true. But he had had the dining-room made over since his father's death. He was getting ever richer.

> He went to the theatre. He went to concerts. He took holidays. He had been to London, and more than once. He had a few good friends. He was his own master. . . . His career, which to others seemed dull and monotonous, presented itself to him as almost miraculously romantic in its development.

So Edwin Clayhanger is thinking of his career and its development. One of the specialties of Bennett is that tone of emotion, in the characters themselves and in the reader, which is associated with the continuous and fatal lapse of time. This is not that concentrated excitement over the issue of some drama taken at its height and played out within a few days or a few weeks. It is the slow-growing and penetrating sentiment that comes only with a sense of the continuity of lives encountered at recurring periods over a long course of years. It is likely to run strongest at times when death puts its full stop to the career of some one of the characters and causes the others to regard their lives in the perspective of the generations. Thus in "The Old Wives' Tale" there is the death of Mr. Baines and Mrs. Baines in the first book, in the second book the death of Samuel Povey; and in the fourth book we witness the end of Gerald and Sophia and Constance. And in the meantime life is punctuated for Constance by the growth of Cyril from babyhood to manhood, and by the Christmas post-cards received from Sophia down through the years.

In the James type of novel our intimacy with the characters grows in the spiritual dimension of thought through the infinite expansion of the moment. But here it is the literal dimension of time, with its constant incremental cumulation of feeling, that makes us intimate with the people of the story and gives them their incomparable air of solidity and reality.

4

The chronicle of "The Old Wives' Tale" covers a period of more than forty years, from the sixteenth year of Constance Baines to her death at fifty-eight. This is even longer than the period covered by "Vanity Fair." And one might look for similar methods of composition in books so like in panoramic effect. But Arnold Bennett, even in those extensive "chronicles" (as Mr. Muir calls them), has been noticeably affected by the dramatic tendencies of his day.

To begin with, Bennett has an exceptionally clear sense of the artistic value of the chapter as a unit of composition. He knows in advance precisely what material he is going to include in each chapter, what contribution it will make to his steadily moving story, just how much weight it will have to bear from the superincumbent mass of his carefully planned structure. He knows how it will begin and by just what stages it will move to its definite conclusion. He has as sharp a sense as Eliot, James, or Zola for the "discriminated occasion." A chapter is most often conceived by him as the vehicle for a particular scene or act of his drama. And within the chapter he distinguishes clearly between the successive moments of the action, the successive tableaux which make up the act. To this end he often divides each chapter into numbered sections, each of which presents a separate moment or tableau. This is his method in "The Old Wives' Tale," "Clayhanger," and "Hilda Lessways."

It is evident that he exercises fastidious care in the opening and closing of chapters and sections. He is a very objective writer compared with James, mostly occupied with action, movement, event. For this reason it is even more obvious in Bennett that he begins the chapter regularly in the midst of a constituted scene. A very large number of chapters open with the speech of one of the characters on a definite occasion. It may be that weeks or years have intervened between this and the preceding chapter, and it may be necessary to give some brief account of what has passed in the interval. But first he will set the new scene going. If it is an act or an attitude which is to be recorded rather than a spoken word, the first sentence is phrased in such a way as to plant us firmly in the new situation, however much later it may be in time. "Mr. Povey was playing a hymn tune on the harmonium, it having been decided that no one should go to chapel." "Constance stood at the large, many-paned window in the parlour. She was stouter." "Then she was lying in bed in a small room, obscure because it was heavily curtained." "They had been to Versailles and had dined there." "Matthew Peel-Swinnerton sat in the long dining-room of the Pension Frensham."

The same care is used in giving to each section its distinct value as a scenical component of the action. Thus in the minor mechanical points of story-telling, Bennett illustrates the concern for neatness of form that was a dominant feature of the novel in his period. And the care bestowed upon the smallest units of composition is made to serve that "sense of time" which it is the object of this type of novel to produce through the cumulative effect of many little events following one another steadily through a long course of years.

When we turn to the larger outlines of the story, we note that there is in "The Old Wives' Tale" a much smaller number of characters than in "Vanity Fair," and much less of social diversity. There is less complication of issues, and the author has not the necessity of passing constantly from one set of characters to another to keep going his various threads of plot.

And even within his compact family group, Bennett has taken pains to simplify and keep separate the several lines of action. This he has accomplished notably by his division of the story into four books and his allocation to each book of the matter appropriate to it. In the first book we have the simple group, all assembled in the same house: Constance, Sophia, Mrs. Baines, Povey. The center of interest is not absolutely determined here, but on the whole it is felt to be Sophia, because it is between her and Mrs. Baines that the issue is most sharply drawn, and she is the young person to whom our sympathies go out most strongly. If this book is entitled "Mrs. Baines," it is more by way of signalizing that she has no part in the later books —the marriage of her daughters is the end of her. In the second book the center is clearly Constance, in her relation to her husband and her son. In the third book the center is absolutely and without exception Sophia. In the fourth book the center of interest is the relation between Sophia and Constance, brought together again in their old age. The first and second and fourth books are laid in Bursley; the third in Paris. When one considers that each one of these four books is as long as many an ordinary novel, one is all the more impressed with the sense for dramatic composition displayed by this writer of chronicles in the manner of Dickens and Thackeray.

The great thing to note is that, instead of alternating the chronicles of Constance and Sophia throughout the second and third books, during the twenty-five years of their separation, Bennett had the inspiration to keep them absolutely distinct, following through first one and then the other without interruption.

But, some one will say, Bennett did this naturally and indeed inevitably, for the reason that the two sisters did not meet during all these years: it was not the author's technique but the nature of the material which determined this arrangement. The answer is that we can make no such artificial distinction between technique and subject-matter. The technique is, to be sure, the natural expression of the subject-matter favored by a given writer. But it is equally true that the choice of a certain type of subject-matter is determined by the technical preferences of the author. Or, better, the undifferentiated mass of human life arranges itself for different authors and for different schools according to certain typical patterns. What first impresses the reader of "The Old Wives' Tale" is the pattern of the lives of Constance and Sophia Baines, beginning and ending together, but in the long middle years flowing sharply apart; and one cannot question that this was a leading feature of Bennett's original artistic motive in writing their history.

That the separate following of Constance and Sophia

through the middle books of "The Old Wives' Tale" is more than a happy accident is made clear by the Clayhanger series. Here Bennett follows almost identically the same plan, and here there were actually several meetings of the characters concerned during the time that he keeps their stories separate and distinct. The first novel is "Clayhanger"—itself a longer book than the average—which covers the life of Edwin from 1872 to 1892, including his several meetings with Hilda. The second is "Hilda Lessways," covering her life through a part of the same period. In the third of the series, these two persons, now married, are carried along together like Constance and Sophia Baines in the fourth book of their chronicle.

The most remarkable feature of the author's technique in this series is that the meetings between Edwin and Hilda before their marriage are twice recounted at length, the first time from the point of view of Edwin in "Clayhanger," the second time from that of Hilda in "Hilda Lessways." Here again, in an extended chronicle, we have a striking instance of the dramatic principle of composition which prescribes the careful maintenance of a limited center of interest.

XXI

VARIATIONS: GALSWORTHY

ANOTHER English writer of the same period even more widely identified than Bennett with the sort of chronicle which is carried through a series of novels covering a long period of years is John Galsworthy. The six novels comprising "The Forsyte Saga" and "A Modern Comedy," together with the several short stories which link one novel with another, make up the most monumental example in English of that predilection for novels in series which has been a leading feature of the early twentieth century.

Other famous examples are: in French, Romain Rolland's "Jean Christophe" (1904–12), Marcel Proust's "A la Recherche du temps perdu" (1913–26; English translation under the general title "Remembrance of Things Past"), Roger Martin du Gard's "Les Thibault" (1922 ff.; English translation in three volumes beginning with "The Gray Notebook"); in Dutch, Louis Couperus's "Books of the Small Souls" (1901–1903); in Polish, Ladislas Reymont's "The Peasants" (English translation 1924–25); in Swedish, Selma Lagerlöf's "The Ring of the Löwenskölds" (1925–28); in Danish, Martin Andersen Nexö's "Pelle the Conqueror (1906–10) and his "Ditte" (1919–21); in Norwegian, Sigrid Undset's "Kristin Lavransdatter" (1920–22) and her later series beginning with "The Axe" and ending with "The Son Avenger" (1925–27); in Norwegian and English, O. E. Rölvaag's series beginning with "Giants in the Earth" and ending with "Their Father's God" (1924–31).

In England, besides the series of Bennett and Galsworthy, there have been the following: J. D. Beresford's "Jacob Stahl" (1911–15), Dorothy Richardson's "Pilgrimage," comprising nine novels between 1915 and 1927, Henry Handel Richardson's series entitled "The Fortunes of Richard Mahony" (1917 ff.), Ford Madox Ford's series of four novels beginning with "Some Do Not" (1924), and G. B. Stern's series beginning with "The Matriarch" (in England, "Tents of Israel," 1924). In America there have been Louis Bromfield's series beginning with "The Green Bay Tree" (1924) and ending with "A Good Woman" (1927), Edith Wharton's "Old New York" (1924) and the incompleted series by John Dos Passos (see Chapter XXXIX) and by T. S. Stribling, "The Forge" (1931) and "The Store" (1932).

Earlier examples of such novels in series dating from the 1890's are Huysmans' "Là-Bas," "En route," "La Cathédrale," and "L'Oblat," Pontoppidan's "Emmanuel," "The Promised Land," and "Dommens Dag," Sienkiwicz's "With Fire and Sword," "The Deluge," and "Pan Michael," and Fogazzaro's "The Patriot," "The Sinner," and "The Saint." And they all perhaps go back, in general scheme, to Balzac's Comédie Humaine (1829–47) and Zola's series of "Les Rougon-Macquart" (1871–93).

This whole subject has been studied by Miss Elizabeth Kerr in a master's dissertation, on file in the University of Minnesota library, entitled "The Sequence Novel: Fictional Method of a Scientific Age." Miss Kerr makes much of the fundamental unity of conception running through the various works of the series in the most characteristic of these products.

Another general feature of all these sequence novels is that, while they cover a long period of time and tend to include a large number of characters in the aggregate, each separate novel is limited in time, in the number of characters, and in the special dramatic issues involved; so that, just as each novel has its own title, it has generally its own distinct unity of design, and is capable of being read by itself and standing alone. And yet there is never any question about the intimate connection of each of these novels with all the rest in the series. There is very often one central character who is carried through the whole series and who most often carries with him a large number of the other people from book to book.

On the other hand, the separate titles and the completeness and self-sufficiency of each novel in the series distinguish them sharply enough from books like "Tom Jones," "Roderick Random," "Peregrine Pickle," and the three-decker English novels of the nineteenth century, in which, for the most part, the separate volumes are no more capable of standing alone than the separate instalments of a novel published serially.

It is quite likely that the exigencies of publishing and the conditions of the book market were in large part responsible for the formal self-sufficiency of these novels in series. They had to be made to stand each by itself, since the reading public could not be asked to wait several years for the completion of this year's story or go back before reading it to buy and read the story of several years ago.

But this purely practical consideration fell in, I think, with the taste of the times for stories dramatically limited according to the general formula of the well-made novel. The Georgian reader did not have the Victorian's tolerance for the Epilogue, such as we find it in George Eliot, for example, in which the author tells us briefly what happened to his characters during the twenty-five years following the fall of the curtain. The twentieth-century reader does not relish this sketchy messing about with future events; he does not care to be told just how each character received the due reward of his virtuous life. He likes his curtain neat and definitive. If there were further developments, that is another story, which may well be taken up in another book.

as Couperus takes up the sequel of "Small Souls" in "The Later Life" and the other novels of his tetralogy.

2

In the case of Galsworthy it is important to remember that when he wrote "The Man of Property" (published in 1906), he had not conceived the idea of the "Forsyte Saga" as a whole. This definitive study of the rich bourgeoisie of London was followed immediately by the "Country House" (1907), "Fraternity" (1908), and "The Patrician" (1911), studies of the squirearchy, the professional class, and the aristocracy, respectively, and making up altogether a kind of social survey of the well-to-do classes in England. At that period Galsworthy's idea seems to have been to make his study of English society *in extenso* rather than to specialize intensively in the manners and customs of the Forsytes. It was not till 1917, after he had published several other important novels, that appeared the short story "An Indian Summer of a Forsyte," which takes up the chronicle of Jolyon Forsyte and Irene; not until 1920 appeared the second novel of the series, "In Chancery"; and not till 1928 appeared "Swan Song," the sixth and last one of the series.

It would indeed have been impossible for Galsworthy to project in 1909 any of the novels beginning with the third. For they deal, among other things, with events in political history which were many years in the future; the action of "To Let" takes place in 1920, after the World War, that of "The Silver Spoon" in 1924–25 during the first Labor government, that of "Swan Song" in 1926 during the famous general strike.

The idea of continuing the chronicle of the Forsytes in the form of a family "saga" was an afterthought of Mr. Galsworthy; and this, for one thing, results in an even greater distinctness of the component parts than is the case with the sagas of Rolland, Proust, and Sigrid Undset. "The Man of Property" is as complete, independent, and well unified a novel as "Fraternity" or "The Country House"; and if the later novels of the series do imply the background of the earlier ones, it is none the less true that each is carefully devised to stand by itself.

This is, I think, more especially true of "In Chancery" and "To Let." In the second series, "A Modern Comedy," one feels that Mr. Galsworthy is carried forward more by the momentum already acquired than by any powerful creative impulse; each book follows immediately on the year in which the action is placed, as if the author were somewhat hastily and perfunctorily keeping his chronicle up to date. One grows rather tired of the monotonous reappearances of Soames in his double rôle of anxious financier and doting father. There is some effort to give distinctness to each book by varying the public interests of Fleur's husband, Michael Mont, and by certain episodes in the private life of Fleur. But on the whole, these episodes lack definition, and one's final impression of the series is a sense of indeterminateness greatly in contrast with the sharpness of outline which characterizes the earlier novels. It is unmistakably the earlier series which gives Mr. Galsworthy his place among novelists of distinction.

"The Man of Property" is a study of the possessive spirit as it affects the lives and manners of a typical English family engaged in big business and finance. Here and in the later novels of the series this spirit of possession is set in opposition to a Beauty which the Forsytes do not take into account in their philosophy, but which in spite of them comes in to upset their plans and disturb their emotional life. In "The Man of Property" this opposition is dramatized in the relations of Soames Forsyte, the solicitor, and his wife Irene. They were married without love, on the explicit understanding that if they did not hit it off he was not to hold her bound by the marriage tie. But when, in the course of the story, Irene declares that such a condition exists and demands her freedom, Soames repudiates the agreement and holds her bound. It is not in him to relinquish what is, for him, only another form of that most precious of all things, property.

The matter is brought to a head by the love which springs up between Irene and Soames's architect, Bosinney. This young artist is, like Irene, unaffected by the Forsyte scale of values. He has been engaged by Soames to build their new house at Robin Hill. He is a man of original imagination and taste and is carried away by his desire to make the new house a thing of unusual beauty, so that he considerably exceeds the amount agreed on with Soames for the cost of the building. At the opening of the story he is engaged to marry June, the daughter of Soames's cousin, Jolyon Forsyte, but the intimacy which develops with Irene in their consultations over the house leads to their falling in love. Soames would doubtless have met the extra cost of the house with no more than a little grumbling if it had not been for the stealing of his wife's affections, but, stung in the quick by this invasion of his property rights, he brings suit against Bosinney, determined to ruin him financially.

Of the concluding events of the drama I will mention only the death of Bosinney, run down by a bus while wandering distracted in the London fog. The story all centers around the building of the new house at Robin Hill and the growing realization by the Forsytes of the existence of a passion with which they are unable to cope; the action takes place from June 1886 to December 1887, covering roughly the period during which the house is building.

"In Chancery" takes up the story of Soames and Irene in the years 1899–1901. They have long been living separate but not divorced. Soames cannot realize the definitiveness with which Irene has turned against him. He makes a crude effort to win her back, and, that failing, he invokes the machinery of the law to divorce her, so that he may marry again and have issue. He succeeds in putting her in the wrong by methods which are a biting satire on the English divorce laws of the time; but in the course of doing so he raises up a champion for Irene in the person of his cousin Jolyon, June's father. This member of the Forsyte clan, now a widower, is the one who holds their philistine philosophy in its least pure form. His sensibilities are outraged by Soames's brutal persecution of Irene; he comes to admire her fineness of nature; and love springs up between them. So that the jealous Soames has the misery of seeing his wife in love with that one of all his relatives with whom he has least in common. The dramatic character of this story is most simply indicated by the brief formulation: Soames by insisting on his right of property in his wife's affections, succeeds merely in driving her into the arms of Jolyon.

In "To Let," while Soames and Irene and Jolyon are still principal characters, the story is better defined as the drama of their children. Fleur, Soames's daughter by his second wife, and Jon, the son of Irene and Jolyon, accidentally meeting in the year 1920, fall in love without knowing anything of the history of the parents. But the bitter heritage is one they cannot throw off, and in spite of their love, and of Fleur's determination not to let any old history come between them, it is impossible for Jon to marry so much against the feeling of his father and mother. The dramatic character of this story is very simply formulated: the ugly working of the sense of property in one generation brings about the grievous frustration of love in the following generation.

It will be evident that each one of the novels which make up "The Forsyte Saga" is distinct and independent and sharply defined in its lines of action. This does not mean that Galsworthy exhibits the dramatic tendencies of the well-made novel in anything like their completeness. His attitude toward the Forsyte clan is that of a sociologist or anthropologist making a study of the manners of some primitive people. Author and interpreter, he is never tired of pointing out the characteristic manifestations of the "possessive spirit" and indicating how typical they are of the British people or of human kind in general.

One of his main intentions is to illustrate the great diversity of types included under the head of Forsytism, and the many modifications which come about with the passage of time. Especially in "The Man of Property" his scheme implies the featuring of a large number of different members of the Forsyte family in their several homes, who, one after the other, take the center of the stage for the moment. Mr. Galsworthy never at any period of his writing had a marked predilection for continuities of action involving a single person or group which tend to build up scenes like those on the stage.

But with all these abatements there is much of the dramatic in the general composition of his narratives, as one might expect from an author who is so famous as a writer of plays. Through all the comings and goings of the Forsytes in "The Man of Property" one never forgets the central theme of Soames's relations to his wife. The various branches of the Forsyte family are all following with extreme interest the developments at Robin Hill. They are all fascinated and troubled by the exotic charm of Irene, fascinated and outraged by the strange incomprehensible phenomenon of Bosinney; and from their several strongholds they are watching the growth of that storm-cloud on the horizon which threatens the smug security of their order.

It has often been pointed out what a peculiar method Galsworthy employs in his treatment of Irene and Bosinney, though this is essentially the same method that Mrs. Wharton follows with regard to the Countess Olenska in "The Age of Innocence." These characters, who are meant to be the most sympathetic to the reader, are never presented directly but always through the eyes of the Forsytes. As Mr. Leon Schalit points out:

> In the whole "Saga," only Irene and Bosinney, the two lovers, remain opaque. This is clearly deliberate . . . The whole Irene-Bosinney love affair is hinted at, rather than related. . . . Instead of directly describing the moods of the two lovers he will get them by showing the thoughts and feelings aroused in the observer by the sight of the lovers.

Mr. Galsworthy has thus managed a sort of reversal of the method of the restricted point of view very suitable to his intention in this book. Instead of following the story through the eyes of the two most sympathetic characters, the lovers, he follows it through the myriad eyes of the philistines, all centered upon the two mysterious and disturbing persons. It is an excellent device for unifying the diverse material and giving it pattern. And it was probably the best possible method for making his study of the natural history of the Forsytes.

In the two later volumes the pattern is greatly simplified by virtue of the fact that he has set the Forsytes so firmly on their feet in "The Man of Property" and has no further need for characterizing them in detail. But here again we have to deal with the principle of contrast which, as Mr. Schalit has pointed out, is a leading compositional device in Galsworthy. Contrast and, we may add, correspondence or parallelism of themes, repetition of themes, and the use of symbolic themes. Winifred's reluctance to divorce Monty, her Forsyte instinct for holding on to him as to something that is hers, is the shadow of Soames's feeling about Irene, and her suit for divorce is the parallel of Soames's. Jolly and Val reproduce two peculiar blends of Forsyte and non-Forsyte as well as repeating the Soames-

Jolyon feud. And of course in the passage from Soames to Jolyon, from Jolyon to Soames as center of interest, in the passage from the Soames-Irene to the Soames-Annette relation, the principle of contrast is being followed.

This is the clue to the unity of effect of the whole. The alternation is not between blocks of diverse characters carrying on diverse action in a complicated intrigue, as in Dickens, but between finely contrasted or graded specimens of true Forsyte, mongrel Forsyte, and non-Forsyte humanity, considered always by reference to the Forsyte view of life.

And then, finally, the Forsyte view of life is symbolized in public affairs by the Boer War, in which the characters take such a vivid interest. The British attitude toward the Boers is like that taken by the Forsytes toward private property, and the principle of suzerainty invoked to justify the war in South Africa is the same as that invoked by Soames in his relations with Irene.

The lines of "To Let" are even simpler than those of "In Chancery"; but here too there is a considerable use of contrast and parallelism. Altogether, throughout the entire series of Forsyte novels, as well as in Galsworthy's other work, there is much cunning artistry lavished upon the elaborate system of cross-reference and implication. And much could be said of the deftness and refinement of touch displayed by Mr. Galsworthy in the development of his method.

What is probably more urgent, however, is to signalize the relative want of force, depth, and solidity in his effects when brought into comparison with the greatest of his contemporaries, like Thomas Mann, Marcel Proust, Sigrid Undset, or with such of his predecessors as Fielding, Tolstoy, George Eliot, Zola, or Thomas Hardy. While the work of these men gives the effect of painting in oils, rich, deep, and luminous, the effect of Galsworthy is rather that of water-colors, at its best full of life, charm, and delicacy, at its worst thin, sketchy, and superficial. In the last analysis, of course, these differences must be traced to unlikeness of temperament and imaginative power. But it is interesting to speculate on features of technique which go along with such variations in effect.

3

There is one rather mechanical aspect of technique which may have something to do with the relative want of solidity in Galsworthy's effects. And this is most conveniently studied in connection with his handling of the chapter divisions.

In Tolstoy, as we have seen, the chapters are very short and each one is generally confined to a single occasion and to one center of interest; often the same occasion and the same center of interest is continued through a considerable number of chapters, with corresponding gain in momentum. In George Eliot the chapters are very much longer and confined to a single occasion and a single center of interest; often a considerable number of chapters is confined to the closely related events of one day. In "Adam Bede" the first sixteen chapters (261 pages in my edition) are devoted to the events of four successive days.

In Galsworthy the chapters are for the most part quite short; and while they are generally confined to the events of a single day, they show a decided tendency to pass from one center of interest to another and from one place to another. There is almost never in Galsworthy any considerable number of pages devoted to a single scene, in one place, with the same characters participating throughout. And almost never does he follow the same character straight through a long succession of chapters or pages.

There is nothing in all Galsworthy to compare for steadiness of view on a single character with the chapter in "Buddenbrooks" (XI, ii) ending, "This was one day in the life of little Johann," or that section of "The Magic Mountain" which recounts the experience of Hans Castorp lost in the snow. There is nothing comparable, in the way of solid and leisurely development of a situation, to the opening chapters of "The Return of the Native" or of "Adam Bede." There are no single chapters in Galsworthy comparable for handling, with authority and *in extenso,* a single occasion involving a considerable number of persons, with any one of a dozen chapters in Zola's "Nana," or those in "L'Assommoir" presenting the fight at the *lavoir,* or the wedding of Gervaise, or the night when she takes to the streets. There is no series of chapters comparable for continuity of tragic interest with those in "Adam Bede" recounting Hetty's "Journey in Hope" and her "Journey in Despair," or those following on the wedding of Tess Durbeyfield, or those leading to the death of Eustacia Vye and Wildeve. There is no situation so fully rendered and with such authority of realistic art as that of Sophia Baines on the night of the public execution at Auxerre, or that of Emma Bovary on the last day of her life.

The difference is partly one of emotional force. Galsworthy simply has not the power of the great writers to present in all their poignancy the supreme moments of human passion and suffering. That English reserve and detachment which have sometimes been represented as artistic merits in him are also the gage of his low temperature emotionally. He is a graceful swimmer near the shores of human feeling, but he never ventures into the deep waters. His characters suffer, like well-bred people, from sentimental deprivations which are real enough in their way. But they remain well bred in the very core of their being; they suffer the mild pains of the well-to-do. They do not seem to have come up against the stony walls which break the hearts of common people. They do not feel the pinch of life as Edwin Clayhanger feels it, or Esther Waters, or Michael Henchard, or Kristin Lavransdatter.

Nor is one conscious in Galsworthy of the sheer weight of realistic observation which in the greater writers is one measure of their intellectual stature. He does not look at anything so hard and long as Thomas Mann has looked at disease, for example, in that chapter of "Buddenbrooks" beginning, "Cases of typhoid fever take the following course," or as Bennett looked at the old printing-machine in "Clayhanger," let alone the way in which Hardy looked at Egdon Heath or in which Balzac regarded the Maison Vauquer in "Le Père Goriot."

He does describe in considerable detail the interiors of various Forsyte houses, with much aptness of phrase and deftness of draftsmanship. But somehow one does not have the sense of three dimensions which similar descriptions give one in Balzac, Hardy, or Bennett. And while he has a good deal to *say* of the representative character of his settings, they do not carry with them the intellectual overtones of the great masters. No physical object in Galsworthy stands so unmistakably for symbol and fact at one and the same time as Maggie's slop-pail in "The Old Wives' Tale."

Galsworthy does not have in high degree that faculty to make one *see* which indicates in an author intenseness of visual imagination. No scene in his work is so vividly illuminated as that moonlight scene in the Adirondack wilderness in "The Master of Ballantrae" in which the Indian fakir exhumes the body of the buried master. No spot of earth is so magically set before us as the stretch of road to Casterbridge followed by Fanny Robin on her way to the poor-house, or the interior of Captain Anthony's cabin in "Chance." Galsworthy has none of that power, possessed by Hardy and Dickens and Victor Hugo, of following with intent curiosity the movements of a figure seen in a landscape. He has not the faculty of bringing all the powers of vision to a focus upon some single spot or figure thus made to absorb the entire imaginative energies of the reader.

Now, genius is a mystery. These various faculties—emotional, intellectual, imaginative—are not to be reduced to the mechanical terms of technique. But there is nevertheless some relation between creative genius and the methods which it follows to attain its ends. And Galsworthy's comparative want of force is associated with his inability to regard any person, place, or object steadily for any length of time.

Probably the longest series of chapters in any of his books confined to the events of a single day is found in Part II of "The White Monkey," chapters I–VII (pp. 115–184). But here at once one remarks that with virtually every chapter there is a change of center. The first chapter is Soames's, the second Victorine's, the third Michael's, the fourth and fifth Fleur's, the sixth Michael's again, and the seventh Victorine's. And not merely that. But within the several chapters there is a constant change of scene as the person concerned passes from one place to another and is engaged with different people. In the first chapter Soames takes part in four distinct scenes—with Annette at Mapledurham, with strangers in the railway carriage going up to London, with his man Gradman in the office of his law firm, and in the Board Room of a joint-stock company with the chairman of the board.

This is perfectly typical of Galsworthy's procedure. His characters never can stay in any one place or in the presence of one group of people. They are forever scurrying restlessly about like ants. This makes impossible anything like a really constituted and well-developed scene. And since he is forever passing from one character to another, there can be nothing like that continuous following of a single character which we have throughout "Clayhanger" or the entire third book of "The Old Wives' Tale."

Very often, moreover, it is in midstream—within the chapter—that he chooses to change horses. This is particularly true in "The Man of Property," which remains, in spite of everything, probably the most important of his novels. Over and over, in individual chapters, no sooner is our sympathetic interest engaged with one character than we are asked to transfer it to another, with necessarily a loss in emotional force. Consider for example Chapter XI, entitled "June's Treat." It begins with an account of a dinner at Soames's house, including Soames, Irene, Bosinney, and June, the dialogue rendered objectively from the point of view of an imaginary observer. There follows an account from June's point of view of her attending the theater with Bosinney and the unaccountable coldness of her fiancé, culminating in his refusal to take her on Sunday to see the new house. The reader is ready to give his whole heart to June in this pitiful situation, when suddenly the author turns from her and Bosinney to persons so entirely strange to us that it is with a great effort that we can place them at all. We read of June:

> The house had been mercifully darkened for a crisis, and no one could see her trouble. Yet in this world of Forsytes let no man think himself immune from observation. In the third row behind, Euphemia, Nicholas's second daughter, with her married sister, Mrs. Tweetyman, were watching. They reported at Timothy's, how they had seen June and her fiancé at the theatre.

There follows half a page of the conversation of these ladies, presumably on the following day. We then come back to June and follow her in her disconsolate return to her grandfather's house. Then more than a page is devoted to Old Jolyon's reflections. And the chapter ends with June. "And upstairs in her room June sat at her open window where the spring wind came, after its revel across the park, to cool her hot cheeks and burn her heart."

This may be a convenient way to get the story told and to touch on the wide range of persons and interests involved. But it is obviously impossible on any such system to make a really deep impression on either the sensibilities or the imagination of the reader. (Which may indeed be one reason for the great popularity of Galsworthy with readers who wish to spare their sensibilities.) It is an exceptional chapter in "The Man of Property" in which there is not one or more such excursion away from the person and place that may be supposed to interest us most deeply, into the lives and thoughts of others on quite other occasions. And even when we remain technically within one and the same scene throughout the chapter, there is often so constant a shift from objective to subjective, from one person to another as the center of observation, or from the thoughts of one person to those of another, that our interest and sympathy are distributed and dissipated as in some of the less successful panoramic tableaux of Hogarth.

Thus Galsworthy's fictions are made up, not of fairly large units of uniform narrative character, as is the case with Dickens, Eliot, Flaubert, Tolstoy, or any of the most powerful of the old masters, but of innumerable small bits of fragments assembled like the bits of colored glass in Gothic windows. This method has proved a very successful one for giving a general impression of the Forsyte clan in all its diversity, and it has evoked no protest from readers who like a story that moves forward with liveliness and sparkle. Mr. Galsworthy has had as many and as enthusiastic readers as any novelist of equal distinction in our time. But I cannot but think that this scrappy and facile method of composition is the counterpart of a certain want of depth and vigor of conception, a certain languid paleness of temperament reflected from the author upon his characters, so that they constantly make one think of the mannequins displayed in the show-windows of smart department-stores.

I find myself drawn in spite of myself to breathe the word "sentimentalism" in this connection. I do not question the honesty and fineness of spirit of this writer, nor the truthfulness of his portraiture so far as it goes. But it does not go very far. It does not go very deep. It stays too consistently within the range of view of nice people. There is a kind of sentimentalism which results from simple want of intellectual thoroughness, from an imperfect analysis of the motives and forces involved in human action. And this is the sort one detects in the conception of Galsworthy's Irene. He certainly has a deft and facile brush stroke, but one wonders whether his colors are such as will stand against the corrosive action of time.

XXII

VARIATIONS: SIGRID UNDSET

THE objection to Galsworthy's method is not simply that his narratives are built up of many small units rather than of massive scenes. This is, to a considerable extent, the system of Arnold Bennett, of Knut Hamsun, Sinclair Lewis, and many other powerful contemporary novelists. But generally speaking, in the authors mentioned, there is some principle of composition which saves them from that scrappiness of effect which we have observed in Galsworthy. Most often it is the assemblage of the small narrative units around a single center of interest over long stretches, so that each new fragment, each new circumstance adds its increment of power and significance.

The novels of Willa Cather have almost always a single center of interest. In "A Lost Lady" (1923), which is probably, all things considered, her best piece of work, it is that Mrs. Forrester whose charm and weakness are both portrayed with so much humanness and delicacy of touch. There is also young Niel Herbert, through whose eyes, for the most part, this rare creature is shown. It is he who makes clear to us the "value" for Mrs. Forrester's character of her railroad-builder husband—her appreciation of him, her loyalty to him. "That, he felt, was quality; something that could never become worn or shabby; steel of Damascus." And it is in the mirror of Niel's disillusionment that we trace the growing shoddiness of her character as the love of pleasure more and more takes the place of what for Niel was the ideal element in her nature. Thus the book is doubly unified—through the subject itself, and through the extra provision of an instrument within the story for focusing the subject.

I do not mean for a moment to suggest a parity between the delicate and shallow pencilings of Miss Cather and the really serious social studies of Mr. Galsworthy. Even Mr. Galsworthy would hardly have been content with the tenuous and sketchy motivation of Niel Herbert. He is a happy device, but hardly more than a device. Miss Cather's undertakings are never so difficult as Galsworthy's, and her achievements are relatively easy ones. Still, she is an artist of distinction within her narrow range; and the neat composition of books like "A Lost Lady" and "The Professor's House" (1925) will serve to illustrate our present point.

The point is better made, however, by bringing into the comparison an artist of Mr. Galsworthy's own caliber, whose general subject is virtually the same—philistinism in contemporary life. Mr. Lewis may not write, typically, with the sympathetic insight into the sentiments of nice people, nor with the moderation and restraint, of Mr. Galsworthy. He altogether eschews the mild elegancies and prettinesses of the English writer. His satire is of a drier, purer brand. But for that very reason his art is more sharp-edged; his effects stand out in bolder relief.

His "Babbitt" (1922) is at least as significant a social document as "The Man of Property," and at least as "real." On the side of composition it bears some resemblance to Mr. Galsworthy's work, in that the dramatic or scenical method has been put aside for what we might call the incremental. It is a portrait of a typical philistine business man, built up with many little strokes of the brush. What gives it its massive power is, for one thing, the almost unbroken maintenance of George F. Babbitt as the center of action and point of reference. Almost nothing happens in the absence of Babbitt. Almost nothing is related of which he is not at least a witness, whether or not realizing the full implications of what he sees. So that the thing grows steadily in force and momentum.

There is even less plot than in Galsworthy. In place of plot, we have a significant evolution in the attitude of Babbitt toward the social order of which he forms a part. There is a long block of chapters, say from XII to XXII, which trace his steady rise to popularity and a kind of affluence through his shrewd and energetic playing of the game—subscribing heartily to all the loud vulgarities, the social superstitions and hypocrisies which constitute the creed of his class. But there is something in Babbitt which makes him restless under the oppression of this philistinism. It is partly conscience and open-mindedness; it is partly the dreariness of his home life and the desire of the "old Adam" in him to have his fling. So that we may distinguish another long block of chapters, XXIII to XXXIV, which trace Babbitt's revolt. He is of course not strong enough to carry through his rebellion against the organized and dominant forces of the Boosters' Club and the Good Citizens' League. He finds that his wife means more to him than the furtive pleasures of Bohemia. And the story ends with a sort of cringing submission to an order of things which is too strong for him.

It is this continuity of theme and issue which, taken together with the single center of interest and the consistency of tone, give to "Babbitt" its bold and simple outlines—its effect of composition. Under the head of continuity, it should be remarked, further, that Mr. Lewis is capable of devoting one quarter of the whole book, the first seven chapters, to a single typical day in the life of his central character—something unparalleled, so far as I know, in the work of Galsworthy.

It may of course be urged, on the other hand, that Lewis's work lacks the live effect given by the variation of coloring, the nuances of Galsworthy's method. And I do not pretend that Lewis's is the ideal way of presenting human nature; that it has, for example, the depth and intimacy of Thomas Mann or Emile Zola. There is too often the note of burlesque. There is too much generalizing of the subject by the author. The characters and incidents too often have the effect of cleverly chosen documents or exhibits. One feels this most strongly perhaps in "Arrowsmith" (1925), where the author's scorn for ballyhoo in science and his deep-felt admiration for the true scientist call for a treatment less "smart" and topical, and more in the key of imaginative writing.

But one cannot deny the truth, the representative importance, of these documents; nor can one deny Mr. Lewis's skill in arranging his material so as to have the fullest effect in the forum of public opinion.

2

Probably the best example we can find of positive genius in handling this manner of narrative is Sigrid Undset. Her work is as fine an instance as we can cite of a feature of story-telling technique so characteristic of our time that it is worth a special chapter. It is a technique which corresponds to a special way of regarding life. The story-teller is inclined to conceive of life as made up not of a few broad and massive movements, culminating in a limited number of critical scenes, but rather of an infinite succession of small waves breaking on the shore of human experience and little by little modifying its shape and aspect. And there is a corresponding disposition to a finer modeling of the outlines. In this technique the ordinary chapter is a composite arrangement of many small bits of story. The action is slow; and while the plot may be there, the emphasis is rather on the feel and texture of life under certain conditions.

In "Kristin Lavransdatter" (1920–22) there is an epic breadth of movement, an encyclopedic inclusiveness of family life in its broader aspects, extending to a comprehensive survey of a whole social order. There is no want of distinctness of outline and intention; at times the effect is sharply dramatic, with a worked-up suspense over the outcome of matters of life and death. But what is most remarkable in the art of Sigrid Undset is not the adequacy and boldness of the culminating dramatic scenes but the fine modeling of those parts that make the bulk of the narrative, in which is built up little by little the domestic situation of Kristin—the infinite detail and variety of documentation, the minute intimacy and concreteness of the rapidly succeeding pictures of her life as mother and wife and mistress of the house. Very well suited to the author's intention is the use of rather long chapters divided into many smaller sections separated by double spacing.

Thus in the opening chapter of "The Mistress of Husaby" (the second book of the trilogy), we first see Kristin arriving by boat at the landing-place at Birgsi, pale and woebegone with the double strain of pregnancy and travel by sea, and then the following morning met by Erlend's friends and trying to disguise her illness and low spirits. In the second section we see her riding across the hillside toward her husband's home, escorted by a troop of lively young men. Then we follow her into the church, and into the house where she is to be mistress. The fourth section shows her three days later, after the departure of the guests, reviewing her impressions of the new household, the ill husbandry that prevails there, and the contrast with her father's well-regulated establishment. In the following section this theme is made dramatic in a conversation with her husband's kinsman Ulf. There follows a section devoted to further specification of the arrangement and conduct of the house. Then come the more dramatic sections: that in which Erlend accidentally makes the discovery that Kristin is pregnant and angers her by showing himself more concerned at the scandal than happy in the prospect of their having a child; and those in which he takes her to visit a neighboring estate, and they quarrel on the way, ending with their reconciliation and companionable return home.

Thus, in twelve separate sections, are briefly touched perhaps a score of distinct moments in the early married life of these passionate lovers—some of them distributed over several weeks, and others following rapidly upon one another in the course of one day's horseback excursion—which develop scenically the strained emotional situation that is to characterize their whole life together and gradually disclose the first rift in their happiness. Each distinct picture drives in its little golden nail, as James would say, and the drama grows in intensity and depth of significance with every light deft touch of the artist's brush.

Some attention should be given to the practice of punctuating the narrative by double spacing between the sections. Such punctuation, so important in this kind of composition, is entirely wanting in Galsworthy. And this fact sets him apart from the large number of novelists of our time who have made use of it.

There are several ways of indicating the sections of which a chapter is made up, with the passing from one occasion or one point of view to another. The double-spacing regularly used by Sigrid Undset is a more occasional feature of Hamsun and Edith Wharton, of Louis Bromfield ("Early Autumn"), Sherwood Anderson ("Many Marriages"), Willa Cather, and many other contemporary writers. In Mr. Anderson's "Dark Laughter" a line of dots serves the same purpose; in Aldous Huxley's "Point Counter Point" it is a line of asterisks. Where the division into sections is more regular, as in Bennett, Lewis, Rölvaag, Bromfield ("Twenty-Four Hours"), the common device is to divide the chapter into sections indicated by roman or arabic numerals. Writers who use this method are likely to be such as deal in the "extravert" type of characters, characters who live greatly in the fact; and each section brings its neat and definite increment of objective incident or drama.

Now, such indications of separateness are essentially devices for punctuation, intended for the greater convenience of the reader. And if we find the work of Marcel Proust, for example, difficult reading, one obvious reason is that, in a narrative very little brightened and diversified by dialogue, he has made the least possible use of paragraph division, lines of dots, double spacing, or any other major mark of punctuation; and the result is a certain Teutonic solidity of page after page of unbroken prose, which frightens the most enterprising reader.

But the matter goes deeper than that. The disposition to take advantage of these aids to clearness is indicative of a certain fastidiousness of taste which makes for neatness and order; it often implies a superior concern for the niceties of classification and arrangement, and, further still, a sensibility to the attraction of the perfectly finished phrase. The points of contact between the several parts of the narrative are like the points of contact between musical phrases; and the writer concerned to indicate clearly where they fall has much in common with the musician concerned to observe with preciseness the pauses in a piece of music and to render with exact finish the effects of staccato and legato. The very fact of using the devices that indicate the points of contact and transition tends to make the writer more sensitive to the strategic values of these points in the narrative. In order that the several moments shall produce the surest effects in combination, it is important that each one should infallibly produce its own particular effect with distinctness and the exact degree of emphasis assigned to it.

The point of highest strategic importance in the section is likely to be the end. What is said there may be very quietly said; its deeper significance may be implicit rather than explicit; but we know how often, in books as in life, the most significant things appear thus disguised and unstressed. In life there are many little things that give one a clue to the importance of remarks of most demure aspect: something in the inflection of the voice, an instant's hesitation, a slight gesture, the sentence left unfinished.

Many skilful novelists, especially among the French, make frequent use of the line of dots following a statement to indicate a pause. And writers like Sigrid Undset are well aware of the value of double-spacing. It is instinctively accompanied on the reader's part by however brief a pause for reflection, and so the author does well to place at the end some word which he would like to have sink into the reader's consciousness.

There is, moreover, an esthetic gain in the intimation given by the slight break in the text that one thing is now complete and another is beginning. However closely the two moments are related, they are yet distinct, and with this slight pause we have the impression of starting at a later point, with the cumulative effect of one thing added to another. Time itself flows in to give an air of finality to the past experience. And still further, this little device may lend a special flexibility and mobility to the narrative. With the intimation given by the break, the author may often dispense with an elaborate transitional phrase, and, by the same stroke, with some generalizing statement that would water down the concreteness of his pictured story. And so the action moves forward with crispness and sparkle, and with ever accelerated motion.

No sufficient illustration of these effects can be given without more extensive quotation and more detailed comment than is here possible. Instead, something may be said of the breadth in general compositional scheme made possible by this technique. Many an exquisite detail may be worked in which would perforce be excluded from a chapter designed to trace the broad unbroken line of a single dramatic scene. There is here room for many a circumstance which might, at first blush, seem irrelevant, but which is full of subtle overtones, establishing harmonic relations of the rarest beauty, and which in the end falls into place with great precision in the larger compositional effect.

Such, in "The Cross," is a tiny section included in the chapter which presents the misery of Simon after his breach with Erlend, at a time when he has become acutely conscious of his unabated love for Kristin. He has been musing on his own life, the child he has had by Halfrid, and how his life might have been altered if that child had lived. In that case he would not have busied himself so in saving the life of Erlend, and Kristin might have been sitting now at Jörundgaard, a widow . . . "And he himself going about, maybe, rueing that he was a wedded man! There was naught so witless but that he could believe it of himself now . . ." Then follows the section in which he has set out in the wet spring snow, with the birds, toward evening, starting to pipe and trill in the woody thickets.

> As a cut in the skin bursts open again at a hasty movement, a chance memory gave him pain . . . Not many days ago, at his Easter feast, they—a whole troop of them—had stood about, basking in the midday sun. High above them, in a birch-tree, sat a robin, piping out into the warm blue air. Geirmund came round the house corner, limping, dragging himself along on his staff, with one hand on his eldest son's shoulder. He looked up, stopped, and mimicked the bird. The boy, too, pursed his mouth and whistled. They could copy well-nigh every bird note. Kristin stood a little way off, amidst of some other women. Her smile was so fair as she listened . . .

And that is all. The intention is clear enough. The author, at this point, wishes to remind us of the acuteness and the ideal quality of Simon's love. She does not wish to tell us of it in bald and general terms, nor to bear down upon it with any but the lightest stress. And she thinks of this beautiful way of conveying to us the impression desired, quite incidentally, in the form of a vivid remembered picture naturally suggested by the aspect of the country as Simon rides on his way. It is too slight a touch to be admitted in a narrative conceived in strictly dramatic terms, but one which we could hardly spare.

And finally, before leaving the matter, we should note the contribution of this technique of chapter-division to the emotion of time that is so beautiful a feature of the chronicle as a whole. This is felt by the reader more and more strongly with the passing of the years over the head of Kristin, with the inevitable awesome procession of events that make of her a lover, a married woman, a mother many times over—the tragic alienation from her husband, the growing up of her children and determination of their fates, the death one after another of her dearest ones, and her gradual withdrawal from the worldly life. The reader has a sense of vast stretches crowded with milestones deeply scored with human suffering and labor.

Such would be the effect of the skilful telling of this story according to any technical system, from the mere force of the saga itself. But there is a more immediate and intimate evocation of this time-sense all along the way, which arises from the division of the narrative into its minor units of human experience. With the passage from one section to another, with its new increment of incident and passion, we seem to hear the very ticking of the clock, the ceaseless quiet swing of the pendulum that measures off the lives of men and weaves like a shuttle the web of time and destiny.

XXIII

THE UNITIES

Sigrid Undset has taken us a long way from the well-made novel with its special dramatic ideals. Her books are distinctly of the chronicle or biographical type, with the long lapse of years, and do not admit of that neatly limited dramatic issue which we have found in James and his ilk. Her panoramic inclusiveness has room for considerable historical episodes and a very large number of characters. And while the greater part of the narrative is presented from the point of view of Kristin, there is nothing like the rigorous limitation of view observed by James and many of his followers.

Coming back to these matters of limitation, we cannot but observe the growing tendency in the last thirty years to a narrower and narrower observance of the "unities" of time and place in the novel. In the Forsyte series of novels, the limitation of time grows with the years, as if Galsworthy were coming more and more under the domination of this fashionable tendency. While "The Man of Property" (1906) covers a year and a half in all, and "In Chancery" (1920) as much as two years, "To Let" (1921) is confined to the period from May to October of one year, and each one of the later books of the series is similarly confined to the period from spring to autumn or from autumn to spring. It should, however, be observed that already in "The Country House" (1907), Galsworthy had limited his time still more strictly, the whole action taking place between the twenty-eighth of April and the third of the following June, or slightly over one month.

Many of the novels of Hergesheimer are limited to a period shorter than the average in Galsworthy: "Java Head" (1919) three summer months; "Cytherea" (1922) and "The Bright Shawl" (1922)—within the framework supplied by the memories of the elderly gentleman—rather less. In Hemingway's "The Sun Also Rises" (1926) the period is reduced to two months; in Huxley's "Antic Hay" (1923) to a month or so, and in his "Point Counter Point" (1928) to a little over a month, if I reckon correctly. Ethel Sidgwick's "Le Gentleman" (1911) passes between some time in June and July 14. Norman Douglas's "South Wind" (1917) brings us down to somewhat less than two weeks, while the sirocco blows, and Phil Stong's "State Fair" (1932) to a little more than a week. Frank Swinnerton's "Nocturne" (1917) offers a novel in which the entire action is confined to the events of a single night, thus anticipating Joyce's performance in "Ulysses" (1922).

"Ulysses," though a most unusually long book, is all confined to the events of twenty-four hours, and has presumably influenced the practice of many novelists. Mr. Bromfield advertises this aspect of technique in the very title of his "Twenty-Four Hours" (1930). Virginia Woolf in "Mrs. Dalloway" (1925) follows Joyce, among other things, by confining the action to less than a twenty-four-hour day.

Rex Stout, in "How Like a God" (1929), while he includes a considerable history in the retrospective musings of his central character, yet limits in a particularly curious way the occasion on which all these musings take place. The man is climbing the stairs to an apartment on an upper floor. The stages of his ascent are indicated by passages in italics at the head of each of the sixteen chapters, with what happens on his arrival briefly disposed of at the end of the sixteenth. The body of each chapter consists of that part of his history reviewed during a small stage in his ascent. Thus the whole of the story passes through his mind in the brief time required to climb these stairs. It is a very interesting technical performance, and illustrates the culmination of several tendencies in current novel-writing. There is first the tendency to tell the story backward, as so often in Conrad, as in Sherwood Anderson's "Many Marriages" (1923) and "Dark Laughter" (1925).

The looping backward from a constituted present, again, generally accompanies the tendency to present the story through retrospection on the part of one of the characters. There is much of this in Joyce, in Virginia Woolf. In Miss Cather's "The Professor's House" Professor St. Peter, caught in the web of domestic commonplace and of academic routine, lets his mind dwell frequently upon his childhood and other more romantic periods in his life. The most colorful circumstance of all was his acquaintance with Tom Outland, inventor and amateur archæologist; and it is his retrospective musings on Tom Outland which lead to the introduction of the young man's diary, giving an account of his discovery of a lost Mexican pueblo on the top of a desert mesa. This constitutes the second of the three books into which the novel is divided. It crosses the otherwise somewhat drab story with its band of vivid color, making of the whole a composition of considerable charm. Moreover, the way it is introduced enables the author to keep her story proper within the orthodox limits—since Richardson's "Clarissa Harlowe"—of twelve calendar months, and to give to the whole an air of compactness and of current reality.

Miss Cather is not so successful in her evocations of the past in "Shadows on the Rock" (1931). There is here a very large amount of biographical and historical information to be conveyed, and it is conveyed not so much through retrospection on the part of the characters as through straight exposition by the author. "Shadows on the Rock," however, belongs to the special genre of historical novels, and is not to be judged by the ordinary standards of novel-writing. It is the almost unique distinction of Sigrid Undset that she is able to give to remote historical events the sort of reality that we associate with contemporary life. If Elizabeth Madox Roberts has been able, in a lesser way, to do something of this kind in "The Great Meadow" (1930), that must be judged again as a very special achievement.

In "Dark Laughter" virtually the whole story is presented through the musing reminiscences of Bruce Dudley and Aline; in "Many Marriages" a great part is presented in this way and still more through the account of his life given by the father to his daughter, all on the night when the story comes to its crisis. This one night occupies three fourths of the whole book, and the action of the rest covers only a few weeks' time, so that "Many Marriages" is another striking example of limitation in time. In all these books the tendency is to make the dramatic present—the here-and-now—which is the culminating moment of the story—a sort of framework for the earlier stages, given in retrospection. And the most formal and deliberate example of this technique is "How Like a God."

Another curious example of a similar technique is Christopher Morley's fanciful invention "Thunder on the Left" (1925). The framework of this story is a children's birthday party at a seaside resort. In the course of the party one of the children makes a wish before blowing out the candles of the birthday cake. He wishes to spy upon the grown-ups and learn whether they really *do* have a good time. And this results in the magical projection of these very children into man's estate some twenty-one years later and in the same place. The body of the story presents the life of these grown-up children gathered together for a picnic. But in the end we return to the original birthday party and realize that the inserted narrative is a mere flight of the fancy. The inserted narrative covers less than two days' time, and the framework here-and-now only the few hours of the children's party.

Mr. Morley, however, was not the first to make some actual here-and-now the point of departure for a fanciful flight from reality and return to it. In Cabell's "Jurgen" (1919) the middle-aged pawnbroker, coming home to his wife in the evening after putting up the shutters of his shop, incurs the gratitude of the great god Koshchei, who made all things as they are, by having a kind word to say for evil —that is, for things as they are—and is rewarded by being restored to the vigor and intellectual curiosity of youth. And so, transmogrified by the fine shirt of Nessus, he is permitted to go through a great variety of adventures which in the long run do *not* give him a good time, but make him glad to return to his scolding wife Lisa and all the comforts of use and wont. His imaginary return to youth is the exact opposite of Martin's imaginary promotion to maturity, his adventures have an air of romantic improbability, and the moral of the tale has rather a different complexion. But there is a close resemblance in the technical schemes of the two books. In "Jurgen" the imaginary adventures of the hero are supposed to occupy just a twelvemonth, while the framework here-and-now brings him back to the same evening on which he set out.

What we have been discussing so far is the aggregate time covered in a novel as a whole. As for continuities of action within these limits, it is obvious that where a whole story covers but a few weeks there is likely to be a close succession of days, with seldom any intervals to be bridged. This is notably the case in "South Wind," "Cytherea," "Antic Hay," "The Sun Also Rises." And it is also likely that certain individual days will be developed at considerable length. In "South Wind" there are many instances of days to which several chapters are devoted, and one day, that of the volcanic eruption, continues to hold the stage through no less than seven chapters. In "Point Counter Point" the first twenty-four hours occupy the author's attention through the first twelve chapters (155 pages in my edition), or more than one third of the book. It is still more obvious that where the aggregate time is one day or less we have an extreme case of that continuity of action which we noted in the novels of Dostoevski. We follow Mrs. Dalloway hour by hour through the twelve hours of her exposure. And while "Ulysses" is divided into a number of major episodes which make up the twenty-four-hour panorama of Dublin life, these episodes are continuous one with another, and each one is developed at such length that it has the massiveness and solidity of a story by itself.

As for the "unity of place," this is rather the rule in the novels mentioned in this chapter. "Java Head" all takes place in the village of Salem; "The Bright Shawl" (within its reminiscent framework) in Havana; "Le Gentleman" in Paris or its environs; "South Wind" on the little island of Nepenthe (presumably Capri); "Ulysses" in Dublin; "Mrs. Dalloway" in a fairly restricted portion of London; "Twenty-Four Hours" (following the example of Dos Passos's "Manhattan Transfer") on Manhattan Island; "Thunder on the Left" in and about the house of Martin's parents at their summer resort; "Many Marriages" and "Dark Laughter" each in its little village of Wisconsin and Indiana, respectively.

Very few of the novelists I have cited in this chapter as examples of the "unities" suggest the well-made novel except in such mechanical and superficial ways. Mr. Douglas in "South Wind," and, following him, Mr. Huxley in books like "Crome Yellow," "Antic Hay," and "Point Counter Point" are concerned not so much with people's dramas as with their intellectual hobbies. They are interested in people who have something amusing to say. Their books suggest but vaguely the problems of those caught in the web of actual living, the heat and stress and urgency of daily life. What they like is a pattern of talk, in which each character utters opinions with due regard for the exigencies of wit and rhetoric or for the special variety of silliness and futility of which he is the representative.

One is constantly reminded in them of Thomas Love Peacock and the neat little dialogues which he strings along the tenuous romantic plots of "Headlong Hall" (1816) and "Nightmare Abbey" (1818). And when one has pointed out their kinship with Anatole France, one has sufficiently suggested that, while they are very much in a literary tradition, and a fine one, they do not grow from the main stem of the tree of the novel. The novel proper has been from its inception a "bourgeois" genre, and the novelist has always taken his people seriously as people, if only in the way of satire.

When it comes to Joyce and his following, we have such a radical departure from the main technical procedures of the novel that we shall have to consider them as primarily a reaction against the ideals of the well-made novel. But no literary revolution involves a complete reversal of the methods of its predecessor, and the widespread observance of the unities of time and place in books so unlike the well-made novel in essence must be regarded as a heritage from that type to its successors and supplanters. Indeed, it is the paradox of the situation that the limitation of time and place, which was one of the characteristic tendencies of the well-made novel, was carried to much greater extremes in the type of novel which is in the main a protest against it.

XXIV

POINT OF VIEW: HERGESHEIMER

THE disposition to observe the limited point of view in third-person narratives is of course widespread during the period considered. It is symptomatic of this trend that the first of George Moore's novels to be written from the point of view of a single character was "The Lake," published in 1905, whereas in the great novels of his earlier time there is no evidence of his having considered this point of technique. "The Sun Also Rises" and "A Farewell to Arms" are novels of a single point of view, but they are in the first person, which James considered a naïve and inferior medium, and belong to the great traditional class of autobiographic novels.

Quite recently, in "Dusty Answer" (1927), Rosamund Lehmann gave a triumphant instance of the vogue of the limited point of view. The special beauty of her achievement is, through the consciousness of a sensitive girl, to have presented so convincingly half a dozen corrupt and sophisticated characters. It is not the mere pictorial composition itself that is the technical beauty of the work, the relation of these sinister beings to the young and innocent Judith. It is the skill with which these characters are rendered to our understanding purely in terms of Judith's emotion.

Another extremely interesting recent example of this technique is Rex Stout's "How Like a God." In this case, it is neither the first nor the third person that is used, but the second. In the introductory pages to each chapter, we are informed of Bill's progress up the stairs, and this is told in the third person. But in the chapters themselves we have him reviewing the history which has brought him to this stairway on this occasion. And it is his inner discourse which is thus rendered. He is talking to himself, as it were, reminding himself of all he has been through—of the long chain of causes leading to his present psychological predicament. And so, through the body of this story, the leading character is always "you."

In the later novels of Sherwood Anderson there is a strong tendency to have the entire story told from the point of view of the characters and to keep to that of a given character over a long space. In "Many Marriages" the point of view during more than half the book is unbrokenly that of John Webster, the maker of washing machines, who feels impelled in middle age to leave his wife and his native town, and to explain to his daughter the reasons for the failure of his married life. During the latter half of the book there is one clearly defined passage of about ten pages in which we follow the thoughts of his wife, who is being abandoned and whose sensibilities have been outraged by the brutal unveiling of her most private life, and several distinct passages in which we follow the thoughts of the daughter, who has been converted to her father's way of viewing things. But for the most part, even in the second half of the book, it is the thoughts of the man which are being followed, and the book closes with an account, entirely from his standpoint, of his departure with the woman Natalie. Quite similarly in "Dark Laughter" the main body of the narrative is given through the impressions, the musings, the retrospection of Bruce Dudley, a factory worker in Old Harbor, Indiana, beginning with the first five books (129 pages), but with other large blocks assigned to the points of view of Bruce's employer and his employer's wife. In both of these novels, the author is virtually nowhere as commentator or independent source of information.

The novelist who has most constantly resorted to the technique of the limited point of view, and who has within each work most consistently maintained the limitations assumed, is Joseph Hergesheimer. In "Linda Condon" it is through the impressions of Linda that the entire story is given to us; in "Cytherea" through those of Lee Randon; in "The Bright Shawl" through the imagination of Charles Abbott, an old man sitting in his chair and recalling the adventures of his youth in Cuba. Not merely is each of these persons the invariable center of the stage in his own story, but whatever there is of interpretation is given to it by this central person. If the reader is occasionally able to appreciate qualities in certain of the characters not quite understood by Linda Condon, say, so young and inexperienced as she is, if some things are passed on to us over her head in the dialogue in which she takes part, that is, of course, a recognized means of enlarging the scope of this technique; the same enlargement has often been made by James, and notably in his story of a little girl, "What Maisie Knew."

More interesting, however, than any of these books are "The Three Black Pennys" and "Java Head," in which Hergesheimer makes use of James's technique of alternating and limited points of view. In "The Three Black Pennys" (1917) it is, more strictly, not alternating but successive points of view that are offered. What Hergesheimer takes for his subject here are three successive periods in the history of a family of Pennsylvania iron-founders, with episodes in the lives of three men of the family, the last two descendants of the first. These three Pennys are called Black Pennys because of an ancient Welsh strain in them which crops out once in several generations, showing itself in a disposition to solitude and a want of conventionality. "Opposition's their breath." They are quite different in age and general condition. The first is young, the second middle-aged, the third an old man. The first is closely bound up with the family iron-founding; the second has become a big business man; the third has retired altogether from his connection with the business and become a literary and artistic dilettante. But there is some effort to stress the influence of heredity in character—"the past inexorably woven into the pattern of the future"—and still more, and more successfully, a kind of mystic sense of the reliving by later generations of experiences and sensations from the past. The last Howat returns to die in the old stone house at Shadrach Furnace, where the story began with the first Howat. As he dies there he sees "a pattern of flying geese wavering across the tranquil sky," which is an exact repetition of a vision of his remote ancestor who bore the same name. And in many ways the author has done his utmost to give us a feeling of the continuity of experience in these successive avatars. So that if the three episodes are rendered through the point of view of three different men, far separated in time, still in a sense one may say that it is one man, or one essence, that of the Black Penny, that is followed throughout.

A somewhat similar method is used by Hergesheimer in his most recent book "The Limestone Tree" (1931), in which he presents ten separate episodes from the "saga" of certain Kentucky families of honorable and bloody memory. Each episode is given from the point of view of a character closely associated with its main action. It is a striking evidence of the degree to which Mr. Hergesheimer is committed to this method that he should have applied it to a narrative of events so solidly factual in character, in which there is little occasion to dwell on the impressions of the person chosen for mirror of the action. Indeed, there is something a bit quaint and unconvincing about certain phrases reminiscent of "Cytherea" or "The Golden Bowl" applied to a backwoods character like James Abel. But, for all that, this limitation of the point of view in each episode does constitute a happy principle of organization: better than mere chronology or the author's whim it determines the order in which each event comes out, the place and occasion that brings each episode to its dramatic climax. It helps to project the reader more immediately into the spirit of the time. It is an example of the value of this method in the short-story form.

Most interesting, most charming, and most dramatic of all Hergesheimer's novels is probably "Java Head," a story of the town and seaport of Salem in the eighteen-forties, just as the carrying trade is leaving her for Boston, with the substitution of steamboats for sailing-schooners. In this novel Hergesheimer's handling of the point of view is curious and delightful. The book is divided into ten chapters, and each one of these chapters is confined to the point of view of a different person, except that two of them are given from that of Gerrit, the most important character. The story is told straight forward, but the author has managed to render the action of each chapter in terms of the impressions of the character chosen for that part.

These persons are not all of the first importance in the story, but each one gives his special quality to the part of which he is the witness. They are of many different sorts, in age, character, and experience. There is Laurel, aged eleven, proud of being too grown up for pantalettes but all absorbed in girlish interests, candy, and play; there is salty old Jeremy, the grandfather, given to stories of the old sailing-ships; blue-eyed, quixotic Captain Gerrit, impatient of the hypocrisies and devious ways of the land; unscrupulous Edward Dunsack, crazed by opium, enamored of the sophistications and luxurious ways of the Orient; Nettie Vollar, an illegitimate child, rebelling against her grandfather's view of her as a sinful creature; Taou Yuen, Gerrit's Manchu wife, gorgeously painted, polite, superior, full of Chinese superstition and high philosophy.

It is a picturesque, and at moments an exciting, story that Hergesheimer tells through these so various recorders, and it is a technical feat of no mean order thus to keep us interested in the story without any undue consciousness of the varying media. What they do is to lend each one the color of his temperament to the chapter over which he presides, so that the whole is like some beautiful fan of many-colored leaves.

But after all, the dominant effect is decorative rather than dramatic. There is here, as in all of Hergesheimer's work, a large stress upon costume, period, setting, picture. The careful and charming seasonal notations, the much that is made of the nautical element and of the colorful cargoes, the painstaking reproduction of historical details like the drilling of militia for the Fourth of July, the visit of President Polk, and the politics of the merchant marine; the exterior trappings of life of the period—carriages, candles, wine-glasses—all this reminds us of Amy Lowell and D. H. Griffith. And the characters themselves are most interesting, in the last analysis, regarded simply as a decorative arrangement in colors.

Still less dramatic is the conception of stories like "Cytherea" and "Linda Condon." It is rather with a lyrical inspiration that Hergesheimer burns incense before the altar of his Platonic Love—the shadowy love that unfits Lee Randon for the domestic life of wife and children, or enables Dodge Pleydon to find in Linda the inspiration for his career as a sculptor. Of the same quality is that passion for patriotic service that inflames Charles Abbott in Cuba, under the symbol of a bright shawl.

The very inevitability which Hergesheimer ascribes to the passion of love in "Cytherea" and "The Three Black Pennys" makes it an unfit motivation for drama strictly speaking. With all the realism of external circumstance, these characters want the moral—the social—actuality of characters in James, who are bound to meet and solve the problem of conduct. There is here no psychological mystery, no situation with elements unsolved, no game of intricate moves to be played out. The leading prepossession of Hergesheimer is the Pateresque problem of finding words to render qualities. It is for this reason that, with all the other marks, Hergesheimer does not quite meet the ideal requirements of the well-made novel.

The technical influence of Hergesheimer is a continuing one in current American fiction, especially with writers undertaking to revive certain historical aspects of American life with something of the realist's sober eye. In Wallace Irwin's "The Days of Her Life" (1930), a story of San Francisco in the eighties and nineties, each of the sixteen chapters is devoted to one day in the life of the heroine, Emma Beecher, from June 9, 1881, to July 9, 1899. Thus the single point of view is maintained throughout, and the long course of years in this panoramic survey is reduced dramatically to a limited number of particular moments. In William McNally's "House of Vanished Splendor" (1932), the history of a certain wealthy family of Minnesota which traces its decline over a period of more than thirty years, the sixteen chapters are distributed among the seven leading characters, so that each of them has from one to three chapters conducted from his special point of view. Thus, through the medium of books like "Java Head" and "The Three Black Pennys," something of the James tradition in technique survives in work as different from his in general intention as could well be imagined.

XXV

THE WELL-MADE NOVEL: SEDGWICK, WHARTON

The two authors who most nearly follow the method of James—though in smarter and more attenuated form—and who in certain cases represent the well-made novel in its ideal state, are the American women Anne Douglas Sedgwick (Mrs. Basil de Sélincourt) and Edith Wharton.

In "The Little French Girl" (1924) Miss Sedgwick has turned out a story startling, and almost laughable, in its feminine reproduction of the themes and procedures of James. Her handling of the point of view is quite as meticulous, and even more regular or patterned than that of James. The book is divided into four nearly equal parts: the first and third are assigned to Alix Vervier, the little French girl, the second and fourth to Giles Bradley, the young Englishman with whose family she spends two winters. It is with absolute scrupulousness that the author identifies herself throughout each part with the person to whom it is assigned. Her subject is perfectly typical of James, involving a delicately developed contrast between the French and English temperaments and ways of arranging life; and this contrast is built up, as in the later novels of James, through the impressions of the two characters. The characters are motivated, as in James, by their sentiments, which resolve themselves, when analyzed, into a highly refined sense of honor in personal relations.

But what makes this so perfect a type of the well-made novel, where Anderson and Hergesheimer fall short of it, is Miss Sedgwick's handling of the plot. Like James, she makes great use of the technique of gradual revelation, each situation being developed to its fullest possibilities, before some new item of fact comes in to create a new situation for the characters to explore. For, like the characters of James, these people are forever exploring, seeking to understand and appreciate. Strong emotions are involved in their understanding of the situation; they have not always arrived at the same point of understanding, and one of them may have reasons for keeping his knowledge from the other; and the dramatic character of the dialogue often arises from the need of one to spare the other knowledge which he has attained, and at the same time to justify himself in the eyes of the other for the interpretation which he puts on things.

In the first part, Alix comes to stay with the Bradleys in England, and is in a perpetual process of taking in the English attitudes toward life. There is also a very particular matter involving the character of her mother, whom she adores. A certain young woman who goes under the pet name of "Toppie," a high-strung and puritanical person, had been in love with Giles's brother Owen. Before he was killed in the World War he had been intimately acquainted with Madame Vervier. Toppie knows that he had visited Madame Vervier while on leave, but not how often he had visited her. Alix knows of the several visits, but does not understand what interpretation to put upon them. It is only Giles who has reason to think that his brother was more intimate with Madame Vervier than either Toppie or Alix could bear to realize. And the dramatic climax of the first part comes with a scene in which, in Alix's presence, he lies to Toppie about the number of Owen's visits in Paris. Alix does not understand why he should lie about it, and Giles is hard put to it to justify himself in her eyes without revealing too much of his thought about her mother.

In the second part, Giles accompanies Alix on a summer

visit to her mother's seaside cottage in Brittany. There it is his turn to take in the French ways and to speculate on the exact relation of Madame Vervier and the charming young André de Valenbois. The climax of this part comes with the scene in which Madame Vervier, anxious to get her daughter safely out of the milieu in which she lives, lays all her cards on the table, makes it perfectly clear to Giles that André is her lover, and proposes that he (Giles) shall marry Alix. His reply is that he is in love with some one else—Toppie, of course. A second and higher climax comes on his return to England, when he attempts to give Toppie an account of Madame Vervier. In his wish to shield Toppie from his own knowledge, he only succeeds in making himself appear ignoble, and in his effort to justify himself, he makes matters worse for Toppie by letting her know that Madame Vervier is not, as she had always assumed, a widow, but has a husband living. One is reminded of Lambert Strether's gradual enlightenment concerning Madame de Vionnet.

How the author complicates this knot and then unties it, I will leave to the reader to discover for himself. What I wish to note is the skill, the neatness, the precision, with which she conducts the characters through the game of move and countermove, always along the line of their respective spiritual predicaments, and always within the framework of the chosen consciousness. This work does not have the solidity and depth and brooding intensity of James. The author does not dwell so long on the moments of thought, on the mere subjective process. The style is lighter; the narrative goes forward with a lighter movement, carrying a lesser weight of baggage. But for all these reasons it is perhaps a better exemplification of what is implied in my term "the well-made novel."

It should be noted that "The Little French Girl" is perhaps unique in the work of Miss Sedgwick for the completeness with which it carries out this formula. It represents a sort of culmination in her work of these tendencies, which are stronger in all her later novels than in the earlier ones, so far as I have examined them, though in none so strong as in this. In "Philippa" (1930) everything is presented distinctly from the point of view of one of the four principal characters, and generally each one is given a long block to himself before a change is made to some other. The author lets the characters do it all. In "The Old Countess" (1927) there are but two persons, the married couple, Graham and Jill, who render through their alternating impressions the character of Madame de la Mouderie and her protégé, as well as the tragedy in which they are themselves involved.

Once or twice we go behind the impressions of the character, and learn what he himself looked like to others on the occasion he is recording. Such exceptions, however, are extremely rare; and it is true enough for the most part that in these later novels Miss Sedgwick observes with scrupulous exactness, if not with the regularity of "The Little French Girl," the principle of the restricted point of view.

In her earlier work this is much less true. In "Franklin Winslow Kane" (1910), while there is very little that does not come to us from the impressions of the characters, there are so many of these whose impressions are followed, and the changes are so frequent, that much of the effectiveness of this method is lost.

Again, in "Tante" (1911), in addition to the injudicious distribution of the point of view, there are many passages which are in the purely expository manner of an author who finds it more convenient to speak to us directly. While the bulk of the story is from the point of view of either Gregory or Karen, the principals, this honor is sometimes given to a person so insignificant as Miss Scrotton; and there are many scenes presented in a straight objective manner, so that we who have been watching Madame von Marwitz from before the footlights (through the eyes of

Gregory and Karen) may be duly informed of what she is actually like behind the scenes. This is the usual old-fashioned method; it is like the method of James in "Roderick Hudson" and "The Tragic Muse"; whereas the method of "The Little French Girl" and "The Old Countess" is more like that of "The Golden Bowl" and "The Wings of the Dove."

The upshot of this comparison is that, while Miss Sedgwick was all along greatly under the influence of James, she followed him at a considerable interval. The culmination of his technique comes in her just twenty years after its culmination in him. It comes, let us observe, at the very moment when all the progressive tendencies in the novel are showing a marked reaction against most of what he stands for.

2

The same thing is true of Edith Wharton, whose first striking use of the later James technique is in "The Age of Innocence" (1920). "The Valley of Decision" (1902) may be left out of account altogether. It is a ponderous historical novel in the tradition of "Romola," suggesting George Eliot in the close-knit, competent, rather formal style, and in the minute and conscientious scholarship displayed.

"The House of Mirth" (1905) has a subject more suggestive of James—the shifts and compromises of a young woman brought up to the luxury of society life but without a sufficient income. Lily Bart, by her intelligence and charm as well as by her situation, reminds us of Charlotte Stant, Kate Croy, and Fleda Vetch. It is inevitable that her story should be told largely from her point of view. But Mrs. Wharton has not conceived this as an artistic principle to which sacrifices must be made, and she finds it more convenient to present many passages of the story from the point of view of Selden, and even of such insignificant characters as Mrs. Peniston, Mrs. Stepney, Gerty Farish, and Trenor. Mrs. Wharton sometimes leaves the point of view of her heroine to tell us how she looked, or passes lightly from her thoughts and feelings to those of her companion.

Lily dropped down on the rock, glowing with her long climb. She sat quiet, her lips parted by the stress of the ascent, her eyes wandering peacefully over the glowing ranges of the landscape. Selden stretched himself on the grass at her feet, tilting his hat against the level sun-rays, and clasping his hands behind his head, which rested against the side of the rock. He had no wish to make her talk; her quick-breathing silence seemed a part of the general hush and harmony of things. In his own mind there was only a sense of pleasure, veiling the sharp edges of sensation as the September haze veiled the scene at their feet. But Lily, though her attitude was as calm as his, was throbbing inwardly with a rush of thoughts.

An occasional passage such as this shows that, while Mrs. Wharton has a distinct tendency to make much of the impressions of her important characters, she had not at this date the intention of rendering her story exclusively through these, but followed naturally the traditional method of objective narrative.

This is even more striking in novels like "The Fruit of the Tree" (1907) and "The Custom of the Country" (1913), in which the interest is distributed over a larger number of principal characters, who succeed one another alternately as the center of the picture, and give way often to quite secondary characters where the exposition requires it. Very frequently, in "The Custom of the Country," the author begins her chapter (XIV, XV, XXXVII, XXXVIII) in a purely objective manner, setting the stage and marshaling the characters for half a dozen pages before any one of the persons emerges and begins to interpret the action in terms of his own impressions.

And there is a particular reason why, in this book, Mrs.

Wharton cannot maintain the James technique of restricted point of view. The central person, Undine Spragg, a common young woman from the back country, who uses her beauty as a means of making successively more brilliant marriages, and so raising herself in the social scale, is a noble forerunner of Lorelei in "Gentlemen Prefer Blondes" (1925). But Mrs. Wharton does not tell her story, like Anita Loos, in the diary manner. And the irony with which her career is chronicled does not admit of our losing ourselves in her point of view. Her vulgar smartness is a very different thing from the sensitive intelligence of Fleda Vetch or Lily Bart, and cannot be expected to render more than the gross and superficial aspects of the world she views. So that with the best of intentions, with the modern disposition to let the character speak for herself, the author cannot very whole-heartedly identify herself with Undine Spragg, and we are forever conscious of her critical gaze upon the motives and behavior of her shoddy heroine.

But any reader coming to "The Custom of the Country" directly from, say, "Vanity Fair" will be struck by the enormously greater use made in the later novel of the impressions of the characters themselves—even Undine's—as the means of rendering the action. This tendency toward intensifying the point of view is perhaps what should be emphasized in a discussion of any of these earlier novels of Edith Wharton rather than their departure from the limited point of view.

Meantime, in several very short novels or novelettes she had been experimenting with the absolutely limited point of view. In "Madame de Treymes" (1907), strongly reminiscent of "The American," of "Madame de Mauves," and of other stories of James, long and short, the point of view is, without exception, that of John Durham, the counterpart of Christopher Newman and Longmore, Americans similarly caught and bewildered in the mazes of French aristocratic society. In "Ethan Frome" (1911), inside the framework provided by the imaginary narrator, the point of view is exclusively that of Ethan Frome. Thus Edith Wharton followed exactly the evolution of James in this matter, even to the first application of the restricted point of view in stories long enough to be published each in a single volume, though not long enough to be classified securely as novels.

In "Summer" (1917) the same technique is extended to a novel of almost average length; and after "The Age of Innocence" this technique is the rule rather than the exception. In "A Son at the Front" (1923) and "The Children" (1928) the story is given altogether from the point of view of the central character. In "Hudson River Bracketed" (1929) it is given alternately from the standpoints of the two principals. But none of these novels of Edith Wharton after "The Age of Innocence" is on a level of interest with "The House of Mirth" or "The Custom of the Country." Taken together they are symptomatic of the overwhelming trend in her toward the restricted point of view. But of all her books, it is "The Age of Innocence" that stands out as the best example of the well-made novel in its various implications.

3

This book is a historical novel in the sense that, published in 1920, it is laid in the New York of the 1870's, the "age of innocence," and that much is made, in a deft and unobtrusive way, of the physical aspect of old New York, the cultural interests, and, above all, the social and moral tone, of the four hundred of the time. Much is made, again, of the quaint exclusiveness of the few families who are acknowledged to be paramount. As for the moral tone, alluded to in the title, the great thing is the disposition of good society of the seventies to ignore the existence of anything "unpleasant," to convey delicate meanings, if they must be conveyed, by implication without the use of words, never frankly to face realities that do not conform to the prevailing ideal, and inexorably to purge society of any person who has offended against the conventional code.

It is this social ideal which is represented by May Welland. There is in the end something impressive in the quiet, selfish cruelty with which she holds her fiancé and husband to his obligations, even using her prospective motherhood (of which she is not even certain) to "hold up" him and the woman he loves. It is not to her own happiness so much as to a kind of idol, a jealous god of respectability, that she compels their sacrifice. And since they do sacrifice to this god, they thereby acknowledge his authority, and a kind of rightness in his ideal. On this point, indeed, the irony, the satire breaks down, since the author has an air of subscribing, herself, to the moral code in question.

The story is very simple. The Countess Ellen Olenska, an American woman who has married abroad unhappily and run away from a dreadful husband, has now returned to New York and wishes to be taken back into the fold. In spite of a certain ambiguity in her history and status, she is backed by the right people among her connections, and arouses the interest of Newland Archer, a young lawyer engaged to marry her cousin May Welland. He is deputed by the family to persuade her not to sully their name by suing for divorce. In this mission he succeeds, and meantime falls in love with her. But when he declares his love it is already too late, for he has won her over so completely to his idea of decency that she cannot conceive of finding her happiness at May's expense. And so Newland marries May and sees nothing more of Ellen for a long time.

But now it becomes a question of her going back to her unspeakable husband—a solution greatly to the taste of the New York relatives. Newland opposes this; their love flames up again; and it is a question whether they may flout the idol to which they have sacrificed. But this is prevented by May's confiding to Ellen that she is pregnant, and the family have the satisfaction of packing Ellen off again to Europe. Such is the story, except for an epilogue chapter reviewing Newland's life of good works over many years, and ending with the visit of his son Dallas to Madame Olenska in her Paris apartment.

The book is remarkable for unity and simplicity of action. There are, of course, other characters than these mentioned, and other tenuous threads of plot, but no loose threads—everything is skilfully woven in and pertinent to the main action. Each chapter, almost without exception, makes one discriminated occasion, the French ideal of a scene of drama. Leaving out of account the epilogue, the entire action covers about two years' time. But most of this time falls between chapters, near the beginning of the second book, and the drama proper occupies two periods of several months each, with a close-knit, continuous thread of limited issues.

What more than anything else contributes to the unity and compactness of the drama is that Newland Archer is present in every scene, and that everything is shown from his point of view. The author may begin a chapter with what seems like an objective account of a scene or of certain circumstances necessary to our understanding it, but invariably, in such a case, within a page or two she reminds us that what she has described or chronicled is what was seen by Archer or known to him: "As he mused on these things"; "these things passed through Newland Archer's mind as he watched the Countess Olenska"; "Newland Archer, standing on the verandah of the house, looked curiously down upon this scene." And much more commonly the chapter begins with him directly.

Quite as remarkable as the consistent point of view is the consistency with which this view is directed upon a particular object or issue. Three persons are presented—one the person seeing, and the others the two persons seen, and the limitation helps Ellen Olenska and May Welland as much as it does the man observing them.

In particular, the limitation of what we know and think of Ellen to what Newland thinks and knows gives her reality, artistic distinctness, and intensity. And at the same time it provides the story, as the author controls what new information she shall release from point to point, and keeps our curiosity and concern at the same white heat as Newland's.

This is most striking of all in the first book, in which the "exposition" is carried forward step by step with the story. The great question here is as to the actual character and status of Ellen, from the moment when, in their box at the opera, Newland heard the remark of old Sillerton Jackson on the public recognition given the countess by the Mingotts, "I didn't think the Mingotts would have tried it on." In the following chapter Newland is made to wonder at the Countess's disrespectful way of referring to New York; later, at her inviting him to call—an act so unconventional—what did *that* mean? The gossip of dinner tables makes him speculate on the exact circumstances of her leaving her husband and what degree of reprobation attached to her behavior. This ambiguity is intensified by her relations to the dreadful Mrs. Struthers, whose home is the meeting-place of amusing and talented bohemians, and to Julius Beaufort, the banker of notorious reputation. When Newland urges her, in the common interest, not to divorce her husband, there lurk in the background certain vague charges which her husband has made against her. He cannot get her to make a specific statement as to the nature of these charges; he wonders if she has it in mind to marry her lover who helped her away, and in just what sense he was her lover.

All these questions come to a head in the final chapter

of Book I, the *scene-à-faire* of this drama. Here, in true James manner, the two persons are like players in some dark game; with each new play, with each new revelation of fact or motive, the situation takes a new turn; and the scene moves forward from surprise to surprise. Newland, fearing that he has not strength to hold out long, has been urging May to hasten the date of their marriage, and she has become aware that he is interested in some other woman, and has offered to set him free. When now he tells Ellen of May's offer, she wants to know about the "other" woman—does she love Newland? When he reveals that *she* is the other woman, she replies that *he* is the one who has made their love impossible by persuading her not to divorce Olenski. . . . It next appears that it is not her husband that she has feared or anything that he has "on" her; she has merely wished to avoid bringing scandal upon him and May. . . . And now Newland is determined that he will not marry May, that he must have Ellen. . . . Ah, but that is impossible, and it is he himself who has made it impossible. Ellen has come to realize that she cannot rightly love Newland unless she gives him up; she cannot be happy unless she remains true to the ideals which he has taught her. . . . But even then, we feel, she might have yielded to the urgency of Newland; she is, we suspect, on the point of yielding, when a telegram arrives from May announcing that she has consented to advance the date of the marriage as Newland had wished. And this chapter and this book end with Newland's announcement to his sister that he is to be married in a month.

4

If Edith Wharton shows her expertness more in one thing than another, it is in her dialogue. But it is the dramatic continuity of issue that gives its point to the dialogue and determines that it shall have structural, functional value as well as interest for itself alone. In "The Age of Innocence," certainly, she does not indulge herself with talk which is merely entertaining, which is devised for setting forth certain pet opinions of the author or for displaying the humors and eccentricities of the characters. Some aspects of New York society tone are amusingly hit off in certain passages of dialogue, but she manages to subordinate this interest strictly to that of her theme and make it serve the major issue. Her dialogue has some of the point of Thackeray's, but it is more dramatically knit together.

It is in general pointed and crisp from pruning and selection and from concentration on an issue. She is very deft in the springing of new items of information, carefully prepared, the timing of curtains, the isolation of significant bits. There are no long fat speeches of explanation, as so often in Hugh Walpole, for example; it is all broken up into half-utterances, challenges, questions, meanings developed through the give-and-take of dialogue. The chapters are short, and the chapter-divisions serve to set in provocative relief the culminating lines, like Sillerton Jackson's remark at the end of the first chapter, "I didn't think the Mingotts would have tried it on."

Very fine is the breathlessly awaited pronouncement of old Mr. Van der Luyden in Chapter VII. The Van der Luydens are the acknowledged arbiters of taste in the four hundred; upon their reaction depends the reception given Ellen by every one that counts. It seems that the Leffertses —influential, but not omnipotent—have pronounced against her. And now Newland and his mother have come to appeal to the higher court. The preliminary conversation with Mrs. Van der Luyden is not detailed, nor the Archers' presentation of Ellen's case. A word or two is recorded of solemn remark on Mr. Van der Luyden's daily custom of reading the "Times" in the afternoon. Emphasis is laid by the Archers on the fact that he ought to know of what is going on in Ellen's case. Everything is centered on the Archers' suggestion that this is all a dodge on the part of Lawrence Lefferts.

"The *Leffertses!*–" said Mrs. van der Luyden.

"The *Leffertses!*–" echoed Mrs. Archer. "What would Uncle Egmont have said of Lawrence Lefferts's pronouncing on anybody's social position? It shows what Society has come to."

"We'll hope it has not quite come to that," said Mr. van der Luyden firmly.

And so we know that Ellen's case is won.

It is above all the thing not said that counts in the dialogue of Edith Wharton, and the full implications of the little said. Everything said by Ellen is telling because of our concern to know what lies beneath it, and everything said about her—especially by May—is exciting because of our feeling of a latent hostility, our uncertainty how much is known and thought. The effect of wit is produced by clipped and weighted remarks left full of hidden implications. There is a passage in which Newland is discussing Ellen with his mother and his sister Janey:

"I hope you like her, Mother."

Mrs. Archer drew her lips together. "She certainly lays herself out to please, even when she is calling on an old lady." [She is referring to herself.]

"Mother doesn't think her simple," Janey interjected, her eyes screwed upon her brother's face.

"It's just my old-fashioned feeling; dear May is my ideal," said Mrs. Archer.

"Ah," said her son, "they're not alike."

And so the thing is left, without comment, to make its own effect.

The dialogue of Edith Wharton often reminds one of James's in its way of linking speech to speech, one character catching up the phrase or point of the other's remark by way of challenge, question, matching of the idea and carrying it farther:

"I want," she went on, "to be perfectly honest with you—and with myself. For a long time I've hoped this chance would come: that I might tell you how you've helped me, *what you've made of me*—"

Archer sat staring beneath frowning brows. He interrupted her with a laugh. "And *what do you make out that you've made of me?*"

She paled a little. *"Of you?"*

"Yes: for *I'm of your making* much more than you ever were of mine. I'm the man who married one woman because another told him to."

Her paleness turned to a fugitive flush. "I thought—you promised—you were not to say such things today."

"Ah—how like a woman! None of you will ever see *a bad business* through!"

She lowered her voice. *Is* it *a bad business*—for May?"

And so the interchange continues through the next three pages.

The trick is James's. But then one thinks at once of the great difference in the way it is turned. The dialogue of Edith Wharton is so much slighter, brighter, smarter, wittier than that of James. The issues are so much more obvious; the story moves forward so much more swift and sparkling. One does not have in her the feeling of threading a long and arduous labyrinth. The development of situation in James is carried out with all the fullness and relentlessness of Ibsen. In Wharton one thinks rather of something in French comedy.

There are many other superficial reminders of James in "The Age of Innocence." We cannot forget that Archer is the family name of the heroine in "The Portrait of a Lady." And as for Newland, we remember that Christopher Newman is the hero of "The American" and Chad Newsome that of "The Ambassadors." The Countess Olenska reminds us of Eugenia Young, morganatic wife of the Prince of Silberstadt-Schneckenstein, who, in "The Europeans," comes back to the bosom of her Boston family under circumstances so similar; she reminds us also of Madame Merle in "The Portrait of a Lady." And if, in the end, she turns out capable of a spiritual fineness which is not like anything in the character of Madame Merle or Eugenia Young, this very spiritual fineness is again in the formula of many another James heroine. When she says to Archer, "Then you'll help me?" we are reminded of the similar appeal of Madame de Vionnet to Lambert Strether. When Archer nearly gets her to agree to "come to him" once, it is a repetition of the situation between Merton Densher and Kate Croy in "The Wings of the Dove." When at the end, Newland Archer sends up his son Dallas to see the Countess Olenska, and, seated on a bench in the park below, reflects, "It's more real to me here than if I went up," we have a situation and a reflection that might be found in any one of a dozen stories of James.

And yet, in Edith Wharton, as in Anne Douglas Sedgwick or in Ethel Sidgwick, we have a follower of James as different from him as she is like him. Even in her handling of the point of view—perhaps most of all in her handling of this very problem—we find the difference. In "The Age of Innocence" and many other stories she is as strict as James in the observance of the limited point of view, but the effect is not the same. Everything is rendered through the consciousness of Newland Archer, but nothing is made of his consciousness.

Newland Archer is one of the palest and least individualized characters ever offered to the public by a distinguished writer of fiction. He is hardly more than a device for projecting a situation and characters much more real than himself. We do not dwell with him in the narrow prison of his predicament as we dwell with Fleda Vetch or Maggie Verver; we do not puzzle out with him the strange writing on the wall as we do with Merton Densher and Lambert Strether. The limited point of view is here a compositional device of great value; it serves to focus the attention upon the simple issues. It gives sharpness and precision. But it does not serve as in James for enrichment and deepening of the effect. It is not a means of steeping us imaginatively in the special and rare solution which is the essence of a unique personality.

For this very reason Mrs. Wharton is a more popular writer than her master. There is so much less weight of the "subjective" to make the story drag. And if she has adopted the "dramatic" device of the limited point of view, she has avoided that over-emphasis on the conscious process which makes it bad "theater." So that here again, as in Miss Sedgwick, it is an attenuated version of Henry James which best illustrates the ideal of the well-made novel.

PART FOUR: TRANSITION

Un critique intelligent devrait, au contraire, rechercher tout ce qui ressemble le moins aux romans déjà faits, et pousser autant que possible les jeunes gens à tenter des voies nouvelles.

—GUY DE MAUPASSANT: Preface to "Pierre et Jean"

. . . that is to say, art as I understand it,—rhythmical sequence of events described with rhythmical sequence of phrase.

—GEORGE MOORE: "Confessions of a Young Man"

XXVI

CRITIQUE OF THE WELL-MADE NOVEL

It is time to remind ourselves of the general intention underlying the movement we have been tracing. More or less consciously, all along, the main writers of the period considered have been aiming to make of the novel a distinct literary form, as different as possible in procedure from the philosophical essay, the historical chronicle, with which in the beginning it was so closely associated. At the same time they have been trying to make of it something more than that miscellaneous vehicle of entertainment which it meant to many of the most gifted Victorians. A single subject, embodied in a dramatic situation, developed logically, without interruption and without interference, to its inevitable conclusion—this was their idea of a novel. And in pursuance of this idea, great gains were made in the art of novel-writing.

But, at the same time, great sacrifices were made and great losses suffered, and inevitably this movement was preparing the reaction against itself, which was all along going on sporadically, but which was brought into full swing with the publication of Joyce's "Ulysses." I have already spoken of losses suffered by the novel from the withdrawal of the author. With the effort to make the novel dramatic —that is, self-impelling—there was a notable tendency to do without that critical spirit which was furnished by the author's comments.

Enough has been said in these pages implying disparagement of the technique of Thackeray and Fielding; it is high time to acknowledge that few minds of equal solidity and critical power have in our day occupied themselves with the English novel. Among the faculties associated everywhere with the English spirit is the burly male faculty of common sense, and whatever else we may boast of the spiritual achievements of the days since Thackeray, common sense is not what stands out as typical. The critical spirit is strong in Samuel Butler and in Norman Douglas; but few will pretend that we have in these writers spirits as well balanced, as sane as Fielding, Scott, Austen, or Thackeray.

They certainly do not show in high degree the geniality, the humor, the wit, which were once the leading traits of English fiction. J. B. Priestley is widely advertised as a writer who revives in our day the subjects and manner of Dickens. But it is surely a chastened and watered Dickens that we find in "Angel Pavement," and no one would think of preferring this pale sobriety to the fine inebriation of "Martin Chuzzlewit" and "Great Expectations." William Dean Howells has been greatly neglected in these pages because, with all his preoccupation with truth (in a narrow range), he had so little notion of form. But there were qualities of charm displayed in, for example, "A Hazard of New Fortunes" which it is vain to look for in contemporary fiction. Much has been made of the strategic errors of Meredith in handling psychology and of James's improvement in this matter. But no one would think of comparing James with Meredith as a wit or thinker. No one thinks of taking Henry James as guide, philosopher, and friend.

It is not, of course, the fault of any formal ideal in art that humor, philosophy, and geniality have so largely disappeared from twentieth-century literature. It is a general condition of the spirit in our bewildered, disillusioned times. To have humor, philosophy, and geniality, it would seem, we must be ready to make certain assumptions; we must rest secure upon certain principles generally assumed as true. And in the past two generations we have been too busy—we are still too busy—questioning the assumptions of earlier times to rest secure in anything.

But there is this to be said of the connection of the well-made novel with the disappearance of these excellent qualities. The rigorous selectiveness, the formal neatness which have been the growing ideals of the novel, have tended to eliminate from fiction all sorts of elements fine in themselves but irrelevant to the particular issue. There has been a tendency to squeeze the sponge and leave it dry. The well-made novel has on the whole favored writers not strongly endowed with humor, not given to an overflow of genial philosophy.

The subject is full of paradoxes. The very tendency to dramatize the consciousness of the characters has on the whole favored writers relatively weak in the power of dramatizing—of differentiating and projecting character. Very often the author who insists on identifying himself with a person in his story is simply yielding to the temptation of making that person react as he himself would do under the same circumstances. And so what he gives us is no more than a sort of spiritual autobiography. One feels this to be true of Mr. Anderson in "Many Marriages" and "Dark Laughter." What makes these books important is that Mr. Anderson is so largely sincere in his account of his soul under the names of John Webster and Bruce Dudley, and that, while presumably drawn from his own experience, these characters are representative of so large a category of men. I doubt if as much can be said of Mr. Hergesheimer's projection of himself (is it?) in "Cytherea." One is conscious here of a certain erotic sentimentalism, a kind of dressing up of the passion of love—a rationalizing of the vagrant impulse—which is a widespread feature of our "modern" attitude toward the emotions. One feels it, for example, in Mr. Swinnerton. And there is doubtless a touch of it in Anderson and Lawrence.

But when it comes to the well-made novel, there is another variety of sentimentalism in the treatment of love, for which I can find no better term than ethical sentimentalism. It is something that flourishes in the soil of English fiction. It has its root in the assumption that love is definable purely as a sentiment, and the general tendency to ignore its connection with the reproductive function. I should not like to have the term sentimental applied to James, but I have no doubt that he is responsible for a vast amount of sentimentalism of this variety in his many followers.

If the charge of sentimentalism is to be brought against James, it is because of the disposition of his characters to translate all passions into terms of sentiment, and so make them "nice." A legitimate passion does not need to be made nice; it is just naturally nice if nothing is said about the passional element in it. An illegitimate passion may be given a semblance of niceness by some kind of rationalization. Such is the passion of Charlotte Stant and the Prince Amerigo; it is given a semblance of niceness by the fact that Milly and her father are such good pals that there is nothing left for the others but to leave them alone and "play together."

It is possible that temperamentally James knew nothing of the passion of love and so found it easy to do without it. Intellectually he was well aware of it, and whatever Charlotte and the Prince may have to say about their relation, he was not taken in by it. If there is a strain of sentimentalism in James, it is because of his almost exclusive concern with nice people, and with passions masked in terms of sentiment.

The reason why his sentimentalism never slops over is the predominantly intellectual stress in his treatment of sentiment, and the rich and powerful imagination with which he conjures up these people and their world. The Venetian painters give a highly idealized picture of life, but it is all bathed in a light that makes it real at the same time that it maintains the illusion of ideality.

2

If the strain of sentimentalism is stronger in the followers of James, it is because they have less powerful imaginations, and while they try for a realism greater than his, their stress tends to the emotional.

Edith Wharton is by no means a striking example of the sentimental strain. She is too much a woman of the world for that. Her impeccable taste never permits her a lapse into the ridiculous. In "Ethan Frome" she has even risen, for once, into a simple and tragic realism which can stand comparison with almost anything in fiction. But she does have a predilection for nice people and nice sentiments. She does tend to interpret the psychology of her more sympathetic characters in terms of her own impeccable taste.

When it comes to what should be the great scenes of emotion, this author finds herself in an insoluble dilemma. She wishes to indicate the emotion, and she wishes to avoid anything that would be in bad taste, and what she falls into is the conventional and banal. Ellen and Newland are discussing her husband's letter, at the height of their great scene. Ellen speaks:

"I had nothing to fear from that letter: absolutely nothing! All I feared was to bring notoriety, scandal, on the family—on you and May."

"Good God," he groaned again, *bowing his face in his hands.*

The silence that followed *lay on them with the weight of things final and irrevocable. It seemed to Archer to be crushing him down like his own gravestone;* in all the wide future he saw nothing that would ever lift that load from his heart. He did not move from his place, or raise his head from his hands; *his hidden eyeballs went on staring into utter darkness.*

"At least I loved you—" he brought out.

On the other side of the hearth, from the sofa-corner where he supposed that she still crouched, he heard *a faint stifled crying like a child's.* He started up and came to her side.

"Ellen! What madness! Why are you crying? Nothing's done that can't be undone. I'm still free, and you're going to be." He had her in his arms, *her face like a wet flower at his lips, and all their vain terrors shrivelling up like ghosts at sunrise.* The one thing that astonished him now was that he should have stood for five minutes arguing with her across the width of the room, when just touching her made everything so simple.

. . . .

She spoke in a low even voice, without tears or visible agitation; and *each word, as it dropped from her, fell into his breast like burning lead. He sat bowed over, his head between his hands,* staring at the hearth-rug, and at the tip of the satin shoe that showed under her dress. *Suddenly he knelt down and kissed the shoe.*

She bent over him, laying her hands on his shoulders, and looking at him with eyes so deep that he remained motionless under her gaze.

This is very good story-telling, very good theater. But as a rendering of emotion, of what goes on between two people in "real life," how flabby and inadequate! As imaginative writing, what a mere string of smart clichés! The trouble is that Mrs. Wharton has considered each time the propriety of the gesture and not its rightness. It is this sort of thing that so often makes us say of her people: Just where have I seen this figure before? . . .

Miss Sedgwick's strength lies in the portrayal of bad, mean, selfish, picturesque characters—Madame von Marwitz in "Tante," Madame Vervier in "The Little French Girl," Madame de la Mouderie in "The Old Countess"—who are never seen from their own point of view, but always through the eyes of the people we like. As for the wholly sympathetic characters, they are mainly valuable for the light they throw on the others, and of course we are eager to see them victorious over such adversaries. But they have not much character themselves. Or they are simply too good to be true.

Such is Giles Bradley in "The Little French Girl." He is not really a man at all, but a nice woman's conception of a nice man. Without his love for Toppie the book would have been cut short in the middle, but his love for Toppie is merely a demonstration of his English sentimentality. He does not seem to realize—nor his creator either, for that matter—what a perfectly horrid creature she is.

More than once the author gives a feminine turn to the reflections of her hero. Or, to put it more exactly, a sentimental turn. "The Little French Girl" was published during the first great vogue of A. S. M. Hutchinson, that most glib of sentimentalists in our day, and one seems to catch here and there a whiff—oh, just a soupçon—of that influence. Madame Vervier and Giles have been discussing what effect, if he had lived, Owen's affair with her would have had on his feeling toward the two women. He would have been strong enough, she says, not to grow to hate her because of the need for keeping Toppie in the dark.

Was it true? Giles wondered, sitting there before her, his head bent down while he stared up at her from under his brows, frowning and intent. Could Owen, ever, have been as strong as that? And would it have been strength? No; madame Vervier might have armed him against remorse; but she did not know Toppie. *Toppie's radiance would have fallen back, dimmed, startled, from the presence of the thing hidden* yet operative in her life and Owen's. *A canker would have eaten; bitterness and darkness would have spread.* Either her *radiance would have withdrawn from him,* or, *beating too strongly at his defences,* it would have discovered all. *Dismay, devastation would have broken in on them,* and if Toppie could still have forgiven it would have been with a sick and altered heart. But he could not talk to madame Vervier about Toppie. The strange thing was, as he saw *Toppie's radiance,* that he felt himself safe from the torrent, and that he began to understand madame Vervier.

Too much Toppie was the trouble with Miss Sedgwick's world; and this was doubtless partly responsible, by way of reaction, for the too much tom-cat of Lawrence's, Hemingway's, Hecht's. Miss Sedgwick is an exquisite artist within her limits; but her limits were very narrowly drawn. Somewhat wider were Mrs. Wharton's, and she made a brave effort to make them wider than they were. But she was hampered by the conventions of her world—which was a feminine version of James's. For persons occupying a world so neatly ordered it would be easier than for some one like Lawrence to observe the conventions of the well-made novel.

3

There is one great merit in the handling of the restricted point of view by Mrs. Wharton and Miss Sedgwick. The subjective passages, in which the character muses and reflects upon his situation, are kept well within bounds. In James the artistic intention calls for extremely extended passages of this sort, much more extended than the patience of the average reader can bear. But there is, I think, no watering. The problem of the moment is often a very subtle one, and the author's imagination dwells upon it broodingly so as not to lose one shade of what it means to the character. In many writers under James's influence, the exploitation of this part of the narrative is carried to tedious lengths.

In Hugh Walpole, for example, there are pages upon pages of this sort of thing which the judicious reader will know how to skip. One trouble is that the characters are so much alike, all tarred with the same faint brush of suffering and soulfulness. In "The Duchess of Wrexe" (1914), which is probably his best novel, a large part of the narrative is given over to the thoughts and feelings of Rachel, of Breton, Roddy, Lizzie Rand, and Dr. Christopher. And while these people have very different parts to play in the story and the author has done his best to differentiate them in character, they all think alike, and, what is more, all feel alike. They are all so nice in their sentimental reactions, so troubled in spirit, going through so languidly and yet convulsively their exercises in the moral gymnasium which is life!

Opposed to them is a malignant old woman, Rachel's grandmother, the Duchess, who is supposed to sum up in some vague way all that is evil and mean in social life—the old, selfish, autocratic tradition of the Beaminsters. The Duchess knows that her granddaughter is in tacit rebellion against her ideals, and she marries her to her favorite, the pagan Beaminster, Roddy, with the deliberate intention of crushing her spirit and bringing her to heel. "Her grandmother was determined to destroy the honesty and truth in her and had chosen a Beaminster for her agent and now waited happy for the death of Rachel's soul."

Her motivation is anything but clear. Mr. Walpole always wants to make his characters too widely representative. "The Duchess of Wrexe" is one of the many novels of the time which were intended to chronicle the changing social order, with presumably the change in ideals. This is a leading motif of the Forsyte Saga. It is the constant subject of H. G. Wells. Something of the same intention is seen in Rose Macaulay's "Potterism" (1920) and "Told by an Idiot" (1923). Only, while it is perfectly clear, in Miss Macaulay and Wells and Galsworthy, what changes in social custom and alignment, in economic theory and political ideals, are being discussed, and while none of these writers suggests that the soul of man is undergoing beneath our eyes some radical alteration, the whole matter is shrouded by Walpole in a mist of transcendental vagueness, in which we know only that, in some mysterious manner, the death of the Duchess signalizes the approach of the millennium and the emergence of Soul. Ethical terms which have no clear application (honesty and truth), metaphysical terms from Carlyle (shams, Real and Unreal), are all messed up with terms from social theory (progress, the new Individualism, the end of a Period); and throughout it is implied that the opposed terms of an ethical dualism are somehow to be assigned respectively to the old and the new generation. The relief of Mafeking, with the riotous London crowd, soberly enough interpreted by Soames Forsyte in "In Chancery," is made by Walpole's people the occasion for an orgy of confused speculations.

There is a speculative citizen of the world named Brun who has no part in the story but makes an occasional appearance for the sole purpose of putting strained interpretations on simple events. He has a curious generic resemblance to Gabriel Nash of "The Tragic Muse." In addition to his political-social theory, he has a picturesque and most elusive moral theory having to do with a Tiger which each one of us carries hidden somewhere in his heart, and which, if our soul is to live, we must sometime face and conquer. This is not the first or last appearance of the Tiger in Walpole—a mythical beast lineally descended from James's Beast in the Jungle and Blake's "tiger burning bright in the forests of the night."

This Tiger belongs to a region of Mr. Walpole's imagination which makes him rather skilful in creating an atmosphere of mystery and terror. He has done this quite successfully, for example, in "Fortitude" (1913), in "The Dark Forest (1916), and "The Secret City" (1919). "The Dark Forest" is a story of the World War as experienced by English and Russian Red Cross workers on the eastern front.

Mr. Walpole has used somewhat the method of Conrad in "Heart of Darkness" (1902) for gradually working up his mysterious terrors, and he has obviously been influenced by Dostoevski in the psychology of his characters. But the moral degradation of the ivory-hunter Kurtz in "Heart of Darkness," while so long a matter of shadowy guesses and intimations, is sufficiently real and itemized in the end to justify the shudders to which the reader is subjected. And the psychology of Dostoevski, while he keeps it obscure through long stretches of his story, is solidly enough based in a coherent religious philosophy. Strange as the Russians may seem to us, there is nothing in them so factitious and fantastic as these two pairs of men in "The Dark Forest," rivals in each case for the love of a dead woman and racing each other to Death under the impression that the one who first arrives in the realm of the shades will possess the desired woman. If the idea is not so simple as this, that will be because it is more confused. Something of the same fantastic quality attaches to the cathedral in Mr. Walpole's famous novel on that subject (1922), which has been so often compared to Ibañez's novel with the same title.

It is this pretentious haziness of ideas that stands in the way of any serious study of human nature, and gives that air of unreality to the situations in which Mr. Walpole's characters find themselves. Mr. Walpole was a close friend of James, who evidently regarded him as one of his most promising disciples. And he perhaps considered that in "The Duchess of Wrexe" he was developing a James situation. We read of Rachel's "desperate efforts to analyze a situation that was, in definite outline, no situation at all." But the situations in James, while they are often baffling enough for the people involved, never want definite outline. What Mr. Walpole lacks, to be a proper disciple of James, is the imaginative precision which is maintained through all the windings and subtleties of thought, as well as James's freedom from the sentimental stress. If there was a certain softness latent in James, it came out with a vengeance in some of his followers, and was a dominant note in pre-war English literature.

An uncritical subjectivism is often a weakening element in twentieth-century fiction. And not merely fiction in English. It is a notable feature of the later volumes of Couperus's "Books of the Small Souls." There is here none of the spiritual sophistication practised by Mr. Walpole, but I have an impression of some of the softness, and the monotony of reflections by persons not sharply enough characterized.

In Galsworthy, again, there is an effect of the automatic in the passages, more and more frequent in his later novels, in which the characters are shown musing, for the most part, on the state of the world—on the money market, the decline of mind, the rising tide of socialism, or psycho-analysis, vitamins, and the influence of the press. It is mainly Soames Forsyte who is thus made to connect the private history with developments in the world at large. But in the final volumes of the saga, Mr. Galsworthy has taken to recording the views of Michael Mont as well. There is here no question of undue sentimental stress. But the method of subjective drama has come to seem like a mechanical trick—a substitute for whatever it is that is wanting in the characters. It has somehow gone to seed, this subjective method, and if it is ever to flower again, some process of renewal is called for. It is this process which is undertaken by Messrs. Joyce and Co.

4

The well-made novel was the flowering in the twentieth century of a tree that had its roots in the nineteenth. To the more forward-looking spirits of the twentieth century it must have seemed to suffer from too much—not form, for some of them have been greatly concerned with form—

but formalization. With its tight little plot, its exclusion of everything that did not bear directly and obviously on the theme, and its old-fashioned idealistic definition of its theme, it must have seemed to the new men rather quaint and prim and stiff.

The story had ceased to exist for itself. Everything was focused on the characters conceived as problems of conduct. The primary interest was in the soul. It was the soul of the character that determined the action of the story.

But note—and this is most important for understanding the motives of the reaction against the well-made novel—that while the interest was centered in the soul of the character, the *soul was defined by the action of the story*. This is just as important as the proposition reversed—that the action was determined by the soul of the character. The soul of Fleda Vetch is constituted for us by the predicament in which she finds herself between her love for Owen Gereth and her loyalty to his mother and Mona. The soul of Newland Archer is constituted by his position between his wife, typical of narrow New York, and Ellen Olenska, typical of a larger living. Everything that we know of these souls is crystallized like particles of some chemical along the slender threads of the sharply defined dramatic situations.

These are remarkable examples of what we may call the classical spirit in the formal conception of the novel. In the classical spirit is a dominant bent for clarification, simplification, *definition*. And observe that in the well-made novel it is the rational, the logical faculty that is in play in the definition of souls. The narrative of their spiritual predicaments is conducted in intellectual terms, in terms of sentimental (that is, formalized, intellectualized) ideals. It is a definition of the characters in terms of a sentimental ideology, and a highly simplified one. And the men and women of our time who have written "Women in Love," "Lord Jim," "Ulysses," "Pilgrimage," "Mrs. Dalloway,"

"An American Tragedy," "Babbitt," "Manhattan Transfer," "Holiday" must feel in the presence of the well-made novel as the romantic poets of 1798 and 1830 felt in the presence of Dryden and Pope, of Racine and Voltaire.[1] They must have felt that the writers of the well-made novel had defined and defined until they had defined away a large part of the soul itself. For the process of definition is a process of limitation. And limitation, if carried too far, means thinning out, impoverishment, loss of color and substance and the vibrancy of the living thing.

1 That the well-made novel is by no means dead is shown by the appearance and the great popularity in 1932 of Charles Morgan's "The Fountain." This book has a very interesting theme—the effort of a man of our time to practise the mystic discipline of the spirit. The subject is developed with considerable power, though in the end the author fails to show how the contemplative life can be reconciled with the sentimental. Mr. Morgan writes well and is a fine and subtle craftsman. If in psychology, in sentiment and form, his face is turned nostalgically to the past, he gives at any rate a striking reminder of the artistic resources commanded by writers of a school now regarded as somewhat old-fashioned.

XXVII

THE REALIST REACTION: DREISER

One of the strongest of influences leading to the break-up of the well-made novel, at least in America, has been the movement toward extreme realism. This movement dates back into the nineteenth century, at least as early as Stephen Crane's "Maggie, a Girl of the Streets" (1891), and "The Red Badge of Courage" (1896). Its main exponent in the present century is Theodore Dreiser, whose career as a novelist is exactly contemporary with Edith Wharton's, "Sister Carrie" appearing in 1900 and "An American Tragedy" in 1925. Mr. Dreiser does not give the impression of being an author greatly concerned with questions of form as such; and if his novels constitute a reaction against the conventional pattern of the well-made novel, this is incidental. They are fundamentally a reaction against conventional ways of regarding human nature. They are one continuous protest against the prime assumptions of the genteel novel.

For essentially that is what the well-made novel for the most part is, a survey of humanity from the standpoint of genteel good taste. It is mainly confined to the limits of good society; and where, as in "The Custom of the Country," it offers glimpses of more vulgar reaches of human experience, they are shown unmistakably as they would appear to one established in fortune and family of at least three generations' standing. This is highly rarefied air, in which it is possible to bring certain sentiments to an extreme pitch of perfection. These sentiments are about equally compounded of good taste and ethical conformity. Indeed, the two qualities are hardly to be distinguished on this level of social evolution. And to question the general prevalence of these qualities in any society worth considering, as well as their absolute validity as standards for society in general, might in itself be construed as an evidence of bad taste and immorality on the part of the questioner.

This was about the state of things in the American novel when Mr. Dreiser arrived to view life in the larger perspective of Balzac and the French naturalists. In order to realize the extent to which the genteel tradition prevailed, one has but to read Frank Norris's "The Pit" (1903). This story made, with "The Octopus," a brave attempt at realism in the treatment of contemporary business methods, at least as much as was involved in the production of wheat, its distribution, and the trading in it on the floor of the Chicago Board of Trade. And this marked a distinct innovation and progress toward the bold handling of business in Dreiser's "The Financier," "The Titan," "The Genius" (1912, 1914, and 1915, respectively). But so far as the treatment of society and private relations goes, "The Pit" gives one a sense of quaint formality, of a willingness to accept conventional patterns in human motivation and behavior which reminds one of Edith Wharton's "The Fruit of the Tree" (another novel dealing with business) more than of "The Financier" and "The Titan."

In the genteel novel the fact of wealth and social position is something taken for granted, something to start with, and carrying with it the notion of a certain degree of refinement, an ordered social status and a fixed standard of personal conduct. And all that remains is to plan out the social comedies and sentimental dramas suitable for production on this narrow stage. But Mr. Dreiser was born into a world in which none of these things was established. He was born into it and was himself a part of it, as he so candidly and eloquently lets us know in his autobiographical writings, such as "A Book about Myself" and "Dawn." And what he saw on every side of him, what he knew with the practical and intimate knowledge of personal participation, was a world more like the jungle than like the world of Edith Wharton and Hugh Walpole.

It was made up of men and women starting poor, vulgar, ignorant, emotionally starved, but—so far as they were strong—determined to win for themselves wealth, luxury, culture, social estimation, and the gratifications of love. They were not snobs—that was not at all the way they appealed to Theodore Dreiser—they were simply vital forces pushing forward irrepressibly to take their place in the sun. All about them were swarming millions of their kind, through the milling jam of whom they must force their way forward. The methods were the age-old methods of competitive business, never before perhaps displayed on so grand a scale as in the America of Dreiser's time: tireless work, organization, speculation, coöperation with those who can aid you, abandonment of those who cannot serve you, political graft and intimidation. The mental equipment was imagination, feline cunning, the gambling instinct, indomitable courage . . . and the devil take the hindmost! For those who won, the rewards were unlimited power, grand houses, picture galleries, and a choice of women, demanded by the insatiable craving to gratify the ego. The race was to the strong.

Meantime the weak were striving, in their own ineffectual way, for much the same prizes—conceived with less imagination and pursued with less perseverance and ruthlessness. Most were doomed to envious mediocrity, and many heedless ones were destined to be caught in the toils of the law (Clyde Griffiths in "An American Tragedy," Stener in "The Financier") or to ignominious defeat and death (Hurstwood in "Sister Carrie"). Generally speaking, the women were condemned to checkmate in the ruthless game of hearts (Jennie Gerhardt, Angela in "The Genius," Roberta in "An American Tragedy," innumerable women in "The Titan"). The woman, with her disposition to loyalty, her more absolute adherence to the conventional standards governing the married state, her relative weakness economically and biologically, would mostly get the worst of it in this clash of egoisms.

In his attitude toward this jungle life of human beings, Mr. Dreiser is not a satirist. He has neither the genial irony of a Thackeray nor the often smart and brittle mockery of a Sinclair Lewis. He is in deadly earnest. He does not take a tone of superiority or set himself apart from his characters. He does not regard them as philistines or as sinners. These people are, one feels, very much the sort he takes himself to be, with the same problems, ambitions, cravings, discouragements. And whether they are winners or losers in the struggle, he is pretty closely in sympathy with them, even though, in his wider vision, he may see them in their littleness, helplessness, and futility. He understands the selfish urgencies that move people to unsocial behavior, and equally well the misery and ruin that so often follow in the wake of such behavior, most often for others but frequently also for themselves. His tone is that of a brooding, compassionate, philosophical observer.

So far as there is a note of criticism in his picture, it is in reference to judgments and standards which he regards as conventional, artificial, and often—as he seems to imply—hypocritical. The one thing that moves him to impatience is the genteel assumption of the prevalence in society of standards which *do not prevail,* and the easy relegation to the background of selfish types of behavior which seem to him well-nigh universal. His great motivating passion as a writer is simply to tell the truth. Or to put it the other way round, his passion is to give the lie to the prevailing idealistic assumptions of fiction of his day in English. In "An American Tragedy" his intention seems to be to picture a young man in no way unusual, to show how natural he is in all his desires and actions, and how, without being in the least a criminal type, he is driven, all in the course of nature, to commit the most heinous of crimes.

Dreiser's realism does not exhaust itself upon the general outlines of action and motivation. There is plenty left over for the minutest details of psychology. Here again his aim is not to conventionalize, to simplify in the direction either of prettiness or meanness, but merely to record the natural facts of the case, without exaggeration or extenuation. Thus in "The Genius," when Eugene Witla has gone to New York, leaving his Angela behind in the West, we are told of the letters he writes her, in which, without intending to deceive, he does give a false impression of the depth of his personal feeling:

> At night he would return to his bare room and indite long epistles to Angela, describing what he had seen and telling her of his undying love for her—largely because he had no other means of ridding himself of his superabundant vitality and moods. They were beautiful letters, full of color and feeling, but to Angela they gave a false impression of emotion and sincerity because they appeared to be provoked by absence from her. In part of course they were, but far more largely they were the result of loneliness and the desire for expression which this vast spectacle of life itself incited.

The mere plain truthfulness of such quiet observations serves to clear the air like a window opened on a room sickly with the scent of withered flowers.

The genteel tradition Dreiser pushes aside altogether and goes straight back, for his models, to Balzac and perhaps the later French naturalists. His effort is to vision society not from the standpoint of a clique, but with the broad comprehensive view of a scientific observer, outside of all cliques and patterned societies. If I suggest a possible inspiration from the French naturalists, it is because his work is strongly colored by the terminology and deterministic assumptions of nineteenth-century science, which were so strong an element in Zola and his group. But it may have been direct from science, rather than from literature, that Dreiser took his disposition to regard human behavior as one manifestation of animal behavior in general, or even—to use his more frequently recurring term—as a chemical phenomenon.

If time allowed, it would be worth while to distinguish between the somewhat crass scientism of Dreiser and the decidedly more humanistic philosophy of Balzac, of Flaubert and Zola. These French writers had very firmly in mind a model of social well-being and ideal behavior against which to measure in all boldness the aberrations of degraded and perverted humanity. They all had in mind certain social ideals as a salutary force for constraining men and subjecting them to the collective will of society, necessary for its very existence. The most abused of these French writers is Zola; but it must not be forgotten that he believed in science as a means of diagnosing the ills of society with a view to their eventual cure. He would not write as a moralist, but he believed in the wholesome effect of his work in the long run. As he wrote in his early notes while projecting the Rougon-Macquart series:

> There is an urge towards liberty and justice. I believe that it will be long in arriving, while holding that we may be led to a better state. But I believe above all in a constant march toward truth. It is only from the knowledge of virtue that a better social state can be produced.

These Frenchmen were born into a long-established traditional order, extremely elastic, it is true, and subject to modification, but with little suggestion of the barbaric chaos of Mr. Dreiser's unformed America. And it was impossible for them to forget for an instant that, along with the forces of animalism and egoism, along with the savage struggle for existence, there was a social will and a social order which could never be radically contravened and set at naught.

What is important, however, is not to point out the relative crudeness and exaggeration of Dreiser's realistic philosophy, but to emphasize what he has in common with the great French novelists—his fearlessness, his honesty, his determination to have done with conventional posturings and evasions. It was extremely important that we should have some one bold enough to set down in the English language just as he saw it the unvarnished truth about American business life, American social life in its major reaches, and the sex-psychology of American men and women. And every serious writer of the present day is deeply under obligation to the brave pioneering of Theodore Dreiser. It is he, more than any other writer, who has borne the brunt and odium of this ungrateful task. And he it is who should have the praise.

2

When we turn from the consideration of substance and ask what Mr. Dreiser has done for the novel as an art form, it is first to be noted of course that, if he has given adequate expression to his thought, he has met at least the minimum requirements of shaping art. And then it must be added that he has made no specific original contribution to novelistic technique, and is not among the most skilful of novelists when it comes to nice points of craftsmanship.

His books are solidly built around a central idea. They are documented in a manner worthy of his admired Balzac and even suggestive of the more colossal structures of Zola. No novelist could have gone into the operations of business and politics more thoroughly and still maintained our unflagging interest. He manages to make us appreciate the excitement of the stock-exchange and follow intently the organization of gas companies and street-railways, of advertising agencies and magazine mergers, and the interrelations of politics and business. And at the same time he makes clear how all these matters bear upon the intimate emotional life and cultural status of individuals.

In two instances he has succeeded in giving a notably dramatic cast to his huge and copious material. "The Financier" is largely built round the great financial panic of 1871 following on the Chicago fire. The young broker Cowperwood is caught with half a million dollars' worth of municipal loans on his hands; he makes a brilliant and heroic fight to stave off failure; he is driven to the wall by politicians who see a chance to take over his much coveted street-railway stock, and sent to the penitentiary as scapegoat of the political machine. The continuous strained action and suspense of this culminating phase of his Philadelphia career occupy nearly three fourths of the story, giving one of the most striking examples one could find of the "dramatic present." Another equally striking example is that part of "An American Tragedy" dealing with Clyde Griffiths's murder of his sweetheart Roberta, which again, if we take into account the circumstances immediately leading to the crime, the detective work, the trial, the appeal, and the execution of Clyde, occupies considerably more than half of the story. All things considered, "An American Tragedy" is doubtless the most neatly constructed of all Dreiser's novels, as well as the best written. And it is always a satisfaction to find that an artist is gaining rather than losing with the passage of the years.

The solid documentation, which suggests Balzac, suggests a defect in technique which is even greater in Dreiser than it is in the French writer. He relies too much on formal exposition. He imagines that if he has described a character to us we can see him; that if he spends three or four thousand words telling us all about a character, then we know all about him; that what an author has explained becomes *ipso facto* the possession of the reader. Accordingly he overloads the text with details, important enough and interesting enough if only they might somehow be assimilated to the imaginative fabric of the story.

Again, he does not know how to get from one moment in his story to a later moment without giving an extensive summary of what was going on in the interval. In "The Titan" and "The Genius" chapter after chapter is given up to such perfunctory summaries, in which there is nothing to sustain us but the memory that there have been interesting times before and probably are interesting times ahead. Of course what inevitably happens is that the reader skips. And where the intelligent reader skips, the writer might just as well have spared his pains.

Mr. Dreiser, in short, is singularly defective in the faculty for conceiving his story in scenes. He has taken seriously his philosophic obligation to tell the truth, but has thought very little of his artistic obligation to "make us see." He is entirely innocent of any intention concerning point of view. He keeps himself, on the whole, pretty well out of the story. But he seldom considers from page to page whose story it now is. Whatever needs explaining must be explained at the moment it comes into his head, without regard to whether or not it will spoil an intimate effect for the imagination or the feeling. That is, his approach to his art is almost exclusively intellectual. He has so much matter to deliver from his mind to the reader's mind. For the reader's imagination he has no care. In keeping with his indifference to the scenical, he has no conception of what a chapter may mean in the way of imaginative composition of subject-matter. His chapters are chronological rag-bags rather than the imaginative units which Zola's chapters, for example, are.

His handling of dialogue is typical of his want of concern for the niceties of writing. Dialogue is one way of enlivening exposition, and he uses it with the average frequency of serious writers. Of course there are moments of dramatic confrontation and struggle in which it would be practically impossible to avoid the spoken word. There is nothing remarkable about his dialogue. He is a plain realist, and does not attempt to make his people's talk pointed or witty. Neither does he attempt to signalize it as commonplace or vulgar. It is commonplace, but without intention. It is not slangy, racy, colloquial. It is ordinary speech, but without any special notation of the rhythms of ordinary speech. There is no hint of the deliberate marking of the accents such as we have it in Hemingway's dialogue. Dreiser is not thinking of the way talk sounds; he is thinking simply and solely of the subject-matter, of what is conveyed. But the best things, the subtlest and most poignant things are not conveyed by words that *mean* so-and-so; they are conveyed by words that *sound* so-and-so.

Much fault has been found by critics with Mr. Dreiser's style, and I do not mean to add anything here on that ungrateful subject. Only this: His style is all of a piece with his general want of concern for imaginative writing as such. As wholes, his books are of extreme interest because of the large spirit, the passionate intelligence which informs them. His writing does not bear too close inspection in detail, because he has not approached it with an esthetic intention. His people are true like historical personages. Intellectually we believe in them. We are certainly interested in them. We want to know how their stories come out. As imaginative creations, with some exceptions (Hurstwood, Jennie Gerhardt), they scarcely exist, and they move through scenes that scarcely exist, however conscientiously built up. There are in his books no *belles pages,* no enchanting moments, no passages that thrill us with minute precision of rightness, such as abound in Hardy, Gorki, Maupassant, Hudson, Thomas Mann.

For all that, he is one of the strongest forces tending to antiquate the well-made novel . . . and that *because of what he has to say.*

3

Dreiser is very unlike the new men, the modernists. He shows no interest in technical experiments and inventions. He makes no attempt to add a fourth dimension to the three dimensions of plain realism. He tells a simple story, straight forward. He is scarcely more interested in psychology as such than is Hardy. Like Hardy—much more than Hardy—he is literal, matter-of-fact, extravert, moving in a world of "substantial things." The lives of his people are made up of what they do and what happens to them. In his books there is no psychopathic divorce between thought and action, between motive and behavior. Compared with the new men, the generation of Joyce, he is a classical figure.

XXVIII
THE MODERNISTS

When we speak of the new men, we must start with Conrad, who began writing in the eighteen-nineties, before James was through and before Dreiser had begun. For Conrad was the great experimentalist of his day. He was as ill content with ready-made ways of putting a story together as with ready-made ways of interpreting character. And he did more than any one else to limber up the stiff machine of fiction. And then we must take into account the solitary figure of Lawrence, who, being a painter, brought to fiction some of the subtleties of pictorial art, and, wrestling with the mysteries of sex psychology, stumbled on a technique suited to that elusive subject. These writers are transitional; and as such it will be most convenient to regard Dorothy Richardson, though she was so radical in some of her methods. It is most convenient to consider these three writers together and apart from those who came in with Joyce, whom I call expressionists. But in characterizing the modernists as a whole, in brief anticipation, and in broad contrast to the school of James, it is possible to lump together these transitional writers with those who followed them.

The new men are naturally affected by the new psychology. Modern psychology does not conceive the soul as something which can be adequately rendered in terms of a single dramatic action with a highly simplified issue. It is not something to be caught in the net of neat intellectual definition. The soul is not that simple entity offered to us in most works of fiction. It is a vast fluid, or even vaporous, mass, wide-spreading far beyond the feeble village lights of our conventional reading of character, deep-sounding into our nervous and animal organization, into childhood, heredity. It runs out and down far beyond thought, beyond memory and consciousness. It is not uniform and homogeneous, but varying and full of a great diversity of tinctures and infusions. There are all sorts of debris and driftwood floating on the surface, and huge water-soaked logs lurking far below. At the bottom is mud, and in the depths are octopuses and starfish and all kinds of undreamed-of monsters. The soul is not one identity but many identities grouped about many centers and often at war with one another, or indifferent and unaware of one another's existence.

For the most part it is no identity at all, but a kind of dreaming welter of sensations and reactions so instantaneous and spontaneous that we never become conscious of them. In many aspects the soul is not individualized as belonging to this or that ego, but is a mere jet of the vitality common to our race or sex or social group. Our consciousness, which is a small part of our soul, does not proceed logically or coherently except at certain times and for certain periods under the pressure of some urgent practical need. For the most part it follows an association of ideas so freakish—though natural—that we cannot chart its progress, running off constantly into what seem irrelevancies as judged by reference to any recognized dominant interest. The soul is supremely indifferent to past and future, near and far. It is a highly specialized faculty of our rational mind that has devised these conventions, these instruments for controlling material things and guiding conduct. Each soul is attached to an individual physical organism; but through the imagination, through the infinite nervous connections between organism and organism, souls have a large capacity for interpenetration. A large part of the life of the soul may be regarded in the light of group actions and reactions.

In short, it becomes more and more awkward and queer to use the term "soul" to cover the phenomena in question. We might try the word "psyche," which is not quite so heavily weighted with discordant connotations.

The new writers are as much concerned as the old ones with the psyche as the focus of life experience. Only, with their modern conception of the psyche, they grow more and more impatient of the quaint little patterns into which the old psychological novelists had tried to force this protean creature, and their disposition to ignore all sorts of things that go to make up human personality. And the new writers have felt the need to break up these conventional patterns. They have wanted new technical devices, new procedures, for rendering the psyche. In general the new features of their technique are expressions of what is called the romantic as opposed to the classic spirit in art.

Instead of regularity of form, they show a tendency to what at first blush appears a freakish changefulness and unpredictability. Analysis will show that, for the most part, form is not with them so freakish as it seems, perhaps not freakish at all. Only, their principles of form are not those which have been traditional for the novel. They are not determined by the plot, as with Fielding or Trollope; neither are they determined, generally, by that simple dramatic issue which is the form taken by plot in the well-made novel. So that, in their reaction from the particular rigid form favored by their predecessors, we may speak, provisionally, of their tendency to *deformalization*.

Instead of uniformity and simplicity, they tend to diversity and complexity. In this respect they show a superficial resemblance to the earlier Victorian novelists, with their abundance and colorful variety of material. And yet the spirit and technique and dominant preoccupations of the new men are so different from those of the Victorians that no one would dream of comparing the two schools.

Instead of concentration around a limited issue, they show an eccentric tendency, a tendency to fly off in many different directions.

Instead of continuity of action, they show a tendency to discontinuity. A continuous action seems to them too unlike ordinary experience, with its freakish, accidental interruptions, its overleapings of time and circumstance. They feel that the sense of life is often best rendered by an abrupt passing from one series of events, one group of characters, one center of consciousness, to another.

Moreover, they don't particularly care about neatly finishing off a given action, following it through to the fall of the curtain. As the eye, from a line of spaced dots and dashes, has the faculty of supplying what is not there and tracing an uninterrupted line, they know the imagination has the faculty of filling up the gaps in an action presented in fragments, of getting the impression of an entire life from a mere hinting indication of the high moments. Again, they feel that the imagination is stimulated and rendered more active, is actually exhilarated, by broken bits of information, as the nerves are stimulated by the discontinuity of an electric current.

Want of continuity, yes—but not of a sort of rhythm, a sense of movement, of wave-like progress. This rhythm is not metrical like that of verse, but is constituted by repetition, by recurrence of themes, by a kind of lyrical agitation of the stream of consciousness. The word "rhythm" is here used in the sense in which it is applied to the similar quality of well-constructed pictures, especially the abstract paintings which are called post-impressionistic.

Instead of dramatic effect, these men go in for something more like lyricism.

They show a tendency to throw overboard terms intellectual, logical, sentimental. They rely more on impressions of the senses—on a mere succession of sensations—for rendering the psyche. Their idea is perhaps to make the effect at the same time more real and less sharply defined. There are two ways in which this greater reality is brought about by the exploitation of sensations. So largely, by this means, one gets rid of the author's intellectual formulation of the thought-process, which is likely to interfere with directness of presentation and throw its conventional film over everything. And then this method conforms to the actual thought-process, which is chiefly made up of items of sensation, rather than being a connected chain of logical reasoning.

The new men do not represent a sharp and complete break with tradition. In particular, some of them have learned a great deal from the well-made novel. But it will be seen how much they were in reaction against most of its main tendencies. And in general their motive has been to give new life to a form which, in the hands of the writers of that school, had become so impoverished and anemic.

XXIX

IMPRESSIONISM: CONRAD

"I have been keenly interested in the discussion of a number of questions, I have been a haphazard and pampered prophet, I have found it amusing and profitable to write stories and—save for an incidental lapse or so—I have never taken any very great pains about writing. I am outside the hierarchy of conscious and deliberate writers altogether. I am the absolute antithesis of Mr. James Joyce . . . Long ago, living in close conversational proximity to Henry James, Joseph Conrad, and Mr. Ford Madox Hueffer, I escaped from under their immense artistic preoccupations by calling myself a journalist."

The words are those of Mr. H. G. Wells, and they remind us how unmistakably Conrad belongs in the hierarchy of conscious and deliberate writers. Conrad was the most restless and ingenious experimenter of his time, the one who brought the greatest variety of technical procedures to bear upon the problem of the novelist. According to Mr. Edward Garnett, Conrad "never theorized about technique and . . . on asking me why I had never written on the art of fiction and receiving my reply that the subject was too difficult for my brains, he declared that it was also too difficult for his and that he had never formulated any rules for his own practice." On the same page, however, Mr. Garnett gives several instances of Conrad's extreme preoccupation with technique in the work of others.

It is obvious that, while Conrad never formulated any rules, he was forever trying out new methods, hitting upon this or that new procedure, it may be, by instinct rather than by deliberation; but it was the instinct of a man profoundly concerned with method, forever on the look-out for some new way of cheating oblivion and saving his chosen art from the dry-rot of monotony and academicism. Given his temperament he could never be content with the neat little formula of the well-made novel, with its crystalline simplicity of logic and its steady rigor of method. Life must have seemed to him much too complex, much too vast and elusive a creature to be caught in any such net—and still more that illusion of life, which, rather than the thing itself, is what such writers are most concerned to capture and display.

His own most famous account of his intentions as a novelist is given in the preface to "The Nigger of the Narcissus":

> My task which I am trying to achieve is, by the power of the written word to make you hear, to make you feel—it is, before all, to make you *see*. That—and no more, and it is everything. If I succeed, you shall find there according to your deserts: encouragement, consolation, fear, charm—all you demand—and, perhaps, also that glimpse of truth for which you have forgotten to ask. To snatch in a moment of courage, from the remorseless rush of time, a passing phase of life, is only the beginning of the task. The task approached in tenderness and faith is to hold up unquestioningly, without choice and without fear, the rescued fragment before all eyes in the light of a sincere mood. It is to show its vibration, its colour, its form; and through its movement, its form, and its colour, reveal the substance of its truth—disclose its inspiring secret: the stress and passion within the core of each convincing moment.

There is probably no serious novelist of the time, unless it be Mr. Wells, who could not have subscribed wholeheartedly to this credo. But there is none but Conrad that could have written these words. There is none that has this excitement, this accent of almost hysterical emotion. There is none for whom the art of writing was more difficult, more agonizing; Mr. Ford even asserts that he hated it. "Conrad hated writing more than he hated the sea." Of all English writers of his time none was so bent double under the weight of what Mr. Wells calls "their immense artistic preoccupations."

This may be partly because Conrad was writing in a foreign language, one he had learned to speak since he came to man's estate, in which he was perpetually liable to little slips in idiom, and which he pronounced so badly—so frequently misplacing the accent—that it was hard to understand him when he read aloud.

Still more his subject-matter, interesting as it was on its own account, must have created difficulties not encountered by friends like Galsworthy and Bennett. This exotic matter, hidden rivers in Borneo, Malay princes seeking to recover their lost kingdoms, the savage secrets of sea and jungle; these incredible heroes—Lingard, Heyst, Razumov—maintaining the point of honor in the midst of treachery and corruption; these heroines, the creation of man's power of idealizing women, savage as Mother Eve and steadfast as the pole-star—Lena, Rita, Jewel, Aïssa, Flora—it was no mean task throwing the illusion of truth over subjects so strange and fantastic.

It is not merely that he used the subject-matter of romance, that he occupied and immensely enlarged the realm of Cooper, Stevenson, and Kipling. He was not content to work the traditional motives of chivalry, fealty, bravado, and revenge. Life was not so simple as that, nor so monotonous. His grotesque imagination fills his pages with monsters and vermin: Willems, Jones, Kurtz, Schomberg, Pedro, Ricardo, Ortega, Scevola. He loves to trace the slimy involutions of morbid psychology. And when it comes to his heroes, he loves to envelop them in a cloud of Slavic mysticism.

Conrad resented Mencken's stress upon his Slavic strain;

he never tired of expressing his dislike for the Russians, and especially for Dostoevski. But where do we come so near as in Dostoevski and the Russians to the psychology of a Lord Jim, a Baron Heyst? And where but in Dostoevski did Conrad get the plot, the psychology, the very technique of "Under Western Eyes"? One of the most curious of minor resemblances to Dostoevski is that series of titles assumed by Blunt in "The Arrow of Gold," *"Je suis Américain, catholique et gentilhomme."* We know that Blunt is drawn from a real person of the same name, and the real person may well have described himself in just these terms. But it is at least a striking coincidence that Kirillov in "The Possessed" should have signed himself, also in French, *"Gentilhomme, séminariste russe et citoyen du monde civilisé."*

Of course Conrad hated the Russians on patriotic, on political grounds, and he was a decidedly political-minded man. He wanted to be identified, himself, with "Europe," and insisted that the true classification of Poland was with Europe and not with Slavic and Asiatic Russia. Again, he may have disliked in Dostoevski the specifically religious cast of his "mysticism." And then, is it not possible that he was affected unconsciously by the very natural desire to make little of an artist by whom he had been so greatly, if so unknowingly, influenced? In any case, the point I wish to make is that Conrad was much concerned with twists and puzzles of psychology—growing out of the character's *Weltanschauung*—which, if not Russian, are at any rate "central European," and most decidedly not English. He certainly shared with Dostoevski a profound feeling of the mysteriousness, the almost transcendental character of human motives. This psychological cast is something as exotic as his subject-matter, and is another reason why he found so arduous the novelist's task of making his reader *see*.

Now, the most obvious means of making the reader see

is simply the use of adequate words. And that Conrad most earnestly cultivated this means we have, what we hardly need, the testimony of Mr. Ford Madox Ford (then Hueffer), who collaborated with him in the writing of three novels, and that at a most critical time in Conrad's career. Both Ford and Conrad were enthusiastic devotees of Maupassant and Flaubert, whose stories they knew so well in the original that when one would begin reciting some well-written passage the other would take up the recitation and carry it on to the end. What they worshiped in these French writers was the *mot juste* and the cadence, the Goncourt ideal of *écriture artiste,* with the perfect "rise and fall." Their notions of style were not identical, Conrad being inclined, Ford thought, to make his writing *trop chargé*. This was one thing Wells admired in Conrad, and he begged Ford not to collaborate with him for fear he should spoil his magnificent "Oriental style."

Conrad's Oriental style is one of the features for which he is most admired. But over and over again, especially in his earlier novels, before Ford came on the scene, one must feel that he would have profited by the critical spirit of the Englishman. Conrad had often the tendency to use too many words. It is as if in his search for the *mot juste* he tried out three or four or a dozen words, and then, instead of keeping the one which just suited his need, he kept them all. And for this, I imagine, Flaubert is somewhat to blame—the Flaubert of "Salammbô" and the "Tentation de Saint Antoine." Conrad was too much under the spell of these sonorous rhythms, and did not sufficiently consider that French rhythms will not always stand transplanting into the more matter-of-fact English.

But this, after all, is but the defect of his quality. This is not simply fine writing and panache. Conrad's emotion is too warm and turbulent to be confined within the dry dikes of the *mot juste*. Over and over again, when he broods upon man's destiny, his great heart, and the futile stir he makes upon the vast impassive face of Nature, he reaches heights of imaginative splendor which would be impossible to a more critical artist.

2

It is notable, however, that Conrad's eloquence is most frequently resorted to in his earliest stories, before he had hit upon devices for "making us see" more structural and less dependent on mere style. In the course of his later writing he found a considerable variety of such devices for bringing the subject into focus. To begin with, there are the various techniques for identifying the author (and so the reader) with the principal actor, making him feel his suspense, his curiosities, his irritations, putting him at the same point of view, physically and morally, as the character.

This method came very natural to Conrad in a good many of his stories which are hardly more than transcripts of his personal experience. "The Shadow-Line" (1917), for example, is a first-person account, with only insignificant variations from fact, of Conrad's voyage from Bangkok to Singapore in the bark *Otago,* his first command.

Something of the same thing is true of tales like "Youth" and "Heart of Darkness" (1902), although Conrad in these cases provided a special framework for his stories. Experiences which were his own—almost literally exact throughout in "Youth," somewhat more worked up and highlighted in "Heart of Darkness"—he attributes to a Captain Marlow. He has the captain narrate his adventures orally to a group of men. The author describes the place and conditions under which the stories were told, thus furnishing a sort of stage for his little drama. And so they are provided in advance with a certain emotional tone, which goes far to give them artistic unity and precision of effect. Moreover, their being told by word of mouth to a group of sympathetic but matter-of-fact listeners, necessarily affects the style, somewhat chastening Conrad's Orientalism, making it seem, so far as it lingers still, a peculiarity of Captain Marlow's temperament, and altogether contributing to the plausibility, the verisimilitude—a most important consideration in the art of making us "see."

"Heart of Darkness" is a much more difficult artistic achievement than "Youth," much more of an effort of the creative imagination. It was based on Conrad's voyage to the head-waters of the Congo and his personal impressions of the geographical and social conditions of that exploited country. Many of the characters were taken from life. Kurtz was suggested by one Klein, the company's agent at Stanley Falls. But what Marlow made of Kurtz and his way of doing it, that is the story.

Kurtz is a personal embodiment, a dramatization, of all that Conrad felt of futility, degradation, and horror in what the Europeans in the Congo called "progress," which meant the exploitation of the natives by every variety of cruelty and treachery known to greedy man. Kurtz was to Marlow, penetrating this country, a name, constantly recurring in people's talk, for cleverness and enterprise. But there were slight intimations, growing stronger as Marlow drew near to the heart of darkness, of traits and practices so abhorrent to all our notions of decency, honor, and humanity, that the enterprising trader gradually takes on the proportions of a ghastly and almost supernatural monster, symbol for Marlow of the general spirit of this European undertaking. The blackness and mystery of his character tone in with the savage mystery of the Congo, and they develop *pari passu* with the atmosphere of shadowy horror.

This development is conducted cumulatively by insensible degrees, by carefully calculated releases of new items, new intimations; and all this process is *controlled* through the consciousness of Marlow. Thus we have a triumph of atmospheric effect produced with the technique of the limited point of view, a story in a class with "The Fall of the House of Usher" and "The Turn of the Screw."

Relatively unimportant are the autobiographical novels written by Conrad at this period in collaboration with Ford, "The Inheritors" (1901) and "Romance" (1903). These were Ford's stories to begin with, and we may probably assume that this first-person narrative was the technique he had adopted before Conrad came into the partnership.

A very special and complicated technique is used by Conrad in "Under Western Eyes" (1911). About half of the narrative is told in the third person and follows without intermission the point of view of the leading character, the Russian student Razumov. But this part is based upon a document, Razumov's diary, which has been transposed into the third person, edited and abridged by an English professor who knew Razumov and some of the other persons involved in Geneva. The other half of the story is told in the first person by the English professor himself. Thus the whole narrative is conducted, in several large blocks, from the point of view of but two persons—one the central character, and the other some one only incidentally involved, essentially a spectator. And everything in the history is authenticated by either a written document of the chief participant or by the testimony of an eye-witness.

This story is told with a great air of plausibility, and the special technique admirably serves Conrad's purpose of showing the case of Razumov, as it were from both the inside and the outside. This is at one and the same time a psychological study in the manner of "Crime and Punishment" and a story of political intrigue, with elements of suspense and mystery. And I don't know how better Conrad could have carried forward these two strains of interest than by the complicated method he has chosen.

This is not the only case in which Conrad used an imaginary diary as the basis for his narrative. "The Arrow of Gold" (1919) is set forward, in notes at the beginning and end, as based upon a MS. of Monsieur George himself, meant for the eye of one woman, a childhood friend of his. If we are to believe Conrad's statements to his friends and his account in his autobiographical "Mirror of the Sea," the main characters and events of this story are drawn from life and Monsieur George is Conrad himself. In this case the MS. and the third-person narrative are, in the first place, simply a disguise, a means of turning autobiography into fiction by making them look like fiction passing itself off for autobiography.

However this may be, the single point of view is magnificently used for more than one purpose in the interest of vividness and verisimilitude. Of the five parts, the first four are mainly occupied with what we may call the exposition. In particular, they gradually reveal the character and history of the heroine, Rita de Lastaola, now living in Marseilles, former mistress of the sculptor Allègre, reputed mistress also of Don Carlos, the Spanish pretender, and generous patron of the Carlist cause. (Monsieur George is himself engaged in smuggling guns into Spain for the use of the Carlist troops.) Along with this is the unfolding of the character of the American adventurer Blunt, his relations to Rita, and the growth of George's infatuation for Rita. It is a marvel in the art of working up curiosity, suspense, and atmosphere through the judicious release of items of information, each one of which whets the reader's appetite as much as it satisfies it.

The fifth part, much longer than any of the others, brings the sensational climax of the story, in which Rita and Monsieur George are shut up in a room together without weapons, and in danger of their lives from an insane jealous lover of Rita's, and are thus driven, as it were, into one another's arms. Here again the limited point of view is superbly employed for securing vividness of effect. It is an art which Conrad has used with great success in many of his books. It consists in giving to a particular moment a sharp isolation, in which it stands out, in its physical and moral features, in lightning-like illumination against a background of midnight obscurity. There are many fine examples in "Lord Jim" and in "Victory."

Quite remarkable in this kind is the physical limitation of view in the climax scene of "Chance" (1913). It is by accident that Powell, the ship's officer, finds himself looking through the transparent glass of Captain Anthony's cabin window. It is only a certain portion of the cabin which he can see, but this includes the captain's table, his bottle, his glass of whisky, and a thick curtain which shuts off his quarters from other parts of the cabin. A peculiar stirring of the curtain arouses the apprehensions of Powell.

He became suspicious, with no one and nothing definite in his mind. He was suspicious of the curtain itself and observed it. It looked very innocent. Then just as he was ready to put it down to a trick of imagination he saw trembling movements where the two curtains joined. Yes! Somebody else besides himself had been watching Captain Anthony. He owns artlessly that this aroused his indignation. It was really too much of a good thing. In this state of intense antagonism he was startled to observe *tips of fingers* fumbling with the dark stuff. Then they grasped the edge of the further curtain and hung on there, *just fingers and knuckles and nothing else*. It made an abominable sight. He was looking at it with unaccountable repulsion when a hand came into view, a *short, puffy, old freckled hand* projecting into the lamplight, followed by a white wrist, *an arm in a grey coat-sleeve, up to the elbow, beyond the elbow, extended tremblingly towards the tray.* Its appearance was weird and nauseous, fantastic and silly. But instead of grabbing the bottle, as Powell expected, this hand, tremulous with senile eagerness, *swerved to the glass, rested on its edge for a moment* (or so it looked from above) and *went back with a jerk.* The gripping fingers of the other hand vanished at the same time, and young Powell, staring at the motionless curtains, could indulge for a moment the notion that he had been dreaming.

I have given but a small fragment of the whole passage, but it will serve to suggest the nightmare vividness effected by the sharp physical limitation of vision. The reader will also note the careful control of tempo in this narration. It is only by degrees that the weird hand and its movements are revealed. The whole technical process reminds us of the "slow-up" and the "close-up" which are such powerful devices of the moving-picture producer.

The actual physical items are delayed in each case by a noting of the imaginative effect, the psychological reactions of the spectator—a matter of supreme importance in Conrad's technique. He knows how to combine so artfully the psychological with the physical limitation of the point of view. It is this which distinguishes him so sharply from the ordinary romancer.

The same combination is found in high degree in the climax scenes of "The Arrow of Gold." And these scenes have also the advantage of being very greatly prolonged. This one situation—this one desperate night in the house of Rita's sister—is altogether the most extensive of any in the book, with a cumulative excitement rarely matched in fiction. The effect of physical limitation is particularly intensified in the long scene in Rita's chamber, with the insane cousin raving in the adjoining room, and Rita and George straining every nerve to maintain absolute silence. Then after the overturning of the candelabrum, they are in complete darkness, and the terrible dialogue between Rita and her mad cousin comes to George through the sole medium of his hearing.

No one will ever know just how much of fact Conrad had to go upon in the development of this scene. I am inclined to think that his imagination far outran the facts through the whole book. But, however that may be, it was the writer of fiction, using all the devices of his craft, who made of the scene something so real for the reader. And it was, to be specific, his trick of "isolating" (with the help of the limited point of view) which enabled the author here to make us *see.*

3

Indentification with a leading character is a means very little used by Conrad in his earliest novels. It is as if it were a trick he had not learned. "Almayer's Folly" (1895) and "An Outcast of the Islands" (1896) are certainly "written"—rather too well written, *trop chargé,* if I am to trust my taste. Their subject-matter is perhaps the most fascinating at Conrad's disposal, the same as that of the later part of "Lord Jim," to which he returns again in "Rescue." They have to do with one of those hidden rivers of Borneo, with the few white traders who have been able to find their way up this jungle-bordered stream, and with the shady, infinitely complicated politics of the native Malays. No lover of Conrad can afford to miss these glamorous and amazing narratives.

But I cannot regard them as over-successful in the manner of the telling. As for the technique of identification, this would be very difficult to apply in any great degree to such material. Thus in "Almayer's Folly," the leading character is Almayer, and it is, more than any other, his point of view which is given. But it is hard indeed for us to identify ourselves at all continuously with so weak and shoddy a soul. And then the exigencies of the story seem to require that we should constantly leave him for the doings and thoughts of others: his daughter Nina, the Dutch officers who come to visit him, and a great variety of native politicians and lovers, Babalatchi, Dain Marools, Mahmat, Taminah.

The third of Conrad's novels was the very short one, "The Nigger of the Narcissus" (1897) which was originally intended to be a short story. It is based upon actual experiences of Conrad while serving as second mate on a ship of the same name in a voyage from Bombay to London, together with suggestions from several other sea voyages. But Conrad makes very little use of the autobiographical method for giving singleness of effect, and the introduction of himself into the story seems to have been an afterthought. Impressive as this story is, from its subject-matter and from Conrad's unique and eloquent interpretation of that subject-matter, technically it appears as a kind of exercise in story-telling, *in the course of which* only he stumbled upon methods which might come in as a supplement to the mere power of words.

The ordinary sea story is a very simple affair. It is likely to be presented as the experience of some one individual, whether told in the first or the third person. It is very matter-of-fact, with virtually no occasion for niceties of psychological interpretation, and no feeling for the need of pictorial art in the representation of the ship, the sea, or the seamen. Conrad's story is the antithesis of all this. It is an account of the illness of a negro sailor, James Wait, and its effect upon the imaginations and emotions of his shipmates. They are men brave in the presence of extremest danger, but cowardly before the thought of Death incarnate in this imposing and tubercular negro. Both Wait himself and the rest of the crew are compelled to believe, or pretend to believe, that he is not really sick, but simply shamming. And then comes about a paradox in their psychology. For the captain, too, out of compassion for the dying negro, pretends to believe that he is not really dying but only malingering; in the presence of all the crew, he harshly condemns the sick man to imprisonment in his cabin, and then the crew, angry with the captain for his harsh treatment of their pet, come very near to mutiny.

The reader of this abstract will knit his brows over such seemingly topsyturvy psychology. And indeed, in the book, it is not so simple as I have made it, and hardly so credible. It is the last word in subtlety and sophistication, and a good many pages are given, first and last, to its elucidation.

Conrad is, of course, as much concerned to portray these men from the outside as from the inside. A large part of the book is made up of a rapid succession of brilliant word-pictures, presenting the men and the officers and James Wait; singly and in groups; in the forecastle and on deck, forward, amidships, and on the poop. They are shown as they seemed to themselves in their own thoughts, as they seemed to one another, or as they would seem to an imaginary observer; the men as they appeared to the officers and the officers as they appeared to the men. We have individual scenes, and we have generalized accounts of what went on over long periods of time. We have set conversations on particular subjects, and we have typical babels of sailors' voices shouting fragments of speech on every conceivable topic. And in addition to all this we have frequent descriptions of the ship, in the manner of Masefield: general accounts of ship's business, pictures of the ship on the sea as it would have appeared to a distant observer, pictures of the sea as it appeared from the ship, and many particular pictures of parts of the ship as seen from other parts on board.

The entire book occupies well under two hundred pages. And within this brief span Conrad has presented his subject in every manner known to narrative art, from every conceivable angle of vision, from every conceivable point of view, physical and psychological. His subject is the *Narcissus* and everything about that boat during a six months' voyage. And he seems to have started out with the intention of "putting across" that subject by the mere magic of the written word. The Oriental style is very much in evidence throughout, whether in description, psychology, or meditation.

On men reprieved by its disdainful mercy, the immortal sea confers in its justice the full privilege of desired unrest. Through the perfect wisdom of its grace they are not permitted to meditate at ease upon the complicated and acrid savour of existence. They must without pause justify their life to the eternal pity that commands toil to be hard and unceasing, from sunrise to sunset, from sunset to sunrise; till the weary succession of nights and days tainted by the obstinate clamor of sages, demanding bliss and an empty heaven, is redeemed at last by the vast silence of pain and labour, by the dumb fear and the dumb courage of men obscure, forgetful, and enduring.

But Conrad's instinct outran his theory. He began his story in the omniscient manner of the traditional author, and for a long space it is all told in the third person. There is no suggestion at all that the person writing was anywhere on that boat as witness or participator in the action. Then suddenly, on page 36, and between sentences, there is a shift from the third to the first person. It is a question of the attitude of the crew to James Wait, and suddenly the crew are no longer "they" and "them" but "we" and "us." It would appear that the writer is one of the crew and sharing their experiences and emotions. The first person is maintained pretty steadily through ten pages, and then we return to the third. And throughout the rest of the book there is a constant alternation between the objective third person and the first person which implies participation by the writer. Very often there is a shift from the third person to the first on one page and back again on the next.

Generally speaking, we may say that the most vividly realized passages are those in which the writer identifies himself with the crew (or possibly with the officers) by the use of the first person. It is clear that, however blindly Conrad may have started out in the objective manner, his instinct led him inevitably to the technique of identification. But there is no indication until the very end of the story of who this writer is who makes himself so anonymous a member of the group described as "we," nor even very certainly whether he is an officer or one of the crew. It is only in the last three pages that he becomes individualized as "I," sharply distinguished from the common sailors, whom he so much admires and regards in comradely fashion, but with the unmistakable air of a superior.

Thus in "The Nigger of the Narcissus" we see Conrad actually in process of learning, of accidentally stumbling upon a trick which was to serve him so very well in the greatest of his later stories. To experiences which he had personally lived through he was trying to apply the traditional impersonal manner of fiction, and only as it were in spite of himself fell into the personal manner of one who was there. In later stories we shall see him applying the personal manner of one who was there to what were largely fictitious inventions.

4

It would be too simple to suppose that Conrad's want of singleness of view in his earlier novels, and again in later ones like "The Rescue" (1920) and "The Rover" (1923), was the result of mere artistic inexpertness. He could never have been contented with the crystalline simplicity of the well-made novel. He was too much in love with variety, contrast, picturesqueness. He had an instinct for those effects in art which come from informality, from happy accident, and an air of studied carelessness. Moreover, he must have felt a certain flatness in the art of the well-made novel, a two-dimensional effect. And he was concerned himself to present his subject *in the round.* All art, he said, "must strenuously aspire to the plasticity of sculpture, to the colour of painting, and to the magic suggestiveness of music." Well! It is clear how difficult it would be to attain to the plasticity of sculpture while confining one's point of view rigorously to that of some one character, however gifted. And as for the magic suggestiveness of music, where shall one find a fictitious character fit to compete with a Conrad in such evocations?

And then, moreover, Conrad's conception of human nature was one which made much of its mystery, its protean elusiveness. No one angle of vision would suffice to catch it in its completeness. The problem, for any situation or any character, is to find the perfect focus for one's photograph. But there is no one perfect focus, and one must constantly experiment, constantly seek for a better and a better position. And in the end, in order to give even an approximately just conception of the subject, one must draw together all these hasty sketches into one composite picture. Thus in "An Outcast of the Islands" the main subject is Willems. But the truth about Willems is all bound up with the truth about Lingard, and Almayer, and Aïssa, and Babalatchi. And each one of these is called upon in turn to shed the light of his view upon the others.

One of the most interesting features of Conrad's Malay stories is the light thrown upon the character of the whites by the natives—the native comment on the folly, greed, cruelty, treachery, and indomitable power of the white race. But while there is a good deal of life in these stories, a great loss of force is sustained through the interference of one point of view with another and the more frequent indeterminateness of the point of view.

Conrad's problem was to secure the advantage of the many points of view without losing that of coherence. It was to make a real composite of these many pictures taken from so many diverse angles, to make a *synthesis* of material so disparate. And he solved that problem most successfully through the help of Captain Marlow.

This person he had created in the short story "Youth," and also used in "Heart of Darkness" before the completion of "Lord Jim" (1900). "Lord Jim" was intended to be likewise a short story, but was apparently begun without the idea of introducing Marlow. The first three chapters are told in the ordinary manner of third-person omniscience. They give a general account of Jim in the days when he was a water-clerk in Eastern ports, then return to his childhood home and training, and sketch his voyage as chief mate on the *Patna* in the Indian Ocean up to the time of the collision. Then, in Chapter IV, Marlow is introduced as one of those later attending the trial of Jim and his fellow-officers for deserting their ship. From that time on to Chapter XXXVI, the story is represented as being related by Marlow to friends in moments of relaxation after dinner. The concluding chapters were read later, in the form of documents under his London reading-lamp, by one of the party of Marlow's auditors. But the documents are mainly written in the hand of Marlow, one of them a letter, and one a long narrative of the later events while Jim was living in Patusan.

Virtually the whole of the story therefore comes to us from one who knew Lord Jim and was deeply interested in letting us know the truth about him, but who was not a professional writer. By far the largest portion comes not from his pen but from his mouth, in the form of a story told aloud over the after-dinner cigars. And this at once has the most magical effect upon the style and tone. The Oriental style, in this word-of-mouth narrative, gives place largely to a natural, anecdotal manner, the manner of one speaking with authority of things of which he knows, and yet—in such a strange story—striving for plausibility, striving to convert his audience to sympathy with his point of view, arguing with them over the character of his hero, producing evidence for his knowledge of this or that episode. All this gives to the narrative an amazing air of authenticity; puts it in a class with that extraordinary feat of Defoe's in "The Apparition of Mrs. Veal."

But this is only a beginning of what Marlow does for

"Lord Jim." This character is, seemingly, much more a sneer creation of the imagination than Almayer, Willems, Lingard, or Doña Rita. And yet Lord Jim is more vividly realized than any of them, perhaps the most vividly realized of all Conrad's characters.

His motivation is subtle, paradoxical, obscure, and a matter of speculation. But that is one reason why he is such a good subject for Conrad's—and Marlow's—hand: this young Englishman who had, in a crisis, forfeited his honor as a seaman and an officer, who was haunted for years by the sense of his disgrace and driven from one inferior occupation to another, from one port to another, by his desire to escape his ill fame; and who then, among the savages of a remote trading-post, "made good," "mastered his fate," and so won back his honor and his self-respect. Marlow befriended him, sympathized with him, understood him in fleeting intuitions from time to time, but never really "knew" him. At the time when Marlow went back home after Stein had sent Jim to Patusan, he says:

> "I cannot say I had ever seen him distinctly—not even to this day, after I had my last view of him; but it seemed to me that the less I understood the more I was bound to him in the name of that doubt which is the inseparable part of our knowledge. I did not know so much more about myself."

Marlow himself is well motivated, and his interest in Jim. He is interested in Jim, just as Captain Brierly is, the judge at his trial, and the French lieutenant who took charge of the *Patna* after Jim's desertion. They have all faced the doubt of how they would have acted in a similar crisis, whether their honor was strong enough to stand the test. "I did not know so much more about myself." Marlow wishes most devoutly to believe in Jim, in order that he may believe in himself, in human nature in general, in the possibility of the ideal in this world. It is most important to him that Jim should maintain his illusion of being somehow not damned, or find some momentary flash of revelation in the midst of a world of illusion.

One reason why Jim is so vivid a character is precisely because Marlow found him so elusive, because he was forever trying so hard to "see him distinctly." This is what leads to the sharp isolation of this or that scene.

It is also what leads Marlow to his frequent change of the angle of vision. The truth about Jim, as about any human being, he seems to think, is something which can be approximated only by regarding him from many different points of view. Much of this story comes to Marlow from the lips of Jim, much from other witnesses: the French lieutenant, the trader Stein, Jim's native wife Jewel, the pirate Brown, and others still. For much of the story Marlow is himself an eye-witness. Thus there is brought to bear upon Jim's case the light of every variety of temperament and of attitude toward Jim determined by every variety of interest and motive. This book is streaked and spotted with colors as brilliant and variegated as any futurist painting. The thing has a splendor and vibrancy of life not conceivable on the sober canvas of the well-made novel.

And yet it has the steady progression, the steady concentration on a single subject, of a novel by Wharton or James. It is Marlow who is responsible for this. He it is who directs and controls this restless and ranging exploration, always having in mind just what dark corner we are seeking to illuminate. It is he who receives on the lens of his speculative mind light-rays coming from every conceivable direction and focuses them all so rigorously upon the one point which he wishes to make visible to our imagination.

5

In "Chance" Conrad employs this method a second time in a full-length novel. And this is what, in spite of its relatively less enchanting subject-matter, its relative thinness of substance, makes of "Chance" one of the two or three most successful of all Conrad's novels. It has to do with Flora de Barral, daughter of a financier who has been in prison for dishonest operations with other people's money, and her elopement from the house of her host, a Mrs. Fyne, to marry Mrs. Fyne's brother, the sea-captain Anthony. During a considerable part of the story even the reader is in the dark about the character and motives of Flora, which are meanly understood by the Fynes; and this and the actual relation between her and Anthony furnish the main mystery, the element of suspense in the story.

These things (after the first chapter) all come to us as Marlow relates them to "me," that is, let us say, to the author. Some of them Marlow has from personal observation, but more from conversations with Mr. and Mrs. Fyne, with Flora, and with young Powell, officer on the *Ferndale*. And so here, as in "Lord Jim," the facts come to us strained through several personalities, which are like colored screens modifying the original picture and adding each one its own increment of interpretation. A graphic representation of the process will show how very complicated it sometimes is. For all that happened on the *Ferndale,* the sequence is as follows:

Powell . . . Marlow . . . me . . . the reader

The reader receives from the author an account of a narrative given to him by Marlow, who had the information from narratives of Powell.

This is not a purely theoretical picture of a process which has no real psychological significance. The author lets the reader know of Marlow's manner of telling his story, and of certain disputes which arise between him and Marlow in the course of the narrative with regard to its interpretation. Marlow in turn has his comments to make on young Powell, whom he regards as an entirely reliable witness but a somewhat naïve one, whose view of things has to be supplemented by the imagination of some one better acquainted with human nature. Or again, for certain passages in the earlier life of Flora, Mrs. Fyne passes on to Marlow information which she had from Flora; so that we have the following:

Flora . . . Mrs. Fyne . . . Marlow . . . me . . . the reader

Four screens have been interposed between the reader and the original source of information. In fact, I believe that in some instances it is Fyne who passes on to Marlow what Mrs. Fyne had from Flora, so that the graph should read:

Flora . . . Mrs. Fyne . . . Fyne . . . Marlow . . . me . . . the reader

The proof of the pudding is in the eating. The justification for all this complication of method is the richness and depth of effect, the amazing three-dimensional lifelikeness of characters and episodes which have received the benefit of so many successive treatments. From each one of the media through which it is strained, whether they be sympathetic, antipathetic, or indifferent, the subject retains tinctures and incrustations of humanness which individualize and make it live as no mere expressive words of an author can do.

To begin with, Marlow's telling the story to "me" relieves it of that formality which clings to the ordered and written words of the professional. And here again, as in "Lord Jim," Marlow has a difficult task of interpretation, of reconstruction. There are certain scenes for which he can have had no direct information—such as the scene between Flora's inhuman governess and her young man—and which he has had to build up inferentially. There are many phrases in which Marlow lets us know that he has arrived at his view of things by a process of reconstruction. The very limits of his knowledge make more convincing whatever he knows for sure.

"Angry or simply sad but certainly disillusioned, he wanders about and meets the girl one afternoon, and under the sway of a strong feeling forgets his shyness. This is no supposition. It is a fact. There was such a meeting . . . Don't you think that I hit on the psychology of the situation? . . . Anthony arrived at the cottage. In the evening. I knew that late train. He probably walked from the station. The evening would be well advanced. I could almost see . . . You will understand that I am piecing here bits of disconnected statements."

Then back of Marlow lies Fyne. He is a minor official, fussy and unimaginative, but more inclined than his wife to give the benefit of the doubt to Flora. Back of him is his wife. She is a sturdy, stupid, philistine member of the intelligentsia, and she is a woman with all the meanness of her sex in her interpretation of a sister woman. Then finally somewhere back of them all is Flora herself, made savage and taciturn by the terrible burden of life upon her slender shoulders, skittish and enigmatic, hard, fierce, and hysterical, whom Marlow himself has saved from an attempt at suicide. I say nothing here of the mere story-interest of her enigma: what did she say in that famous letter to Mrs. Fyne? I am now considering the human richness of portraiture, the subtlety of shading, the lifelikeness, that come of her being made the subject of so much and varied interpretation.

6

And now we come to another feature of Conrad's technique that is particularly favored by the use of Marlow as narrator. This is his apparently freakish and eccentric chronology. At this point it is worth while quoting certain statements of Mr. Ford with regard to the technical theories evolved by him and Conrad at the time of their collaboration. They will throw light on more than one feature of Conrad's technique, and most of all on his chronology.

It became very early evident to us that what was the matter with the Novel, and the British novel in particular, was that it went straight forward, whereas in your gradual making acquaintanceship with your fellows you never do go straight forward. You meet an English gentleman at your golf club. He is beefy, full of health, the moral of the boy from an English Public School of the finest type. You discover gradually that he is hopelessly neurasthenic, dishonest in matters of small change, but unexpectedly self-sacrificing, a dreadful liar, but a most painfully careful student of lepidoptera and, finally, from the public prints, a bigamist who was once, under another name, hammered on the Stock Exchange. . . . Still, there he is, full-fed fellow, moral of an English Public School product. To get such a man in fiction you could not begin at his beginning and work his life chronologically to the end. *You must first get him in with a strong impression, and then work backwards and forwards over his past.* . . .[1]

There seem to be two main reasons for the manner of narration which departs widely from the chronological order of events. One is suggested in the last sentence quoted; it is a question of the reader's interest—of story-telling strategy. It is too cumbersome, too dull, to try to get in at the beginning all you know about your character. The thing is first "to get him in with a strong impression"; and then, to give him the development which he deserves, you "work backwards and forwards over his past." The other reason is a question of naturalness, lifelikeness, and getting away from the formality associated with an author. "The object of the novelist is to keep the reader entirely oblivious of the fact that the author exists—even of the fact that he is reading a book." It is obvious how this applies to the Marlow device. But it applies also to the chronology.

We agreed that the general effect of a novel must be the general effect that life makes on mankind. A novel must

1 Ford, Ford Madox: *Joseph Conrad: a Personal Remembrance.*

therefore not be a narration, a report. Life does not say to you: In 1914 my next-door neighbor, Mr. Slack, erected a greenhouse and painted it with Cox's green aluminum paint. . . . If you think about the matter you will remember, *in various unordered pictures,* how one day Mr. Slack appeared in his garden and contemplated the wall of his house. You will then try to remember the year of that occurrence and you will fix it as August 1914, because having had the foresight to bear the municipal stock of the City of Liège you were able to afford a first-class season ticket for the first time in your life. You will remember Mr. Slack—then much thinner because it was before he found out where to buy that cheap Burgundy. [And so on for another page of divagations around the subject of Mr. Slack's greenhouse.]

We accepted without much protest the stigma "Impressionists" that was thrown at us. In those days Impressionists were still considered to be bad people: Atheists, Reds, wearing red ties with which to frighten householders. But we accepted the name because Life appearing to us much as the building of Mr. Slack's greenhouse comes back to you, *we saw that life did not narrate, but made impressions on our brains.*

It is very curious how little use of this method Conrad and Ford made in their novels written in collaboration, compared with the novels of Conrad alone, written at about the same period or later, and the novels of Ford written since the war. I regret very much that space will not allow me to discuss those remarkable novels of Ford "No More Parades" (1925) and "A Man Could Stand Up" (1926), with their beautiful application of all these theories; not to speak of "The Good Soldier" (1915), in which is to be found another interesting statement of his theory that stories should be told "in the way persons telling a story would tell them."

As for Conrad, he had always shown a disposition to get his character in first with a strong impression and then work backward over his past before going on with the dramatic present which brought the story to its climax. There are striking instances of this method in "Almayer's Folly," "The Rescue," and virtually every one of his novels. But in the novels which represent his earlier technique these blocks of backward narrative have too much the air of mere "exposition," as if the story had outrun itself and the author had to go back and catch up. And for the most part, within these extensive blocks of narrative the chronology is straightforward, and so we cannot say strictly that the author is "working backwards and forwards" over his character's past. It is in "Lord Jim" and "Chance" that this method is most successfully and consistently applied. Let us take the case of "Lord Jim" and indicate in the most summary fashion possible the backward and forward loopings of the story. And, to make it more graphic, let us assign a letter of the alphabet to each main period of the action.

The story begins with a general account of Jim as water-clerk at various Eastern ports after the collision and the trial (say, KLM). It then goes back to give an account of Jim's life from the beginning up to the moment of the collision (A-E). In the fourth chapter we are present at the trial of the officers of the *Patna* for abandoning their ship (H), at which time Marlow made the acquaintance of Jim. We then have from Marlow an account of the look of these dishonored officers on their first appearance at the port where they were tried (G), and of an encounter he had much earlier with the German skipper before the sailing of the *Patna* (D). We return to the trial (H) and look forward to the suicide soon after of the presiding judge, Brierly (J). Then Jim begins to give Marlow an account (through several chapters) of what happened on the *Patna* and afterward (E and F), and we have also Marlow's account of his conversation with the French lieutenant who boarded the vessel after the collision (F). Several chapters are given to Marlow's dealings with Jim immediately after the trial (I), with a forward glance to Marlow's last glimpse of Jim after his visit to Patusan (R). Next we have Jim's experiences in various ports (KLM), leading to Marlow's consultation with Stein (N). We next pass to the visit paid by Marlow to Jim in Patusan (Q), and—here I am greatly simplifying—fourteen chapters are given to an account of this visit (Q), alternating with accounts of what Jim had to tell Marlow, during this visit, about his first arrival at Patusan and his life there (P). This part ends with Marlow's farewell to Jim (R). I will not attempt to outline the rest of the book.

All this certainly sounds bewildering, and it looks still more bewildering if we put together the letters representing the sequence of events as narrated and compare them with the actual chronological order. The true chronological order would be:

A, B, C, D, E, F, G, H, I, J, K, L, M, N, O, P, Q, R, S, T, U, V, W, X, Y, Z

The order in the book is, by chapters:

KLMP, WA, E, B, E, E, H, GD, HJ, FE, E, E, F, F, F, FK, I, I, R, I, KL, MN, N, Q, QPO, OP, P, QP, P, P, P, QP, P, P, Q, Q, Q, R, ZV, YX, S, S, S, TY, U, U, U, WXY

A similar picture of chronology in "Chance" or "Nostromo" would give an equally topsyturvy alphabet. And in "Nostromo," indeed, the effect upon the reader is almost as bewildering as the picture would suggest. In "Chance" and "Lord Jim," however, the effect is nothing like so peculiar as one would expect, and the method has its justification.

In the first place, there is the mere consideration of storytelling strategy. The method *does* enable the author to get in first a strong impression of the character, of this or that situation, and so catch the reader's attention, before bringing the light of retrospection and anticipation to explain and modify the impression. It is the actual strategy of many an excellent raconteur. It is for this reason a system which gives naturalness to Marlow's narrative.

But the esthetic rationale goes much deeper. It is Conrad's sense of the elusiveness of human nature which leads him not merely to view his subject from so many angles and strain it through so many media, but also to keep moving his camera backward and forward in time so as constantly to get the subject into some new illuminating perspective. It is as if human nature were a rare and skittish bird which he must approach with every circumstance of precaution and which must by all means be taken by surprise. The method of James is to lay regular siege to Life; the method of Conrad is to lie in ambush for it.

7

Conrad's material in "Nostromo" (1904)—character, incident, setting—is perhaps richer than that of any of his other books. In fact, it is much too rich even for a book of this size, the longest of his novels. The political history of Costaguana alone is enough for one big book, without the silver-mine of the Goulds. Conrad has introduced into this story more major figures than in any other. The chronological looping method is used throughout, with evident good intentions but with very dubious results.

It is unsatisfactory because no one character or group of characters holds the center of the stage long enough for us to grow comfortably interested in him or it. During the second part, Martin Decoud is much more at the center than Nostromo. The titular hero does not begin to take his due place in the story until the end of the seventh chapter of the third and last part (page 411 in a book of 600 pages), and he does not hold it steadily from there on. And with all the bewildering distribution of interest and confusion of chronology, there is no Marlow to direct the exploration of the wilderness, to show the point of this or that excursion away from the present moment and the present center of interest.

The result is that only the most resolute lovers of Conrad can push their way through the tangled underbrush of this well-nigh pathless forest. Mr. Jean-Aubry calls it "his longest, most complicated, most powerful work." Priceless things are buried there under a complication of tropical growth. Mrs. Gould and Dr. Monygham are alone worth an expedition to recover them. But no one should undertake such an expedition without being warned of its perils and ardors. Conrad's letters are full of references to the long desperate struggle he had in its composition, and the reasons are obvious. With such a sodden weight of matter to be assimilated, with nothing like a real center of interest anywhere in the book, and with no Marlow to keep things in their places, nothing but superhuman powers would have enabled him to realize his ideal of making us see.

The book is of course a most striking example of what I have called the *deformalization* of the novel. And it was not labor altogether wasted. The "impressionistic" method outlined by Ford does go far to give life and naturalness to the story. But it must be acknowledged that Conrad here indulged in excesses of such impressionism. In "Victory" (1910) he managed without Marlow, partly because he did have a center of interest. But the great triumphs of his technique are "Lord Jim" and "Chance," in which his impressionism was chastened and controlled by the use of the word-of-mouth narrator Marlow.

XXX

IMPRESSIONISM: LAWRENCE

TO BEGIN with, let it be said that I do not pretend to understand the psychological state of Lawrence himself, which had so much to do with his choice of subjects and his characterization. Mr. Middleton Murry has made a diabolically clever study of his friend, and has shown from book to book how one character after another is either drawn from Lawrence himself or else is a presentment of what he would have liked to be. No one can pretend to know Lawrence without having weighed all the evidence cited by Mr. Murry. Unfortunately, apart from the pseudo-piety and dubious hero-worship which accompany this analysis of his friend's pathological state, there is a fundamental obscurity and confusion in Murry's picture of that state. He makes it clear that, owing to what is called a "mother-fixation," Lawrence was never able to make a happy emotional adjustment to women. But what remains hopelessly obscure in Murry's account is whether the impotence of Lawrence—for that is what, in plain terms, he attributes to him—was a physical or a sentimental impotence.

Well, it is a commonplace of criticism that the writer's misery is often our good luck.

> Aus meinen grossen Schmerzen
> Mach' Ich die kleinen Lieder.

Lawrence was a tortured soul throughout the forty-five years of his life. But what he suffered, and what he thought and observed under the stimulus of this suffering, was sufficient to furnish forth a dozen remarkable novels, not to mention his poems, plays, and miscellaneous writings. He was "crucified into sex," and he gave the world the benefit of that experience. Few of his books are to be recommended to the very young or to any readers who have a need for being spared a too close view of the psychology of sex. His theoretical psychology is said by professional psychologists to be wrong-headed. This does not prevent his books from being strewn with psychological truths—revealing attitudes, situations, emotional states—so rich and convincing that he makes most writers of his time look trifling and almost childish by comparison.

There are things about his style which I do not like. The cockney taste of Keats and Leigh Hunt was not a circumstance to that of this miner's son. This applies to what he says as well as to the manner of saying it. He blurts out so many things to which it is the instinct of genteel good taste not to refer at all. He makes men go bathing together naked and admire one another's beauty—which, of course, is simply "not done." But, then, we know how much farther the indiscretions of genius carry us in the arts than the taboos of good taste. And there is more of the splendor and terror, the flutter and glimmer and vitality of human experience in one chapter of Lawrence than in whole volumes of Willa Cather.

Lawrence was practically untouched by the ideals of the well-made novel. There is no suggestion whatever, in his typical work, of the dramatic focusing of a restricted point of view. It is true that in "The Lost Girl" and in "Aaron's Rod," there is a simplification resulting from each one of these novels being the story of a single person—the first that of Alvina Houghton, the second that of Aaron Sisson. In each case, as the story proceeds, it becomes more and more exclusively that of Alvina or of Aaron, and automatically the single point of view establishes itself.

In his first published novel, "The White Peacock" (1911), it was probably by intention that the story is told in the first person by a man who was witness to virtually all that went on. This Cyril was the brother of the principal woman character, Lettie, and a dear friend of the principal man, George. Mr. Murry is doubtless right in identifying Cyril with Lawrence. He was born, like Lawrence, in September, was given, like him, to painting, and was endowed with his emotional and artistic sensitivity. So that what we have is the author putting himself as a character into the story. He has, however, no part of his own to play. He is simply a shadowy third party to every situation in which the others are involved. They are sometimes very intimate and delicate situations, in which it is hard to believe that the others would have allowed him to trail along; so that he introduces an element of unreality into the story. This typical novelistic device was particularly unsuited to Lawrence's genius.

None of these three is among the great typical novels of Lawrence. "Aaron's Rod" has considerable importance in the development of his ideas on love, but has comparatively little of that mystical poetry in the psychology of love which is his distinctive contribution to the novel. "The Lost Girl" is a delightful book, a relaxation from his more severe preoccupations, a marvelous flight from reality. "The White Peacock" is the most charming of neglected works of genius. It is true that the story has a sad ending, and that it *is* a work of genius. But these are the only reasons I can think of why it should have been neglected. I know of no work in prose or verse more overflowing with the beauty of English country and the circumstances of farm life. In its own way it is as fine as Meredith, as Hardy, as John Cowper Powys in "Wolf Solent" (1929). Human relations and sentiments in great variety are touched off in a narrative swift, firm, sensitive, penetrating. There is something joyous in the spontaneous flow of impressions from this unjaded pen; Lawrence's mind has not yet set into that hard, jagged mold that makes the strength of his later novels at the same time that it gives them their cruel and repellent quality.

It is perhaps of Meredith that Lawrence most reminds one in the technical handling of his material. The two are alike in the essentially lyrical and romantic character of their genius, in their tendency to expatiate in detail, in their almost complete innocence of technique as it would be understood by Eliot, Stevenson, Turgenev, James.

They are worlds apart in philosophical tone; Meredith is as notoriously "sound" as Lawrence is notoriously "morbid." And they are very different in their attitude toward their characters. In this matter Lawrence is much more "modern" than Meredith. He does not patronize his characters; he does not paw them about and tell us what we ought to think about them. He has little irony and no humor. His attitude toward his characters might be described as purely scientific if it were not that it is so fervently, even feverishly, sympathetic. He appears very little in the rôle of discursive philosopher. While there is a good deal of abstract theorizing on human relations in the later books, it appears mostly in the dialogue; he leaves it to the people themselves. And if they are rather more given to this sort of speculation than the general run of people, they are not more so than the characters of "Jude the Obscure" and "Point Counter Point."

The finest and most representative of Lawrence's novels are "Sons and Lovers" (1913), "The Rainbow" (1915), and "Women in Love" (1921). "The Plumed Serpent" (1926) is an extremely interesting and colorful book; but the heroic stirring of the Mexican soul beneath the overlayings of Spanish Christian sentiment is a theme too fantastic to be taken seriously, and too difficult of combination with Lawrence's constant theme of erotic psychology. "Lady Chatterley's Lover" (1928) has its own stark beauty, and is a document of unmistakable importance. It represents Lawrence's last desperate effort to adjust his own emotional difficulties, or to find an ideal formula for men more happy than he in their sex life. The formula is far too simple, being found in a mechanical detail of physiology in the art of love-making. There is a tendency all through Lawrence to wish to throw off the intolerable burden of emotional relations by some such trick of legerdemain, to reduce sex relations to physiology and be done with them. But this was something manifestly impossible for so sensitive a soul, one that lived so constantly in his emotions, if indeed it is possible for any civilized human being. It is all very well to say that we make too much of our emotions; that we should live cool and collected, with reason and wisdom in control and our sentiments battened down under hatches. But we are not made that way; and ordinary normal human relationships are an affair of tenderness and tears, excitement, strain, struggle, discouragement, and hope, of vanity bleeding and pride laid low. This was obviously the case with Lawrence, who never quite won to a normal human relationship. And if all of his characters had succeeded in simplifying their sex life as did the gamekeeper who was Lady Chatterley's lover, his books would have an altogether different significance, an artistic importance altogether inferior to what they do have.

2

Lawrence's main intention and preoccupation are such as accord ill with "dramatic" tendencies in novel technique. His characters are not so much unitary souls arranged in patterns as centers of radiation quivering with the interchange of impulses. It is not the situations in which they find themselves which primarily concern him, but the feelings they have toward one another; and not so much the feelings on one side or the other as the *inter-*

play of feelings. His all-embracing intention is, seemingly, to show the materialization in human lives of the elemental life-impulse—we might say the procreative instinct, but I think he would object to having it defined so narrowly—the welling up into conscious life of the great subterranean waters of unconscious vital force. The persons are not conceived primarily as actors interesting in themselves for projects undertaken, or for the dramatic patterns resulting from their conflicting interests. The author is not interested in social forms or the social spectacle for themselves. His characters are simply jets of the great dark stream of energy, carriers of energy and the cosmic will. He is not so much concerned with the forms taken on by the energy as with the energy which takes on the forms; not so much with the dramatic moment as with the process which passes through the dramatic moment.

He is not primarily interested in producing individual characters which live by their idiosyncrasy, like Dickens, in shutting you up with a loved person in a fearful predicament, like Charlotte Brontë, in assembling social documents, like Balzac. He wishes to illustrate the variegated manifestation of the life-impulse, the manifold coloration of the stream of life; but his main concern is with the stream, and—in the stream—with its *flow*. Plot appears not in the form of intrigue with mysteries to be solved, misunderstandings to be ironed out, conflicts of interest to be settled, moral issues to be brought to a conclusion. The plot is simply the line of movement of the elemental life-force—a sinuous, rapid, shifting, wave-like movement; the movement of waves of no such slow and massive stuff as water but much more subtle and swift, like some form of radiation. The dramatic situations are simply the maladjustments, correspondences, counterbalances of erotic impulse personified. Human beings appear as the modalities of the elemental urge.

A great specialty of Lawrence is his creation of a charged

emotional atmosphere. This derives partly from his treatment of the emotions not in the dramatic, or in the sentimental, or in the moralistic fashion, but as manifestations of physico-psychic phenomena which are the play of the elemental life-forces—the individuals being considered as carriers of so much fluid energy. This accounts for a certain indefiniteness or intangibility in the causes of a given feeling, or in the very character of the feeling, which does not appear as the desire for a well-defined object or pointed up in a particular dramatic issue. It is not the virtues and social qualities of an individual which make another fall in love with him, but something more elemental, less amenable to definition.

The average novel takes love for granted, and then makes it the issue in a situation constituted by obstacles put in the way of gratification, by misunderstandings between the persons involved, by points of honor, conflicts of obligation or jurisdiction. In such cases the interest is more in the geometrical figure thus outlined—for example, the notorious triangle—than in the obscure forces brought into play. The dramatic situation is thought of as a problem to be solved by moral or sentimental algebra.

With Lawrence, love is conceived of in terms suggesting chemical affinities, the attraction and repulsion of forces not definable in moral-sentimental-social terms. Sometimes we think of chemical affinities; sometimes of psychic auras affecting one another; sometimes of bodies of different magnitudes and weights exerting varying degrees of pull upon one another; most often—and it is a common figure with Lawrence—of electrical phenomena: positive and negative, polarization, incandescent wires, voltage, interference, short circuits. In his "Fantasia of the Unconscious" he says:

A family is a group of wireless stations, all adjusted to the same, or very much the same vibration. All the time they quiver with the interchange, there is one long endless flow of vitalistic [sic] communication between members of one family, a long, strange *rapport,* a sort of life-unison. It is a ripple of life through many bodies as through one body.

Similar figures recur throughout his books, especially in the love passages.

> It was a dark flood of electric passion she released from him, drew into herself. She had established a rich new circuit, a new current of passional electric energy, between the two of them, released from the darkest poles of the body and established in perfect circuit. It was a dark fire of electricity that rushed from him to her, and flooded them both with rich peace, satisfaction.

This passage from "Women in Love" refers to the sensations of two lovers in actual bodily contact, but Lawrence is just as often talking of an interchange of sensations between persons merely in the presence of one another or thinking of one another, of the emotional character of the abstract relation as such, if we can speak of any relation as being abstract. Thus in an article published in "Scribner's Magazine" in the year of his death he writes:

> A woman is a living fountain whose spray falls delicately around her, on all that come near. A woman is a strange soft vibration on the air, going forth unknown and unconscious, and seeking a vibration of response. Or else she is a discordant, jarring, painful vibration, going forth and hurting every one within range. And a man the same. A man, as he lives and moves and has being, is a fountain of life-vibration, quivering and flowing toward some one, something that will receive his outflow and send back an inflow, so that a circuit is completed, and there is a sort of peace. Or else he is a source of irritation, discord, and pain, harming every one near him.

Much stress is laid by Lawrence on the state of *awareness* which exists between two persons. The ordinary writer does not mention such a phenomenon. He takes for granted that persons are aware of one another if they are brought into relation. What he stresses is what they think of one another, what they seek from one another. But Lawrence stresses awarenesses which are more elemental, more fundamental in psychology, and less specifically motivated. It is not that two persons can do such and such things for each other, or wish such and such things from each other, or that they have reason to hate each other, but that they are psychic entities existing within range of each other and have certain affinities which unite them in a grapple of loves and hates, in origin undifferentiated as to specific cause, but manifesting themselves naturally in specific cases.

Thus the relation between Will Brangwen and his little daughter Ursula in "The Rainbow": "Between him and the little Ursula there came into being a strange alliance. They were aware of each other. He knew the child was always on his side." On her part there was "the dim, childish sense of her own smallness and inadequacy, a fatal sense of worthlessness . . . Still she set toward him like a quivering needle. All her life was directed by her awareness of him, her wakefulness to his being. And she was against her mother." This is independent of and antecedent to any specific reasons for their being allies, unless the obscure one of blood-kinship, of father-daughter relation.

Naturally much is made of the state in which persons first become aware of one another. Thus again, in "The Rainbow," when Anna's father tells her that her cousin Will is coming to church with her, "Anna glanced at the strange youth again. She felt him waiting there for her to notice him. He was hovering on the edge of her consciousness, ready to come in. She did not want to look at him. She was antagonistic to him." It is not explained why she was antagonistic. It is something elemental, something antecedent to conventional reasons. It is, I suppose, an instinctive anticipation of the sex combat which she is destined to carry on with him throughout her life.

Much attention is given to the feelings of people at their points of contact, especially feelings denoting a want of connection, a failure of the forces involved to flow together. The offs and ons of sexual attraction are marvelously presented. And here again they are presented not as occasioned by specific stimuli in the form of things done or said to please or offend, not subject to reasons so superficial and readily explained, but as occasioned by the underground working of physico-psychical laws, of forces and combinations of conditions incalculable. We have the impression of lights going on and off as a result of hidden touches, imperfect contacts becoming perfect, short circuits; or, again, of rival bodies exerting pull on one another and aware of such a pull.

> And he remained wrathful and distinct from her, unchanged outwardly to her, but underneath a solid power of antagonism to her. Of which she became gradually aware. And it irritated her to be made aware of him as a separate power. She lapsed into a sort of sombre exclusion, a curious communion with mysterious powers, a sort of mystic, dark state which drove him and the child nearly mad. . . . Then suddenly, out of nowhere, there was connection between them again. It came on him as he was working in the fields. The tension, the bond, burst, and the passionate flood broke forward into a tremendous, magnificent rush, so that he felt he could snap off the trees as he passed. And when he arrived home, there was no sign between them. He waited and waited till she came . . . She was sure to come at last, and touch him. Then he burst into flame for her, and lost himself . . . The hour passed away again, there was severance between them, and rage and misery and bereavement for her, and deposition and toiling at the mill with slaves for him.

This was Tom Brangwen and Lydia Lensky; and then, in the next generation, we have the same history going on with Anna and Will. In the latter case much is made of the struggle of wills as of two opposed forces, not in the dramatic sense of two persons between whom there is a definite issue, but simply of two forces wishing to dominate, to push one another to the wall, to destroy one another. Most remarkable perhaps, and most mysterious, is, in the third generation, the struggle between Ursula and Anton, powerfully drawn to each other sexually, and yet unable to make satisfying contact, unable to find that vital fulfilment which is the be-all and the end-all of these dark forces.

We have here the clue to the world-wide difference between the themes of Lawrence and those of the ordinary novelist. What his people are all seeking is nothing more precisely defined than this "vital fulfilment." We read in "Anna Karenina" of an English novel in which the hero was "almost reaching his English happiness, a baronetcy and an estate." The psychological novel has made some progress since the time that Tolstoy wrote these words; but still the great mass of all novelists in English set for their heroes and heroines objectives almost as precise and external as a baronetcy and an estate. Lawrence is perhaps the only English novelist who has taken for his specialty what can with any propriety be called the psychology of sex.

And that is the main reason why he has been so long taboo. For a large proportion of what is called morbid in him is simply—whether morbid or not—the regular accompaniment of the relation between any two individuals who are seeking "vital fulfilment" and are obliged to make an adjustment of wills and temperaments. Naturally the most interesting point for study is that at which adjustment is difficult. And this being Lawrence's specialty, the emphasis necessarily falls upon what used to be called the "disagreeable."

3

I have dwelt on the element of mystery in the emotional reactions of Lawrence's characters; I might have called it irrationality. But I do not mean to imply that it is arbitrary or does not have its determining cause in the obscure levels of the unconscious. Lawrence knew what he was about. He was a pioneer explorer in a dark Africa, beyond the reach of the post-office and the motor road. But he was proceeding by plan, with chart and compass. And most of what is obscure in him takes on a significant meaning to any one who will acquaint himself with what is known—or guessed—of the psychology of sex. Let him begin, of course, with Freud.

Of all his novels, "The Rainbow" is the most comprehensive textbook of this subject. There is a remarkable account of the emotional relationship of mother, father, and child, through two generations. Twice in the story we have the father, baffled in his urge toward the mother, turning to the daughter for his emotional fulfilment. In the case of Tom Brangwen and his stepdaughter Anna, we have a man who really loves the child and treats her with sensitive understanding and patience, so that she is finally won over to him, and then the relation of the parents is gradually adjusted, so that the child has a feeling of security in their union. The case of Will Brangwen and Ursula is that of a stupid, self-absorbed father who, in spite of his love for his daughter and his emotional dependence on her, is really insensitive to her spiritual needs, is weakly brutal or indifferent in his treatment of her; so that she, in her sensitive pride, shuts up against him, comes to see the world as hostile, and is badly "conditioned" for her own emotional problems in maturity.

There is reference to a dozen other phenomena familiar among students of psychoanalysis, or simple commonplaces of modern psychology, though Lawrence refrains almost invariably from using the hackneyed technical terms: the unconscious process of "self-maximation" through love; "transference" and "sublimation"; the "inferiority complex"; a sex psychology which takes a religious form; etc.

But Lawrence's dominant subject, in "The Rainbow" as in all his work, is what has been called the battle of the sexes, a subject treated in highly simplified form in the plays of Strindberg and Ibsen. This battle of the sexes is incident to the complexity of circumstance under which two individuals meet—the elemental urge to fulfilment running everywhere upon obstructions—difference of temperament, difference of power, conflicts of will, faulty emotional synchronization, and so on.

The battle resulting from difference of quality or power in love is illustrated in the rather mysterious case of Ursula and Anton. Apparently the author wished to present the contrast between a woman who loves the soul as well as the body of a man and the man who can love only the woman's body. A great cause of sexual conflict lies in the fact that the woman is fulfilled through child-bearing, while the man continues to crave an intense fulfilment through the woman. This is illustrated in the married life of Tom and Lydia. The battle of the sexes is naturally fed by everything of opposition in the temperaments of the two lovers, whether it is incidental to their individual idiosyncrasies or, still more, something inherent in their contrary character of male and female.

This latter is the note that recurs the oftenest throughout Lawrence's work. It is very strongly sounded in "Sons and Lovers." Paul Morel is typical of Lawrence's men in his unwillingness to give himself fully to the woman; whereas Miriam is typical of his women in her passion to absorb the man completely, to leave nothing of him over, unexhausted by their love. In this case there is a special reason why Paul cannot give himself unreservedly to Miriam. For "Sons and Lovers" is primarily the story of a mother-fixation. Paul's love for Miriam is a desperate attempt to free himself from his excessive attachment to his mother. But this he cannot do. He cannot give to Miriam what has already been made over to his mother; and thus comes about that torturing dichotomy of his emotional being, and the disharmony between him and the woman who wants all his love and to whom he can give but half.

There is every reason to believe that this is, almost literally, autobiography; and Mr. Murry finds in this mother-fixation the clue to all of Lawrence's work. I cannot but think that he simplifies over-much. It is undoubtedly true that Lawrence's relation to his mother absorbed far too much of his emotional powers, and made him more than ordinarily rebellious against the sentimental demands of women. It made him exceptionally dependent on women, and by the same token exceptionally alive to the man's desire to keep back something of himself in the love relation. But what it made him alive to is, I fancy, a feeling not altogether peculiar to himself or to persons who have been unfortunately conditioned by unwise mother-love.

Perhaps it is not a question of male and female. Perhaps this desire to keep something back—to maintain some independent realm of spiritual being through all the fire and intimacy of passion—may be felt by women as intensely as by men. But here it is a man who writes; and to him it seems that he and all other men are struggling against the tyranny of the female, who wishes to exhaust in the sex relation all the spiritual capacities of the male.

This is essentially the theme of "Women in Love," and the person in this story who represents the triumph of the male point of view is Birkin, who married Ursula Brangwen with the understanding, reluctantly granted, that he should be allowed to keep his spiritual freedom. He has earlier had an intimacy with another woman, Hermione, who represents another type of female domination.

> Fusion, fusion, this horrible fusion of two things, which every woman and most men insisted on, was it not nauseous and horrible anyhow, whether it was a fusion of the spirit or of the emotional body? Hermione saw herself as the perfect idea, to which all men must come: And Ursula was the perfect Womb, the bath of birth, to which all men must come! And both were horrible. Why could not they remain individual, limited by their own limits? Why this dreadful all-comprehensiveness, this hateful tyranny? why not leave the other being free, why try to absorb, or melt, or merge? One might abandon oneself utterly to the *moments,* but not to any other being.

The particular form taken, in "Women in Love" as in "Aaron's Rod" and other later novels of Lawrence, by this desire to escape from absorption by the woman was the consummation of a supplementary friendship with a man; and it grows more and more clear that this friendship—which Lawrence vainly sought, himself, in his own life—was to be the impersonal friendship of teacher and disciple. Here, if you like, is where the crazy streak comes out. For this very great artist was determined to be a leader and savior of men. Not content with the "sublimation" of art, he must also further satisfy his unfulfilled emotional life by taking on him the mantle of a prophet. But we can surely forgive him for making the mistake, if it is a mistake, of Wordsworth and Shelley.

4

Lawrence's technique is the natural outcome of his preoccupation with intimate sex psychology combined with his painter's eye, his vivid awareness of the external world. He is always primarily occupied with the subjective experience of his people, their sensations in the presence of one another, but at the same time he is aware of how they look from the outside, of their tone and manner, the setting in which they play their parts, what they say and do; of all that gives them objective reality. It is therefore impossible for him to maintain strictly the point of view of any character, keeping to the subjective aspect of things. He is forever passing back and forth between subjective and objective, within the chapter, within the paragraph, within the sentence. The characters are seen together in their setting; or they are themselves aware of their setting as something outside themselves; or one of them is seen and felt by the other, taken by himself or in his setting.

It is impossible, given his intention, to stick to the point of view of one character rather than another. It is, as I have said, the *interplay* of forces in the electromagnetic field lying between the characters that concerns him; and that implies a constant shift back and forth between the characters so as to record the sensations on both sides, as well as sensations conceived in terms common to both.

Thus if one examines the chapter in "Women in Love" entitled "Continental," one finds the five principal persons involved, Gudrun, Gerald, Birkin, Ursula and Loerke, presented in every possible combination, so far as center of interest or point of view is concerned: each one taken by himself (that is, five separate arrangements); each one in combination with each of the others (ten more arrangements, if my arithmetic is right), and then all together and in combination with the other guests at the alpine hostelry.

Then again the sinuous trail of the elemental life-force often leads him over more ground and more varied than is consistent with the "dramatic" ideal in the novel. In "The Rainbow" he undertakes to give an intimate record of the dealings of this impish spirit with no less than three generations of the Brangwens. In "Sons and Lovers" more than a third of the book is occupied with the life of the older Morels and the growing up of the children, before we come to the love life of Paul; and this latter theme, which occupies the rest of the book, involves the recording of ten or a dozen years, rather evenly distributed along the whole line of the narrative.

Lawrence does not carefully date his action like Galsworthy and Bennett; nor does he, like them, draw a sharp line between what happened this year and what happened ten years later. The thing seems to keep going on steadily like time, growth, and evolution.

He has little sense for the "discriminated occasion." Very seldom does he develop any one scene with an eye to suspense, momentum, and climax. The elemental force plays fitfully in and out, growing intense or fading away. His chapters are typically very long and cover a great number of occasions—brief, particular occasions—with short transitional passages of summary and generalization, emphasizing the continuity of the process.

In characterization his method is rather suggestive than formal. Generally speaking, his characters are vividly individualized; and while you may not altogether understand them, there is no question about your knowing them. Sometimes, however, he is led astray by his psychological theories, or by his preoccupation with the undifferentiated life-impulse. During a large part of "Women in Love" the reader is likely to confuse the two sisters, Ursula and Gudrun, by intention so different, though strong in family likeness and certainly more like to each other than to any other heroine of fiction. This is partly due to his neglect of point of view, and his constant shift of center.

His style is brilliantly original, experimental, impressionistic. It is oftentimes faulty in idiom, and faulty in the typical romantic way of trying to push expressiveness far beyond the possibilities of language. It is the style of a poet. And the poet is felt, too, in the very great use of symbolism and of incidents rich with overtones of feeling and hidden correspondences of thought. Such are the superb chapters in "Women in Love" entitled "Rabbit" and "Moony." In the latter there is a fine symbolism in Birkin's stoning the reflection of the moon-goddess (the accursed Syria Dea) on the waters of a pond. And there is perhaps no better bit of "modernistic" description in all Lawrence.

> Then again there was a burst of sound, and a burst of brilliant light, the moon had exploded on the water, and was flying asunder in flakes of white and dangerous fire. Rapidly, like white birds, the fires all broken rose across the pond, fleeing in clamorous confusion, battling with the flock of dark waves that were forcing their way in. The furthest rays of light, fleeing out, seemed to be clamouring against the shore for escape, the waves of darkness came in heavily, running under towards the centre. But at the centre, the heart of all, was still a vivid, incandescent quivering of a white moon not quite destroyed, a white body of fire writhing and striving and not even now broken open, not yet violated. It seemed to be drawing itself together with strange, violent pangs, in blind effort. It was getting stronger, it was reasserting itself, the inviolable moon. And the rays were hastening in in thin lines of light, to return to the strengthened moon, that shook upon the water in triumphant reassumption.

The term "impressionist" is even more properly applicable to Lawrence than to Conrad. The impressionist painter saw his subject differently from his predecessors. He saw it less in terms of the outline which is known to be there and more in terms of the mass which strikes the eye. And his technique was to build up an impression of the mass by laying spots of color side by side. James is a pre-impressionist in the novel by virtue of the precision with which his issue is defined by the tight little line of his plot, the steadiness with which he maintains a chosen point of view—what may be called the exact fixation of each element in the narrative. Lawrence, in poetry and the novel, is an impressionist because he is not concerned with the dramatic shape of the thing but with the living "feel" of it. When Miriam asks Paul why it is that she likes so much one of his sketches, he replies, "It's more shimmery, as if I'd painted the shimmering protoplasm in the leaves and everywhere, and not the stiffness of the shape . . . Only this shimmeriness is the real thing. The shape is a dead crust."

It is this shimmeriness which is the chief contribution of Lawrence to novelistic technique. And it is this which makes him—before Joyce—the most notable example of the reaction against the well-made novel. Unless, indeed, he was simply unaware of the well-made novel or indifferent to it, and so not capable of reacting against it. He has remained outside its sphere of influence. He has taken a line of his own. He is, in the novel, very little of the dramatist and very much of the poet.

XXXI

IMAGISM: DOROTHY RICHARDSON

THE term "impressionist" applies even better to Dorothy Richardson than to Lawrence. Indeed, she carries the technique of impressionism so much farther than he does, and with so much more apparent deliberateness of intention, that she has a decidedly more "modernist" air than Lawrence. In some respects she belongs rather with Joyce and his followers. She shares with Joyce the credit of having originated in English the "stream-of-consciousness" type of fiction. But the personality of Miss Richardson is so utterly different from that of either of these frightful males that, for this reason if there were no others, it is more convenient to find an entirely separate category in which to place her.

The term that on the whole sheds most light in her case is "imagism." Her long series of novels under the general title of "Pilgrimage" was begun during the great vogue of the imagist poets. The first three books—"Pointed Roofs," "Backwater," "Honeycomb"—appeared in, respectively, 1915, 1916, and 1917, the years of publication of the three anthologies entitled "Some Imagist Poets," which followed upon the volume entitled "Des Imagistes," published in 1914.

These poets were strongly influenced by the French symbolists. They were fundamentally lyric poets, and their dominant tendency was to render life not in terms of story or dramatic characterization, nor, again, in terms of abstract thought and sentiment, but in terms of impressions.

And these impressions they endeavored to convey, as Miss Lowell says, not through "vague generalities" but by images which "render particulars exactly." They represent a widespread tendency of the time, a tendency which, in its essence, is still largely present in American poetry, as these stanzas from Mr. Archibald MacLeish's "Ars Poetica" will bear witness:

> A poem should be equal to:
> Not true
>
> For all the history of grief
> An empty doorway and a maple leaf
>
> For love
> The leaning grasses and two lights above the sea—
>
> A poem should not mean
> But be

It is obvious that a prose narrative can never conform altogether to this ideal of a poem. But the novels of Dorothy Richardson come as near to it as anything can come and continue to be a prose narrative. I base my description of them largely on the first three, which are much the most charming and interesting, as well as being more significant in an account of the experimental novel of to-day. They are books that can hardly be said to have a social or philosophical theme. They are altogether lacking in formal characterization. There is no dramatic issue. And there is the almost irreducible minimum of story.

There is certainly no story in the sense of some relationship developing, some plot engineered, some opposition overcome. Miriam Henderson, in "Pointed Roofs," simply teaches a year in a German school, receives impressions of Germany, fails to please the Fräulein, and comes home. In "Backwater" it is much the same thing with Wordsworth House, the dismal London school, except that there she does please, and leaves by her own desire. In "Honeycomb" she passes a season as governess in a delightful country-house and receives impressions of men, women, and violets.

It is true that, on one occasion in "Backwater," she spends so much time with Max at a dance that she loses Ted, and then Max dies in New York. But all this of Ted and Max occupies an infinitesimal part of the whole narrative, and only the brief scenes with Max at the party are shown. Nothing is more remarkable than the complete disappearance of the unnamed *him* [Ted] after the first section of Chapter I in "Pointed Roofs." And so with Max in "Backwater" after the party; he is only once alluded to, where Miriam tells Miss Haddie of his death. Real events are almost invariably brought in indirectly or incidentally: Harriett's and Sarah's engagements in letters, that of Sarah slipped in in connection with another topic.

It is clear that Miriam in the depths of her nature is very much concerned with the question of a man—some one to take away that sense of loneliness which she both cherishes and shrinks from. She must indeed be aware of this herself, however obscurely; at any rate it is hardly conceivable that she should not be thinking sometimes of Ted and Max, who seem so important when they are mentioned.

And yet these, from a story point of view, most important of characters are almost altogether ignored, so that we may say the record is highly incomplete. And why? Perhaps because this nice seventeen- or eighteen-year-old girl is too delicate or too indeterminate-minded to allow herself to dwell or be moved to dwell on the thought of particular men. It is, shall we say, the strongest factor in her life, but it is below the surface of consciousness, and she is no Freud to drag it up into the light? Or perhaps this Miriam Henderson is definable psychologically as a strictly virginal nature, or as otherwise inaccessible to the appeal of the opposite sex. That she is intensely conscious of men is clear enough throughout, and most obvious in "Honeycomb." She hates men for their self-satisfied smile . . . "because a woman says one thing one minute and another the next. Men ought to be horsewhipped, all the grown men, all who have ever had that self-satisfied smile, all, all, horsewhipped until they apologize on their knees." Many psychologists would say that the strain of emotional deprivation comes out in her exhaustion, and her appeal to God—when she hears from home of a dance and thinks of her pinched life—"Why do you make me suffer so?" Practically nothing had been said of her suffering, though a good deal had been said of her fevered effort to be religious-minded, as well as her delight in the romantic stories of Carey and Ouida.

Well, that is it, in the end; the thing is done indirectly. The conscious surface of her impressions is given and vastly more is implied, with only here and there a discreet admission of more. Never was there so convincing a rendering of what a man might describe as the Daphnean furtiveness of a woman's mind.

It is not as if the author were there to interpret for us. The fundamental assumption of Miss Richardson's method is that the author should not be there. May Sinclair, in her introduction to "Pointed Roofs," makes an admirable statement of the author's attitude according to this system.

> Obviously, she must not interfere; she must not analyze or comment or explain. Rather less obviously, she must not tell a story, or handle a situation or set a scene; she must avoid drama as she avoids narration. And there are some things she must not be. She must not be the wise, all-knowing author. She must be Miriam Henderson. She must not know or divine anything that Miriam does not know or divine; she must not see anything that Miriam does not see . . . She is not concerned, in the way that other novelists are concerned, with character. . . .

As Miss Sinclair says, we have virtually no narrative. The prevailing tense is not the preterite as in Jane Austen or Thackeray, but the imperfect. "Miriam was practising." "The conversation was growing boisterous." "The girls were all settling down to fancy work." For this is not an account of what Miriam did, nor of what she was after (little is said of her secondary aims, like being a successful teacher; this is simply implied in her impressions of school life), nor even generally of what she *thought*. Even that is too active, too like an American heroine taking a line, grappling with life. And Miriam is passive.

It is an account of what was going on in her presence, what impressions were coming to her, of how such life as she tastes and touches tastes and feels to her. Miriam's thoughts and aspirations are for the most part too tenuous to be put in words; they are to be merely suggested through her moods in the presence of beauty, her antipathetic reactions to common talk, her pleasant reactions to German *Gemüthlichkeit,* etc.

As for what Miss Sinclair says of the non-interference by the author, much of that has long been implied in the ideals of "subjective drama." But no one had ever carried it so far as Dorothy Richardson. In his later novels James tries to identify himself as completely as possible with one or another of the characters. Only he feels that he should be there to render, to interpret the character's view of things. And it is ever the style of Henry James—his manner of putting ideas together, his stately and finicking process of thought—which dominates the landscape. This is necessary, he thinks, to keep things orderly, and to make us understand the bearing of the character's thoughts upon the point at issue. But in Dorothy Richardson there is no point at issue. She does not wish to keep things orderly or to make us understand. She wishes to make us *feel* with her character. She wishes to do away as far as is humanly possible with all extraneous interpretation, and with any suggestion of a style which is not Miriam Henderson's. She wishes indeed, as Miss Sinclair says, to "take Miriam's nature upon her," and so to follow the very idiom of her thoughts.

2

There have been novelists before her remarkable for the degree to which, in this or that part of their books, they followed the characters' own idiom. It was made a reproach against Zola that, in "L'Assommoir," he told his story of the slums of Paris too much in the language of the people. And this reproach he turned into a boast. In his preface of 1877, after discussing the morality of the book, he says: "The form itself has frightened readers. Some have got angry with the very words. . . . My work is my defence. It is a work of truth, the first novel about the people, which does not lie, and which has the smell of the people."

In a portrayal of drunken and degraded types, he makes large use of the picturesque argot of the Paris streets, not in passages specifically his own, but in the more extensive parts in which he is presenting the characters' view of things, whether in talk or in their thoughts and attitudes of mind. Indeed, it is often hard to determine, in a given place, whether what we have to do with is actual speech or the unspoken language of thought. Neighborhood feeling and community opinion are often the subject, and one passes insensibly from what is said out loud to what is said in the heart; from what is said or thought on a given occasion to views habitually held. In a tract against vice and the degrading social conditions which foster it, Zola does not think of assuming the tone of the preacher, or of denying the liveliness and colorfulness of life even in such vile conditions. He trusts his story to point its own moral. His descriptions of eating and drinking and fighting are conducted with a Rabelaisian gusto. The tone of the whole book is strongly tinctured with the racy idiom of the streets. This is one reason for its extraordinary vividness and vitality. And the vividness and vitality being those of life itself, even at its worst, make of it a work of art, and save it from having a predominantly depressing effect.

It is impossible, in translation, to do any proper justice to a technical feature involving the most intimate flavors of vernacular speech. For those who cannot read French, I suggest that there are passages in Dickens where somewhat the same method is used for dramatizing the characters' thoughts, though in a lighter and less serious vein.

A foreign work which suffers less in translation than Zola's is Knut Hamsun's "Growth of the Soil" (1917). This is a story of Norwegian peasants, and here, even more constantly than in Zola, the thoughts of the characters are rendered in terms of their familiar speech. A good example is the third chapter of Book II, in which Axel, while cutting wood, is accidentally pinned beneath a falling fir tree, and lies there helpless with his thoughts until at last he is rescued by Olline. I will quote but one paragraph, at the point where his enemy Brede has found him there and gone away refusing to help him:

> Silence. Axel strains away at the tree once more, lifts it a little, and brings down a new shower of snow. Gives it up again and sighs; he is worn out now, and getting sleepy. There's the cattle at home, they'll be standing in the hut and bellowing for food, not a bite nor a drop since the morning; no Barbro to look to them now—no. Barbro's gone, run off and gone, and taken both her rings, gold and silver, taken them with her. Getting dark now, ay, evening, night; well, well. . . . But there's the cold to reckon with too; his beard is freezing, soon his eyes will freeze too as well; ay, if he had but his jacket from the tree there . . . and now his leg—surely it can't be that—but all the same one leg feels dead now up to the hip.

"All in God's hands," he says to himself—seems like he can talk all godly and pious when he will. Getting dark, ay; but a man can die without the light of a lamp. He feels all soft and good now, and of sheer humility he smiles, foolishly and kindly, at the snowstorm round; 'tis God's own snow, an innocent thing! Ay, he might even forgive Brede, and never say a word. . . .

So Hamsun and Zola give intimacy and color to their narratives by careful observance of the characters' own locutions and turns of thought. But, for all that, they tell a story of objective events in which their presence is constantly required to explain, summarize, describe. In "Pilgrimage" either Miss Richardson is giving us plain autobiography or else she has really succeeded in identifying herself completely with Miriam Henderson. Her whole task is to select from the impressions beating in on Miriam's consciousness those which will best represent her temperamental reaction to life. So that we may say that the picture is limited by the range as well as the tone of the heroine's conscious life. Here we have, perhaps for the first time in a third-person narrative, an absolute rendering of the character's point of view.

The narrative is simply the stream of consciousness of the heroine, a stream growing ever fuller by the contribution of many small affluents. The intention is evidently to give us a broad impression of the feel of life under certain conditions. The whole is made up of many detached impressions grouped, with an instinctive sense of thematic relationships, in chapters and sections following one another mainly in natural time sequence.

The book is not a record of conscious thought directed to some clearly defined practical end; so it has a kind of fluid indeterminateness. Such logical connection as the impressions actually have for Miriam—such bearing as they have on conduct—is not set down formally, since that is not necessary for her; for her it does not need to be made specific. And, then, much of it is acknowledged as vague, not worked out, the meaning or bearing of particulars not clearly apprehended. And in general the intellectual and practical bearings of the whole experience are left unstated; even the emotional states are seldom characterized in abstract terms.

This is probably because the author believes that life comes to us as sensation and mood; that it comes thus particularly to young people first breasting the unexplored ocean; and most of all, to young girls with their cultivated ideal of reticence and vagueness. It is long before they begin to work out clearly and precisely what they want, precisely what they think and feel, and, above all, precisely what their own sensations mean. It is a kind of dream world in which they live, a world of symbols to which they have not the key.

It has heretofore been the convention of story-telling, for the sake of story pattern, to represent people as fully conscious voluntary actors, simplifying and sharpening outlines in the interest of dramatic issues. Here is a new order of truth: life as unanalyzed and not wholly differentiated dream stuff. And being so extremely natural, and at the same time so novel, it strikes us as realism such as we have seldom known.

3

Of course there are philosophical implications and intimations all along the line. Miriam is, we gather, on a pilgrimage to some elusive shrine, glimpsed here and there and lost to view. She is after something variously indicated, from point to point, as reality, beauty, happiness, the "shine on things," the "little coloured garden." She goes to town on an errand, down a road which, people didn't realize, "was big enough to be full of waves and waves of something real, something cool and true and unchanging." In a rose garden, "she seemed to have reached the summit of a hill up which she had been climbing ever since she came to Newlands." She minded no longer the thought of her father's debts. "The disgrace sat only on the muscles of her face. . . . Deeper down was something cool and fresh—endless—an endless garden." In the dentist's surgery, in "The Tunnel," she has the same mystic experience. "Up here there was something that had been made up here, real and changeless and independent. The least vestige of tumult would destroy it. It was something which no one could touch." She feels that there is an essential happiness hidden away in people's hearts. "Perhaps that is why people in life are always grumbling at 'annoyances' and things; to hide how happy they are."

This "little coloured garden" which she is forever seeking to enter compensates her for the humiliations and deprivations of her life. More and more she finds that she can only enter it alone; that the presence of others, and particularly of men, destroys it, draws a film over it. And this, of course, is extremely important in any account of her Daphnean psychology.

This mystical element in Miss Richardson has a strong family likeness to that of Virginia Woolf, who followed her in the use of the "stream-of-consciousness" technique. It also reminds one of that which often recurs in the work of May Sinclair. But in Miss Sinclair, it is much more likely to be stated in formal terms and to be made more obviously the subject of the book. In Miss Richardson, at least in the earlier books of the series, it is something that peeps out at one from behind bushes and disappears around the corners of hedges. Miss Sinclair follows more the ordinary direct method of narration, the method of statement, definition, formulation.

But one might just as well say that Miss Richardson's is the direct method. It is all a question of metaphysics. It is a question of whether the phenomena themselves are real, or the ideal essences which underlie phenomena. The ordinary method is the more intellectual. It makes for intelligibility, for intelligible form, for meanings defined and portable. But one is perfectly at liberty to say that it is not the realistic method of picturing life.

Life is not formulated until we apply reason to it, the faculty which has been cultivated for the abstract purposes of thought and the practical aims of conduct. But reason is the last faculty to be developed and applied by ordinary mortals. And it has a way of dissecting the life out of experience. It has a way, Miriam Henderson thinks, of distorting the facts. And she has a perpetual feud with males because of their disposition to put things in categories and leave them there to writhe and languish. Dorothy Richardson might perfectly well contend that her way is the direct one because it presents the items of Miriam's experience without attempting to formulate them.

She has, for example, delightful ways of indicating the happy moods of young girls without saying anything about them. Her description of a girl smoking her first cigarette, in "Backwater," is not merely a gem of delicate description; it is a marvel of implication. She was a very young girl, in a morning moment of clear untroubled well-being; she had become self-supporting. "She had chosen to smoke and she was smoking, and the morning world gleamed back at her . . ." Some of her dialogues are incomparable for the amount of furtive suggestion she can get into them. Miriam has just received her appointment to teach. The sisters are planning a party, and Harriett has some news for Miriam:

"What about Saturday?"

"It's all right, Ted was at the club."

"Was he!"

"Yes, old scarlet face, he were."

"I'm *not.*"

"He came in just before closing time and straight up to me

and ast where you were. He looked sick when I told him, and so fagged."

"It was awfully hot in town," murmured Miriam tenderly. She went to the piano and struck a note very softly.

"He played a single with a duffer and lost it."

"Oh, well, of course, he was so tired."

"Yes, but it wasn't that. It was because you weren't there. He's simply no good when you're not there, now. He's perfectly different."

Miriam struck her note again.

"Listen, that's E flat."

"Go on."

"That's a chord in E flat. Isn't it lovely? It sounds perfectly different in C. Listen. Isn't it funny?"

"Well, don't you want to know why it's all right about Saturday?"

There, making all allowance for difference of sex, temperament, and circumstances, is the way Mr. Hemingway so often gets his effects—by implication, by understandment, by symbolic representation. Only, Mr. Hemingway confines himself so rigorously to things said and done, whereas Miss Richardson is constantly drifting along in her character's stream of consciousness, passing by natural association of ideas from one thought to another, backward and forward in time, and crossing with easy flight all barriers of space and logical classification.

Often her heroine is simply passing from item to item of her little store of experience, dispensing altogether with verbs and grammatical connectives, with a sketchy incompleteness of expression. Sometimes in her thought she is addressing people who are absent or referring to them in some connection which it takes nimble wits to follow. Sometimes the emotional connotation of a present experience remains indefinite though strong, leading into dark places of the memory. Often she is on the track of an impression for which she can find no word.

And often words are found much more expressive than Mr. Hemingway would allow his characters, who are all so shy of being literary or even adult. The German pastor seen by Miriam without the aid of her glasses is "a dim black-coated knowledge." The next moment, "Fräulein Pfaff's smiling voice sounded from the little door." For some reason the Fräulein did not care for the friendliness of Miriam and Pastor Lahmann. And "she turned and drove Miriam from the room with speechless waiting eyes."

It is hard to give an impression of the stream-of-consciousness manner of narrative with the quotation of less than several pages. But the following brief passage will have to do. Miriam is trying to go to sleep, and has been musing painfully upon the need for thrift and the want of fun in her scrimping life:

> Save, save. Sooner or later saving must begin. Why not at once. Harry, it's no good. I'm old already. I've got to be one of those who give everything up.
>
> I wonder if Flora is asleep?
>
> That's settled. Go to sleep. Get thee behind me. Sleep . . . the dark cool room. Air; we breathe it in and it keeps us alive. Everybody has air. Manna. As much as you want, full measure, pressed down and running over. . . . Wonderful. There is somebody giving things, whatever goes . . . something left. . . . Somebody seeing that things are not quite unbearable . . . but the pain, the pain all the time, mysterious black pain. . . .
>
> Into thy hands I commit my spirit. *In manus* something. . . . You understand if nobody else does. But *why* must I be one of the ones to give everything up? *Why* do you make me suffer so?

4

As for Miss Richardson's relation to the imagist poets, I will quote two sections from a chapter of "Honeycomb" which might be included almost entire in an anthology of free verse. A reader acquainted with French and German schools of verse between 1900 and 1920 will discover her kinship with the unanimists, the futurists, the expressionists, and other coteries who once made a stir in the literary world. American readers will think of Amy Lowell and John Gould Fletcher.

The West End street . . . grey buildings rising on either side, feeling away into the approaching distance–angles sharp against the sky . . . softened angles of buildings against other buildings . . . high moulded angles soft as crumb, with deep undershadows . . . creepers fraying from balconies . . . strips of window blossoms across the buildings, scarlet, yellow, high up; a confusion of lavender and white pouching out along a dipping sill . . . a wash of green creeper up a white painted house front . . . patches of shadow and bright light. . . . Sounds of visible near things streaked and scored with broken light as they moved, led off into untraced distant sounds . . . chiming together.

* * *

Flags of pavement flowing along–smooth clean grey squares and oblongs, faintly polished, shaping and drawing away–sliding into each other. . . . I am a part of the dense smooth clean paving stone . . . sunlit; gleaming under dark winter rain; shining under warm sunlit rain, sending up a fresh stony smell . . . always there . . . dark and light . . . dawn, stealing . . .

Most of the imagist poets were strictly speaking impressionists—realists—in their concern for landscape effects, the passive subjection of their imaginations to the inflow of impressions. But in their inspirer, Ezra Pound, there is a strong suggestion of post-impressionist intention and method. He is so much more likely to proceed from the idea and to assemble in an abstract composition disparate and corresponding elements. This is often true of H.D., who—perfect imagist that she is—deals so largely in physical impressions that are symbols of unstated emotional attitudes, and, again, assembles them in patterns that give a strong impression of intellectual abstraction, as in her Sapphic "Fragment Thirty-Six."

The same thing is true of many free-verse poets who are not definitely associated with the imagist school. In all of Sandburg there is a marked strain of impressionism. But in his longer poems, like "Smoke and Steel," "And So To-Day," "Good Morning, America," the general composition can hardly be conceived without reference to some of the larger canvases of the post-impressionist painters. And his shorter pieces, like "Cadenza" and "Broken-Face Gargoyles," often suggest expressionist painting by the abstraction, the simplification, the rigorous elimination of merely descriptive elements.

Still more obviously in line with post-impressionist methods in painting are the poems of Wallace Stevens, Hart Crane, E. E. Cummings, Allen Tate, and T. S. Eliot. The most remarkable examples of such abstract composition in verse are Mr. Eliot's famous poems "The Waste Land" and "Ash-Wednesday." I shall return to this subject in the following chapter. I have introduced it here by way of suggesting, that, while Dorothy Richardson and James Joyce are both as different as they can be from the pre-war type of novelist, and while they are the two great originators of the "stream-of-consciousness" movement, they proceed, in some respects, from opposite poles of esthetic theory. For Joyce is essentially a post-impressionist, whereas Miss Richardson is essentially part and parcel of the general impressionist movement in art.

This distinction, however, is rather suggestive than scientific, and need not be maintained with too much rigor. The post-impressionist painters do not represent a complete and instantaneous break with the impressionists. They learned much from their predecessors and they arrived at the extremes of abstraction by way of transitional work like that of Cézanne. And besides, in applying these terms to poetry and fiction, it is well to bear in mind that we are simply indicating an analogy, though it is one which will serve to suggest the somewhat parallel development of the arts in our time.

PART FIVE: EXPRESSIONISM

On comprends qu'une semblable manière de composer, si différente de l'ancien procédé visible à tous les yeux, déroute souvent les critiques, et qu'ils ne découvrent pas tous les fils si minces, si secrets, presque invisibles, employés par certains artistes modernes à la place de la ficelle unique qui avait nom: L'Intrigue.

—Guy de Maupassant: Preface to "Pierre et Jean"

Il y eut un temps où on reconnaissait bien les choses quand c'était Fromentin qui les peignait et où on ne les reconnaissait plus quand c'était Renoir.

—Marcel Proust: "Le Côté de Guermantes"

XXXII

POST-IMPRESSIONISM: JOYCE

JOYCE'S "Ulysses" (1922) represents the most complete reaction against the main tendencies of the well-made novel. Indeed, it represents the most complete break, in our time, with the entire historical tradition of the novel. If it were not for the widespread influence it has had on other books which are obviously novels, we might leave it out of our account as being a freak of nature, a thing *sui generis,* and hardly in any proper sense a novel at all.

It is, to be sure, a fictitious narrative in prose, and that is a large part of any definition of the novel. But it has hardly more of a plot than "Tristram Shandy." And without a plot, it lacks a main ingredient of the "dramatic" which is a defining feature of the well-made novel. In the well-made novel the plot was greatly reduced and subordinated to the psychological interest; or, rather, identified with it. The plot was strictly confined to some narrow spiritual issue. But this issue, which limits the plot, gives it its sharp definition and makes it a plot. It is as neatly molded round this dramatic issue as a morning coat was fitted to the waist of a gentleman drinking tea in 1910.

In "Ulysses" there is no such issue, no plot, but simply a series of everyday occurrences serving as a framework on which to hang the psychical fabric whose texture it is our pleasure to study. Stephen Dedalus, Irish poet and school-teacher, has a talk with his friends in the tower where he is living; conducts a class at his school; visits a newspaper office with an article on the foot-and-mouth disease written by his master, Mr. Deasy; discusses Shakspere with friends in the library; takes part in a conversation with medical students in a maternity hospital; gets rather drunk and visits a bawdy house, goes home with Leopold Bloom and takes a cup of cocoa before saying good night. Leopold Bloom, Jewish canvasser for advertisements and amateur scientist, gets breakfast for his wife, Marion; visits the post-office, where he finds a letter from a girl-friend; goes to a funeral; visits the newspaper office in connection with an ad; writes a letter to his girl-friend in the bar of a hotel; is kicked out of a saloon by a violent anti-Semite; sits on a bench and has a mute flirtation with a sentimental young girl; goes with Stephen Dedalus to Nighttown and takes him home for a cup of cocoa; goes to bed with his wife and puts himself to sleep with pleasant thoughts. Marion Bloom indulges in a long reverie in which she reviews her own emotional history and all her relations with her husband, ending up with a vivid recall of the first time that she said yes to him. In connection with all these occurrences we are introduced to many persons important in one way or another to the principals.

The whole record has the most amazing air of reality, and, except for one thing, gives as strong an impression of life as any novel in the English tongue. The one thing lacking is passionate motivation of action. The principal characters are intimately known, their past history, their habits, mental and physical, even their motivation from moment to moment. But whatever it is they are after—and this too we know in a general way if we are very discerning readers—it is never brought to a head in dramatic action or issue. No one commits murder or feels impelled to do so; no one robs a bank; no one tries to get the better of another by trickery or force. The passion or sentiment of love is almost nowhere represented, in spite of certain protoplasmic phenomena of a sexual character.

The nearest approach to story is the striking up of a

kind of friendship between Stephen Dedalus and Leopold Bloom. Stephen's father in the flesh is an unsatisfactory person; and Bloom's dearly loved son had died in early childhood; so that each one has need for his psychological complement in the father-son relation. And so when Bloom picks up Stephen from a gutter in Nighttown and takes him home for a friendly chat and a cup of cocoa, we may say—at least it has been said—that the story reaches a sort of culmination. And it is clear enough that the Bloom-Stephen relation was intended to correspond somehow to the Odysseus-Telemachus relation in the Odyssey.

But after all, the acquaintanceship of Bloom and Stephen is but one of dozens of strands out of which this multifarious web is woven. And, having in mind the whole narrative, it would be absurd to say that the ruling passion of Stephen Dedalus is the craving for a father, or that of Bloom the craving for a son. There is no suggestion that Stephen actually finds in Bloom the makings of a satisfactory father, and very little more indication that Bloom feels strongly drawn toward Stephen with paternal sentiment.

If Leopold Bloom has any ruling passion, it is the craving to compensate in his own mind for the sense of inferiority which oppresses him. There is plenty of reason assigned for his sense of inferiority—the scorn in which his race is held, his want of any great success in business, his inability to satisfy his wife's emotional demands or to command her faithfulness. And he is very busy "compensating."

But this business does not take the "dramatic" form of action. For the most part it takes the obscure psychological form of "fantasy." He imagines the voluptuous pleasures of the Orient, congenial to his racial inheritance; he imagines himself making love to Gerty MacDowell (but it is all imagination); in the great scene in Nighttown—cast in dramatic form—after he has been besieged by a dozen reminders of his own futility (all in his imagination), he makes his recovery by imagining himself Lord Mayor of Dublin, the world's greatest reformer, emperor-president and king-chairman. He marries the Princess Selene, the splendor of the night. He administers justice, answers hard questions, delivers political harangues, and performs miracles. Before going to sleep he indulges in a perfect orgy of consolatory imaginings. He imagines a large number of schemes for making quantities of money with little effort. He imagines himself young again and capable of "exercising virile power of fascination in the most immediate future after an expensive repast in a private apartment . . ."

Leopold Bloom is, in short, an amiable and pottering introvert. He is a middle-aged man, attached to his comforts, *l'homme moyen sensuel,* unsuccessful, and unprovided with any practicable scheme for attaining success, but drifting along from one sensation to another, expanding and contracting, putting out and drawing in feelers, like so much jellyfish. He has no strong objective, no organizing principle for his energies. He has no ruling passion even, unless it be the wish to think well of himself; and that he takes out almost altogether in day-dreams.

Something of the same thing is true of Stephen Dedalus, though his is a more complicated character and harder to define. He is a young man, profoundly disillusioned, and governed, as much as anything, by scorn and disgust for most of what he sees about him. It is true that he is a poet and that he is presumably going about his poet's business as stated at the end of Joyce's "Portrait of the Artist as a Young Man": "I go to encounter for the millionth time the reality of experience and to forge in the smithy of my soul the uncreated conscience of my race." But this guiding principle, if it is there, is quite lost in the hullabaloo of his own thoughts and the general hullabaloo of Dublin life in which he is so deeply immersed. He seems to have lost control of sheet and tiller and to be drifting about at the mercy of every gust of wind. The note of suffering is more distinctly sounded in his case than in Bloom's, but this too is a thin cry lost in the Rabelaisian hubbub of the pot-house.

Perhaps his ruling passion is, like Bloom's, the craving to think well of himself. But Stephen also is much of an introvert, and given to fantasy as a chief means of satisfying this need. In the line of action the best he can do is to put over on his learned disputants a new theory of the personal psychology of Shakspere, or to smash (symbolically) the chandelier in a bawdy-house. If Stephen Dedalus is, as has been with good reason supposed, in some sense modeled on Joyce himself, there is one important omission. There is little suggestion in Stephen Dedalus of the positive organizing principle, the mere force of character, that made possible the writing of the "Portrait of the Artist as a Young Man," let alone "Ulysses."

We are all familiar with people like Bloom and Dedalus. They line the tables nightly at the Dôme and the Rotonde, and their disabled hulks are scattered about the shores of the business world. It is obvious why they do not lend themselves well to plot and drama—to what has been heretofore the staple of the novel. Laboring under this paralysis of the will to action, they do not take hold upon life constructively, but allow themselves to be dispersed among the backwaters of fantasy and sensation. One result is that the narrative of Joyce is "subjective" to a degree never before known.

2

The subjective element becomes noticeable in fiction, as in everyday psychology, when an interval occurs between the stimulus to action and the resulting act. It is necessary for the character to choose a "line," and the period between stimulus and action results in an emotional strain through suspense, the state of hopeful anticipation, or anxiety. The subjective element is likely to be increased with every prolongation of this emotional or thinking phase, in which, with the persistence of the state of indecision, doubt, fear, hope, the strain is aggravated and intensified.

Higher degrees of subjectivism are distinguishable in authors who like to analyze the subjective predicament of the character into its minuter component elements. This may be for the purpose of intensifying our consciousness of the predicament by dwelling on it at length and in detail, and giving us a sense of great intimacy with the feelings of the characters. It may be thus a dramatic intention which determines the employment of the method. Or it may be simply that the author is so much more interested in the subjective element that he goes in for detailed analysis for its own sake. Whether the effect is good or bad depends partly on the taste of the reader. It also depends on the talent of the author, his vividness of imagination, the sureness with which he takes his stand at the emotional center of human experience. Examples of great success in this method are to be found in Conrad and James. In Pirandello, we have an approximation to the effects of Conrad in "Il fu Mattia Pascal" and to those of James in "Si Gira."

This procedure is analogous to that of the close-up and the slow-up, or *ralenti,* in the moving picture. In the close-up we have a magnified and so more detailed presentation of a face or other feature, not necessary for the action, but often very effective for rendering the feeling, the esthetic intention, and for letting the impression of the character sink in. In the *ralenti* the movement, which at the ordinary rate is perceived as one rapid curve, as undifferentiated outline, is slowed up to such an extent that we are able to distinguish its successive moments. We are perhaps less aware of the drama of the thing, but we are more aware of its magic, its poetry, its metaphysics. In its merely physical phase, this procedure is best illustrated by some subject like a horse taking a hedge or a volley at tennis, in which we can follow with great precision the movement of the horse's legs, the special technique of the tennis-player. Wonderful combinations of close-up and *ralenti* are found in the masterpieces of Charlie Chaplin and Emil Jannings.

In the analogous procedure in fiction, there is a tendency to exhaust the content of the moment presented, there is an *infinite expansion of the moment.* We are made aware of many details in the subjective state which otherwise would be passed rapidly over or ignored in the interest of action and the effect of the whole. This method is the exact contrary of Smollett's, in whose work ("Peregrine Pickle" and "Roderick Random") a chief attraction lies in the swift passage from incident to incident, the sense of rapid motion like that we have in an automobile. For the reader interested in psychology, this subjective close-up may procure one of the highest gratifications within the gift of fiction, enabling him to extract the last drop of human significance from a given subject. The danger is that author and reader may lose a due sense of the relation of feeling and thought to action, the behavioristic reference of all subjective states, and so there may come to pass a disintegration of the psychological complex, a divorce between motive and conduct.

But now suppose an author whose intention is precisely to display such a psychological disintegration. What we should then expect is what we have in "Ulysses." The trinity of sensation-motive-conduct is broken down. Action is so slight and inconsecutive that it hardly counts, and we cannot have a proper behavioristic reference of the subjective states. Motive, which is so largely judged by reference to action, appears in a weak and sickly condition. What dominates the landscape is sensation—actual and imaginary.

The great point of likeness between Henry James and James Joyce is their extreme subjectivism. The great point of difference is the comparative want in Joyce of the behavioristic reference. He is concerned very little with action, and very much with what goes on in the consciousness of Bloom and Stephen. And it is not to explain their action that he displays their souls; it is their souls themselves that interest him—or, rather, the flux of sensation and thought that constitutes the identity of each. A new psychology has intervened between James and Joyce, and it is no longer possible to talk of souls. The people of James are unitary beings, responsible for their choices and judged by the fineness of their perceptions. The plot of the story is the process of their enlightenment proceeding inevitably to their choice of the better alternative. The subjective close-ups of James are meant to have their bearing on the dramatic issue, and are limited, in the long run, by this intention. In Joyce there is nothing of the kind to limit the close-ups. So that what first sharply distinguishes him from James is his carrying so very much farther one of James's leading tendencies.

The same thing applies to the author's disposition to self-effacement. However James may try to identify himself with his characters, there is ever the elaborate structure of his personal style. This is necessary, he thinks, to guarantee the coherence of his character's experience. But coherence is not what Joyce is concerned with. It is, on the contrary, the hasty reader will conclude, the very height of incoherence. The *monologue intérieur,* which occupies the bulk of this volume and is the feature most frequently imitated, seems devised to illustrate the freakishness and inconsequence of the subjective process when not strictly controlled by some practical objective. One idea leads to another by associations that shoot off at a tangent; one stream of thought is overlaid and undermined by any number of diverse streams, which are sure to seep through the roof or well up from beneath and distract its flow just at the point where it seems to be getting somewhere. The psyche which is defined by the continuity of this welter appears to be passive under the compulsion of eye and ear continually flooding it with new associations, and still more under that of memory and imagination.

And what doubles the confusion is the unwillingness of the author to show us the way, even to indicate the point and plausibility of hiatus and ellipsis. The silent monologue is for the most part carried on in the very idiom of the character, with whatever there is of idiosyncrasy in the way his thoughts follow one another. Once again, in applying James's idea of self-effacement, Joyce has developed the formula to the point where it is unrecognizable.

Let us set down two considerable passages from "Ulysses," taken from the beginning of the section in which Stephen is shown pacing the shore and musing:

> Ineluctable modality of the visible: at least that if no more, thought through my eyes. Signatures of all things I am here to read, seaspawn and seawrack, the nearing tide, the rusty boot. Snotgreen, bluesilver, rust: coloured signs. Limits of the diaphane. But he adds: in bodies. Then he was aware of them bodies before of them coloured. How? By knocking his sconce against them, sure. Go easy. Bald he was and a millionaire, *maestro di color che sanno*. Limit of the diaphane in. Why in? Diaphane, adiaphane. If you can put your five fingers through it, it is a gate, if not a door. Shut your eyes and see.
>
> Stephen closed his eyes to hear his boots crush crackling wrack and shells. You are walking through it howsomever. I am, a stride at a time. A very short space of time through very short times of space. Five, six: the *nacheinander*. Exactly: and that is the ineluctable modality of the audible. Open your eyes. No. Jesus! If I fell over a cliff that beetles o'er his base, fell through the *nebeneinander* ineluctably. I am getting on nicely in the dark. My ash sword hangs at my side. Tap with it; they do. My two feet in his boots are at the end of his legs,

nebeneinander. Sounds solid: made by the mallet of *Los Demiurgos*. Am I walking into eternity along Sandymount strand? Crush, crack, crick, crick. Wild sea money. Dominie Deasy kens them a'.

Won't you come to Sandymount,
Madeline the mare?

Rhythm begins, you see. I hear. A catalectic tetrameter of iambs marching. No, agallop: *deline the mare.*

Open your eyes now. I will. One moment. Has all vanished since? If I open and am forever in the black adiaphane. Basta! I will see if I can see.

See now. There all the time without you: and ever shall be world without end.

They came down the steps from Leahy's terrace prudently, *Frauenzimmer*: and down the shelving shore flabbily their splayed feet sinking in the silted sand. Like me, like Algy, coming down to our mighty mother. Number one swung lourdily her midwife's bag, the other's gamp poked in the beach. From the liberties, out for the day. Mrs. Florence Mac Cabe, relict of the late Patk Mac Cabe, deeply lamented, of Bride Street. One of her sisterhood lugged me squealing into life. Creation from nothing. What has she in the bag? A misbirth with a trailing navelcord, hushed in ruddy wool. The cords of all link back, strandentwining cable of all flesh. That is why mystic monks. Will you be as gods? Gaze in your omphalos. Hello, Kinch here. Put me on to Edenville. Aleph, alpha: nought, nought, one.

A few pages later, when something has brought to mind his student days in Paris:

My Latin quarter hat. God, we simply must dress the character. I want puce gloves. You were a student, weren't you? Of what in the other devil's name? Paysayenn. P.C.N., you know: *physiques, chimiques et naturelles*. Aha. Eating your groatsworth of *mou en civet*, fleshpots of Egypt, elbowed by belching cabmen. Just say in the most natural tone: when I was in Paris, *boul' Mich'*, I used to. Yes, used to carry punched tickets to prove an alibi if they arrested you for murder somewhere. Justice. On the night of the seventeenth of February 1904 the prisoner was seen by two witnesses. Other fellow did it: other me. Hat, tie, overcoat, nose. *Lui, c'est moi.* You seem to have enjoyed yourself.

Proudly walking. Whom were you trying to walk like? Forget: a dispossessed. With mother's money order, eight shillings, the banging door of the postoffice slammed in your face by the usher. Hunger toothache. *Encore deux minutes.* Look clock. Must get. *Fermé.* Hired dog! Shoot him to bloody bits with a bang shotgun, bits man spattered walls all brass buttons. Bits all khrrrrklak in place clack back. Not hurt? O, that's all right. Shake hands. See what I meant, see? O, that's all right. Shake a hand. O, that's all only all right.

You were going to do wonders, what? Missionary to Europe after fiery Columbanus. Fiacre and Scotus on their creepystools in heaven spilt from their pintpots, loudlatinlaughing: *Euge! Euge!* Pretending to speak broken English as you dragged your valise, porter threepence, across the slimy pier at Newhaven. *Comment?* Rich booty you brought back; *Le Tutu,* five tattered numbers of *Pantalon Blanc et Culette Rouge,* a blue French telegram, curiosity to show:

—Mother dying come home father.

The aunt thinks you killed your mother. That's why she won't.

The section from which these passages are taken begins with no statement of what character is involved, where he is or what he is doing. We are left to gather that from indications farther along. We are never told that Stephen is engaged in trying out the principles of Aristotle's psychology with his feet and his eyes. That we must gather from the terms themselves and from the allusion to Dante's phrase for Aristotle, "master of those who know." We gather from certain German words that Stephen had been studying Aristotle by the light of German commentators or German metaphysics. The old women walking on the beach come in without introduction, and they bring with them, without explanation, one of the mystical motifs which run through the reflections of Stephen—the "strand-entwining cable of all flesh" which establishes the continuity of life since Mother Eve—and we are left to figure out as best we may Stephen's whimsical demand to be connected (by telephone, as I take it) with Edenville, whose number is naturally nought, nought, one. No glossary is furnished, and we are thrown back on our own knowledge of Greek and German and French. We are not informed that *Paysayenn* is an English way of representing phonetically the French pronunciation of the letters P.C.N.

By this time (page 37 and following) we have learned that Stephen is given to addressing himself in his imagination in the second person; and so we assume that the "you" who in Paris carried punched tickets to prove an alibi was Stephen Dedalus, and that the shooting of a post-office official who prevented him from cashing his mother's money-order is the humorous dramatization of an impulse never carried out, as is likewise his jovial reconciliation with the murdered man when the "bits all khrrrrklak in place clack back." Certain hints in earlier scenes give us, if we are sharp, the clue to the telegram which summoned Stephen back to his mother's death-bed. Putting things together, we make out that Stephen, in his rebellion against his mother's faith, had refused to kneel down and pray for her when she asked him. It is for this reason that his aunt thinks he killed his mother, and "that's why she won't" . . . whatever it is she won't. This is, I suppose, a matter of supreme importance in the motivation of Stephen; but it is slipped in in the same incidental fashion as any most trifling circumstance.

3

Now, let it be stated at once that, in this manner of narrative, Joyce is not moved by mere cantankerous caprice. He is simply carrying one step farther that disposition of the author to keep himself out of the picture which we have noted as involved in the "dramatic" tendency. And already, in "A Portrait of the Artist as a Young Man," he had made a clear statement of the esthetic intention which was to be so much more completely realized in "Ulysses."

Stephen Dedalus was there setting forth for his friend Lynch the distinguishing features of what he calls the lyrical, the epical, and the dramatic forms. The lyrical form is that "wherein the artist presents his image in immediate relation to himself"; the epical that "wherein he presents his image in immediate relation to himself and to others"; the dramatic that "wherein he presents his image in immediate relation to others." He seems to regard the three forms as progressive, the dramatic being the final form in literary evolution.

> The personality of the artist, at first a cry or a cadence or a mood and then a fluid and lambent narrative, finally refines itself out of existence, impersonalizes itself, so to speak. The esthetic image in the dramatic form is life purified in and reprojected from the human imagination. The mystery of esthetic like that of material creation is accomplished. The artist, like the God of the creation, remains within or behind or beyond or above his handiwork, invisible, refined out of existence, indifferent, paring his fingernails.

So then it is no mere bent for riddling and teasing which leads Joyce to omit those painstaking explanations with which it has been customary to guide and enlighten the reader. It is the desire to "present his image in immediate relation to others," getting rid of the personality of the author, that colored medium which has been wont to interpose itself between the subject and the reader. It is the same passion for pure dramatic "projection" of the subject itself which directed Browning in the composition of "My Last Duchess," "A Tocatta of Galuppi's," "Caliban upon Setebos." And the obscurity of Joyce has the same origin as Browning's, and the same excuse in so far as it is successful in securing its end, which is that of dramatic immediacy.

> 'Will sprawl, now that the heat of day is best,
> Flat on his belly in the pit's much mire . . .

Primitive Caliban talks of himself in the third person, as he might talk of some other creature. But at times, in the heat of his imagination, he rises to the more exciting first person, and his imaginings take on the character of present actualities:

> Put case, unable to be what I wish,
> I yet could make a live bird out of clay:
> Would I not take clay, pinch my Caliban
> Able to fly?—for, there, see, he hath wings,
> And great comb like the hoopoe's to admire,
> And there, a sting to do his foes offence,
> There, and I will that he begin to live . . .

One can find in Browning every peculiarity which makes difficult reading of the passages quoted from "Ulysses." And Joyce and Browning are both using much the same technique as Carlyle in "The French Revolution"—that compact, allusive, elliptical manner, feverishly dramatizing, scorning the formal style of history, passing rapidly back and forth among the tenses, the moods, and the persons.

Carlyle, to be sure, cannot keep himself long out of the picture, Scots moralist and transcendental philosopher. But he has a marvelous faculty for putting himself at the point of view of his character. Also, a most uncanny faculty for reproducing the tone of his documents: French memoirs, Prussian "Dry-as-dust" chronicles, Kantian-Fictean metaphysics.

Joyce, when he gives us Bloom, gives him to us unmixed, in the very rhythm and tempo of his ruminations, the very idiom and dialect of his thinking, strangely compounded of Oriental dreaminess, scientific speculation, and the hard matter-of-fact of the small business man. When he gives us Marion, it is all pure instinctive female, without a trace of logical or rhetorical coördination, without even the division of sentence and phrase. And there are a dozen other distinct manners suited to the personalities of the leading characters, or of groups of characters taken in the lump.

There is the style of that Irish patriot who makes the assault on Bloom in Barney Kiernan's bar, the lively colloquial style of bar-room narrative:

> I was just passing the time of day with old Troy of the D.M.P. at the corner of Arbour hill there and be damned but a bloody sweep came along and he near drove his gear into my eye. I turned around to let him have the weight of my tongue when who should I see dodging along Stony Batter only Joe Hynes.—Lo, Joe, says I. How are you blowing? Did you see that bloody chimneysweep near shove my eye out with his brush? . . . So we turned into Barney Kiernan's and there sure enough was the citizen up in the corner having a great confab with himself and that bloody mangy mongrel, Garryowen, and he waiting for what the sky would drop in the way of drink.

There is, again, the style of Gerty MacDowell, full of sentimental clichés, with loose-hung sentences running off into bathos. There are innumerable whisky-inspired passages of babble and tumult, Rabelaisian "discourse of the drinkers." Each one of these characters and scenes has been conceived by the artist in his imagination and "reprojected" upon the screen of his work, while he himself "remains within or behind or beyond or above his handiwork, invisible . . . paring his fingernails."

In Stephen Dedalus at least, it might be thought, we have the personal style of Joyce, who has put so much of himself into that figure. But no. Whatever his origin, even Dedalus is a dramatic creation, distinct from his author, projected away from himself. If in his ruminations he reproduces something of what has passed through the mind of James Joyce, it is at any rate not in the style of the author seated at his table before his white sheet of paper, setting things in order, devising cadences worthy of Newman, Flaubert, or Huysmans. It is the style of a poor befuddled poet pacing the sands with the vague intention of visiting his uncle, but with memories and sensations crowding in on him pell-mell—fragments of Aristotle and music-hall refrains, sewer smells and midwives with their black bags, imaginary dialogues, souvenirs of Paris, self-reproaches, sniggering anecdotes, and half-formed lines of verse. It is ideas associated in the casual and incoherent way that ideas run before the author takes them in hand to sort them out and set them in order.

And once we get used to this system of writing, once we "catch on," we have strongly the sense, which the author intended us to have, of being in immediate contact with "life" itself. In the ordinary novelist the "life" that is the author's subject is found embedded in a firm matrix of the author's style, and is redolent, willy-nilly, of the author's personality. In Joyce the subject has been disengaged from this setting, this matrix, and exposed by itself, even at the cost of its falling to pieces for want of support. And falling to pieces, as I have said before, the characters seem to be.

4

So then, plot having gone by the board, and with it to a considerable degree the psychical coherence of the characters, what is left to hold together this great amorphous mass and give it form? It is here that Mr. Stuart Gilbert is indispensable, with his detailed account of "Ulysses." Mr. Gilbert has shown that Joyce has a principle of organization as formal as it is unique in fiction. "Ulysses" is nothing more nor less than a symphonic poem, characterized by a rigorous and insistent development of themes. Underneath the apparently freakish play of the surface runs the continuous rhythm of recurring motifs.

First of all, there is the close correspondence of each of the eighteen sections to one of the episodes of the Odyssey. This correspondence is not merely a matter of the general outline of the episode. It is carried out in a thousand obscure allusions scattered through the narrative and lodged like ore in the most secret rifts and veins of rhetoric and reverie. Along with this is the thematic development, in each episode, of allusions to some bodily organ, to some one of the arts, some type-word or symbol, often to some color, together with the application in each case of a special narrative technique appropriate to the subject-matter. For example, the scene in the newspaper office, corresponding, with humorous exactness, to the Homeric episode of Æolus and his windbag, develops with infinite ingenuity the theme of the lungs, that windy organ of rhetoric; it offers examples of every trick known to the Greek rhetoricians (Mr. Gilbert cites ninety-five of them); and its special technique is the enthymeme, consisting of a syllogism with one premise omitted. Besides all this, there are other recurring motifs, such as the mystic doctrine of metempsychosis; the theme of paternity, biological and spiritual; the preoccupations of theology and Aristotelian metaphysics; certain anthropological themes; and of course the psychological motifs of inferiority and compensation, with a dozen related notions from Zurich and Vienna.

Now, what most needs saying, in reference to all these motifs and correspondences, is that they are not used for the development of plot, nor are they, for the most part, necessary to the motivation of character. So far as fiction goes, they are a pure luxury—the unbridled play of the poetic or musical faculty. Incidentally they are the element in "Ulysses" (and what I am now saying applies still more forcibly to "Work in Progress," not yet published in its entirety) which has least affected such novelists as have more or less come under Joyce's influence. These themes, serving as threads to tie the book together formally, are something extra, something superadded to the "slice" of Dublin "life" which is his obvious subject. And yet, while they reveal the hand of the artificer, they still leave him invisible, somewhere within or behind or beyond or above his handiwork, and, God knows, indifferent.

This is something that Mr. Gilbert seems to miss. He takes so seriously the theme of metempsychosis, for example, or that of the mystic omphalos, never suggesting that Joyce may have been writing with his tongue in his cheek. And he does not, I believe, bring up the question of what point there may be in making this silly pedestrian day of Bloom correspond from moment to moment with the glamorous return of Odysseus. The *point* of this juxtaposition of contemporary Irish futilities with heroic Greek adventure is obviously the ironic exposure of contemporary Irish futilities. But never does Joyce interpose to make his point. And never does he resort to his personal style as an author to develop any of the other motifs. They are woven into the dialogue, into the musings of the characters, who do not realize that they are being made the means of developing a set of themes. As for the author, he is everywhere and nowhere.

There has been a deal of talk about Joyce's realism. It is true that he is a realist, if that means that he has no sentimental or moral ax to grind, or if realism is taken to signify the formidable assemblage of lifelike detail. What is equally to the point is that he is in the line of the symbolists, as Edmund Wilson has shown in his learned and subtle book entitled "Axel's Castle." In technique he transcends realism by not confining himself to the three dimensions of a literal transcription of life. He takes liberties with the facts. In the Walpurgisnacht or Circe episode, for example, the fantasies of Bloom and Dedalus are not labeled fantasies, as realism would require, but are hypostatized into dramatic figures and scenes. The End of the World appears as a man with a Scotch accent; Bella's fan takes voice to utter reproaches to Bloom; and Bella turns into Bello in the middle of the page as Virginia Woolf's Orlando changes his sex in his sleep.

Mr. Gilbert has pointed out the appropriateness of the technique of "gigantism" in the episode of the Cyclops (that in which Bloom is driven out of Barney Kiernan's by the antisemitic "citizen"). What is this gigantism? It is an ironic transposition of the actual scene into an altogether different and seemingly loftier key. These poor soused Dubliners stand at the bar and discuss the topics of the day: the death of Paddy Dignam, the foot-and-mouth disease, the Irish language, and their drinks. And somewhere out of Eternity there comes a weird light to throw their shadows on some apocalyptic screen: monstrous swollen, misshapen shadows as of mythical heroes, carrying out in pantomime on some prodigious scale the ideal implications of their petty words.

But just how is this managed? The actual scene is given in the pot-house vernacular of the anonymous narrator, including a literal citation of what was said by the persons present. And then at frequent intervals, without warning, appear paragraphs, in every variety of mock-heroic and parody, in which the actual speech or act is presented in its ideal form. Here is a brief example in which the ideal event precedes the actual:

> And lo, as they quaffed their cup of joy, a godlike messenger came swiftly in, radiant as the eye of heaven, a comely youth and behind him there passed an elder of noble gait and countenance, bearing the sacred scrolls of law and with him his lady wife, a dame of peerless lineage, fairest of her race.
>
> Little Alf Bergan popped in round the door and hid behind

Barney's snug, squeezed up with the laughing, and who was sitting up there in the corner that I hadn't seen snoring drunk, blind to the world, only Bob Doran. I didn't know what was up and Alf kept making signs out of the door. And begob what was it only that bloody old pantaloon Denis Breen in his bath slippers with two bloody big books tucked under his oxter and the wife hotfoot after him, unfortunate wretched woman trotting like a poodle. I thought Alf would split.

And here is the conclusion of the whole scene in its actuality followed by its ideal transcription:

And the last we saw was the bloody car rounding the corner and old sheepface on it gesticulating and the bloody mongrel after it with his lugs back for all he was bloody well worth to tear him limb from limb. Hundred to five! Jesus, he took the value of it out of him, I promise you.

When, lo, there came about them all a great brightness and they beheld the chariot wherein He stood ascend to heaven. And they beheld Him in the chariot, clothed upon in the glory of the brightness, having raiment as of the sun, fair as the moon and terrible that for awe they durst not look upon Him. And there came a voice out of heaven, calling: *Elijah! Elijah!* And He answered with a main cry: *Abba! Adonai!* And they beheld Him even Him, ben Bloom Elijah, amid clouds of angels ascend to the glory of the brightness at an angle of forty-five degrees over Donahoe's in Little Green Street like a shot off a shovel.

So, like a fourth dimension, the mock-ideal shadow is added to the three dimensions of the actual to make up this Carlylean equation. Other striking instances of fourth-dimensional devices might be cited. When it comes to "Work in Progress," the fourth dimension is everywhere. For the dream state of mind there set forth is compatible with the most crazy juggling of times and spaces. In the symbolism of this fantastic epic, there is a sort of ideal equivalence of many different periods and settings, and many different characters from myth and history merge into one.

This is the poetical method of T. S. Eliot in "The Waste Land," as he explains to us in the notes. "Just as the one-eyed merchant, seller of currants, melts into the Phoenician Sailor, and the latter is not wholly distinct from Ferdinand Prince of Naples, so all the women are one woman, and the two sexes meet in Tiresias." Tempting as is the riddle of "Work in Progress," it shall not here concern us. For in "Work in Progress" there is hardly a hint of an actual slice of three-dimensional life such as makes the substantial basis of "Ulysses." So that it would prove quite unprofitable to consider it in the light of a novel. Even in "Ulysses" we have, in many ways, a resemblance less to other novels than to contemporary poems—Ezra Pound's "Cantos," Hart Crane's "The Bridge," and Eliot's "Ash-Wednesday" and "The Waste Land."

One way of placing Joyce would be by the analogy of post-impressionist painting. The technique of James might be likened to that of painting before the advent of impressionism. His aim is truth in the representation of nature. Truth is the whole burden of his literary criticism. A very special truth he seeks, truth selected and set in a particular light. That is where the art comes in. But still he is the painter sitting down before a landscape to render it with faithfulness. This is the attitude of the impressionist as well as of his predecessors. Only, the impressionist saw his landscape differently and developed a special technique for rendering it. I have shown in what sense we might apply the term "impressionist" to Conrad, Lawrence, and Dorothy Richardson.

But the post-impressionist is not primarily concerned with the representation of nature. His aim is, out of elements derived from nature, to make an abstract composition for rendering some truth of his own conceiving. His truth may be of the utmost significance in the ideal world, but it is not necessarily a fact of nature. Or rather, say, his truth is a combination of facts never found combined in precisely this way at any given moment in nature. He may therefore ignore or amend perspective, which is an attribute of three-dimensional nature. Any new dimension taken into account brings in a new perspective. His abstract design may involve a measure of deformation or conventionalization of the objects presented. It is clear that Joyce's "Ulysses"—not to mention "Work in Progress"—corresponds in fiction to post-impressionist painting, by virtue of the prominence in it of abstract composition. But this, as I have pointed out, is a note in Joyce which is by no means uniformly echoed in writers whom he has influenced, whereas it is a dominant note in several contemporary poets. It makes him rather difficult to classify. He has vastly influenced the technique and the substance of the novel. But he has perhaps as great affinities with Aristophanes as with Thackeray. He is as close to Dante as to Henry James.

XXXIII

THE BREADTHWISE CUTTING

THE leading character in André Gide's "Les Faux-monnayeurs" ("The Counterfeiters") is a novelist named Edouard, who is in many respects modeled on Gide himself. He is writing a novel (entitled "Les Faux-monnayeurs," like the book in which he figures), and among the things he has to say about his intentions in this book, is the following:

"A slice of life," said the naturalist school. The great mistake of this school is cutting its slice always in the same direction; in the direction of time, lengthwise. Why not breadthwise, depthwise? As for me, I prefer not to cut at all. Understand me: I should like to get everything into this novel.

Now this, in a way, is what Joyce has done in "Ulysses." He has not cut his slice of life lengthwise. He has no plot involving incidents following one another in the direction of time. He has confined his entire narrative to one day, and within that day he has spread wide, breadthwise, and plunged down far into psychology, depthwise. As for the depthwise plunge, enough has been said. It is one substitute he has offered for the want of plot. The other substitute is breadthwise cutting, comprehensiveness of view. The funeral of Paddy Dignam and the parturition of Mrs. Purefoy are not elements in a plot; they are the two poles of human life philosophically regarded.

Every moment dies a man,
Every moment one is born.

Between these two poles are appetite and physiology (eating, drinking and elimination); love, represented by the lusty swarming of Marion and the weakly eroticism of Leopold Bloom; with the preoccupations of business, politics, patriotism, science, music, and letters.

If there is a theme, it is perhaps the "uncreated conscience" of Stephen's race. The ultimate effect is a vivid and rather desolating impression of Dublin, of the Irish people, and, through that, of the race of man in its present state of jovial futility. It is such a picture of the state of man, without grace, as might have been offered by Paul or Augustine if they had concerned themselves with literary art. Some such undertaking has been carried out in earlier times by Tolstoy, by Victor Hugo, Balzac, and Zola; but always with them the composite picture of mankind, of human nature, has been ranged lengthwise along the line of a plot, and almost invariably whatever was introduced into the picture was made to bear upon a specific dramatic issue, something to be resolved.

For the most part, in "Ulysses," everything is given some relation to one of the three major characters, Stephen, Leopold, and Marion. In all but one of the seventeen sections one or more of these persons is present virtually throughout. But as if to signalize his more comprehensive intention, the author inserts a section in the midst of the book in which some hundred people are shown, in a succession of fleeting glimpses, each one occupied in a characteristic way during the middle of the afternoon. And while Bloom and Stephen do come in along with their fellow Dubliners, their appearance is so casual, their stay so short, that they seem of no more importance than any one else; they are lost in the crowd.

This chapter, corresponding to the episode of the Wandering Rocks in the Odyssey, is apparently designed to render the bewildering complexity of human interests and occupations. There are priests, lovers, policemen, undertakers, typists. There are lawyers and shopkeepers of every description. There are the young sisters of Stephen Dedalus, scheming to squeeze a penny out of their tight-fisted father. There is Paddy Dignam's son buying pork chops, and Martin Cunningham circulating some list for charity. There is a bicycle race, and there are men discussing horse-races, politics, and Hamlet.

And all these things are going on simultaneously. The chapter is divided into nineteen sections. Each section is devoted primarily to the doings of some one person or group. But into each section is intruded reference to the occupations of a character who is not there. The chapter begins with the religious occupations and meditations of Father Conmee, S.J. The second section presents Corny Kelleher, the undertaker, making up his accounts; but here in the middle we read how "Father John Conmee stepped into the Dollymount tram on Newcomen bridge." The fourth section presents Katey and Boody Dedalus in their close steaming kitchen; and here again appears Father Conmee, walking "through Clongowes fields, his thin-socked ankles tickled by stubble." Any character who has once appeared is likely to turn up in this way for a moment's notice in the midst of business the most foreign to his own—young Dignam with his pork chops shooting meteor-like across Rochford's and Lenehan's talk of betting on the races; the young woman from a suburban hedge removing a ghostly twig from her skirt while Ned Lambert and J. J. O'Molloy are showing some one the historic council-chamber of St. Mary's Abbey. I am not sure but certain characters may not make their ghostly appearance in this way before they have been properly introduced in the section devoted to them.

Thus Joyce undertakes to defy the tyranny of time. His breadthwise cutting of the slice extends straight across the present moment, laying bare the very grain of the meat, the lean larded with fat, and the skin, bone, and gristle all in one slice with the fat and the lean.

And he has a special device in this chapter for presenting all his diverse human figures at approximately one and the same moment. In the eleventh section we are present at a conversation between Dilly Dedalus and her old man, when we read, "The viceregal cavalcade passed, greeted by obsequious policemen, out of Parkgate." The same cavalcade in the next section dashes through Kernan's meditations over business and music. And finally, in the last section, this cavalcade becomes the main subject of the moment. "William Humble, Earl of Dudley, and Lady Dudley, accompanied by lieutenantcolonel Hesseltine, drove out after luncheon from the viceregal lodge." There follows a detailed account of the progress of this "cavalcade," with a reference to some three or four dozen persons, earlier mentioned, who now in succession watch the passing of the viceroy and his lady.

Thus in his "recapitulation" Joyce suggests again the infinite diversity, the incommunicability, of these bits of animated protoplasm, at the same time that he binds them all together in one common interest, turning all their faces to one center, the representative of sovereignty.

2

It may seem a far cry from James Joyce to Virginia Woolf, considering the extreme difference of tonality in the works of these two writers. But Mrs. Woolf has been as anxious as Joyce to cut her slice of life depthwise and breadthwise. And there are many fundamental points of likeness of her intention and technique to Joyce's, especially in "Mrs. Dalloway" (1925). Like "Ulysses," this book is confined to less than twenty-four hours' time, and to one city (London). Like "Ulysses," it is greatly taken up with the stream of consciousness of two or three characters, and has no plot. Like "Ulysses," it is given form, for one thing, by the development of themes in the fashion of music.

Like "Ulysses," it introduces certain characters who have no connection with the leading persons, no bearing upon their fates. Septimus Warren Smith, crazed by his experience in the war, who finally kills himself to escape the oppression of the doctors, has nothing to do with Clarissa Dalloway, the pensive social butterfly whose personality is most fully realized in the giving of parties. His fate and hers are simply complementary colors in the composition of this abstract painting, meant, it would seem, to give a certain impression of London life (or, more universally stated, of Life itself).

If the impression of life rendered mainly through the consciousness of Clarissa Dalloway is utterly different from that rendered through Stephen Dedalus and Bloom, it simply goes to show that life is a different thing for each individual on whom it makes an impression. The artistic problem is much the same for Joyce and Mrs. Woolf, and in meeting this problem she has taken many a leaf out of his book.

One of the most curious of her imitations of Joyce is the incident of the royal automobile in "Mrs. Dalloway." Clarissa has walked over from her West End home to buy the flowers for her party, following the butterfly whim of her thoughts by the way. While absorbed in the loveliness of the flowers in Mulberry's shop, she is startled by what sounds like a pistol-shot in the street. But the sound proves to have come from a mysterious motor-car, now stopped at the curb with drawn blinds, and everybody is speculating on whether it is the Prince of Wales's car, or the Queen's, or the prime minister's.

For we have now left the narrow circle of Mrs. Dalloway's consciousness and are floating around on the wings of rumor. We learn what humorous remark was made by

Edgar J. Watkiss, "with his roll of lead piping round his arm." Among other people held up by the traffic jam are Septimus Warren Smith and his wife Lucrezia, thus first introduced. Meantime the car proceeds down Piccadilly, with every one watching and wondering what representative of sovereignty it carries. Clarissa has left Mulberry's and is wondering with the others. We are half in, half out of, her mind. We follow the car down St. James's Street, with its wake of curiosity and patriotism. We join the crowd around Buckingham Palace and are privy to their thoughts.

The Prince lived at St. James's; but he might come along in the morning to visit his mother.

So Sarah Bletchley said with her baby in her arms, tipping her foot up and down as though she were by her own fender in Pimlico, but keeping her eyes on the Mall, while Emily Coates ranged over the Palace windows and thought of the housemaids, the innumerable housemaids, the bedrooms, the innumerable bedrooms. Joined by an elderly gentleman with an Aberdeen terrier, by men without occupation, the crowd increased. Little Mr. Bowley, who had rooms in the Albany and was sealed with wax over the deeper sources of life but could be unsealed suddenly, inappropriately, sentimentally, by this sort of thing—poor women waiting to see the Queen go past—poor women, nice little children, orphans, widows, the War—tut-tut—actually had tears in his eyes . . . The car came on.

Suddenly Mrs. Coates looked up in the sky. The sound of an aëroplane bored ominously into the ears of the crowd.

We have now bid farewell to the royal car, which has occupied ten pages, as well as to Clarissa Dalloway, who has for the moment faded out of the picture. With Mrs. Coates and Mrs. Bletchley and a host of others we are watching the plane and trying to see what ad it is spelling out in smoke. The Smiths are looking up too, from their seats in Regent's Park, the two of them pursuing their separate thoughts on the subject of Septimus's mania. And through them we are introduced to Maisie Johnson, fresh from the country, who inquires the way to the Tube station, and thinks them queer; and through her to Mrs. Dempster, who is feeding the squirrels and reflects that "that girl don't know a thing yet," etc. After a few more random contacts, we come back to Mrs. Dalloway, returned home again. " 'What are they looking at?' said Clarissa Dalloway to the maid who opened her door."

One may guess [1] that Virginia Woolf, in writing "Mrs. Dalloway," had in mind, as her real subject, something like this: what life seems like on a fine day in London. Or perhaps, more broadly, the sensation of being alive. She must proceed from a center, and she has chosen for that a cultivated middle-aged woman of fashion planning to give a party. Clarissa is a woman of some imagination, capable of straying rather far in fancy over the lighter aspects of London life.

But the author realizes how narrow a range of experience is implied in Clarissa Dalloway, her family and friends. She needs the Septimus Smiths to bring in the tragic note, whose breath comes, indeed, to Clarissa when Dr. Holmes, at her party in the evening, makes allusion to the suicide of poor Septimus. But even that is not enough. She needs something like the Wandering Rocks episode of "Ulysses" to fill the background of her stage with supernumerary figures, quite unconnected with her foreground characters, but still necessary to suggest the hordes of undistinguished people, each with his own troubles, faiths, preoccupations, who make up the mass of British humanity. And so, like Joyce, she brings in a spe-

[1] In her preface to "Mrs. Dalloway" in the Modern Library edition Mrs. Woolf leaves us still pretty free to speculate upon her idea in the book. Septimus Smith did not at first exist, but was introduced to be Clarissa's "double." The first intention was to have Clarissa kill herself or die at the end; but this was happily abandoned.

cial section—set off, it is, with breaks in the text—starting with the royal "cavalcade," carried over into the ingenious invention of the airplane, and passing on smoothly from one person to another, one person giving his hand to another, as in an old-fashioned square dance. Most of these characters never show their noses again. But they have served their purpose of giving to this slice of life breadthwise extension in the present moment.

3

Before going on to other examples of this tendency in novels since Joyce, we should turn back to the work of a great German writer of our time who was doing something of the sort before the war, and whose influence is probably in some cases more important than that of Joyce. Jacob Wassermann published "Das Gänsemännchen" ("The Gooseman") in 1908, and "Christian Wahnschaffe" ("The World's Illusion") in 1919. In both of these books the slice is cut lengthwise, in the direction of time, and there is a provision of story quite sufficient for the general taste. But there is also the evident intention to cut it depthwise (in the manner of Dostoevski) and breadthwise, in the sense of including many characters who are unnecessary to the story and yet important for the philosophic intention.

The "world's illusion" of the English translation means evidently the illusion under which worldlings live—the wealthy, the selfish, the self-indulgent, the ephemerids of art and luxury. *Wahn* means illusion. It will be remembered that Professor Teufelsdröckh of "Sartor Resartus" lived in the Wahngasse, or street of illusion. But his tower rose high above the street, into the purer element of transcendental philosophy.

The Wahnschaffes are a wealthy manufacturing family, all of them taken in by the illusion of the worldly life and its values: money, power, luxury, social esteem. The son Christian is at the opening of the story the ideal exemplar of the worldly life. He is beautiful, athletic, companionable, pleasure-loving, and always firmly and graciously selfish. From all unpleasantness he turns away—from ugliness, poverty, mental effort, from suffering, sickness, and death. His intimate friend is the aristocratic worldling and *bon viveur* Bernard Crammon. Toward Crammon's illegitimate daughter Letitia he is strongly drawn because of her beauty, her youth, her charm of sentiment and movement. But at the critical moment he is repelled by an ugly toad which he sees crawling over the hem of her dress—evidently a symbolic toad! For a while he is fascinated by a brilliant dancer, Eva Sorel, and follows in her train, along with Crammon and a whole group of wealthy and aristocratic men.

But his name Christian is prophetic. A series of tragic deaths among his friends, and instances of misery, suffering, and moral degradation, pierce at last his armor of complacent selfishness. The problem of suffering and social injustice begins to weigh upon him. He begins to see behind the painted scenery of the "world." And from avoiding the unpleasant in the moral world, he now turns to it with a certain fascination.

Somewhere in the depths of misery and degradation, he seems to feel, lurks the secret of the universe; at any rate he feels the need of living down through the circles of hell which are gradually revealed to him in the world of poverty and crime. Instead of the complacent worldling Crammon, he takes for his friend a sort of renegade theological student, the perverse growth of cruel surroundings and a morbid sense of sin, who rewards his kindness with spiritual treachery, and, so far as he is capable, proves his Judas. Christian later gives up all his possessions and becomes a student of medicine in Berlin, living in the most crowded and disreputable tenements. He takes charge of a worn-out, pitiable prostitute, Karen Engelschall, whom he treats with simple courtesy and forbearance, and with unaffected friendliness.

He makes the acquaintance in his slum of a young Jewish woman of the most radiant beauty and candor of soul. When she is murdered under revolting circumstances by the degenerate Niels Heinrich, brother of Karen, and a poor half-witted youth has been accused of the crime, it is Christian's intuition which enables him to identify Niels Heinrich as the actual murderer and bring him to a full confession of the act and its motives. He does not in any way presume to judge or condemn, but by his completeness of sympathy and his genuine suffering over the loss of Ruth, he brings a certain light into the dark soul of the murderer and leads him to give himself up to justice.

In all this he has brought disgrace upon his family, as they think, and in the end he gives up his very name, and disappears completely in the underworld. Thereby he makes final repudiation of the "world" and its "illusion"; and while no such language is anywhere used, it is clear that he has saved his soul. He is no longer Wahnschaffe, but is entire Christian.

This is not at all a product of the school of naturalism. It is a modern legend, a morality, a gospel. In the life of Christian there are obvious analogies to the legends of Buddha, St. Francis, and Christ. Christian leaves father and mother and follows the dictates of his heart.

The work is less realistic than Dostoevski's, but there are many obvious reminders of the great Russian. Christian is very like Alyosha of "The Brothers Karamazov" and Prince Myshkin of "The Idiot." Dreams and visions play much the same part as in "Crime and Punishment." Amadeus Voss, like Ivan Karamazov, holds conversations with the devil. The psychological method by which Christian solves the murder mystery is strongly suggestive of that of certain characters in more than one novel of Dostoevski. Most striking of all the minor resemblances is the recurrent gesture of Christian in kneeling down before persons who stood to him for the misery and even the criminal degradation of the race: to Frau Kroll in her poverty and distress, and even to the murderer Niels Heinrich, not to speak of Eva Sorel, the beautiful dancer, courtezan, and perverse seeker after power. There are perhaps several such incidents in Dostoevski, but the one that comes to mind is in "Crime and Punishment," where Raskolnikov does honor in the prostitute Sonia to the "divine sorrow" of humanity (as Carlyle calls it). It is true that Raskolnikov is himself a murderer, and that Sonia is a woman of the noblest nature who has been driven to her profession in order to keep her family from starving. But what he salutes in her is her misery and degradation. For she is, in some sense, like Karen Engelschall, "the lowest and vilest thing in the whole world."

In point of technique the novels of Wassermann are as different from Dostoevski's as they are like them in spiritual tone. There is always in the Russian a tense and close-knit plot. We have seen how Dostoevski is likely to concentrate the interest strongly throughout the greater part of a book upon one central character. "The Gooseman" and "The World's Illusion" offer relatively little plot, in the sense of intrigue and dramatic issue. There are many characters whose stories are carried along with that of the principal, though not closely involved with it in a plot. In "The World's Illusion" there is Letitia, married off to a dreadful wealthy Argentine, living miserably in South America, and later returning to Europe to lead the life of a social ephemera. There is the story of Crammon, drifting along aimlessly in his self-indulgent way. There is that of Eva Sorel, mistress of the Grand Duke Cyril, yielding more and more to her lust for power. There are the practically independent stories of Christian's sister Judith, perverse product of wealth, and of her two husbands, Felix Imhof and the actor Lorm; of Amadeus Voss and Johanna Schöntag; and of many other characters whose purpose is to show the various phases of worldly complacency or discontent.

Wassermann's system is to sandwich in bits of these various stories all along the line of Christian's progress. Each chapter is divided into short sections anywhere from ten to thirty-four in number. And the chronicle of Christian is seldom pursued through more than two or three of these sections without being interrupted by those of one or more of the characters whose destinies have flown far apart from his.

The intention is evidently to keep up all through a running contrast between the souls who are finding their way slowly and surely toward a right solution of their spiritual problems and those more numerous souls who are going farther and farther astray in the fogs of "illusion." And since nothing properly definable as a plot makes its appearance before we are a third of the way through the second volume, it is clear that this alternation of subjects is in the interest of a breadthwise cutting of the slice. Wassermann is evidently concerned not to relate a private history, or a group of private histories connected in a plot, so much as to give a composite and comprehensive view of human nature in its dealings with the "world's illusion."

XXXIV

DISCONTINUITY: JOHN DOS PASSOS

VERY similar to the narrative formula of Wassermann is that of John Dos Passos in "Manhattan Transfer" (1925). Whether Dos Passos was actually acquainted with the work of Wassermann I do not know; that he was well acquainted with "Ulysses" I think we may take for granted. If I mention these possible influences, it is by way of keeping in mind certain characteristic features of the twentieth-century novel, it is by way of stressing the "modern" note, and in no sense to insinuate a want of originality in Dos Passos. "Manhattan Transfer" is one of the most brilliant and original American novels of the century. Sinclair Lewis appreciated this when the book first came out; and his enthusiastic review of "Manhattan Transfer" was a credit equally to his generosity and his discrimination.

"Manhattan Transfer" resembles "The World's Illusion" and "The Gooseman" in cutting the slice lengthwise as well as breadthwise. The narrative covers the period from about 1898 (date of birth of the heroine, and of the passing of the Greater New York Bill), through the World War, down, roughly, to the date of writing. Many major events are implied, if not actually recorded. The heroine, Ellen, is three times married—to the actor Oglethorpe, to Jimmy Herf the newspaper man, and to the lawyer and politician Baldwin, not to speak of her affair with the Harvard man, Stan. But there is nothing like the murder of Ruth in "The World's Illusion," with its attendant mystery, and in general there is here even less drawing together of the threads into a dramatic issue.

Another main point of resemblance to "The Gooseman" and "The World's Illusion" is the systematic alternation of groups of characters for a purely philosophical and esthetic effect, without regard for plot. In several ways this effect is more pointed in "Manhattan Transfer" than in the work of Wassermann. To begin with, there are no two sections in sequence dealing with the same persons. The chapters are made up, as in Wassermann, of a considerable number of sections, but in passing from one section to another we are always passing from one group of persons, from one social milieu, to another, as in the paintings of Léger and other cubists we pass from one block to another of contrasting color.

Then again, all the characters in "The World's Illusion" are more or less directly connected with Christian, whereas in "Manhattan Transfer" a point is made of introducing a good many people who have nothing whatever to do with either Ellen Thatcher or Jimmy Herf, people they never come in contact with and have never heard of. These people correspond to the Warren Smiths, the Mrs. Bletchleys and Mr. Bowleys of "Mrs. Dalloway." There is, for example, a poor fellow named Bud Korpenning who after years of cruelty at the hands of his father, has killed the old man and come to New York to lose himself in the crowd. For years he hangs about the city doing odd jobs, always poor and miserable, and always in terror of detectives, until at last, about the time of Ellen's first marriage, he throws himself off Brooklyn Bridge. He has nothing whatever to do with the principals or any of their friends or connections; but every so often, in the course of the years, the spotlight leaves the principals, to rest for a fleeting instant on the pitiful haunted figure of Bud Korpenning.

When he is gone there are others to take his place: Dutch Robertson, returning so hopefully from the war, but incapable of finding employment or even a place to make love, and finally ending up as a convicted bank-robber; Anna Cohen, beloved of a Socialist, sweated laborer herself in a dressmaker's establishment, the victim of inadequate fire-regulations; Jake and Rosie of the shady Prudence Promotion Co.; Densch and Blackhead, speculative business men, caught in the slump. And then, besides the recurrent figures, there are others who make but one appearance, contributing their single note to this tone-poem of life in Gotham. Such is the "small bearded bandy-legged man in a derby" who buys himself a Gillette razor outfit in a drug-store and goes home to shave off his beard. In a world so largely made up of laborers and industrialists, he may be said to represent the consumer.

There are of course many characters more or less associated with the principals but quite unnecessary to the development of a plot. Such is Congo Jake, the poor French boy who goes into bootlegging and makes a fortune; various ward politicians associated with Baldwin; various actor-folk associated with Ellen and Oglethorpe; and Jimmy's cousin James Merivale, captain in the American Army and successful business man. Many of these stand for such as profit honestly or dishonestly by the system which victimizes the Dutch Robertsons and Anna Cohens.

The number of characters who thus take the spotlight in "Manhattan Transfer" is much greater than in "The World's Illusion"; and there is a much greater and more representative sampling of types in present-day civilization. Dos Passos is a realist if there is such a thing. Where Wassermann takes his types from the two extremes of wealth and poverty, from the noble and dazzling and from the vilest creatures of the slums, Dos Passos favors those middle reaches of society where the great masses live, and, morally considered, from those levels far below ideal beauty of character, and considerably above the merely mean and vile.

There is still another reason why this alternation of

subjects, this discontinuity of the narrative, is more marked in Dos Passos than in Wassermann. The German writer very soon establishes Christian or Daniel as his leading character, and the other persons are gradually introduced in connection with him and his story. So that when he turns from the hero to one of the other characters, he is turning to some one whom we associate distinctly with the hero. In "Manhattan Transfer," it is the other way round. Not before the middle of the book can we say with assurance that the leading male character is Jimmy Herf and the leading woman Ellen Thatcher, now Oglethorpe. The other characters, though they may in time come to be more or less remotely associated with Ellen or Jimmy, are introduced quite independently. They are numerous and diversified, and, not being related in a plot, they give all the more the impression of a section cut straight across the social organism of New York City.

But we haven't yet come to the end of this subject. For his leading characters, Wassermann undertakes to give their history in its completeness, from year to year, from moment to moment. For the secondary characters, he is content to give us views of them at considerable intervals of time, briefly summarizing the developments that have taken place in the meanwhile. Dos Passos applies this method to leading and secondary characters alike, except that he gives longer and more frequent views of the principals. We see them only at moments that have some particular importance or significance. As for developments in the interval, he does not feel concerned with them; he does not even give them in brief summary. It matters not how many years have passed or how many other people's lives have flowed in between, we plunge invariably into the midst of the new moment with the character in question as if no one else existed and as if there were no such thing as a past lying back of this moment. No, rather as if we, like the characters involved, took the past for granted, carrying it all hidden away in our memories. The author does not tell us what has happened, but lets us infer it from allusions made by the characters in conversation or in reverie—for in the world of thought we do not tell ourselves what has happened to us, but make as it were allusions to it.

In the first section of all we are shown a nurse holding a basket containing a new-born baby. In the third section we are present with Ed Thatcher and his wife Susie in the maternity hospital, and we hear Susie ask Ed if he still wants "to call her Ellen." We put two and two together. We make out later that this is the year 1898, from the head-line of a newspaper read by Ed Thatcher: MORTON SIGNS THE GREATER NEW YORK BILL. (If we don't know history, we look this up in the Encyclopædia Britannica!) The next time we meet Ellen is seven years later; we infer this from a head-line read by Bud Korpenning in the preceding section: RELIEVE PORT ARTHUR IN FACE OF ENEMY. In a later section, Ed and Ellie have been to see Maude Adams and Ellie tells her mummy she wants to be a boy; that is how we know the play must have been "Peter Pan." In a later chapter we have a glimpse of "Elaine" going home from school, imagining herself in danger from the Black Watch; another glimpse of her sitting on a bench at the Battery with her father. And then we see no more of her for fifty pages till she turns up, married, on a train for Atlantic City, just having changed at Manhattan Transfer. The author doesn't tell us she is married, nor describe her man. But we make out something from his saying, "You're my wife now Elaine." As to how she managed to grow up and how she came to be married, we just have to assume that these things happened to her in much the same way as they happen to other girls. How successful this marriage is going to be we can easily infer from remarks she makes to herself after her husband has gone to sleep; but the author never has anything to say about things of that sort.

In the following chapters we have oc asional glimpses of Elaine cutting up with Stan Emery and of how her husband takes it. Then we learn that she has gone on the stage and made a hit. We make this out, for one thing, from the remarks of Harry Goldweiser. (We make out later and independently that Harry Goldweiser is a theatrical producer.) In the meantime she has met Jimmy Herf and they have become good friends, judging from the intimate way in which they talk. And then, some years later, as one gathers from allusions to the war and the armistice, we find ourselves with Ellie and Jimmy in a restaurant drinking absinthe cocktails, and, following the man's thoughts, we infer that they have returned to New York after passing their honeymoon in southern France.

"Gosh . . . let's have another cocktail." He felt paralyzed like in a nightmare; she was a porcelaine figure under a bell-glass. A current of fresh snow-rinsed air from somewhere eddied all of a sudden through the blurred packed jangling glare of the restaurant, cut the reek of food and drink and tobacco. For an instant he caught the smell of her hair. The cocktails burned in him. God, I don't want to pass out.

Sitting in the restaurant of the Gare de Lyon, side by side on the black leather bench. His cheek brushes hers when he reaches to put herring, butter, sardines, anchovies, sausage on her plate. They eat in a hurry, gobbling, giggling, gulp wine, start at every screech of an engine. . . .

The train pulls out of Avignon, they two awake, looking in each others' eyes in the compartment full of sleep-sodden snoring people. He lurches clambering over tangled legs, to smoke a cigarette at the end of the dim oscillating corridor. Diddledeump, going south, Diddledeump, going south, sing the wheels over the rails down the valley of the Rhone. Leaning in the window, smoking a broken cigarette, trying to smoke a crumbling cigarette, holding a finger over the torn place. Glubglub glubglub from the bushes, from the silverdripping poplars along the track.

"Ellie, Ellie, there are nightingales singing along the track."

. . . .

Opposite him the Elliedoll was speaking. "He says the lobstersalad's all out. . . . Isn't that discouraging?"

Suddenly he had his tongue. "Gosh if that were the only thing."

"What do you mean?"

"Why did we come back to this rotten town anyway?"

So then we have passed far beyond the spirit and technique of Wassermann, and are full in the middle of the movement begun by Miss Richardson and Joyce: the suppression of the author and his explanations, the effort at intimacy and immediacy, the elliptical, allusive manner of narrative, the sudden transitions—past and present, thought and speech, real and imaginary, all jumbled together, as in the impression we have of life itself.

2

Of this modernism in Dos Passos I do not wish to speak at present, except in so far as it involves that breadthwise cutting which is our present subject, and which in him, more than in the other writers considered, involves what I have called the effect of discontinuity. All that remains to be done here is to suggest a rationale of this method and show how it suits the general esthetic and philosophical intention of the book. Enough has been said to indicate how well it lends itself to the cross-section view of life. In any such view we see things not as wholes but only so far as the plane of the cutting lays them bare—fragmentary, sharp-edged, lying side by side. There is, again, a great deal of beauty of pattern in this arrangement, the long heavy dotted lines of the main characters crossed in many interesting ways by the lighter falling and rising lines of others less important—poor devils in showers like falling stars, clever fellows steadily going up, and others like rockets shooting skyward to drop back in a swift spiral to the darkness below.

It is hardly necessary to point out the story-telling effectiveness of this succession of shifting views, once we are reconciled to the absence of plot and drama. There is a kind of exhilaration in the rapid passage from one act to another such as is cultivated by the producers of vaudeville, of revues and moving-pictures. But the thing goes much deeper than that.

Mr. Dos Passos' subject, like Virginia Woolf's in "Mrs. Dalloway," is evidently not a story, a drama, but a certain general impression of life. It is, naturally, life seen under a chosen aspect: no one can do it all, or all at one time. Life in his book is localized in New York City. And this man's New York is a riot of sensations and appetites. The dominant impression is that of the din, the stench, the dizzy movement, the dazzle of color; and then the disorder; the pitiful snatching at money, at love, at comfort . . . the wistful glimpsing of a dream and letting it slip . . . the jazzy melody stringing through . . . the brazen pulse of life . . . the sad despair in a whirl of gaiety. There is no respite, no pause, no place of rest, no self-collection and retirement to take counsel of the spirit. The author has a dozen devices for underlining this impression: the prose poems or symbolic preludes with which he introduces each chapter; the symbolic chapter headings, reminding one of the heartless, mechanical aspects of a civilization in which we are caught like rats in a trap: "Steamroller," "Rollercoaster," "Skyscraper," "Revolving Doors."

And here again falls the technique of discontinuity, picture displacing picture in breathless succession in this swift-flitting panorama, with no apparent logic or meaning. These sections in Dos Passos are not numbered as in Wassermann; they are simply separated by an extra space in the text; and they fade into one another like the landscapes seen from a train window, except that there is in such landscapes a continuity, whereas the pictures of "Manhattan Transfer" are as distinct and contrasting as pictures can be. Thus his manner of breadthwise cutting serves to reinforce the general impression—that of the dominance of sensation in human experience, the obsession of the senses. The behavior of these men and women reminds one of the tropisms, the "forced movements," described by Jacques Loeb in the lower animal and vegetable worlds. Life appears as will-less, thought as centrifugal, non-purposive, psychology a mere whirl of undirected sensations.

Of course there is a social philosophy lurking somewhere below the surface of this record. It is apparent in all Dos Passos' work, from "Three Soldiers" (1921) to "1919" (1932). Mr. Dos Passos, we know, is in close touch with the labor movement. He has his economic views, his political affiliations. But what I admire in him, as an artist, is his unwillingness to distort his art with the bias of social theory. He is, in this respect, the antithesis of Upton Sinclair. Mr. Sinclair is a writer whom one must respect for his earnest devotion to humanity; but one can only deprecate his disposition to swamp fiction with the preoccupations of politics and economics. Dos Passos is as much concerned with social problems as Sinclair; but in his representation of life, he goes to the deeper sources of human motivation—to that subsoil of human nature where spread the roots of all social institutions. In "Manhattan Transfer" he has shown us our industrial order as it actually affects human happiness. Or we might put it the other way round: he shows us the traits in human nature which have given us our industrial, our social order, such as it is. And that is more philosophical, more realistic.

As a social theorist, he is, in this book, extremely modest. He shows us the labyrinth in which we wander so hopelessly; but as for the way out, he hardly more than suggests that it may exist. One of the most pathetic and beautiful things about the book is the occasional vague aspiration registered by one or other of these wretched worldlings to escape from their "squirrel-cage"—their suspicion that there may be a better way of life. It is true that their notion of a better way is not remarkable for spiritual refinement; but it is at least a sign of grace.

Gus McNiel, the milk-wagon driver, talks to the bartender about taking up free land in North Dakota and raising wheat. What he does is to go into politics and become a Tammany henchman. Harry Goldweiser proposes to take Ellen somewhere for a night's entertainment; he wants "to get that old feelin' back, understand?" Young Stan Emery deliberately goes to the dogs by way of protest against a world in which he can sight no guiding star. He has no character, but he gives to Ellen some notion of higher values. "Without ever saying anything he made me feel there were other things . . . unbelievable things."

Ellen herself is anything but satisfied with her own way. "There are lives to be lived if only you didn't care. Care for what, for what; the opinion of mankind, money, success, hotel lobbies, health, umbrellas, Uneeda biscuits . . . ?" Unfortunately she does care; she is attached for good and all to this spluttering pinwheel of futility. "She hears the burring boom of a big steamer from the river. Darkly, fearfully afar from this nonsensical life, from this fuzzy idiocy and strife . . ." The net upshot of her spiritual accounting is a fragment of Shelley.

The only one in the whole book who does anything about the situation is Jimmy Herf, the newspaper man. He goes into journalism in preference to business (with his uncle James) because he doesn't like the vision of "Jimmy fed in a tape in and out the revolving doors, noon and night and morning, the revolving doors grinding out his years like sausage meat." But after all, the newspaper is but the organ of the thing he hates, droning from day to day the Burden of Nineveh. And he gives up the newspaper when he has ceased to "have faith in words." The end of the story shows him shaking from his feet the dust of the City of Destruction. Like Christian Wahnschaffe he has repudiated modern civilization.

But what does this mean in a positive way? There is reason to think that it actually did mean something in a positive way to Jimmy Herf—that is, to John Dos Passos. And the first thing it meant was putting down his impression of modern civilization in a book, in "Manhattan Transfer." Since then he has conceived his subject more broadly. He is writing a trilogy or tetratology on the same theme, but embracing American life as a whole. The two novels which have already appeared I shall discuss in Chapter XXXIX.

3

It will now be seen that the impulse to the breadthwise cutting has its origin more or less in an altered social philosophy. The tendency is to throw the emphasis not on individuals, with their particular adventures, their private moral problems, their triumphs and failures, so much as on society conceived as an organism, in which the individuals are important primarily as functions of one another and of the whole. This is much more striking in Dos Passos than in Wassermann. Wassermann still conceives the spiritual problem of his characters in religious—that is, in individualistic—terms, like Dostoevski. He may give the impression that he does not approve of the present economic system, but his cure is for the rich man to "sell all and give to the poor." Sentimentally his face is turned back toward the age of faith.

For Dos Passos, it is clear, social problems are social problems, and I think we may infer that, for him, personal morality is something which needs redefinition in the light of new social ideals. This is one reason why his work has so different an aspect from Wassermann's, an aspect baffling and repelling to many readers. They miss in him a certain sentimental tone to which they are accustomed. But perhaps that is just what makes him the most "modern" of the writers in this movement.

XXXV

LOGIC AND LIFE: GIDE

EXACTLY contemporary with "Manhattan Transfer" and "Mrs. Dalloway" was "The Counterfeiters" ("Les Faux-monnayeurs," 1925), from which novel we have taken our phrase "the breadthwise cutting." In this case we do not have to guess what the author was undertaking to do. Gide is one of the most self-conscious of writers. During the years while he was planning and writing "The Counterfeiters," he kept a note-book, like those kept by James in his later years, in which he made a record of his artistic ideals, his gropings for an idea, and to some extent of his progress in the composition of the book. This note-book he has published as "Le Journal des Faux-monnayeurs." In many respects it corresponds very closely to the note-book of Edouard in the novel itself.

To begin with, there is his wish to be comprehensive, to get everything in. In the "Journal" he speaks more than once of his wish to make his work *touffu,* that is, dense or crowded with matter.

> As dense as I hope to make this book, I can't dream of getting everything in. And yet it is just the wish for that which still embarrasses me. I am like a composer who seeks to juxtapose and overlap, in the manner of César Franck, an andante motif with an allegro.

A question that arose in this connection was whether to have the story told by one of the characters. Gide, who was an admirer and translator of Conrad, had inclined in earlier books to Conrad's way of having the story told by some one who was involved in it. He had also Conrad's fondness for documents. "L'Immoraliste" (1902) is a frame story like "Heart of Darkness," which saw the light in the same year. It was recited by the leading character, Michel, to a group of friends gathered one night on the terrace of his house in Algeria. Thus it has the restricted point of view of a first-person narrative. But it is introduced and concluded by the friend who explains the circumstances under which the story was told; and the whole has the form of a letter written by the friend to his brother, a person in high office, who may be able to help Michel. So that it has the character of one of those documents beloved of romancers. "La Porte Etroite" (1909), again, is told in the first person by some one mainly involved in the story; and then, to give it higher documentary value, there is included a large part of the diary of another leading character.

Thus, in each of these books, Gide manages to reconcile his concern for point of view with his interest in having light fall from several different directions on the same subject.

Point of view is important to any one who conceives fiction in terms of picture. "First of all study the direction from which the light falls; all the shadows depend on that." In "The Counterfeiters" Gide's first thought was to have the story told entirely by Lafcadio. Lafcadio is the name of a principal character in his *sotie,* "Les Caves du Vatican," (1922); I assume that his first intention was to revive him in the new book and give him some rôle like that of Bernard. But eventually he dropped him. "For several days I have been in doubt whether to make Lafcadio tell the story. It would be a recital of events which he discovered little by little and in which he interested himself through curiosity, idleness, and perversity." Later he considers having the story pass through the hands of several narrators. "I should like to provide a succession of interpreters: for example, these notes of Lafcadio would occupy the first book; the second book would be Edouard's note-book; the third a lawyer's brief, etc. . . ."

The reason why he is not satisfied with a single interpreter is that it is too difficult to bring in through him all that he wishes in the way of events and of psychological interpretation. In writing another of his books, he says—but the whole passage is highly worth quoting:

> In the course of writing, I was brought to consider that intimacy, penetration, psychological investigation, may, in some ways, be pushed farther in the novel proper than even in "confessions." In these latter, one is somewhat handicapped by the "I"; there are certain complexities which one can't expect to unravel, to develop, without seeming to force things. All that I see, all that I learn, everything that happens to me in the course of several months, I'd like to work into this novel, and make use of to give it a richer texture. I should like to manage it so that the events are never recounted directly by the author, but rather set forth (and several times, from various angles) by those among the actors on whom these events have had a certain influence. I should like, in the account which they give, for these events to appear slightly deformed; there is a sort of interest for the reader in the simple fact of making his corrections. The narrative demands his collaboration if the drawing is to be right.

There are in this passage half a dozen matters of extreme interest. But I wish to lay my stress for the moment on Gide's desire to work in a great diversity of matter, to have his story spread out over a wide range of human experience. He realizes that this means departing from the usual type of novel (*le type convenu du roman*), and he finds that it involves him in many difficulties, but the difficulties tend to fall away "the moment that he deliberately takes advantage of the queerness" of his undertaking.

> From the moment that I reconcile myself to the impossibility of making this like anything else (and it suits me that it should

be so) why try so hard to find motivation, consistency, a way of grouping everything around a central plot? Can't I find a way, with the form which I adopt, of indirectly criticizing all that sort of thing? Lafcadio for example would try in vain to tie the threads together; there would be useless characters, gestures without significance, talk that leads nowhere, and an action that never gets started.

Gide never quite says in so many words *why* it is he wants to make his work so different from the usual type of novel: why he wants to neglect such excellent principles as motivation, consistency (or consequentiality), and a systematic arrangement of matter around a central plot. But here it is easy to guess what he is after. He is after a nearer approach to the truth of human experience. He wants his work to be *more like life*. And life he has found to be more surprising, more elusive, less formally consistent, than it has been portrayed in "the usual type of novel." He has come under the influence of that tendency to *deformalization* to which I referred in an earlier chapter. And he wants to get away from the logical neatness of the Jameses, the Flauberts, the Bourgets, the Prévosts. He wants to take life by surprise, after the manner of the Conrads, the Joyces.

This is not a new notion with him. In "Les Caves du Vatican" he has already introduced a character who was disposed to "criticize all that sort of thing." Lafcadio has been reading a novel by his distinguished brother, Julius de Baraglioul, and he finds that it is spoiled by excessive logic. The trouble with your hero, he tells Julius, is consistency. "You take such pains to keep him, always, everywhere consistent, towards us and towards himself, faithful to his obligations, to his principles,—that is to say, to your theories." And in the end Julius comes to agree with him.

The logic, the consequentiality, which I demand of my characters,—in order to insure this, I demanded it first of all from myself; and that was not natural. We live disguised, rather than not resemble the picture which we made of ourselves to begin with; it is absurd; in doing so, we run the risk of distorting whatever is best in us. . . .

Pursuing this line of reasoning, he arrives at a brilliant idea for his next novel: a crime committed without a motive. And curiously enough, before the book is over, he breaks his shins against an actual case of murder without motive, or at least without any motive which is clear to the murderer himself. And the murderer is his brother Lafcadio! It goes without saying that he is greatly taken aback at finding so prompt a confirmation of his artistic theory.

In "The Counterfeiters" still more is made of this quaint parallelism and contrast between reality and the logic of fiction. One of the central characters is the novelist, Edouard; and he shares the ambition of Gide to work into his book as much as possible of what he actually experiences. But the culminating event of the book is the suicide of a young boy in a boarding-school; and this event Edouard is unable to get into his story, for the simple reason that he cannot understand it. André Gide understands it fairly well, in its motivation and circumstances, and makes it the climax of his book. But his imaginary author says:

While I don't pretend to give a precise explanation of anything, I shouldn't like to present any fact without sufficient motivation. That is why I don't intend to make use in my *Counterfeiters* of little Boris's suicide; I find too much difficulty in understanding it. . . . I grant that reality may come to the support of my thought, as a confirmation; but not that it should anticipate it. It distresses me to be surprised. The suicide of Boris seems to me like an impropriety [*une indécence*], for I was not expecting it.

In many respects the artistic intentions of Edouard are identical with those of André Gide. But in the present instance he is clearly in a class with Julius, who goes by logic and consistency. He is dominated by the standard of the "usual type of novel." And that is why, as Gide says in the "Journal," "he is unable to write his book. He understands many things; but he is constantly in pursuit of himself, through all the characters, through everything. A true devotion [to his subject] is practically impossible for him. He is an amateur, a missfire." And that, he tells us, is the underlying subject of the book and what makes it so difficult to write.

> There is properly speaking no single center to this book, round which my efforts converge; it is about two focal points, in the manner of ellipses, that these efforts are polarized. On the one side the event, the fact, the exterior circumstances; on the other side, the very effort of the novelist to make a book out of all that. And just there is the principal subject, the new center which throws the narrative off its axis and draws it towards the fanciful and visionary.

Gide does not tell us much about the precise nature of the book which Edouard is writing, and just how the pedantic following of his own logic prevents him from making the best use of his material. But he does show us Edouard theorizing about the proper way of writing fiction, and setting down in a note-book what he observes and what he thinks. And then, all about him, he shows us Life spinning its intricate webs so much faster and farther than Edouard can follow. And while Edouard is losing himself in a cloud of abstract ideas like Carlyle in "Sartor Resartus" (it is Gide's own comparison), Life is piling up concrete facts so startling that Edouard's ideas fade into insignificance.

Edouard does not even appreciate the full import of the title of his novel. On one occasion he is discussing his work with his young secretary Bernard. Bernard has shown himself a little impatient with Edouard's notion of a novel of ideas. And who are these counterfeiters? he asks. What Edouard meant by counterfeiters was certain of his confrères who were offering the public literary products without value, and especially his rival, the novelist, the Comte de Passavant. And his mind was filled with ideas of exchange, devalorization, inflation, etc., which really were supplanting the very characters in his book.

"Did you ever hold in your hand a piece of counterfeit money?" he asked. . . . "Well, imagine a gold piece of ten francs which is counterfeit. In reality it is only worth two sous. It is worth ten francs so long as it is not recognized as false. So then, if I start with this idea that . . ."

"But why start with an idea?" Bernard interrupted impatiently. "If you would start with a fact well set forth, the idea would come of its own accord and take up its abode there. If I were writing *The Counterfeiters,* I should begin by exhibiting the counterfeit money, this little coin of which you were just speaking . . . and here it is!"

And he throws upon the table a ten-franc piece, explaining that it is counterfeit money which he has received in change from a grocer.

Now, what Bernard and Edouard do not realize is that this false coin has been put in circulation by one of a band of young boys several of whom are well known to them both, one of them being Edouard's nephew, Georges Molinier. And what even the reader does not know as yet is that the person responsible for this and other vicious ways into which these boys have fallen is none other than Edouard's rival, the Comte de Passavant. So that while Edouard has been concerning himself with the comparatively mild crime of feeding the public adulterated wares in the form of novels, Reality behind his back is offering the highly significant fact of a generation of school-boys corrupted and turned into criminals. It is this same group of boys in the end who are responsible for the death of little Boris. But Edouard, as we have seen, is shut up so tight in his ivory tower of consistency that he cannot take advantage of this prime exhibit offered him by Reality.

There is still another matter of the very highest importance which Edouard would never be able to get into his book; and that is his own character, his motivation. The Comte de Passavant is his rival not merely for the interest of the reading public, but also for the affections of certain school-boys, and in particular for those of Edouard's nephew, Olivier. The Comte de Passavant is in every respect the evil genius of these boys. Edouard is the soul of benevolence. His aim is to help every one with whom he has to do. But does he understand how far the simple passion of jealousy is the moving power in his behavior? And there is more to it than that. Both Edouard and his rival are by all indications of that race of men who find their emotional satisfaction in men instead of women. Has it ever occurred to Edouard that it might be rather difficult for one of his race to play the good angel to adolescent boys? The question even arises whether this difficulty has been met by Edouard's creator.

It will be impossible for me to recount the plot of "The Counterfeiters," or even to list the many strands woven into it. The important matter is to note the deliberate and systematic way in which the author alternates the many related subjects and methods of approach. Of the forty-four chapters, some dozen only are devoted to Edouard's note-book, which is more or less regularly followed by passages of ordinary narrative. The other leading character, Bernard, makes his appearance in about half the chapters, sometimes in company with Edouard. And all along are interspersed chapters dealing with Passavant, with Bernard's father, with Olivier, with Olivier's brothers Vincent and Georges, and with several other characters, each one of whom has his independent story.

Gide makes no attempt, like Dos Passos and Wassermann, to give a cross-section of society as a whole. And yet this torch seems to light up the darkness in every direction with its fitful illuminations. One has an extraordinary sense of the infinite ramifications of human life, its unpredictableness, its inconclusiveness. As one of the characters says, "In life, nothing is settled; everything keeps going on. [*Dans la vie, rien ne se résout; tout continue*]" The author has dropped a stone into these still waters, and the circles keep widening out, to infinity.

XXXVI

COUNTERPOINT: ALDOUS HUXLEY

THERE are many striking resemblances between Aldous Huxley's "Point Counter Point" (1928) and the novels of André Gide. So striking they are that one is inclined to assume that some of these things in Huxley are reminiscences of Gide. To begin with minor matters, there is the disposition of both these authors to introduce experimental biologists and to spread upon their pages curious facts of natural history. This disposition appears in Gide's "Les Caves du Vatican" (1922) and in Huxley's "Antic Hay" (1923) as well as in the later more famous novels of each author. In "Les Caves" a prominent part is taken by a famous experimental biologist, who collects animals, systematically blinds, deafens, starves them, etc., and makes a statistical notation of their behavior. He is a prototype of Lord Edward in "Point Counter Point," who transplants tissue from one part of an animal to another with the object of determining whether it will grow the same organ in its new locale.

In "The Counterfeiters" there is a young man who interests himself in marine biology. Some of his curious data are appropriated by the novelist, his patron (Passavant), who makes a point of helping himself to whatever he wants wherever he finds it. In "Point Counter Point," the novelist Philip Quarles jots down in his note-book curious facts gleaned from his reading on, for example, the parasitic pigmy males in certain species of Cerativid Angler-fishes. He thinks he might use this information in pointing the parallel between human and animal behavior.

I have spoken of the unmotived crime in "Les Caves du Vatican." If we may borrow the distinction made by Julius, the crime is unmotived, but not the criminal. This Lafcadio has always had an experimental interest in any kind of activity which is bizarre and capable of giving him a thrill. When he throws his brother-in-law out of the door of the moving train, it is just a further experiment upon himself. And it is a failure. Is it too fanciful to see a resemblance between his crime and that of Spandrell, which is the culminating action of "Point Counter Point"? Spandrell has not, in the ordinary sense, any motive for killing the fascist agitator Webley. But his crime does follow, by a kind of Dostoevski logic, from his character as it has been determined by the circumstances of his childhood. (Oh, the author has worked this all out fully!) Spandrell has paradoxically been seeking for religious experience in a life of debauchery. His murder of Webley is one last desperate experiment in religion, so to speak, and a failure. It brings him no nearer to God.

But, after all, the one most obvious parallel between "Point Counter Point" and the work of Gide is this. Both in this novel and in "The Counterfeiters" there is a prominent character somewhat suggestive of the author himself. He is writing a novel in many ways suggesting that in which he appears; he keeps a note-book in which he records things he has observed, plans for his novel, and reflections on the technique of novel-writing.

In each case the fictitious novelist has a leaning toward the novel of ideas.

"Are you not afraid," asked the Polish *doctoresse,* "that in turning your back on reality, you may lose yourself in regions of mortal abstraction and make a novel not of living creatures but of ideas?"

"And what if it should be so?" cried Edouard vehemently. "Because clumsy writers have gone astray, why need we condemn the novel of ideas [*le roman d'idées*]? Under the guise of novels of ideas, they have served us, up to the present, nothing but execrable problem novels [*romans à theses*]. But that is not what I have in mind, you may be sure. Ideas . . . ideas, I confess it, interest me more than men; they interest me above everything."

So Philip Quarles writes in his note-book:

Novel of ideas. The character of each personage must be implied, as far as possible, in the ideas of which he is the mouthpiece. In so far as theories are rationalizations of sentiments, instincts, dispositions of soul, this is feasible. The chief defect of the novel of ideas is that you must write about people who have ideas to express—which excludes all but about .01 per cent. of the human race. Hence the real, the congenital novelists don't write such books. But then, I never pretended to be a congenital novelist.

Again he writes:

The great defect of the novel of ideas is that it's a made-up affair. Necessarily: for people who can reel off neatly formulated notions aren't quite real; they're slightly monstrous. Living with monsters becomes rather tiring in the long run.

This is very like what was said to Edouard by the Polish *doctoresse:*

"You know, in novels, it is always dangerous to present intellectuals. They bore the reader; you never succeed in making them say anything but silly things, and to everything that touches them they give an air of abstraction."

Both Gide and Huxley were aware of the dangers of the novel of ideas. The difference is that Huxley went ahead and wrote that sort of novel, like his author Philip, whereas Gide, more wisely, left the novel of ideas to his author Edouard, but himself wrote a novel about men.

Another very interesting parallel is the notion, held by both Edouard and Philip, of constructing a novel on the analogy of a musical composition. I have earlier quoted

Gide's idea of weaving together an andante with an allegro motif. This idea reappears in Edouard's account of his intentions:

"What I should like to do, understand me, is something like the *Art of the Fugue*. I don't see why what was possible in music should not be possible in literature. . . ."

To which Sophroniska replied that music is a mathematical art, and besides, in considering for the most part nothing but the figures, in banishing pathos and humanity, Bach succeeded in turning out the abstract masterpiece of boredom, a sort of astronomical temple, into which only the rare initiates might make their way. Edouard immediately protested that he found this temple admirable, that he saw in it the goal and summit of Bach's whole career.

The reader of "Point Counter Point" will remember Huxley's remarkable account of the performance of Bach's suite in B minor, for flute and strings, and how he describes the various movements in terms of human emotion:

In the human fugue there are eighteen hundred million parts. The resultant noise means something perhaps to the statistician, nothing to the artist. It is only by considering one or two parts at a time that the artist can understand anything. Here, for example, is one particular part; and John Sebastian puts the case.

But more to the point is the note-book meditation of Philip on the musicalization of fiction:

The musicalization of fiction. Not in the symbolist way, by subordinating sense to sound. . . . But on a large scale, in the construction. Meditate on Beethoven. The changes of moods, the abrupt transitions. (Majesty alternating with a joke, for example, in the first movement of the B flat major Quartet. Comedy suddenly hinting at prodigious and tragic solemnities in the scherzo of the C sharp minor Quartet.) More interesting still, the modulations, not merely from one key to another, but from mood to mood. A theme is stated, then developed, pushed out of shape, imperceptibly deformed, until, though still recognizably the same, it has become quite different. In sets of variations the process is carried a step further. Those incredible Diabelli variations, for example. The whole range of thought and feeling, yet all in organic relation to a ridiculous little waltz tune. Get this into a novel. How? The abrupt transitions are easy enough. All you need is a sufficiency of characters and parallel, contrapuntal plots. While Jones is murdering a wife, Smith is wheeling a perambulator in the park. You alternate the themes. More interesting, the modulations and variations are also more difficult. A novelist modulates by reduplicating situations and characters. He shows several people falling in love, or dying, or praying in different ways—dissimilars solving the same problem. Or, *vice versa,* similar people confronted with dissimilar problems. In this way you can modulate through all the aspects of your theme, you can write variations in any number of moods.

So much for the musical analogy. But there is also a passage in which, just as Edouard defends his plan to skeptical Bernard and Sophroniska, Philip Quarles defends his plan to his wife. She thinks the novel he is proposing will be "rather too queer." But, like Gide in the "Journal des Faux-monnayeurs," Philip contends that it can't be too queer. The queerer it is, the more it will be like life.

However queer the picture is, it can never be half so odd as the original reality. We take it all for granted; but the moment you start thinking, it becomes queer. And the more you think, the queerer it grows. That's what I want to get in this book—the astonishingness of the most obvious things. Really, any plot or situation would do. Because everything's implicit in anything. The whole book could be written about a walk from Piccadilly Circus to Charing Cross.

2

The last sentence reminds us of the kinship of Huxley with Virginia Woolf, Dorothy Richardson, and Joyce. But the particular feature of his "new way of looking at things" makes him still closer akin to Wassermann, Dos Passos and Gide.

> Because the essence of the new way of looking is multiplicity. Multiplicity of eyes and multiplicity of aspects seen. For instance, one person interprets events in terms of bishops; another in terms of flannel camisoles; another, like that young lady from Gulmberg, thinks of it in terms of good times. And then there's the biologist, the chemist, the physicist, the historian. Each sees, professionally, a different aspect of the event, a different layer of reality. What I want to do is to look with all those eyes at once.

Now, this is precisely the type of novel that Aldous Huxley is undertaking to write in "Point Counter Point," as indeed it was what he had always written, in "Crome Yellow," "Antic Hay," "Those Barren Leaves," except that in the later book the multiplicity of views is much greater, the transitions more abrupt, the "modulations" more systematic and deliberate. He undertakes to show us life as it appears to a man (Walter Bidlake) who has got himself involved with a woman of temperament too cold and too sentimental; to his father, an unregenerate old pagan and distinguished painter of flesh tints; to his stepmother, who succeeds in preserving her metaphysical calm through all the irritations of domestic life; to his sister Elinor, whose author husband is so lost in the figments of his brain that he cannot give her the love she craves; to the husband, Philip Quarles, lost in the figments of his brain and the technique of the novel; to Philip's religious-minded mother; to his father, supposed to be a great scholar, surrounded with filing-cabinets and dictaphones, who is really getting himself into a mess with a typist, and makes more headway with his cross-word puzzles than with his magnum opus. (So in "The Counterfeiters" we pass from Bernard and Olivier to the fathers and mothers of the two boys; to

Olivier's brother Vincent and Vincent's cast-off mistress Laura, and so on to Laura's brothers and sisters, her father, mother, and grandfather.)

But we must get back to Walter Bidlake. We are shown his mistress Marjorie, whom he would like to drop, fallen back on mysticism, and then the girl he is in love with, Lucy Tantamount, type of the perverted young woman in search of sensations. She brings us to her father, Lord Edward the biologist, and so to her father's laboratory assistant Illidge. So comes in the political view. For Illidge is a man of wretched origins, who holds a grudge against "capitalism," and will be persuaded by Spandrell to take part in the murder of the fascist leader Webley.

Walter and Lucy are habitués of Sbisa's restaurant in Soho, and there they meet and argue with Spandrell and other types, including Mark and Mary Rampion. Mark Rampion is a painter, a brave, intelligent man, who sees life clearly and sees it whole, and who preaches and practices "integral living"; while Mary is the brave and intelligent woman who has sacrificed her social position to join him in this enterprise. And now I believe I have mentioned all the principal characters with the one exception of Burlap the editor. This highly disagreeable person is a devotee of St. Francis, Mammon, and Venus, whose diverse worship he reconciles by some slimy hocus-pocus.

More than any of the writers we have mentioned, Huxley makes a point of alternating groups of characters with the deliberate intention of ironic contrast, so as to give a sharp impression of the disparateness and incommunicability of these various worlds. He seems to suggest the inexistence of absolute truth, its complete relativity to the temperament, the point of view. It is probable that the author has among his characters a preference for Mark Rampion, as the sole person of good-will who takes all the facts into account and makes a pretty successful synthesis of the manifold elements of a normal life. If there is any unity of pattern, it is given by him. Every other character is to be measured by the degree of his divergence from this norm. But Rampion has little to do in the story but talk, and he is not by any means the most interesting character; so that the dominant impression remains one of multiplicity, diversity, relativity of temperaments and philosophies.

The author makes a point of bringing together in one place a large number of persons of variegated coloration (Chapters I–XI); of bringing together in one chapter simultaneous scenes involving members of one family (XXIV); of presenting several different accounts of the same event as it appears to different persons (XXIX). He likes to pass from one place to another far distant, and show you what the people discussed in the first place are actually doing in the other (V, VI). Above all he likes to "modulate," or play variations on the same theme. In XXXIII he gives us first the suffering of Elinor at the bedside of her dying child; then passes to the house where lies the corpse of murdered Webley, showing the callousness of Spandrell and the sick disgust and fear of Illidge; then goes to the concert in Queen's Hall with Philip, whose son is dying, and makes him listen to the word-play of Willy Weaver; and finally takes us with Illidge to the laboratory, where the murderer has to listen to Lord Edward's speculations on the use of corpses for fertilizer.

All this contrapuntal development is very amusing, but rather too obvious for the best effect. And one thing which contributes to the obviousness is Philip's theory of the "novel of ideas," adopted by Mr. Huxley: "The character of each personage must be implied, as far as possible, in the ideas of which he is the mouthpiece." This is much too simple. You can very seldom judge the actual character of any one from the ideas to which he gives utterance, especially if he is an "intellectual." Most intellectuals are perpetually engaged in throwing up a smoke-screen not merely between themselves and others, but still more between their own real selves and the imaginary selves with which it is their pleasure to live.

But this is not the main objection to this type of novel, in which each character is chosen to stand for something in the world of ideas. The main objection is that the characters are doomed in advance to be mechanical and artificial. They run the danger, pointed out by Gide, of seeming the creations of the author rather than of life.

In the "Journal" he warns himself:

> The poor novelist constructs his characters; he directs them and makes them talk. The true novelist lends his ear to what they say and watches them in action; he hears them talk before he understands them, and it is only after he has heard them speak that little by little he comes to realize *who* they are.

Especially he warns himself against the danger of making his characters address the reader.

> The great error in the dialogues of X . . . is that the characters are always talking for the benefit of the reader; the author has turned over to them his business of explaining everything. Always take pains to see that a character speaks only for the person he is talking with.

Again he warns himself against the disposition of an author to *describe* the character's psychology instead of presenting it dramatically:

> From the first line of my first book, I have sought for the direct expression of my character's state of mind—some phrase which shall be directly revelatory of his subjective state—rather than to portray that state.

In comparison with the novels of Gide or Dos Passos "Point Counter Point" is theoretical and talky. We are more impressed with the ideas of Rampion, for example, or Philip, than made to feel acquainted with them personally. We are not *shown* Rampion living integrally. In the case of Philip there is very little effective dramatization of that intellectual aloofness of his, though Elinor does complain of it. It is not explicit discussion of a sentimental relation that makes it live in fiction, but the intimate presentation of events and predicaments that embody that relation. What we have in Mr. Huxley's novels is the sort of thing offered by Thomas Love Peacock in "Headlong Hall" and "Nightmare Abbey," by Norman Douglas in "South Wind," where each character is an intellectual eccentric. And he certainly shares some of the distinction of style of these writers. What he does not observe is their witty brevity and lightness of tone—he takes too seriously his obligations to realism—though in this respect he has done better in "Crome Yellow" and "Antic Hay."

Huxley is forever describing the character's state of mind and explaining how he got that way, often in general and summary terms. Thus of Walter's feeling for Marjorie:

> It was with that virtue, that refined, cultured, bloodless spirituality that he had fallen in love—with that and with her unhappiness; for Carling was unspeakable. Pity made him a knight errant. Love, he had then believed (for he was only twenty-two at the time, ardently pure, with the adolescent purity of sexual desires turned inside out, just down from Oxford and stuffed with poetry and the lucubrations of philosophers and mystics), love was talk, love was spiritual communion and companionship. [Etc.]

Or the feeling of Burlap for his dead wife:

> These agonies which Burlap, by a process of intense concentration on the idea of his loss and grief, had succeeded in churning up within himself were in no way proportionate or even related to his feelings for the living Susan. [Etc.]

It is all very interesting, though it has not the finesse of Norman Douglas or Anatole France. But it is also in method rather "old hat." It is, at any rate, directly in contradiction to the principles laid down by Gide in the "Journal des Faux-monnayeurs," which is a kind of gospel of twentieth-century technique. Mr. Huxley is aware that he is, in some respects, not in the movement. After Philip's account of the contrapuntal novel, he has a moment of doubt. "But perhaps this is too tyrannical an imposition of the author's will. Some people would think so." Then he recovers confidence in his own plan. "But need the author be so retiring? I think we are a bit too squeamish about these personal appearances nowadays."

The question of the author's appearances is a question of effectiveness of presentation. If the author succeeds in presenting his theme effectively—story, situation, character, states of mind—we shall not quarrel with his personal appearances. This is accomplished by Wassermann and Gide, in their contrapuntal studies, even though they have not taken the excessive pains of Joyce and Dos Passos to cover their own tracks. Our main quarrel is with the author who makes his personal appearance a *substitute* for the artistic presentation of his subject, thinking that talking about the subject is equivalent to presenting it.

There is still another saying of Gide which here comes in apropos:

> The thing to do—contrary to the practice of Meredith and James—is to give the reader an advantage over me—to manage things so that the reader may think himself more intelligent than the author, of a higher morality, and more discerning, and, as it were in spite of the author, may discover many points in the characters and many truths in the story not perceived by the author himself.

That is perhaps the wisest thing ever written about the novelist's art. Any one who has ever published a novel must have had this experience. Some one comes to congratulate him on his work. "On the whole," says the reader, "I admire your work very much, but such and such a character I find most disagreeable." And the author is too much pleased at his success to make the obvious reply, "Well, what on earth did you think I meant him to be?"

XXXVII

COMPOSITE VIEWS

EXTREMELY varied are the manifestations in the last ten years of the disposition to take the cross-section of life breadthwise. Already in 1922 (the year of "Ulysses"), Virginia Woolf in England and Waldo Frank in America were publishing extraordinary works, illustrative of two extreme varieties of this method.

In "Jacob's Room" the intention is primarily to give an impression of the personality of a young Englishman. The author has quite definitely rejected the idea of telling Jacob's story consecutively and in detail. That, she seems to say, is the way with novelists who pretend to know everything, who "construct" a character (to use Gide's phrase) and follow it consistently through a series of events (equally "constructed" or "made up") to a logical conclusion. She is more modest. She has chosen a character who interests her, and undertakes to show, in sketchy outline, what he was up to from early childhood, through his university days and his days in London as a seeker after wisdom, to the time of his disappearance in the war. There is no action worthy of the name; there are no "scenes." There is simply a succession of brief glimpses of Jacob such as one might have of a person one had never "met" but only caught sight of from time to time across a drawing-room. And "what remains is mostly a matter of guess work."

What interests this observer is the essential nature of the young man. But Mrs. Woolf consistently refuses to give us any character sketch of him, to generalize about him. That, she seems to say, is all very well for authors, people who know everything. But in ordinary life that doesn't get you very far. And of course, like all other novelists, Virginia Woolf wants to give in her book the impression of ordinary life. She therefore eschews the method of the novelist—the old-fashioned novelist—and tries to render the effect of this character without making general statements about him.

> It is no use trying to sum people up. One must follow hints, not exactly what is said, nor yet entirely what is done—for instance, when the train drew into the station, Mr. Flanders burst open the door, and put the lady's dressing-case out for her, saying, or rather mumbling: "let me" very shyly; indeed he was rather clumsy about it.

As a matter of fact the way the author characterizes Jacob Flanders is by showing him, in momentary glimpses, as he appeared to a great variety of people, or in relation to them. When he is a little boy it is his mother, calling him in from play on the beach. At Cambridge it is an assortment of university characters, such as they are, for the illumination or the darkening of a young man's mind. In London it is the people he meets in drawing-rooms; those he meets at night clubs, or rubs elbows with at the British Museum. In Greece it is the lady he falls in love with. And everywhere it is the women who love him and the men who cherish him.

Much is made, though always in "hints," of what people think of Jacob, this "silent young man," as one of them calls him. The author likes to skip about among her characters; and sometimes on a single page she will show us half a dozen people in various places, all simultaneously concerned with Jacob. But this is not all. It is true that, in her pictorial composition, all the other figures are placed by reference to Jacob. But many of them are persons who do not know him, entire strangers to him, people to whom he has never given a thought. They happen to be present in the same place with him, on the steps of St. Paul's, or each one in his separate room in Cambridge. They simply belong in the same picture with him. They represent the complexity of human life without which it is impossible to understand him.

Any human being is, after all, but a function of every other human being—"a quantity whose value is dependent on the value of some other quantity." The author is here forever looking for Jacob Flanders, and her search takes her through a crowd of other people whose relation to him is evident only to the philosophic mind.

> The march that the mind keeps beneath the windows of others is queer enough. Now distracted by brown panelling; now by a fern in a pot; here improvising a few phrases to dance with the barrel-organ; again snatching a detached gaiety from a drunken man; then altogether absorbed by words the poor shout across the street at each other (so outright, so lusty)—yet all the while having for centre, for magnet, a young man alone in his room.

Once recognize this functional relationship of each person with every other in our universe, and it is hard to know where to stop. If Jacob's mother is important for an understanding of Jacob, then the neighbors in Scarborough are important for an understanding of Jacob's mother. If Fanny Elmer is in love with Jacob, that gives her an importance as a function of Jacob; but what about the other people in the restaurant where she has left her umbrella—the cashier, who notices that she has left it; the waitress who tries to catch her and return it; the typist crumbling her cake; the coal merchant reading the "Telegraph"; and Mrs. Parsons brushing the crumbs from her furs? Virginia Woolf, in addition to her philosophical cast of mind, has an insatiable interest in people as such, and she finds it very hard to leave any one out. When she goes to the opera she would like to occupy places everywhere at once, in the stalls, boxes, amphitheater, gallery. She doesn't want to miss the contact with any group of patrons. "But no—we must choose. Never was there a harsher necessity! or one which entails greater pain, more certain disaster; for wherever I seat myself, I die in exile: Whittaker in his lodging-house; a Lady Charles at the manor."

This is obviously a dangerous inclination. It might easily lead into confusion and messiness. Everything depends on what Matthew Arnold calls "tact." In the case of Virginia Woolf I am not ready to pronounce judgment. But I think she must be granted "tact" in considerable degree. For the upshot of her method is to give a distinct and rather charming impression of Jacob Flanders himself. And what is more interesting still, she has given an impression of him *in his world*. Which is perhaps as much as to say that her method was the best one for the purpose.

2

The book of Waldo Frank's to which I have referred is "City Block" (1922; new edition, 1932). Of the strange and somewhat morbid beauty of this book I have here no time to speak. It would take us too far afield. And besides, I do not understand it well enough to be able to discuss it adequately. I am now citing "City Block" merely as an instance of the growing tendency to make of the novel a composite picture of many distinct lives.

Perhaps it is not exact to describe this book as a novel. It is, strictly speaking, a group of short stories. But there are two things that give the several tales an interrelationship not customary in this genre. They are, to begin with, confined to the people who inhabit a single block in New York City, and it is the author's evident intention to make in these tales a comprehensive survey of life in a typical social unit. He is interested in the several persons presented, not merely individually but also as members of a social organism.

Probably we had better say psychological organism. For "social" is too fraught with associations. It suggests Balzac, Zola, Dreiser. It suggests sociology—the family, the minimum wage, and the settlement-house. With all this Frank is not concerned. He is concerned with persons as souls. Society he conceives as a sort of psychological continuum, in which the souls, however lonely, are packed close together, so as inevitably to exert pressure upon one another. His conception is highly poetical and mystic, and very difficult of expression in any other terms than those of his own fictitious narrative.

He prefaces his book with the notice: "The author assures the reader that City Block is a single organism and that its parts should be read in order." It will be difficult for any one to say exactly why these tales are set down in this order and no other. There is seemingly a certain progression of mystical experience shadowed forth for the author in this series of tales, which the reader will find impossible to follow without a key. But what will be obvious is the system of introducing in the later tales persons who have appeared, or been referred to, in the earlier ones. In Number One we are introduced to Clarence Lipper, salesman, who has neglected to buy a Christmas present for his wife. The lack is supplied by a certain Mrs. Luve, a woman of dubious life. Clarence Lipper does not come in again, but his wife is a leading figure in Number Thirteen. As for Mrs. Luve, she is the central character of Frank's novel "Rahab," published in the same year with "City Block," and she reappears in story Number Four. In Two are introduced three persons destined to reappear in later tales; in Three, two more.

Often these persons, in their later appearance, are unimportant as actors. They exist mainly as thoughts in the minds of others. Or they first appear in casual and indirect fashion, and later take the center of the stage. Five and Six are concerned with two Jewish storekeepers, their wives, and the cherished child of each couple. In Five it is the Lanichs that have the prominence; while the Rabinowichs are in the background. In Six the Rabinowichs come to the fore. Seven and Eight are virtually continuous, chapters in the history of the same people. Fourteen is the story of Paoli Benati, who "gave these stories to the man that wrote them" and then took his own life.

Thus Mr. Frank has managed to make of his fourteen pieces something more than a collection of tales. Understand it or not, one feels one has been introduced there to —what shall we call it?—a community of souls. The nearest analogy to "City Block" is perhaps Elmer Rice's play, "Street Scene." The one is as phantasmagoric as the other is matter-of-fact. But the two authors have had the same idea—to show us the life not of a man or a clique, but of a street, a city block. It is quite possible to suppose that Mr. Rice may have taken his cue from Mr. Frank. In the "expressionism" of "The Adding Machine" and "Strange Interlude" Mr. Rice and Mr. O'Neill were anticipated by Frank's inventions in "Rahab" and "Holiday." If his own work has been unduly neglected, Mr. Frank may take a kind of satisfaction in seeing his methods acclaimed in the work of others.

3

The same desire to build up a set of short stories into a larger whole, in which, by some compositional device, they are given a semblance of organic unity (if not always an actual unity) is exhibited by a considerable variety of American authors since 1922. It is working from the pole opposite to that of the novel, but it sometimes arrives at much the same point.

Thus in Ernest Hemingway's collection of short stories

"In Our Time" (1925) there is an effort to give a futuristic sort of general pattern to the book as a whole. The stories, each of which stands perfectly well on its own feet, and many of which were separately published, now appear as "chapters," and each chapter is preceded by a brief vignette (a bit of narrative printed in italics), which has nothing to do with the story proper. The first five chapters are all about a boy named Nick Adams. He watches his father perform a Cæsarian operation on an Indian woman; he tells his girl Marjorie that love "isn't fun any more"; he has an adventure with a crazy tramp. In the later chapters Nick reappears—after the war, it would seem—skiing in Switzerland and fishing in Canada with utmost gusto. The intervening chapters are concerned with American soldiers abroad or back home, with various futile and silly American couples traveling abroad, and with a young American boy whose father is a jockey in Turin and Paris. As for the introductory vignettes, they are almost altogether pictures from the war in France, Turkey, Italy, or from bull-fighting, in Spain and in Mexico.

These introductory vignettes remind one of the prose poems in italics prefixed to the chapters of "Manhattan Transfer." Only, in Dos Passos's novel they have an obvious thematic relation to the story. In Mr. Hemingway's book they cut across the story with a shocking effect of irrelevance. Esoterically considered, they may not be so irrelevant. The general subject of this book, as of "Men without Women," is the manly life, the clean life of fight and sport. While Nick Adams is growing up, the war is going on, with its exhilarating challenge to courage and stoicism. In Chapter VI, Nick has arrived himself at the Italian front and is sitting wounded against the wall of a church. With the conclusion of the war, it is bull-fighting which takes its place as recurring motif. A few examples are worked in of men tame, impotent, domesticated, just to give the proper shading, and the books ends with some glorious descriptions of skiing, horse-racing, and trout-fishing.

The separate sketches are extremely well done in that style of deceptive simplicity which is now so familiar to readers of Hemingway and his many disciples. As for the composition of the thing, it is perhaps most sensible to consider it an amusing stunt, or maybe simply a hoax.

Then comes Thornton Wilder with his "Cabala" (1926) and "The Bridge of San Luis Rey" (1927). Each of these is a collection of short stories so closely interrelated by recurring characters that it is felt to be a novel. Each one is a frame story. In "The Cabala"—which has some suggestion of Percy Lubbock's "Roman Pictures" (1923)—a young American in Rome comes into close contact with a group of persons of varied distinction, a sort of esoteric clique, and learns the spiritual history of each one.

In "The Bridge of San Luis Rey" we start from a document, a book by the Franciscan Brother Juniper of Lima. With the falling of the old Inca bridge between Lima and Cuzco in 1714 five persons lost their lives. Brother Juniper is interested to know whether an inquiry into the private lives of these five persons may be made to prove statistically the providential character of God's decrees. The author is not satisfied with Brother Juniper's account of these people and undertakes to set forth what he knows—fully conscious, however, that even he may not have got at "the central passion of Doña Maria's life; nor of Uncle Pio's, not even of Esteban's," that even he may have "missed the very spring within the spring."

The five persons in question are the Marquesa de Montemayor and her servant Pepita; Uncle Pio, an impresario; Don Jaime, weakly son of a great actress, the Perichole; and Esteban, one of twin brothers, foundlings, brought up by a great-hearted abbess. Part Two is an account of the marquesa, especially her unparalleled devotion to her daughter in Spain. Part Three is named after Esteban, and gives an account of his extraordinary love for his brother, his tragic sorrow when his brother falls in love with the Perichole, and his decision to make a voyage with the great traveler Captain Alvarado. Part Four is named after Uncle Pio, but is quite as much concerned with the Perichole, whom he has trained as an actress and loved as a woman. The various characters keep reappearing throughout, including the viceroy and the abbess. Part Five is a sort of epilogue, bringing together the survivors —the viceroy, the captain, the abbess. We are also brought back to Brother Juniper and his ill-starred effort to justify the ways of God to man.

The dominant motif is Love—that unselfish devotion to another human being, or to humanity in general, which covers and obliterates a multitude of sins. Brother Juniper is an inspiration. The several stories are woven together, with infinite cunning and ingenuity, into a single pattern. The narrative is brilliantly done. It is done in the traditional, the classic, rather than the modernistic, manner. There is no whiff of Joyce, Woolf, or Dos Passos. And yet structurally it is of our time. This is no story built around one man, nor founded upon intrigue or dramatic issue, taken in the direction of time. It is a composite picture, a pattern made up of many lives set side by side.

Glenway Wescott's "The Grandmothers" (1927) is a sort of Spoon River Anthology of one family of Wisconsin pioneers. It is the effort of young Alwyn Tower to reconstruct imaginatively the life of his forebears. He takes up chapter by chapter his grandmothers and grandfathers, his great-aunts and great-uncles, his mother and father, his uncles and aunts. There is an elaborate scaffolding of introduction and interpretation. The work is given a certain unity of tone and sentiment through the filial piety of

Alwyn Tower, his almost morbid concern with the past—that tissue of ghostly presences which constitutes his heredity and conditioning environment. In Alwyn's reflections at the death-bed of his grandmother he sounds many notes in that criticism of American life which has taken on such volume in our letters since Van Wyck Brooks and Masters's "Anthology." Throughout this history what impresses him is the abortive idealism of these strenuous lives, the fundamental melancholy deliberately ignored, the fanatical Puritanism, the spiritual pride and failure.

There is no central knot of intrigue or suspense. There is no chronological line of history. Mr. Wescott does not follow the saga-like method of Hergesheimer in "The Limestone Tree" (1931). He has more of the method of Conrad. Alwyn has somewhat the rôle of Marlow or Captain Mitchell. Like Conrad, Wescott likes to insist on the fragmentariness of his information, on the need for imaginative reconstruction; he makes great use of retrospection; he weaves back and forth in time. In some chapters he works in several periods simultaneously, deliberately interchanging distinct planes, in the modernistic manner.

He has not the vividness, the visual imagination of the born writer of fiction. He has so much material that he is swamped by it. We find ourselves reading history. Instead of the actual scene, the present moment, we are dealing with expository summaries. Often this makes hard reading, and, what is worse, a faint or confused effect. We are studying a faded daguerreotype. For all that, the book is a fascinating one. It has the fascination and significance of history. And it has a kind of wistful glamour. Mr. Wescott is a sensitive artist, something of a poet, and "The Grandmothers," in spite of a certain want of accent, is one of the more important examples of the recent vogue for novels which are composite pictures of social groups.

4

The later work of Louis Bromfield is a curious testimony to the prevalence of the vogue I have been tracing. In his earlier novels like "The Green Bay Tree" and "Early Autumn," he is in the tradition of the well-made novel, with a strong suggestion of James and Edith Wharton. In "The Strange Case of Miss Annie Spragg" (1928) he has undertaken a decidedly modernistic study, which has a pertinence here, but which I shall leave to the following chapter for comment.

In "Twenty-Four Hours" (1930) Mr. Bromfield has made a special combination of the traditional and the experimental or "up-to-date" in fiction. Seven men and women of fashion he assembles in an apartment overlooking the East River. When the party breaks up, he follows each one of them through the doings of the night and the following day—now one and then another as the hours pass. One of them becomes involved in the murder of a night-club singer. And thus are brought in a number of underworld figures, who take their turn in the spotlight. Many other persons of humble station—like the doorman of the apartment-house—are likewise followed through the night, thus insuring a sufficient representation from the lower social levels. The principals are reassembled at tea on the following afternoon, together with some new arrivals from Europe. The threads are all neatly tied together; and a gratifying number of weddings is arranged for the fall of the curtain.

Thus Mr. Bromfield has compounded his drink of many ingredients more or less popular to-day, though making their appeal to different groups of readers. He has limited his action to twenty-four hours, and shown a cross-section of urban society. He has followed the alternating system of Wassermann and Dos Passos. He has anticipated Vicki Baum's "Grand Hotel" with his suggestion of many disparate lives going on side by side and strangely touching one another. He has duly exploited the gangster and the night club. And in characterization and narrative manner he has made a tolerable imitation of Edith Wharton. It is a most ingenious piece of work. But it bears the marks of haste and insincerity. I think the public is right to prefer him in his earlier and orthodox phase.

5

The most monumental, and in many ways the most serious, of such composite views attempted in our time, are Evelyn Scott's novels "The Wave" (1929) and "A Calendar of Sin" (1931). The first of these is a composition built around the Civil War. Although it proceeds in chronological sequence and covers the whole period from Fort Sumter to the assassination of Lincoln, it is in no sense a history of the war. It is made up of seventy numbered sections, each one presenting a moment in the life of a separate individual. Some of these sections, especially those concerned with battles, are further broken up into subdivisions dealing with separate moments and individuals, thus bringing the total of pictures up to the number of one hundred. Few of these characters come in a second time, and practically no attempt is made to relate them to one another. Each section confines itself to the chosen individual and such other persons as he is involved with; and, with few exceptions, the point of view is strictly limited to him. The idea is to show the effect of this great political event upon the private lives of some hundreds of typical human beings—men, women, and children, soldiers and civilians, in the fighting zones and at a distance from them. The war itself is the wave referred to in the title. The people affected by it are like corks bobbing up and down on its surface but not necessarily carried along with it. According to the statement from a work on physical geography prefixed to the novel, "Waves travel in some definite direction, but a cork thrown into the water does not travel with the waves. It moves up and down, to and fro, but unless it is blown by the wind or carried by a current it returns to the same position with each wave and does not permanently leave its place."

The most remarkable thing about this story of a war is the way in which the hundreds of characters involved retain each his own private identity. The war has affected their fortunes in one way or another: it has brought them sorrow and death; it has thwarted them or given them occasion to exercise their special faculties. But it has never carried them out of themselves. Miss Scott is evidently strongly impressed with the passion to respect oneself as a motivating force in human behavior, and over and over again she shows us persons in every walk of life, in every kind of action, desperately clinging to whatever interpretation of themselves they find necessary for self-respect, and following, through agony, crime, and death, the line of conduct necessary to confirm them in this interpretation. From the merest child in Richmond, the poorest creole girl in New Orleans, up through Grant and Lee, to Davis and Lincoln, we see them working out, in terms of this national disaster, their own individual salvation. Political events, one feels, are like great tidal waves sweeping across the surface of the ocean of human nature and leaving it essentially what it was before. It is an impressive original conception, and worked out with a wealth of detail, both on the side of psychology and of material fact, such as we have never before seen in American fiction.

"A Calendar of Sin" is a work of less forbidding aspect to the ordinary reader of novels, in that it has much more continuity of story. Here again, however, we have the wide spread of the social vision and the system of alternating groups of characters as in Wassermann and Dos Passos. The action covers the period from 1867 to 1914, with special emphasis on the years of reconstruction in the South, and includes the lives of three generations in some half a dozen families. It begins in Odessa, Indiana, with the aging lawyer Cadwallader Sydney, who leaves his wife and daughter, to begin life again with a young schoolmistress. It reaches out to include James Dolan, the ambitious associate of Sydney; Dolan's brother Charlie, the saloon-keeper; his brother John, the telegraph operator, who marries Sydney's daughter Fanny. Before it reaches this point, the town of Mimms in Tennessee has been brought in: and we make acquaintance with old Judge Gilbert, whose son Geoffrey turned Abolitionist and married a mulatto; Edwin George, who has saved Geoffrey's wife from a mob and is considered no better than a Yankee; his brother Thomas George; and Edwin's rival in the tobacco business, Major Cowley. Both the Georges have several children and Major Cowley has a son, and thus are started no less than eight different stories. The son of John Dolan eventually grows up to marry one of Edwin's daughters; another of the daughters marries the son of Major Cowley; and before the book closes we are reading of the love-affairs of the grandchildren. Besides Odessa and Mimms, we have many scenes laid in Washington, Cincinnati, Memphis, Chicago, St. Louis, in Dakota and in the Southwest.

The division of the book is by years; and, within the year, by the days of the month. On certain days we have the stories of several different persons to follow; and even where it is essentially the same story so far as the action is concerned, separate sections are devoted to the points of view of the several persons involved. Thus for a single day we may have the views of father, mother, daughter, and son, and some of them more than once. Miss Scott is very much concerned with the states of mind of her characters, and most punctilious in observance of the limited point of view. The result is, with the wide variety of viewpoints, to intensify the effect of discontinuity, or disparateness in continuity. It is this which gives so "modern" an air to a narrative which might otherwise remind one of the compendious chronicles of Tolstoy or Thackeray.

What keeps the book from having the modernity of Dos Passos and Joyce is, first, the large freight of exposition which the author carries, rather clumsily. And then the style. The style is her own accomplished and rather formal one. This is cultivated, competent prose, sometimes exquisite in description, a trifle heavy, and decidedly tending to run into iambic pentameters.

What one admires most in Evelyn Scott is her sheer intelligence. It is a thing clear, sharp, analytic, dispassionate—almost inhuman. Her subject is love, the fearful dislocations and disturbances caused in human lives by the indulgence and denial of this passion. Her title is of course ironic. Sin is not a term in her vocabulary, but only borrowed from the poor creatures whose lives were devastated by that dread Gorgon of the mind. In her handling of love and of other human motives, there is as little sentimentalizing as one could hope to find in any human document. She touches human nature with the coolness of a laboratory scientist. That is her strength as a thinker; it is perhaps a weakness in the artist. She has given her book a sub-title, "American Melodramas." I cannot say whether this is ironic or apologetic. Oh, she need have no fear of writing melodrama! If she is not read, it is because she has refrained even from writing drama. I will not say that she does not sympathize, that she does not "understand." She understands too well, far too well. She will not point things up. She will not take sides. She is afraid of being unscientific. She is beyond good and evil.

XXXVIII

EXPRESSIONISM: WOOLF, FRANK

THE term "expressionism" I set here at the head of a chapter to indicate, somewhat loosely, a variety of tendencies opposed to the formerly prevailing literalness in the rendering of life. Expressionism stands, strictly speaking, in opposition to impressionism. Impressionism is, in the main, a variety of realism. It undertakes, by means of a special technique, to give a more precise impression of the look of the object studied. It is quite as literal as the earlier manner of rendering the object, though it has a different system of notation. Expressionism pretends, on the contrary, not to give an impression of the look of the object but to express its meaning or essence. It eschews the letter in favor of whatever symbol is best suited to suggest that interior meaning. It is licensed, at will, to neglect perspective and to make use of any dimension, beyond the three familiar ones, which will help to "locate" more exactly the interior meaning it is concerned with.

I am using the term "expressionism" in a more inclusive sense than that in which it applies to most of the German fiction of the expressionist school (the later Hauptmann, Heinrich Mann, Rudolf Binding, Kasimir Edschmid, Franz Werfel, Max Brod). These men are mainly neo-romantics in whom the expressionist tendency is shown in an avoidance of detailed naturalistic treatment, in a strongly religious bent, and a fondness for legendary, fantastic, and mystical themes (for example, Heinrich Mann's "Die Rükkehr vom Hades," Hauptmann's "Der Ketzer von Soana," Werfel's "Der Tod des Kleinbürgers," Binding's "Unsterblichkeit," Brod's "Leben mit einer Göttin" and his "Tycho Brahe's Weg zu Gott," translated under the title of "The Redemption of Tycho Brahe"). In general conception and style these works are rather conservative than modernistic. The term takes on a broader and more modernistic connotation if we bear in mind the bolder style of the expressionist poets (Holz, Däubler, Stramm, Becher, Werfel) and the bolder technique of the playwrights (for example, Hasenclever, Toller, Kaiser). The technique of Wassermann and Döblin suggests the wider possibilities of expressionism in the German novel. It probably would not occur to the German critics to apply the term to so realistic a work as Joyce's "Ulysses." But the "fourth-dimensional" character of the Walpurgisnacht scene, the gigantism of the Cyclops episode, and many other features of "Ulysses" show a disposition to transcend the old literal realism,—a disposition which may properly be referred to the same expressionistic impulse.

Wassermann and Gide are much more conservative writers than Joyce. But their boldness in technique is shown in the seemingly arbitrary way in which they set down beside one another scenes in several different places, giving, as nearly as possible in fiction, the effect of different lives going on simultaneously. It suggests the mysterious interdependence and solidarity of our spiritual life, which is a characteristic notion of the expressionists. And it is a freer and more imaginative way of making this suggestion than would have been admitted in the old realistic technique.

Again, Gide's craving to get away from too strict a logic in the motivation of character, while it may lead in the direction of truth, is a repudiation of realism. In this matter he makes one think of Wassermann, and both of them remind one of Dostoevski. I believe that Gide is largely in sympathy with his Edouard in what he says about the excessive concern of the naturalists with verisimilitude. For, after all, while Edouard did turn some wrong corners and get hopelessly lost, it is also true, as Gide says, that he has lent him a good deal of himself.

The novel, says Edouard, is the most lawless of forms; novelists can do anything they wish. And it is probably from fear of excessive liberty that the novel has always "clung so fearfully to reality."

> And I am speaking not merely of the French novel. In the same way the English novel, and the Russian, free as they are from all constraint, make themselves the slaves of lifelikeness [*ressemblance*]. The novel has never known that "formidable erosion of contours," that Nietzsche speaks of, and that deliberate departure from life, which made style possible in the Greek dramatists, for example, or the French tragic writers of the seventeenth century. Do you know anything more perfect and more profoundly human than these works? But this is precisely because they are not human except profoundly; they do not pride themselves on appearing human, or at least on appearing real.

This is in a very different spirit from that of Maupassant in his famous preface to "Pierre et Jean." Maupassant gives there the best possible account of the motives which impel any artist to make a careful selection from the circumstances offered him by life, and of course Gide would in the main agree with him. It is in the emphasis that they differ. Maupassant writes:

> To be truthful, then, consists in giving the complete illusion of the truth, according to the ordinary logic of facts and not in transcribing them slavishly in the chaotic order of their occurrence. My conclusion is that the Realists of talent ought rather to call themselves Illusionists.

In the last analysis, Gide is, I fancy, an illusionist in his intention. But he has for the moment a quarrel with "the ordinary logic of facts." He seeks his illusion in that element of mystery which clings to human motivation, and even in the "chaotic order of occurrence" of facts in ordinary life. He is, I think, under the influence of Dostoevski. What else could explain his making so much of the devil in the story of Vincent Molinier, his actual introduction of an angel as a character in connection with Bernard? These are among his least successful inventions; but they are symptomatic.

This sort of thing is much more in the spirit of Wassermann. I have spoken earlier of the conversation with the devil in "The World's Illusion." Still more remarkable are the performances of the gooseman in the novel named after him. This gooseman is, in literal reality, nothing but a funny old statue in the market-place. But when it becomes necessary, for the conversion of Daniel Nothaft, to introduce a god-from-the-machine, the statue comes to life. He visits the hero in his home and harangues him for chapter after chapter; he plays with the children; he changes places with Daniel, and leaves the hero standing all day as a statue in the market. This is all in keeping with the essentially poetic, the mythopœic and didactic genius of Wassermann.

Direct and lineal descendant of the gooseman is the carved stone angel who, in the last chapter of Thomas Wolfe's "Look Homeward, Angel" (1930) raises her arm and moves her ponderous foot for the edification of the hero; and the ghost of the dead Ben with whom he converses in the moonlight is in the same tradition. This is not, in my opinion, the happiest inspiration of Mr. Wolfe in his remarkable first novel. But it shows the way the wind blows.

We have had a good deal of this tendency to the fantastic in English and American fiction of the present century. We have had—not to draw the lines too close—Sir James Barrie's "Little White Bird" (1902), the scientific and utopian romances of H. G. Wells from "The Time Machine" (1895) to "The Autocracy of Mr. Parham"

(1930), W. H. Hudson's "Green Mansions" (1904) and "A Crystal Age" (1906), G. K. Chesterton's "The Man Who Was Thursday" (1908). We have had the philosophical romances of James Branch Cabell, laid in the imaginary realm of Poictesme. And we have had the post-war crop of fantasy: Walter de la Mare's "Memoirs of a Midget" (1921), Aldous Huxley's "Crome Yellow" (1921), Christopher Morley's "Thunder on the Left" (1925). Sylvia Townsend Warner and Norman Matson have introduced us to witches, English and French, in "Lolly Willowes" and "Flecker's Magic" (both 1926). David Garnett has re-introduced the medieval theme of animal transformation in "Lady Into Fox" (1922). And Elinor Wylie has ventured something still stranger and more fantastic in "The Venetian Glass Nephew" (1925).

Several of the books mentioned have already taken their place unmistakably among the prime masterpieces of fiction in English—at least these three: "Green Mansions," "The Memoirs of a Midget," and "The Venetian Glass Nephew." They are fine products of the poetic imagination working in the medium of prose. But there is nothing modernistic about them, except this un-Victorian indulgence in fantasy. For the most part there is nothing modernistic about any of the pieces named, with the mild exception of "Crome Yellow" and "Thunder on the Left." In general they are notable for the smooth unbroken maintenance of the illusion of reality, and for a classical simplicity of method.

There is one fantastic novel of the period which has greater pretensions to the modernistic. And it is for that reason that I dwell upon it here; not because of its excellence—for I do not consider it a great success. This is Mr. Bromfield's "The Strange Case of Miss Annie Spragg" (1928), which is modernistic in somewhat the same way as the books discussed in the preceding chapter. The fourteen loosely bound pieces of this novel are so many variations upon an abstract theme. This theme, which might have delighted the heart of Anatole France or Norman Douglas, is seemingly that of human fertility and fertility cults. It brings together persons, places, and times of considerable diversity. There is the god Priapus, dug up in the garden of an Italian villa occupied by an American lady of religious bent. There is an American spinster in the Italian town who, upon her death, is found to have received the sacred stigmata of the Lord. There is her father, Cyrus Spragg, lusty preacher of the word, who set up his tabernacle in New Jerusalem, Illinois, and founded a cult of which the less said the better. There are, moreover, an Italian priest who has spent forty years atoning for the sin of his youth, a holy nun who has a vision of St. Francis, and a principessa who has been a magnificent lover. There is an Englishman of good family who is cherished by a barmaid, in all innocence, and leaves behind him a monumental History of Prostitution. There are many other curious characters and circumstances. One passes frequently back and forth between Italy and Illinois, Illinois and England; between 1840 and 1870, 1870 and the present time.

This book is what Gide would call a *sotie*. It is amusing in conception, rather sketchy and confused in execution. It will be a curious item for collectors of a philosophic turn.

2

The modernism of Mr. Bromfield has an air of being assumed. Virginia Woolf's modernism is in her bones. She can write novels in many ways, in any way but the traditional one. As further examples of her expressionism, of her revolt from literalness, two of her books must serve, "Orlando: A Biography" (1928) and "The Waves" (1931).

"Orlando" is, by exception among the novels of Mrs. Woolf, a straightforward chronological record of the life of the title-person. Only, this person is one who had lived about three hundred and fifty years at the time the book was written. Under Charles II, while ambassador to Constantinople, he turns into a woman and continues more or less of this sex to the end of the book. He has the secret ambition to be a writer; and in each age he writes according to the style of the period—heroic in the seventeenth century, Augustan in the time of Queen Anne, and (I suppose) expressionistic in that of George V. He is sometimes a bachelor, sometimes a married man, a wife, a spinster; and at one period it was often doubtful whether he was a man or woman, married or unmarried.

The book has been variously interpreted. It is possible to regard it as a history of English literature in its various phases—virile in Elizabethan times, effeminate under Victoria. It is possible to regard it as a kind of wish-fulfilment dream on the part of the author, an imaginative enlargement of her experience. I am inclined to consider it a study in multiple personality, and a protest against the too narrow labeling of anybody. Virginia Woolf has doubtless suffered under the stigma of her sex; and there is a good deal of quiet satire on the way men try to pigeonhole women. This Orlando chose, on the whole, to be a woman, because of certain privileges and superiorities appertaining to that state; but at times he would appear in male disguise and engage in men's activities.

The point of the book seems to be that there is more than one person in each body, that each individual has, at least potentially, many selves, including the "Captain self, the Key self, which amalgamates and controls them all." In the last chapter Orlando drives out to her country-place in her car; and at each turning she summons one of her many thousand selves. She reflects on her variegated nature: "Thirty-six; in a motor car; a woman. Yes, but a million things as well."

Orlando, then, is not a figure drawn from "life." He is

an image, like Hobbes's Leviathan, for making vivid a philosophical abstraction—a truth of human nature which, the author thinks, can be most conveniently and amusingly rendered in this way.

In "The Waves" there is nobody who changes his sex or lives for centuries. But the six persons who are presented are even less than Orlando characters in action, the ordinary subject of fiction; they are mere personalities or psychic entities more or less integrated. Three men and three women, they are shown from early childhood to old age gradually growing into separate and sharply defined personalities. It is, on the whole, very similar circumstances which work upon them in very different ways; for they were born with different potentialities. But it is only drop by drop that life precipitates, for each one, the special essence of his ego.

There is no story, no narrative or dialogue. The book is entirely made up of soliloquies in which the several characters explain themselves to themselves at various stages of their careers—as children playing together, then at school, at college or in society, in business or family life. They begin together in one house, they drift apart. But twice they all come together. They dine together in London to bid farewell to their friend Percival; and years later they dine together at Hampton Court, by way of realizing, each one, what the others are like, and stiffening their own individualities one against another. And then one of them, in a long soliloquy, "sums up" the process.

Soliloquies I call these passages in quotation marks in which the characters utter to themselves their thoughts about themselves. There is no pretense of realism here. Such soliloquy is as sheer a convention as that of Elizabethan plays. "Thoughts about themselves"—but of course not one person in a thousand is so precise in introspection; not one person in a thousand knows so much about himself. Say rather, the way they feel about themselves.

And, of course, expressed not in their language, but in that of Virginia Woolf. The only one of them all who can, by a stretch of imagination, be supposed to talk to himself in such terms is Bernard the poet, the phrase-maker, the representative, if I mistake not, of the author. But, in these soliloquies, they all talk in poetic style, the fluid, fluttering, fanciful, imaged style which we have come to associate with this author. To be sure, she is never the same; she has wide powers of adjustment to different subjects and intentions. In "Jacob's Room" she uses the feminine, evasive manner of Dorothy Richardson, in "Mrs. Dalloway" the allusive, elliptical manner of Joyce, in "Orlando" what she calls "the biographic style." In "The Waves" she reminds us over and over again of that distinguished writer of free verse, Mrs. Richard Aldington ("H. D."). I do not call it imitation, but kinship.

Rebecca West points out, very justly, that Virginia Woolf is a philosopher writing fiction. Of course she is not a systematic philosopher, one who reasons from premises, using abstract terms susceptible presumably of precise definition. She is a person with a bent for speculation, which she applies to human personality. This she undertakes to adumbrate with images drawn from the worlds of reality and fancy. In short, she is a poet.

3

Rebecca West, by the way, is a person who knows what she is talking about. Not only is she a critic of unusual acuteness and originality—fine and rare qualities in a critic—but she is a novelist of versatile powers. And she comes into this chapter with her novel "Harriet Hume" (1929). Like "Orlando" and "The Waves," "Harriet

Hume" is a philosophical study in human personality. This book has a quaint and original style worthy to be mentioned with Elinor Wylie's. There is a pleasant primness and formality about it like that of Mozart or the box-bordered gardens of eighteenth-century letters.

There is no effort at realism. The two main characters, Harriet Hume and Arnold Condorex, are not so much real people as representatives of opposite tendencies in human nature. Harriet Hume, the musician, stands for the contemplative nature, concerned with the eternal verities, while Condorex, the politician, stands for the active life. The contemplative nature is innocent but ineffective in practical affairs; the active nature is capable of great accomplishment but given to compromise. He is too much interested in the art of negotiation, and very successful in negotiating with himself. In short, he is a self-deceiver, understanding neither himself nor the contemplative nature, though he is susceptible to her charm. But she, the contemplative nature, does understand him. She has, in fact, the power of reading his thoughts, and here comes in the element of "miracle." Over and over again she reads his thoughts at critical moments, and thereby makes them both exceedingly uncomfortable.

There are many other elements of sheer fantasy—the legend of three ladies turned into poplar trees, for example, and the appearance in the last chapter of the spirits of the dead. These are queer ghosts too, policemen who drink beer, and Harriet Hume calmly discussing the situation with the man who shot her dead and then killed himself. I am not capable of working out all the implications of Miss West's symbolism; and already I feel that I have been breaking a butterfly on the wheel. But for the general intention, what seems most probable is this: The persons who in the fable appear as separate individuals are really but the two sides of one individual. They are attracted to each other; they go their own ways; they disagree and make each other unhappy; the active one in the end succeeds in killing them both. In life they cannot agree, but in the calm of death they are reconciled.

Thus it would appear that Miss West has reversed the formula of "Orlando." In "Orlando" many diverse tendencies are combined in one person who never could have so combined them in the "realistic" world. In "Harriet Hume" two tendencies which are often found combined in a single individual are made separate in a fable which departs very far from the conditions of "real life." But it is much the same truth that is embodied in such dissimilar myths. And the two novels are expressions of the same reaction against the literalness of the well-made novel.

4

The "soliloquies" in "The Waves" prove, on analysis, to be a curious combination of elements. They represent the "stream of consciousness" of the several characters. They include in one undifferentiated mass what these people perceive through their senses, what they consciously think, and what they feel about themselves and one another without being actually conscious of it. The same combination is found in Joyce, though probably with more sense of the differentiation between conscious and unconscious.

That all the "stream-of-consciousness" writers do not stem from Joyce seems to be indicated by the dates of Waldo Frank's novels "Rahab" (1922) and "Holiday" (1923). There is much in his futuristic manner that makes me guess at German influences; the influence of post-impressionist painting and sculpture is evidently strong in him. What I wish here to dwell upon is his special technique for distinguishing between separate layers or states of consciousness.

In "Rahab" he presents a woman whose spiritual life is

in seemingly sharp contradiction to her material condition and behavior. Circumstances have turned her into an associate of prostitutes and crooks. Or perhaps it is something within herself, along with circumstances, which has drawn her to such associates, something like what drew Christian Wahnschaffe to the depths. (Oh, Sonia, Sonia! woman of Samaria! how large a progeny you have had among the mystics of our day!) By nature this Fanny Luve is a mystic, her soul suffused with some dark faith in life and in herself. At least she has faith that she is on the way to discover a meaning in life, a meaning destined to be revealed to her by some one of the Jewish race. And at the last, through very denial of her hopes, there dawns upon her some light, sharp as a knife-blade—some light, alas! which is no light for us.

I find myself incapable of evaluating the work of Waldo Frank in the whole. I do not know whether it is sound, whether it has a significance on which one can rest as on something solid. With his power in detail I am strongly impressed; with his sympathetic insight into souls; with his imaginative force in conjuring up strange figures—persons and places—that are at once transparent and opaque, having the hard surface of material objects and the teasing lure of myths and symbols. But all that I can do in this study is to point out certain mechanical features of his technique.

He is more merciful than most "stream-of-consciousness" writers. When he wishes to introduce thoughts in the dramatic guise of speech, passing from the third person to the first, he generally indicates this transition by preceding the dramatic passage with a long dash, such as the French use to indicate the speeches in dialogue. Thus we have, distinguished by punctuation, narrative and observation from the principal's point of view, actual speech in quotation marks, and then the speech of thought or soliloquy, with its appropriate indication.

At times Mr. Frank carries his system of notation still farther. There are passages that are not so much ordinary thought, prose thought, as we may say, but something more purely emotional, welling up from the depths of personality. They involve what we may call a poetical definition of the character or the situation as he feels it. These too the author indicates with the long dash, but to these he feels impelled to give the distinguishing form of verse. There is one passage in "Rahab" in which are shown all together the principal characters: Fanny Luve, two of the loose women, her friends, the gambler Mangel, and the judge Mark. There comes upon them all a mood of self-recognition, like those so often shown by Mrs. Woolf in "The Waves"; and like her characters they engage in a mute dialogue of soliloquies. I cannot include it all, but a few excerpts will give a notion of its method if not its quality.

MANGEL:–

—I am made of filth. If I could stop hating myself!
I am a dirty Jew . . I hate Statt . . . He makes me
  feel—this . . . But who is he?
His body is straighter because he has no soul.
(There are times when I would love to kiss his body.)

—My soul is beautiful. My soul says to me:
You are a dirty Jew! . .
What is the use? One picks the smut from one's nose
But one's nose smells on, the smut comes back,
What is the use of having a beautiful soul?
No one tells Statt that he is a dirty Dutchman.

. . . .

SUSAN:–

—I ask myself no question.
O horror, O torrent of horror
If I asked a question.

—The mountainside
Is steep, is snow.
I mount, I mount.
I am erect; my shoulders and my feet
Freeze sharp.

—O the horror, O the torrent, O the flood
Down-pouring . .
If I asked a question.

To a large extent these soliloquies in verse represent latent or implicit thought rather than any of which the character is definitely conscious. And they serve to explain him better than he could possibly do himself. Such a use of them is even more striking in "Holiday." This is, in my opinion, the most successful of all Mr. Frank's novels, though it is clear enough why it has been neglected. In his pure estheticism, Mr. Frank offends too many prejudices, moral and social as well as esthetic. "Holiday" is a study of the psychology of lynching, and—deeper than that—the psychology of race attraction and repulsion. It is laid in a small gulf town, symbolically named Nazareth. There is of course a white Nazareth and a black Nazareth, and behind the two creatures who are the protagonists of this tragedy, are the two piteous groups of white and black people, strangely drawn to one another by the lure of diverse temperaments, and then inevitably set in opposition by fear and hatred.

In many respects the book is remarkable for its originality in technique. But I must confine myself to a single point. At a certain moment, out of a simple conversation between a girl and her father on the subject of negroes, there suddenly emerges a poetical dialogue between the white and the black races. The speech of white and black is doubly distinguished, that of the white race being in prose and in roman type, that of the blacks in verse and printed in italics. It is impossible to give this colloquy entire, but I shall try to choose the most significant passages.

World . . of Nazareth; worlds of Nazareth speaking:

> —I cannot forget you, Niggertown. Night and day you glower. Night and day you shout and laugh, you sing and sway and groan. Always there beside me, Niggertown. Beside my birthright, within my mind like a shadow alive.

—Whah is yo' sister, blossomin' Dixie lan'?
Whah is de sister ob yo' sun and rain?
Yo' sun am smilin' an' yo' rain weeps warm.

> —I walk on soil, and I need soil to live. But earth stays in its place. I plow earth, I scatter seed, I harvest. Upon the willing earth I place my house. . . . You are earth too: and like the earth I need you. Within you I must sow my food and upon you make my ways. Yet you stand up! You shout . . .

—When de sun goes down on Dixie lan'
Mah dusky love shines in de welcomin' night.
Her voice am cool as de melon [etc.]

. . . .

> —All the world's color: and I must hold my pride against the world. Pride is white. History is white. The Christ is white. Honor is white, and birthright. All else . . . color. The sky and sun and the stars, the trees and the thirsty soil: the eyes of my beloved and her lips . . . color, color, foe to my high whiteness. [Etc.]

—You-all don' count. Whah do you come in?
Ah kin raise co'n an' taters
Ah kin hitch mah mule
Ah kin still co'n likker
Ah kin love mah girl.
You-all don' count . . . Whah do you-all come in?

—Shouting, standing, rolling your hot eyes. Leave me be! Be earth! Don't break into my slumber and my dreams!

—You won' leave me be? [Etc.]
Come, blossomin' lan', come, lan' of love and dream
Le's look away fum de white stalkin' ghost.

—I see you everywhere. Like blood. Like earth. [Etc.]

—You won't leave me be?
What kin Ah do fo' you-all? [Etc.]

—My love hungers, I am spent. What's that to you? Get out! . . . Stay down!

—Whar are you? Why should I stay down?
O our village is singin' strong,
An' de crops is in,
An' de cotton's made,
An' de watermelon's ripe. [Etc.]

—I'll crush you! If you're color and love, watch my white hate. I'll hold you! If you are seed and fruit, watch my white drouth exalt the dry well and the blind eyes of my women!

Of the terrible social problem here involved Mr. Frank does not offer the least hint of a solution. His work must be judged on purely esthetic grounds. I will not try to put a value on it. But I do not see how we can fail to acknowledge the boldness and originality of his invention. He has found, for one of the most important features of American life, for a psychological fact of widest scope, a symbolic representation of vivid interest and power.

XXXIX

ABSTRACT COMPOSITION: DOS PASSOS

CERTAIN hard-boiled realists have a freedom in ordering the elements of their composition which corresponds to the poetic expressionism of writers like Mr. Frank and Mrs. Woolf. It lies not merely in the contrapuntal handling of passages from the lives of many unrelated persons (see Chapters XXXIII to XXXVIII) but in the apparently freakish insertion into these private chronicles of more general material which takes the place of philosophical comment and suggests the larger bearings of the history so baldly told. This material has the character (as in Joyce) of themes or motifs, and is often in the broadest sense poetic because of its symbolic correspondence with the plainly realistic portions. And the whole work has that character of abstract composition which makes us think so often in twentieth-century fiction of post-impressionist painting.

Thus in "Manhattan Transfer" the prose poems prefixed to the several chapters, while they are so often descriptive of aspects of the city and city life, serve a purpose far more important than setting. Their implications are more than physical, and, like the chapter headings, they have a reference far wider than the subject-matter of the individual chapters. One chapter is entitled "Metropolis," and the prelude begins: "There were Babylon and Nineveh; they were built of brick. Athens was gold marble columns. Rome was held up on broad arches of rubble." But the reader knows well that what matters is not the materials out of which the Babylons were built but the moral associations of the names and the reminder of how inevitably these cities fell victims to their own greed. One of the preludes deals with the red and green stop-go signals and the herded cars hurrying "towards the glow over the city." One of them is woven of many themes connected with the World War. The chapter entitled "Nicolodeon" is prefaced by an account of all the cheap pleasures purchasable by poor mortals for the price of a nickel. "Steamroller" has a description of how night comes down over the city and "crushes the fretwork of windows and lettered signs and chimneys and water-tanks and ventilators and fire-escapes and moldings and patterns and corrugations and eyes and hands and neckties into blue chunks, into black enormous blocks." The esthetic and the philosophical vision coalesce, and we realize how the great forces of nature deal alike with unorganized and organized matter.

Dos Passos had been reading his Sandburg with understanding, and knew how to give its full eloquence to each material aspect of our industrial life. The reader who remains unenlightened by the text of these stories cannot fail to gather from the commentaries a sufficient notion of the author's attitude toward the civilization he is portraying: an attitude bitter, ironic, tender, compassionate, and withal impregnated with an artist's fascinated passion for beauty. And all accomplished by means of statements as objective as they can be made out of verbs, nouns, and adjectives.

2

"The 42d Parallel" (1930) and "1919" (1932) are in some ways quite distinct in method. They are the first two of a projected series of novels intended to give a panoramic survey of American civilization in our time. The first one deals with the period between 1900 and our entrance into the war, the second (somewhat overlapping) covers the whole period of the war and down to Armistice Day 1919. In each of these novels, there are but five persons out of whose experiences the author has chosen to make up his representative picture. There are many other characters with whom these ten people come in contact, and some of the first five reappear in the second volume as middle-ground or background figures. But it is with these ten persons that we live in intimacy, seeing the rest of the world through their eyes. And for the ten principals we are given a much more detailed and consecutive history than for any of the characters in "Manhattan Transfer." The sections are in general much longer, and the doings of the character in question are followed from day to day, sometimes from year to year. So that we have the impression of a flowing undramatic narrative very different from the dot-and-dash system of the earlier book. It almost suggests the manner of the old-fashioned rambling novel before the advent of "dramatic" ideals.

But several features keep these books from having the aspect of the old-fashioned novel. One is the strict fidelity with which the author confines himself to the point of view of the character in question. So far as I have observed, this confinement is absolute within each section. And what makes it still more notable is the incomparable faithfulness with which the narrative is given, in each case, the tone of the character concerned, though without undue exaggeration of idiosyncrasy. The dominant characteristic of all these people is that they are just ordinary Americans, and the prevailing tone of the whole narrative is that of ordinary American speech and feeling.

In "The 42d Parallel" two of the characters are young men who go from place to place engaging in every variety of unskilled labor. Another is a stenographer coming from an ordinary middle-class family. Her brother, Joe Williams, appears as a leading character in "1919." He is just a boy who can't stand it at home and who, having deserted from the navy, drifts from job to job on merchant vessels. He has enough initiative and pull to get himself made a petty officer in the merchant marine; but otherwise he is a common sailor, concerned about his comforts and appetites, always getting into messes, and ineffectually aspiring to be better settled in life. With characters of this sort Dos Passos realizes that what is called for is a matter-of-fact style plausibly colored with current slang, a style broadly comparable to that of Hemingway or Callaghan.

Slightly higher in the social and cultural scale is Daughter, scatter-brained girl from Texas, who is looking for "life," and is finally killed in a crashing airplane while taking a ride with a drunken French aviator. The tone is set for her in the first sentence of her chronicle:

> The Trents lived in a house on Pleasant Avenue that was the finest street in Dallas that was the biggest and fastest growing town in Texas that was the biggest state in the Union and had the blackest soil and the whitest people and America was the greatest country in the world and Daughter was Dad's onlyest sweetest little girl.

Much more ambitious spirits are found among the people of these books. Such are Eleanor Stoddard and Eveline Hutchins, women of esthetic tastes with an eye to the main chance, who blossom out into interior decorators and end up with fat Red Cross jobs in Paris, occupying the most delicious apartments on the Quai de la Tournelle and collecting love-affairs and antique Italian painted panels. There is Richard Ellsworth Savage, a poor boy, who knows how to get in with the best set at Harvard, and manages to keep his pacifism from spoiling his prospects of promotion in the army. And, king of them all, is J. Ward Moorehouse, who rises fast in the business world, turns public-relations counselor with handsome offices in New York, and ends up as a Red Cross major, installed in the Hotel

Crillon, and sleekly collaborating with Mr. Wilson in the manufacture of the Versailles Treaty. At bottom these four people are all sentimentalists and snobs, and the matter-of-fact chronicle of their doings is discreetly colored with the tasty pink of their spiritual complexion.

Nothing displays the self-denying art of Mr. Dos Passos more eloquently than the rigor with which he has kept himself out of these records. Nowhere has he intruded to tell us what we should think about these people and the civilization they stand for. And yet it is perfectly clear what he thinks. And he has made it clear first of all by his choice of characters to represent his idea and by the plain chronicle of events which are in nowise unusual. Eloquent enough are the lives of common men who, with nothing to guide them, flounder stupidly in the morass of unorganized society. But most eloquent are the careers of the clever, the hard-headed sentimentalists, who know how to take advantage of the current "ideals" and feather their nests with them. The war, as it touched the fighting-men, was long since "done" by Dos Passos in "Three Soldiers" (1921). But not even that picture can compare with "1919" for the ghastly light thrown on what we may call the marginal aspects of war. For most of these people the war was simply one grand picnic, a "show" seen from box seats, a chance to cut loose from the moral restraints of "back home," and then, over and above all that, a good living and a means of making their way in the world. And even more ghastly than the war was the peace, with soft-voiced public-relations counselors conferring with Standard Oil men over the proper disposition of the world's resources.

There is one character with whom we are able to sympathize completely, although he is treated in the same objective, matter-of-fact way as the rest. That is Ben Compton, who makes his entry toward the end of "1919." He is a Jew, "who always said he wasn't a Jew he was an American because he'd been born in Brooklyn and lived at 2531 25th Avenue in Flatbush and they owned their own home." This young man early espouses the cause of the working-class, takes part in many strikes, gets beaten up with the wobblies at Everett, declares himself a conscientious objector, and is finally sent down to Atlanta for ten years for taking part in a meeting in sympathy with the Soviet Government. He is the only one of the leading characters who has devoted himself to any cause more unselfish than the gratification of his own appetites.

3

Dos Passos was evidently determined to stick to plain objective statement of what went on in the lives of his ten characters. But he had in these books an intention no less comprehensive in its scope than in "Manhattan Transfer." And he hit upon three different devices for enlarging the reference of his chronicle.

One of these is called the Camera Eye. It consists of forty-odd short pieces describing moments in the life of a growing boy and then the same boy grown and serving in the Red Cross during the war. There are many suggestions that this boy and man was the author himself. In "The 42d Parallel" he is seen traveling abroad, at school in England, on a river steamer in Chesapeake Bay, going to church, at the university ("four years under the ether cone"). In "1919" he is shown in a great many places during his service in France. Child or man, he sees everything and understands nothing; and these pieces are likely to be a jumble of impressions without logical or rhetorical organization. It is in the Camera Eye that one traces the influence of Joyce and the "stream-of-consciousness" system of notation. Perhaps by the Camera Eye, Mr. Dos Passos wishes to indicate a way of seeing things directly or naïvely before the process of interpretation and elimination has intervened to give a semblance of order to what is seen and fit it all into a consistent and idealistic view of life.

And that is, indeed, the first impression received from these dazzling, bewildering cubist compositions, in which fragments of so many disparate objects are set side by side, often in the same sentence, often with no punctuation of any kind. One has the blood and filth and stupidity of war in the same picture with the loveliest impressions of natural beauty, and with historical associations of the highest dignity. One has reminders of the gross material stakes involved in the war, along with echoes of Milton and Patrick Henry. At first all seems disorder and confusion of mind. And then one realizes that what we have, actually, is a cry for order in a world of confusion, and that each one of these pictures is cunningly composed, according to the best principles of balance, contrast, and proportion, so as to render in terms of art the disgust and loathing of a sensitive spirit faced with the actuality of a war-crazed world. Not every writer could be trusted with the liberties of this method. But I am inclined to think that among these sketches will be found many of the firmest and most glowing pages in the whole work of this extraordinary writer.

The second of the author's devices for enlarging the reference consists in a series of sketches of men prominent in the United States during the period covered. Such are, in "The 42d Parallel," the Socialist leader Debs, the progressive La Follette, the spellbinder Bryan, and the inventors Edison, Steinmetz, Burbank. In "1919" are included Jack Reed, the "playboy" of the Russian Revolution, the liberal or radical writers Randolph Bourne and Paxton Hibben, President Wilson, and the Morgans, four generations of bankers and financiers. It will be obvious how, by his particular "slant" on each one of these head-liners, the author can suggest the tone of his personal commentary on the civilization they represent.

Thus Mr. Dos Passos features the shallowness and insincerity of the liberalism typified by Bryan and the tragic futility of that typified by Wilson. Of writers on social themes the one who has his most hearty admiration is, apparently, Randolph Bourne, the voice of one crying in the wilderness. Of men of action, the two who, by their fighting spirit and their manner of death, arouse the strongest feeling in the reader are two organizers of the I.W.W.—Joe Hill, who was stood up against the jail wall in Salt Lake City, and Wesley Everest, logger, who was lynched at Centralia, after suffering abominable mutilations. Such were the martyrs of the proletarian faith. The book ends with an account of the Washington ceremony in memory of the Unknown Soldier. It is done in somewhat the manner and spirit of Sandburg's magnificent poem on the same subject, "And So To-Day." These two pieces are in themselves interesting examples of abstract composition. And they both render forcefully the commentary of disillusioned America on the false sentiment associated with American militarism.

Dos Passos' third device is named from a feature of the moving-pictures, "Newsreel." There are some forty of these newsreels scattered through the two books. They are made up of newspaper head-lines, stock-market reports, fragments of popular songs, etc. They serve the purpose, to begin with, of indicating the progress of time with their reference to such events as the Boer War, Roosevelt's bolt from the Republican party, the assassination of Jaurès, the Armistice. But, what is much more important, by their jumble of miscellaneous news items they suggest the mentality which produces and is fostered by the newspaper, that epitome of our civilization. Any reader who is puzzled by the way in which news of every conceivable type is all run together in paragraphs without punctuation, and alternated with head-lines in every degree of bold type, need only stop to consider his own manner of reading the daily paper—or at any rate the paper itself, with its almost total want of classification of news, and with its relative emphasis on scandal, disasters, popular amusements, personalities, and political hot air.

But there is more to it than this. Mr. Malcolm Cowley, in a significant and highly favorable review of "1919," remarks that, "in themselves, judged as writing," these newsreels "are not successful." This may be true. But we can hardly judge them in themselves, as pieces of writing, without regard for the cumulative effect they have as an oblique commentary on the narrative. There are certain sinister notes, hardly remarked at first, which make themselves heard more and more insistently as the work proceeds, till finally, like the leitmotivs of Wagnerian opera, they begin to take strong possession of us. And they are all the more impressive in that, as they are combined with other notes, they have distinctly the character of dissonances.

Along with the innocent and frivolous songs of the service men, and the ordinary news from the war and from home, there is the recurrent reference to industries which are benefiting by the war:

HAWAIIAN SUGAR CONTROL LOST BY THE GERMANS, FINISHED STEEL MOVES RATHER MORE FREELY, FERTILIZER INDUSTRY STIMULATED BY WAR, AFTER-WAR PLANS OF ÆTNA EXPLOSIVES, CRUCIBLE STEEL CONTINUES TO LEAD MARKET.

And then, with the Armistice, as the Internationale begins to displace the war songs, we hear more and more of Polish pogroms, of the Japanese menace, of Burleson censorship, and of the violent and forceful putting down of strikes and labor organizations. As the book progresses, the news of the day begins to be less chaotic and bewildering. To a musing reader a consistent thread of meaning begins to run through the head-lines of a single day:

SAYS U. S. MUST HAVE WORLD'S GREATEST FLEET, CANADIANS RIOT IN BRITISH CAMP, GAINS RUN HIGH IN WALL STREET, NE SOYONS PAS LES DUPES DU TRAVESTI BOLCHEVISTE, STRIKERS MENACE COMPLETE TIEUP OF NEW YORK CITY, CALIFORNIA JURY QUICKLY RENDERS VERDICT AGAINST SACRAMENTO WORKERS, BOLSHEVISM READY TO COLLAPSE SAYS ESCAPED GENERAL, BRITISH TRY HARD TO KEEP PROMISE TO HANG KAISER.

These separate items begin to range themselves in a meaningful pattern like the pieces of a puzzle-picture. Certain paragraphs of fragmentary news items begin to stand out as epitomizing the saddest ironies of our social and spiritual life.

. . . eleven men were killed and twenty-three injured, some of them seriously as the result of an explosion of fulminate of mercury in the priming unit of one of the cap works of the E. I. duPont de Nemours Powder Company; in the evening Mrs. Wilson released carrier pigeons . . . *and through it all how fine the spirit of the nation was, what unity of purpose what untiring zeal what elevation of purpose ran through all its splendid display of strength, its untiring accomplishment. I have said that those of us who stayed at home to do the work of organization and supply would always wish we had been with the men we sustained by our labour, but we can never be ashamed* . . . in the dining room music was furnished by a quartet of sailors.

4

So there we have three special thematic devices by which Dos Passos gives to his narrative a larger reference than could be had in the mere chronicle of private lives. Between each section of straight narrative are inserted anywhere from one to four of these briefer commentaries: Camera Eye, Newsreel, sketch of prominent citizen. The effect is to keep one perpetually alive to the wider issues, the broad social background on which the few obscure persons play their parts. Here again we have the fondness for the breadthwise cutting, the composite view. And we have also the disposition to build up a composition out of elements which, however unrelated they may at first appear, are found to have their cunningly related correspondences and to result in the end in significant pattern.

And it will now be clear how well this technique goes with the disposition to regard the novelist's subject as the entire social organism. The author's first concern is no longer with individuals, with their precious moral problems to be met, their precious sentiments to be indulged. His first concern is with that Leviathan, society, striving weakly to adjust itself to the industrial conditions of the new world, more or less blindly struggling forward to the creation of a group consciousness and a group will. It is an unusual combination in one writer, so strong a social significance and so great a command of his craft. And it is this combination which makes Dos Passos one of the most important novelists now writing in English.

XL

ABSTRACT COMPOSITION: DÖBLIN

AN INTERESTING example of abstract composition in a German novel is Alfred Döblin's "Alexanderplatz Berlin" (1930, edition in English 1931). Döblin was already well known as an exponent of expressionism (for example, his "Berge, Meere und Giganten," 1924) before the writing of "Alexanderplatz." The importance of this later book for German readers I am unable to gage; nor do I feel ready to express an opinion on its profundity as a social and psychological document. It is certainly an interesting story.

It has for its theme the moral rehabilitation of a poor, well-meaning fellow who has served his term in prison for a crime of violence. This is a difficult process, owing to the psychological effect of his being an ex-convict and to the milieu in which he has to work out his salvation. The author has taken advantage of the literary vogue of the gangster, and the widespread interest in lives of criminals and others sunk below the level of bourgeois society. He has a genial and breezy manner, which reminds one in some respects of Jean-Paul Richter. There are also suggestions of both Hugo and Dostoevski. The main interest for us in this story is the interesting and original use Döblin has made of suggestions taken from Joyce.

To begin with, he has gone to a great deal of pains to make his book more than the private history of Franz Biberkopf, his hero. Wherever occasion offers, he has introduced general views of the social fabric in which the career of Biberkopf is but one obscure strand. At various points in the story we come upon passages standing forth distinct like outcroppings of rock at an angle found along river banks and giving a notion of geological history. Only, in "Alexanderplatz" it is the present social organism, the stratum of life known as Berlin, where Franz Biberkopf lies embedded like a living fossil, of which the author wishes to give us a representative exhibit.

There is a whole section entitled "A Handful of Men around the Alex" in which he makes a sort of inventory of human life in the neighborhood of this great center of business where Biberkopf has taken to selling newspapers. We have a flying view of operations for building the subway, of the various shops, insurance companies, detective agencies, sundry legal business of a cheap lawyer; of the people who live on the second, third, and fourth floors—their occupations, diseases, domestic relations, amusements, comforts, and discomforts. There are newsreels reminding one of Dos Passos, with a lively and detailed account of murders, street-car disasters, stock-market conditions, jail-breakings, the invasion of the market by American automobiles, and of comic operas being performed at neighborhood theaters. As much is made of street-car lines as by Joyce in "Ulysses," and more than once the author steps off a car with some person and follows him upon his most private errands, with the humane curiosity of a Virginia Woolf, but with a more realistic imagination for the possibilities of the case.

There is other thematic material of a more strictly symbolic order. Such is the detailed and lively account of the Berlin slaughter-houses. (Let all squeamish readers skip.) There is no effort to relate these passages to the story of Franz Biberkopf. The author merely makes a matter-of-fact statement on the necessary dealing with calves and pigs whose flesh is to be eaten. But no one can miss the implied application to the dealings of fate with poor human beings like our hero.

There is one device much used by Joyce and Dos Passos of which Döblin is fond. That is the accompaniment of his narrative with snatches of popular songs and ballads. We all know the obsession of these cheap and sentimental tunes, how they beat out the rhythm of our hectic and driven lives, seeming like the very beat of our pulse, the jerking of our tired nerves, the clack-clack of the belted chain that runs the machine to which we are strapped. Franz Biberkopf is a tuneful German. He celebrates his release from prison by singing "The Watch on the Rhine." As the story goes forward his thoughts are more and more likely to be involved with music-hall songs. They thrust themselves into the midst of conversations real or imaginary—*Ich küsse Ihre Hand, Madame.* Whatever he is thinking, whatever happens to him, tends to fall into rhyme and meter and the tawdry rhetoric of romantic ballads.

> All his crying, all his protests, all his rage was idle prating, evidence was dead against him, and the chains for him were waiting. Though the judges were mistaken (the chase, the pursuit, the damned chase) when his sentence they had spoken (how those damned hounds chased me), what availed his guiltless conscience, since his honor's shield was broken. Man, oh fellow-man, he whimpered, why oppress, why ruin me, did I do you injury? (It goes on, you can't see your way out. And on and on, you run, you can't run fast enough, you can just do the best you can.)

One can imagine the effectiveness, in the native German, of this device for rendering the feverish and ever accelerating rhythm of life for Franz Biberkopf.

One ballad keeps recurring in the latter half of the story. That is the old German ballad of "The Dance of Death." "There is a mower death yclept. Has power which the Lord hath kept. When he 'gins his scythe to whet, keener it grows and keener yet." It goes well with the macabre effect of this typical German work.

Another related set of themes is taken from the Bible.

At more and more frequent intervals, as the story progresses, we find inserted in the realistic narrative quotations from Jeremiah and the Apocalypse, imaginary conversations between Job and Satan, between Abraham and Isaac. The literal quotations from Scripture may be given in the language of our great English version, and are consequently, in the translation of the German work, the most effective of all these symbolic devices.

> So I returned and considered all the oppressions that are done under the sun; and behold the tears of such as were oppressed and they had no comforter; and on the side of the oppressors there was power; but they had no comforter. Wherefore I praised the dead which are already dead.
>
> The dead I praised. To everything a season; a time to rend, and a time to sew, a time to keep, and time to cast away. I praised the dead who lie sleeping beneath the trees.

In basic conception, "Alexanderplatz" derives from the German school of expressionism by virtue of its primary concern with the spiritual life of Franz Biberkopf, and its quasi-religious doctrine of regeneration through suffering. Formally, the modernism (or expressionism) of his method, what makes him more akin to Joyce than to Hugo, is the want of explicit application of the general thematic material to the case of Biberkopf, and the seemingly freakish way in which it is intruded into the midst of his story. There are other features more reminiscent of Dostoevski, Wassermann, and Gide, such as the angels who, at one point, walk beside the hero and talk with him. But in the main this is felt to be a strictly realistic work. And the expressionism (in the broad formal sense) consists in the superposition of the general themes upon the private history of Biberkopf, their interweaving with it. It is these themes, apparently unrelated to it but actually making a spiritual commentary on it, which furnish the fourth dimension for this highly modernistic portrait of a man.

XLI

STREAM-OF-CONSCIOUSNESS

THE type of narrative to which the term, "stream-of-consciousness," applies, has its origin in English in the novels of Dorothy Richardson and Joyce, and has, perhaps, its best exemplification in them. Mr. Joyce himself has pointed out that in a novel by Edouard Dujardin, "Les Lauriers sont coupés," published thirty years before "Ulysses," there is a consistent use of the *monologue intérieur*. I have suggested how Browning and Carlyle anticipated many of the peculiarities of this method, and how Waldo Frank was using features of it contemporaneously with Joyce.

In the followers of Joyce and Miss Richardson, it is probably Mrs. Woolf who makes the most frequent use of the stream-of-consciousness method, especially in "Mrs. Dalloway" and "To the Lighthouse." The method is consistently followed by Valéry Larbaud in his "Amants, heureux amants" (1923) and by Conrad Aiken in his "Blue Voyage" (1927). Dos Passos and Döblin make occasional use of it in passages that seem to call for it. It crops out from time to time in such very different work as Thomas Wolfe's "Look Homeward, Angel" and Nathan Asch's "Pay Day" (both 1930). It is quite consistently used by William Faulkner through the first half of "The Sound and the Fury" (1929), and more intermittently in "As I Lay Dying" (1930). Sherwood Anderson has been influenced by this method in "Dark Laughter"; and even Dreiser has suggestions of it—see Chapters XLVI and XLVII of "The American Tragedy."

It is an infection to which any one is liable; almost any one may sooner or later manifest mild symptoms of this disease. It is probable that it has reached its climax, and that more classical methods of narration will prevail. But the stream-of-consciousness epidemic will have left its stamp upon fiction in English. It represents an enlargement of technical procedures which is too precious to be altogether abandoned.

I have pointed out that the stream-of-consciousness type of narrative is a new and radical development from the subjectivism of the well-made novel. Its defining feature is exploitation of the element of incoherence in our conscious process. This incoherence characterizes both our normal and our abnormal states of mind. The natural association of ideas is extremely freakish. Our psyche is such an imperfectly integrated bundle of memories, sensations, and impulses, that, unless sternly controlled by some dominating motive it is likely to be at the mercy of every stray wind of suggestion.

It is our deliberate attention, called into play by the will to action, that brings order into this chaos. Consciously or unconsciously, we choose to ignore, to forget ninety-nine per cent of all that is actually going on within us. This applies to those of us who are strong and simple, who have the determination and the steadiness of will to bring all our energies to bear upon a definite line of action. But the moment we relax, the moment we let go control of our will and our attention, we fall back into the welter, the chaos of our natural complicated selves.

The novel has generally concerned itself with that which most interests men, action; and the subjective moments are such as bear upon a definite line of conduct. In our day an extraordinary amount of interest has been shown in what we may call passive states of mind, states undirected by what Arnold terms "our sense for conduct." I have pointed out how little of the "sense for conduct" appears in the histories of Miriam Henderson, Leopold Bloom, and Stephen Dedalus, who were all fairly normal people, though leaning strongly toward the "introvert." In their followers, it is remarkable how regularly the stream-of-consciousness technique is applied to abnormal people, or to people temporarily fallen into a state of abnormal passiveness to sensation, in which, again, the association of ideas is not directed and controlled by a "sense for conduct."

The hero of Mr. Aiken's "Blue Voyage" is a man consciously suffering from a "schism in his nature," a writer who does not believe in literature, an erotomaniac, possibly a victim of "schizophrenia"—all the result, he suggests, of certain traumatic experiences in his early childhood. He is traveling second cabin, and has been cut by the woman he loves, the Cynthia of his better nature, who is a first-cabin snob. This serves to aggravate his chronic "inferiority complex," and produces an obstinate state of insomnia—a state in which he cannot stop his mind and imagination from working, cannot keep them in any kind of order. The result is, very naturally, a jumble of fact and fancy, of present physical sensations, memories of his father, of childhood, of love-affairs. Along with the crying of a baby in a neighboring cabin, with the ship's bells sounding the watches of the night, with scraps of poetry, parodies and puns, with the effort to put himself to sleep by counting, there is woven a long imaginary conversation with Cynthia, in which he explains himself, argues with her over the subject of love, and she replies to him, in terms of reproach and scorn; until at last his thoughts and images grow more and more incoherent and "pied" as he loses consciousness and falls asleep.

In Mr. Asch's "Pay Day" the character who is followed through a night of cheap dissipation is a weak brother, a pimply young clerk with an inferiority complex and a bad conscience. The stream-of-consciousness technique shows itself chiefly in a penchant for imaginary disputes between himself and himself, and for dream phantasies thrusting into the midst of his actual experience with an air of equal reality. It is only when he gets good and drunk that the narrative becomes typical of this manner. He is riding in a taxi with several other roisterers, and the fragments of conversation of the various passengers and the taxi-driver are "pied" up in a manner suggestive of the drunken state.

The broken bits of conversation appear rather frequently in contemporary novels. In "Jacob's Room" they are meant to suggest the meaningless babble of "society" as it comes to Jacob's ears. In "Blue Voyage" the medley of smoking-room talk is woven into Demarest's stream of consciousness, along with his own self-searchings, reminiscence, bits from the ship's regulations, and fragments of poetry and popular song. The chapter ends with a dialogue between Demarest and Demarest Two-prime, the latter being one part of his split personality come to give advice to another.

In Döblin's "Alexanderplatz" the composite pictures of Berlin and the contrapuntal themes, like those taken from the Bible, need not be considered strictly as belonging to the stream of consciousness of Franz Biberkopf, though they do affect its coloring and tone. The popular tunes and the ballad rhymes are part and parcel of it; Biberkopf is much given to carrying on dialogues with himself; the "you" and the "I" and the "he" are likely to alternate; the narrative is often swift and elliptical; often falls into a garrulous burlesque manner suggesting Joyce. On the whole, however, there is nothing difficult about this narrative, nothing to make the reader knit his brows. The one place that the stream of consciousness becomes markedly incoherent is where Biberkopf, under the terrible strain of his driven life, goes temporarily out of his head.

Evelyn Scott, with all her insistence on subjective states,

makes very sparing use of the stream-of-consciousness technique. The most striking case is that of a Southern girl in a half-crazed condition just before she plunges a bread-knife into the heart of a Yankee soldier. Similarly, in Mr. Dreiser's "American Tragedy" the chapters which I have mentioned as showing the influence of this technique are those in which Clyde Griffiths is being driven by some power stronger than himself to the murder of his girl.

2

In "The Sound and the Fury" Mr. Faulkner introduces us to a degenerate Southern family, some of whom are sane and mean, or sane and weak; and of the others, one is an imbecile and one is the victim of a suicidal mania. The first two sections, occupying a little over half the book, are devoted to the imbecile and the suicide; and it is here that the author makes his highly original and decidedly bewildering use of the stream-of-consciousness technique.

One day of the imbecile's life is recorded. He is thirty-three years old, but he has retained the mentality of a child of five, and he has so little control of his mental processes that any slightest suggestion will take him back to some earlier period of his life, and he will be living past days over again as if they were here and now. Throughout some ninety pages the record keeps skipping back and forth between this April 7, 1928, and a considerable number of earlier times. The mentality of the imbecile being identical for all these different times, it is often difficult to tell what period of his life is being presented. The only indication given by the author of the shift from one to another is the use of italics at the point of shift. Many characters make their appearance in the several periods, brothers and sister, father and mother, negroes young and old; and it is only what they do that lets us know what relation they bear to Maury. And then, to make confusion worse confounded, it turns out that, for superstitious reasons, Maury's parents have changed his name to Benjamin, so that he is referred to now by one name, now by another. Besides which, there are two characters of different sexes named Quentin, one a brother, and one a niece of Benjy.

A variant of this method is used for the second section, recording a day in the life of Quentin, the suicide, the brother who was sent to Harvard—a day in Massachusetts into which intrude enormous broken fragments of the earlier life of Quentin in Mississippi. Mr. Faulkner has here made an extremely ingenious use of narrative devices derived from Joyce, which I cannot stop to describe in detail. In the rest of the book the method departs less from the normal.

In Mr. Faulkner's next novel, "As I Lay Dying," the story is told in separate snatches by fifteen different people, representing so many different facets of this lurid gem. It has to do with the much delayed burial of a woman by the members of her family. They are poor farmer folk, ignorant, shiftless, "misfortunate" creatures, terribly warped by poverty and privation, in whom the primary traits of human nature appear in their essential starkness. What redeems this horrible story is its extraordinary truthfulness and the extraordinary skill in the telling. These bits of narrative are really soliloquy, narrative recited by the character to himself as audience. The language itself is a marvel in the reproduction of a local idiom.

But what is more remarkable than the language is the psychology—the reflection in these naïve records of the way the mind works for largely instinctive beings, sunk deep as they are in the decaying humus of an ancient culture. It is the author's desire to keep his hands off, not to smooth down these sharp, lifelike contours, which produces the frequent effect of incoherence, or disorder, in these partial records, suggesting the stream-of-consciousness technique.

Here again, it is in the childlike or the disordered mind that the effect is most marked. One of these characters is a very young boy, with curious ideas of death and of what has become of his coffined mother; and another is a man touched by insanity and dowered with something like second sight. It is mainly in the pieces ascribed to these two brothers that the author resorts to his device of using italics to indicate abrupt departures from the present time or the immediate subject. If a technique is to be judged by its results, then one cannot question the rightness of this technique in this novel.

In "Sanctuary" and his book of tales, "These 13" (both 1931), while they show certain modernistic features which would be worth noting if time allowed, Mr. Faulkner has not chosen to make any marked use of the stream-of-consciousness technique. And this may be a significant fact. The relative popularity of this writer is a strange phenomenon, so almost unbearably painful is his subject-matter. But he is one of the greatest literary talents of our day. "The Sound and the Fury" and "As I Lay Dying" are distinguished books; but so are "Sanctuary" and "These 13." If Mr. Faulkner's abandonment of the stream-of-consciousness technique is permanent, it is a notable sign of the times.

3

Dos Passos gives us on the whole a very objective narrative within the separate pieces of which his discontinuous compositions are made up. Such use as he makes of the stream-of-consciousness technique—mainly in "Manhattan Transfer" and in the Camera Eye of the later books—seems highly appropriate to the general razzle-dazzle of our confused and mechanical existence, and causes little difficulty to an interested reader. In his work, again, we observe how this element becomes more marked on occasions where the character has been thrown into a state of mental confusion or unusual strain. Such is the drunken state of Stan Emery which leads to his setting himself on fire. Such are certain moments of Bud Korpenning haunted by the fear of detectives.

Again we have a jumble of "wild and whirling words" when Jimmy Herf comes out of the Pulitzer Building after an all-night shift, tired out, thoroughly discouraged over his married life, but a free man, jubilant at the thought of having thrown up his job as a newspaper reporter. Words are what ails him, the obsession of words on the printed page, painted on signs, on price-tags in store windows—everywhere cheap and lying words. And his impressions on this sunlit day in spring are a farrago of words from advertisements and newspaper items, more or less run together and confused in a manner suitable to their own emptiness and his state of nerves.

Spring rich in gluten. . . . Chockful of golden richness, delight in every bite, THE DADDY OF THEM ALL, spring rich in gluten. Nobody can buy better bread than PRINCE ALBERT. Wrought steel, monel, copper, nickel, wrought iron. *All the world loves natural beauty.* LOVE'S BARGAIN that suit at Gumpel's best value in town. Keep that schoolgirl complexion. . . . JOE KISS, starting, lighting, ignition and generators.

. . . .

Express service meets the demands of spring. O God to meet the demands of spring. No tins, no sir, but there's rich quality in every mellow pipeful. . . . SOCONY. One taste tells more than a million words. The yellow pencil with the red band. Than a million words, than a million words. "All right hand over that million. . . . Keep him covered Ben." The Yonkers gang left him for dead on a bench in the Park. They stuck him up, but all they got was a million words. . . . "But Jimps I'm so tired of booktalk and the proletariat, can't you understand?"

Jimmy sits on a bench in Washington Square and muses on the passing of his twenties. He has a vision of newspaper items giving a nonsensical account of the trial of these twenties before Judge Merivale—that is, before his uncle, the business man, who disapproves of Jimmy's unpractical life. His twenties are all convicted and condemned to deportation as bad citizens. So his fancy runs riot. "And as I sit here, thought Jimmy Herf, print itches like a rash inside me. I sit here pockmarked with print."

Fantasy, or day-dream, is a recurring feature of "Manhattan Transfer" as it is of "Ulysses." The characters are forever taking flight from the pedestrian actuality into some vision of ideal performance. Jimmy as a child, on his way to the candy-store, imagines himself on roller-skates, shooting bandits with an automatic gun. Poor cautious little Ed Thatcher, public accountant, imagines himself taking a plunge in the stock-market and swaggering a millionaire. James Merivale, the hard-boiled banker, imagines himself making a flowery speech, full of the highest sentiments, at a dinner of the American Bankers Association. In each case the vision has the vividness of an hallucination; the imaginary is as real as the actual.

4

This is not, of course, a new thing in fiction. The peculiarity of the new method is rhetorical. It lies in the author's neglect to indicate where the actual leaves off and the imaginary begins. The same thing applies to passages of retrospect and reminiscence thrust into the midst of present experience, to dialogue carried on by the character with himself, and in general to the thousand and one matters to which he makes allusion in his mental comment on the present scene. Times, places, persons, moods are more or less interchangeable, and a cross-section of the character's thoughts is like a view of the earth's strata exposed by a geologic fault.

A more enlightening analogy is perhaps that of the moving picture, especially the sort cultivated in Germany, France, and Russia, with its generous use of cut-back, of symbolic themes, of dissolving views, all meant to give the picture a wider and richer significance than that of a mere story told in chronological sequence. It is probable that the moving picture has had a very strong influence on the stream-of-consciousness technique. And where this technique fails to be effective in the long run, we shall doubtless be able to say: Such and such a method is not practicable for word-pictures, however practicable it may be for pictures taken on a photographic plate.

Other features of the stream-of-consciousness have their origin perhaps in imagist poetry, in some of the many schools of French poetry which marked the period between symbolism and the war, in Dada and later French schools, or even perhaps in German expressionistic poetry. The theorists of expressionism explain that poets of this school proceed on the principle of putting together not so much sentences as words, which are meant to make their appeal directly to the imagination, and which, accordingly, often seem to be wanting in strict logical connection. The aim is to use words in their original picturesque (imagistic) sense, without punctilious regard for grammatical conventions or even for the distinction between parts of speech; verbs, for example, being freely interchangeable with nouns where it will serve the writer's purpose. It goes without saying that, while most of the German poetry of this school has a marked rhythmical effect, a very large part of it is free verse—thought and emotion shaping for themselves such forms as they require.

In all these free-verse movements—in German, French, and English—there is the same impulse to get rid of the excess baggage of formal thought and traditional measured form, to find a more direct expression for the poet's temperament. And in pursuance of this aim, the poets were inventing a kind of imaginative shorthand, which was, in some cases, decidedly effective, but which generally puzzled readers who came upon it unprepared.

What concerns us here is that in the novel the same movement has been going on, stimulated perhaps by the example of the poets, but essentially expressing the same time-spirit. The main difference is that with the poets the new shorthand was a means for expressing themselves, while in the novel it was so largely a device for dramatizing the consciousness of the characters. It did not stop there, to be sure, and traces of it may be found in narrative of the most purely objective kind. Still, its most characteristic use has been in books and passages devoted to the stream-of-consciousness. Certain of the peculiar features of the technique I will briefly indicate.

There is, for example, the tendency to violate accepted conventions in reporting physical facts. Amy Lowell in "The Taxi" has her lover say:

> Streets coming fast,
> One after the other,
> Wedge you away from me.

It has been the custom for a person in a vehicle to think of himself as moving while the streets are stationary. But that is a convention of thinking. It depends on the point of view. It is not the senses that tell us the taxi is moving and the street standing still. And the poets, who wish to freshen up our sense of life by bringing us back to the primary facts of sensation, have taken to giving, where they see fit, a different description of the movement of two bodies which are changing position relatively to each other. They began doing this before Einstein became a household word. One of them was the Italian-French futurist, Marinetti.

And so we are not surprised when we read in Dos Passos: "He looked out through the window. The street stood up on end. A hookandladder and a fire engine were climbing it licketysplit . . ." Or when we read in Frank: "—Here is the Block. Endless long.—How can my feet, pushing little fragments of the snowfull Block, push it behind me? Feet push . . . Feet push, behind, little bits of the Block." And this is but one out of dozens of ways in which poets and writers of fiction in our time have ignored the popular conventions in the statement of facts optical, physical, and psychological. And all, of course, for the sake of greater freshness, intimacy, and immediacy of effect.

Another feature of the stream-of-consciousness may perhaps be traced to certain of the symbolist poets like Tristan Corbière and Jules Laforgue. This is the love of dissonances, of sudden changes in tone from the elevated and poetical to the familiar and ironic. It shows itself, for one thing, in the novel, in the introduction of lines of noble or sentimental verse into passages in which they can only serve for sardonic commentary on the meanness and prosiness of ordinary experience. Sometimes the shriek of dissonance is produced by a burlesque distortion of the noble line. In Demarest's fantastic visions between sleep and waking, he sees old Smith, as a satyr, pursued among tombstones by a skull-faced creature, evidently bent on punishing him for his fondness for chorus-girls. "He is felled like an ox. To what green altar, oh mysterious priest? And all his crispy flanks in garlic drest." Smith is here doubtless a sort of dream-proxy for Demarest himself, thus sacrificed and made ridiculous, in a parody of Keats.

This may easily become a mechanical trick and grow tiresome. Discreetly used, it may be very effective. And it is clear how well it expresses that sense of futility, of the tragic divorce between the ideal and the actual, which is a dominant note of English fiction and American poetry since the war, as it was a dominant note of French poetry before the war. In America too, even before the war, Mr. Eliot was making a most effective use of this mingling of tones, à la Jules Laforgue, this pointing of the mean and the futile with allusions to the fine and the classic; for example, in "Sweeney among the Nightingales" and "Portrait of a Lady." In "The Waste Land" he has erected it into a system. And the same tendency is much in evidence in the poetry of Mr. Aiken, of E. E. Cummings, Wallace Stevens, John Crowe Ransom and still others, some of them fine poets.

Among the many other features of the stream-of-consciousness technique, I will briefly mention two. One is the trick of taking words to pieces and reassembling parts from several words to make up a combination often significant in a nonsensical way, reminding one of "Alice in Wonderland." Thus, in "Work in Progress," a character under the influence of drink is referred to as talking *alcoherently*.

Another is the closely related trick of leaving the words intact but combining them in sentences, paragraphs, and chapters which have but the remotest correspondence to the ordered logic of practical, or rational, thought. This means following the underground associations of ideas straight over into dreamland and delirium. In this, Mr. Joyce has doubtless been somewhat inspired by the amusing, amazing, and sometimes significant performances of Gertrude Stein, in "Tender Buttons" (1914) and "Geography and Plays" (1922). Let it be noted in passing that Miss Stein's novel "The Making of Americans" (1926) is a highly original and worth-while piece of work, in which very little use is made of this riddling method. The device mentioned is much used by Joyce in "Ulysses," and is a main principle of composition in his "Work in Progress," which passes altogether in dreamland, and is meant to represent the manner of associating ideas in the passive state of sleep.

The followers of Joyce make but moderate use of either of these tricks, and their main significance in our discussion is to illustrate the point with which we began. The stream-of-consciousness technique is almost invariably applied to persons of an extremely "introverted" type, to neurotics and those of unbalanced mind, or to occasional states of mind of normal individuals bordering on obsession or delirium: states of mind in which the consciousness is given over to the chaotic play of sensations and associations, undirected by the normal will to rational conduct. And that, I believe, indicates the limits within which this technique is likely to be used in the future.

XLII

THE CULT OF THE SIMPLE

As one looks about among recent writers of promise in the effort to distinguish significant movements, what most strikes one is what I shall call the cult of the simple. The best examples of what I have in mind are the stories of Ernest Hemingway—his books of tales "In Our Time" (1925) and "Men without Women" (1927), his novels "The Sun Also Rises" (1926) and "A Farewell to Arms" (1929); the novels of W. R. Burnett "Little Cæsar" (1929) and "Iron Man" (1930); the tales of Morley Callaghan, "A Native Argosy (1929), and his novels "Strange Fugitive" (1928) and "It's Never Over" (1930); Edward Dahlberg's "Bottom Dogs" (1930); the tales of Erskine Caldwell, "American Earth" (1931), and his novel "Tobacco Road" (1932).

Each one of these writers has his own marked personality, and one can distinguish minor variations in their narrative methods. But by contrast with the regular old-fashioned novel, with the well-made novel, or with the expressionistic novel, their work stands out as having certain common features. In some respects they have points of kinship with Dos Passos, with William Faulkner, with James Gould Cozzens. But their method is much simpler and less modernistic than that of Dos Passos and Faulkner, and less intellectual than that of Faulkner and Cozzens, whose wide range of vocabulary alone sets them in another class. Mr. Cozzens, in his very interesting novels "The Son of Perdition" (1929) and "S. S. San Pedro" (1931), has a strong suggestion of Conrad in subject-matter and the interpretation of character, as well as in more mechanical aspects of technique. And no one would think of associating Conrad with any cult of the simple.

In certain respects the men I am considering reflect prevailing tendencies in present-day fiction. The author is kept as much as possible in the background, except in cases where the author is identical with the leading character, as sometimes in Hemingway and Caldwell. At any rate, there is no one there to manipulate our sympathies or point the moral. There is a minimum of exposition as distinguished from straight narrative. The plots are simple, and the stories move straight forward with practically no need for explanation of antecedent circumstances. Whatever the point of the narrative, emotional or intellectual, these men all prefer to leave it to be gathered from the details of the story. For all the imponderable "values," they prefer the method of implication to that of explicit statement.

These men are as well known for their short stories as for their novels. They take their inspiration, I fancy, from the tales of Maupassant, and very likely also from Joyce in his "Dubliners" (1914). I think I can trace also the influence of Sherwood Anderson in tales like those in his "Winesburg Ohio" (1919). But the new men would doubtless repudiate the romantic sensibility of Anderson. Literal and hard-boiled is what they aim to be. Neo-realistic we might call them in contrast to most of the writers I have been discussing in the last dozen chapters. This whole movement, in these and other writers, is for one thing a reaction against the subjectivism, the psychological trend which has been so strong in serious fiction since the days of Eliot and Meredith. And it is in reaction against both the subjectivism of the well-made novel and that of the stream-of-consciousness writers, against the sentimental subjectivism of Hugh Walpole or Joseph Hergesheimer and against the ironic and Freudian subjectivism of

"Ulysses." All this, they seem to say, is so much artificial stuff of the mind which serves only to wrap up and disguise the natural man. And they are bent on divesting him altogether of ideological trappings, whether ethical, rational, or sentimental-erotic.

2

In spirit, though not in technique, they are doubtless more akin to Joyce and Dos Passos, since they show a decided reluctance to employ any terms that might imply they are "taken in" by ideal values. This is partly a post-war phenomenon, a phase of the "debunking" fever which is so strong in modern literature throughout the world, but which has taken hardest of all in young America. There is a very pertinent passage in "A Farewell to Arms," in which the ambulance officer who has been through the Italian campaign expresses his feeling toward the conventional rhetoric of war. A patriotic Italian had expressed to him the view that "what has been done this summer cannot have been done in vain."

> I did not say anything. I was always embarrassed by the words sacred, glorious, and sacrifice and the expression in vain. We had heard them, sometimes standing in the rain almost out of earshot, so that only the shouted words came through, and had read them, on proclamations that were slapped up by billposters over other proclamations, now for a long time, and I had seen nothing sacred, and the things that were glorious had no glory and the sacrifices were like the stock-yards at Chicago if nothing was done with the meat except to bury it. There were many words that you could not stand to hear and finally only the names of places had dignity. . . . Abstract words such as glory, honor, courage, or hallow were obscene beside the concrete names of villages, the numbers of roads, the names of rivers, the numbers of regiments and the dates.

This will suggest one factor in a philosophy of life, widely prevalent in the modern world, which leads to a very distinct tone in recent literature. Of course we must not make too much of the World War as an occasion for this cynical philosophy, which is at least as old as Byron and which years ago had so brilliant an exponent in Anatole France. In any case we find in these new writers a notable reluctance to employ abstract nouns and adjectives of markedly ideal or rational connotation. Passing a certain judgment on life, these writers are disgusted with any terminology which seems to soft-soap the truth. And being literary artists, they have taken the truth for their subject, so that it is an esthetic pleasure to have it shown in all its nakedness. Plain words for plain things, is their motto. Err on the side of understatement rather than overstatement.

Of course no one can live altogether without some positive philosophy, some code of conduct. And these men all have their admiration for certain virtues. In "A Farewell to Arms" it is pluck that seems to serve the characters in lieu of almost every quality for which fine names have been found. By implication this virtue is ascribed to both of the two lovers. And in one of their conversations the reader will find tucked away what we might call the moral of the book. "Nothing ever happens to the brave." That is the nearest Mr. Hemingway ever comes to professing a system of values.

The greatest of virtues for the novelist has always been love. The true lover was forgiven a multitude of sins. But the present time is one in which no writer dare refer, without apology, to the favorite old distinction between love and lust. In "The Sun Also Rises" four or five men go on an expedition to Spain to see a bull-fight, along with a titled English lady, who is a desperate nymphomaniac. Among them all, this Lady Brett is fondest of the one named Jake; but he, unfortunately, has been physically incapacitated in the war for "making love" to any woman. So that she is obliged, in order to satisfy her imperious needs, to take for lover now one, now another of his companions. The last one is so much in love with her that he asks her to marry him. But she turns out to be a woman of honor. She realizes that he is much younger than she, and determines not to ruin his life. It is a fine occasion for sentimental heroics, but what Mr. Hemingway gives us will be sufficiently suggested by this fragment of a conversation at a bar. It is Lady Brett talking with Jake.

"You know I feel rather damned good, Jake."
"You should."
"You know it makes one feel rather good deciding not to be a bitch."
"Yes."
"It's sort of what we have instead of God."
"Some people have God," I said. "Quite a lot."
"He never worked very well with me."
"Should we have another Martini?"

Mr. Hemingway is evidently determined to reduce life to its simplest elements. And these are physical movements, words spoken, and physical sensations: heat, cold, thirst, sleepiness, pain, and the like. On the subjective side, he admits the "fun" of fishing, camping out, and watching a bull-fight, and such simple states as "feeling fine."

He is never tired of eating and drinking, especially drinking, and this last for two seemingly opposed reasons. In the first place it is a simple physical act, hard to sentimentalize, which brings us down to fundamentals. And then, on the other hand, the hard drinking suggests without any comment the rather desperate and disillusioned state of his people. When Catherine is in the maternity hospital, and her lover's heart is torn with impotent rage and grief (as the old-fashioned novelist would say) Mr.

Hemingway says nothing of the sort, but simply records his physical movements, culminating in his consumption of ham and eggs and copious beer:

> I went down the hall and down the stairs and out the door of the hospital and down the dark street in the rain to the café. It was brightly lighted inside and there were many people at the tables. I did not see a place to sit, and a waiter came up to me and took my wet coat and hat and showed me a place at a table across from an elderly man who was drinking beer and reading the evening paper. I sat down and asked the waiter what the *plat du jour* was.

Here, again, is an earlier passage from "A Farewell to Arms" which will suggest not merely the amount of attention bestowed on alcoholic drinks, but also Mr. Hemingway's sentence-structure and something of the character of the dialogue. The convalescent soldier is in bed reading the papers, with the nurse Catherine keeping him company. A servant has just brought whisky.

> He went out and shut the door. I went back to the papers and poured the soda slowly over the ice into the whiskey. I would have to tell them not to put ice in the whiskey. Let them bring the ice separately. That way you could tell how much whiskey there was and it would not suddenly be too thin from the soda. I would get a bottle of whiskey and have them bring ice and soda. That was the sensible way. Good whiskey was very pleasant. It was one of the pleasant parts of life.
>
> "What are you thinking, darling?"
>
> "About whiskey."
>
> "What about whiskey?"
>
> "About how nice it is."
>
> Catherine made a face. "All right," she said.

The two passages just quoted will give a fair idea of Mr. Hemingway's style. He has evidently been at some pains to keep his sentences of the type called simple. There is one rather exceptional sentence with a relative clause. But in general that is a complication which he eschews, as he eschews all other ways of modifying his predicate with subordinate clauses, conditional, concessive, temporal, etc. That, he seems to feel, would open the door to those sophistications, rational or sentimental, which do but serve to falsify the plain facts of experience. People do not think or feel in complex patterns, but in such simple units as these: "Good whiskey was very pleasant. It was one of the pleasant parts of life."

It is true that people do sometimes take in several facts more or less at once; and that allows him to extend his sentences so as to include several predicates connected by *and,* making up the simplest sort of compound sentence. "It was brightly lighted inside and there were many people at the tables." "We had a fine life. We lived through the months of January and February and the winter was very fine and we were very happy." In this type of compound sentence no preference is given one fact over another; they are all on the same level of importance. "I went down the hall and down the stairs and out the door of the hospital and down the dark street in the rain to the café." To make any selection among such items, to subordinate one to another, to arrange them according to significance, would be to introduce an element of sophistication. Life, as we know, is just "one darn thing after another." Similarly, the one simple adjective, "fine" or "nice" or "pleasant" or "damn good," must serve without distinction for the weather, the whisky, or the emotional life of two lovers.

There is, however, one way of signalizing an experience which is more important than others, and that is by saying nothing about it. In the scene in the hospital room, there is something present much more important than the whisky. That is the feeling of the two lovers for each other. Mr. Hemingway's manner of making us feel this is to leave it out of the account. And this is, in general, the secret of his effects. The movements and words and sensations are recorded; the emotions are left to be inferred.

There can be no doubt that for many readers of sensitive taste he gets his effects. One reason is that he has a faculty for ranging the plainest words so as to give them the expressive accent of natural speech. This is particularly notable in his dialogue. On the surface the talk of his people is often trivial enough in matter and sentiment; but somehow he conjures up, by repetition of apparently insignificant remarks, a feeling of tension and emotional import which is both dramatic and satisfying to the esthetic sense.

We are so tired of the musk and lavender of the "nice" writers that in such works as this we seem to breathe the fresh and honest air of the out-of-doors. And then we realize that mere simplicity, when it is deliberate and artful, can be a most telling feature of "style," whether in dress or in the fine arts. What we have been observing in Mr. Hemingway is a deliberate conventionalization, or "stylization" of story-telling. In its own fashion, it is as conventional as the art of Edith Wharton or Virginia Woolf. Only, for certain readers and in certain moods, there seems to be less nonsense about the conventionalizing of Hemingway. Here for once, we say, is a convention working in behalf of the simple and natural.

3

The types of character featured in this group of writers tend toward the simple and plain in occupation and psychology. It is true that the people in "The Sun Also Rises" and "A Farewell to Arms" are world-weary and "advanced," and so, I suppose, what would often be called "sophisticated." But they are people who sturdily refuse to be intellectual or esthetic, as they refuse to be polite or "moral." No doubt the most correct word to apply to them is uncivilized. They represent a deliberate return to the primitive. They believe with Sir Andrew that our life "consists of eating and drinking"—and also, naturally, of "making love."

In "Men without Women" and "In Our Time" much is made of young boys, sportsmen, and men engaged in rough outdoor pursuits. The best pieces in Mr. Caldwell's "American Earth" render the psychology and interest of a boy. Some of these sketches are done with consummate art. They are deceptively simple, but nothing could convey with more delicate humor and sensibility the charm and naïveté of boyhood than "Molly Cottontail" and "Where the Girls were Different." And there are other pieces in which more brutal subjects are handled with the same artful naïveté.

Mr. Dahlberg's Lorry Lewis belongs to the same great class of vagabond young fellows as Dos Passos's Joe Williams—proletarians who know the insides of orphanages, Y.M.C.A.'s, and cheap hotels, who try their hands at anything from cow-punching to chin-shaving, who do their traveling in box-cars, and who find their women in dance palaces or upon the streets. "Bottom Dogs" belongs to the general type of picaresque novels, biographical and episodic as "Roderick Random"; the style is as lively and hard-boiled as Smollett, and almost pure vernacular. This book is a social document of no little interest, comparable in some ways to Pio Baroja's novels of Madrid.

Mr. Burnett in "Little Cæsar" and Mr. Callaghan in "Strange Fugitive" have taken for their heroes simple men engaged in the risky business of bootlegging; Mr. Burnett has turned to prize-fighters in "Iron Man." In Mr. Burnett, while the simplicity is no doubt deliberate, one has no sense of conventionalization. These are simple records of simple people, and that is all there is to it. And while this work has "human interest," it has few of the overtones of significant art.

An altogether different matter is the primitivism of Mr.

Faulkner in "As I Lay Dying" and the Indian tales of "These 13" ("Red Leaves" and "A Justice"), let alone the brilliant and terrible realism of "Sanctuary." A much richer and more subtle psychology is implied in all these. And there is no suggestion, such as clings somehow to all the work of Hemingway, of a delayed maturity, a spirit which takes delight in its newly discovered cynicism and revels in the uncivilized behavior of civilized people.

Mr. Faulkner's characters are not by any means all primitives, though they tend to be degenerates. His primitivism is a true dramatic projection of the dim and groping soul-life of well-meaning creatures confined to the muddy backwaters of ignorance, indigence, and superstition. And over all his work plays the light of a really intellectual, if tragic, estimate of the whole business. "Better for her if she were dead to-night," thinks the lawyer in "Sanctuary" of the pitiful, scatter-brained heroine of that story.

> For me, too. He thought of her, Popeye, the woman, the child, Goodwin, all put into a single chamber, immediate, profound; a single blotting instant between the indignation and the surprise. And I too; thinking how that were the only solution. Removed, cauterized out of the old and tragic flank of the world.

Very similar in theme to Faulkner's "As I Lay Dying" is Mr. Caldwell's "Tobacco Road." Mr. Caldwell's people are Georgia crackers, as poverty-stricken, shiftless, footless as Mr. Faulkner's Mississippians, and characterized by the same callous selfishness, the growth of extreme proverty and ignorance. The misfortunes which they bring down upon themselves are as grotesquely horrid. Only, in Caldwell's variety of naïveté, they take on a humorous, an almost Rabelaisian cast. And yet, such is the quality of his feeling, the very farcical elements are synthesized in an imaginative whole which is notable for a kind of strange atmospheric beauty.

Mr. Caldwell makes more of the economic conditions

that have reduced his farmer to this pitiable state. For so many years now he has been unable to borrow seed and plant his land to cotton. And yet he does not think for a moment of going to work in a factory, where he could make enough to feed his family. He knows that God intended him to stir the soil when the spring comes. And each spring, when he smells the smoke from the burnt-over lands, he is roused to a fever of ineffectual longing to fulfil his destiny as a tiller of the soil. The crude Hebraic piety of these people makes a strange combination with their want of moral sense. Their ancient and childlike philosophy, expressed in their own simple and characteristic language, keeps recurring in identical terms throughout the book, giving it rhythm and pattern, like the incremental repetition of the old ballads.

In this respect it suggests Hemingway, as Hemingway suggests Anderson, and Anderson, Gertrude Stein. Of the three it is Anderson whom Caldwell most resembles, by virtue of a soft poetic bloom there is on all his work. But he has a quality of his own that sets him apart from all others.

Still another matter is the simplicity of Mr. Callaghan. He has something in common with Hemingway, but he does not follow him in the extreme stylization of his subject. His style is plain, but not militantly so. His tone is quiet, but not so quiet as to startle one. His people are not artifically uncivilized sophisticates; neither are they primitives nor degenerates. The bootlegger in "Strange Fugitive" and the choir-singer in "It's Never Over" are plain, ordinary people, quite unaffected by literary convention, such as one may see any day in taxis in the streets of Pittsburgh or Toronto. Each one, it is hinted, has been unfortunately "conditioned," the one by something in his childhood training, the other by his experiences in the war and the difficulty of getting a new start. So that the one finds it most easy to keep his own self-esteem in the gainful but hazardous traffic in alcohol, and the other falls an easy prey to sentimental complications which are of no benefit to him.

Mr. Callaghan is not dead set against the intellectual formulation of his character's feelings and motives where the story seems to call for it. Thus, of the hero of "It's Never Over," trying to rationalize his impulse to commit murder, he is willing to say:

> He liked to think himself a cool, reasonable man, who never found it necessary to move hurriedly, so looking at himself in the glass, feeling the slight growth of beard, he smiled, pleased by his calmness. It was, first of all, with him a matter of strong emotion, but just as essentially an ethical matter, for he was an educated man who had been taught for years that passions should be governed by reason: one ought to consider, then have a judgment and a conclusion, just as they used to in college in the first classes in logic.

When he goes to confession, the young man hears from the priest of an abstraction which Mr. Hemingway would never admit into one of his books: "the fundamental dignity of the human spirit."

Still, such ideal formulations are extremely rare in Callaghan. And one never scents in him the musk and lavender of the more conventional writers. His descriptions of action are sufficient and effective, but very plain. The great bulk of the record is made up of simple movements and sensations; and these are the principal element in the characters' conscious process. Extremely simple and limited are the adjectives employed to characterize feeling.

> The good, simple, joyful feeling remained with him in the bathroom, shaving, and he sang in his strong voice all the vowel sounds in a scale, between each stroke of the razor looking at himself steadily in the mirror, going up the scale, holding the last note a long time. Fully dressed, he went down-stairs to the front room, and standing by the piano, touching the keys with

only one finger, practised the scales for an hour longer. No one was in the house, everything was the way he wanted it to be.

Emotional effects he gets, almost entirely, like Hemingway, by implication. The conclusion of "It's Never Over" is a scene between two lovers on a street corner exchanging quiet words which are an acknowledgement of the end of their love.

They were at the corner where the car stopped. The wind was blowing and Lillian was holding her hat with one hand and her coat down with the other. A car was coming and they went to speak, but the wind carried the words away. It was such a cold wind it was more important Lillian should not miss the car than they should go on talking.

4

It is doubtless significant that all the writers discussed in this chapter are Americans—one of them, Mr. Callaghan, a Canadian. The English have seldom been able to treat a plain man like a plain man, without condescension and patronizing humor. They have been wonderful with gentlefolk, with peasants, with servants—as seen by their masters—with eccentric types from the lower middle class, viewed from the vantage-ground of their betters. But it is very hard for them to view men except through the spectacles of class. To this rule the two most notable exceptions in the period covered are Bennett and Lawrence.

If there is a movement in the English novel to-day which corresponds to that noted in this chapter, it has not come to my attention. The failure of Mr. Priestley, in "Angel Pavement" (1930), to give a really convincing treatment of clerks in a business office, that of Mr. A. P. Herbert, in "The Water Gipsies" (1930), to render in more than picturesque fashion the life of bargemen, the dreary prolixity of Mr. F. O. Mann in his picture of cockney life in

"Albert Grope" (1931), all serve to remind us of the handicap under which English writers labor by reason of their aristocratic tradition. Even Mr. Wells suffered from this, if I mistake not, in his "Kipps: The Story of a Simple Soul" and "The History of Mr. Polly." In spite of his own plain origins, he was unable to avoid the tone of condescension in the treatment of these "simple souls." The advantages of an aristocratic tradition are obvious enough, and we in America suffer for the want of it. But for every quality there is its defect. For most disabilities there are compensating advantages to those intelligent enough to take advantage of them.

I see no reason for talking about a "proletarian" style of fiction as Michael Gold does. His own "Jews without Money" (1930) is a most interesting picture of the life of the poor on the East Side, but it is not at all exclusively a picture of the proletariat. And I cannot see that the feeling in which his stories are bathed is essentially different from "bourgeois" feeling. Mary Heaton Vorse has given us a genuine account of mill workers and labor organizers in her excellent "Strike" (1930). And her manner of presenting this material is as plain and simple, as honest, as it can be made. But the merit of the book is in treating her characters not as proletarians but as human beings "even as you and me." The advantage of getting down to plain people as a subject for fiction is that it tends to do away with much of the artificiality of sentiment that has become associated with the tea-table and the week-end party.

XLIII
RECAPITULATION

It may fairly be stated that in no period of English literature could the greatness of a writer be gaged by his popularity. The great body of readers are quite unmindful of questions of form, and for the most part indifferent to honesty and seriousness in the treatment of human nature. It is only exceptionally that writers of genius, like Scott and Dickens, are among the best sellers; and it is quite conceivable that the very artistic shortcomings of these men were contributing causes of their popularity. Robert Southey tells us that in his time the most popular English poet was the now quite obscure and negligible John Pomfret. In the early nineteenth century the publisher William Lane made a fortune out of the works of novelists like Mrs. Mary Meeke, Miss Sydney Owenson, and Mrs. Kitty Cuthbertson. These were undoubtedly among the most successful writers of the period, and were eagerly read not merely by milliners' girls and young ladies from boarding-school, but by people of the caliber of Jane Austen and Thomas Babington Macaulay. And yet these books were as silly as most of the movies over which serious people relax their minds to-day, and no one but an antiquarian would now think of perusing "Midnight Weddings" or any of the best sellers of the Minerva school.

Again, let the reader consider the enormous sales, over two generations, of General Lew Wallace and Marie Corelli. If the size of one's audience is any test of greatness, then Marie Corelli had reason to complain, as she is reported to have done, that she was not given a box at the opera next to royalty. She had every reason to suppose that she was the most important writer of her time.

Of the twentieth-century writers whom I have treated at length, a considerable number have never been widely popular, but have grown into classics almost in spite of general neglect on the part of even cultivated readers. It is as if there were a want of agreement between novelists of distinction and the great body of readers, the writers wishing to produce one sort of thing and their patrons wishing to read a quite different sort. This situation is not peculiar to the novel. At the present time it is equally marked in poetry, painting, and music. Can we possibly suppose that Cézanne is even yet as widely and wholeheartedly admired as, let us say, G. F. Watts? And is it not notorious that conductors like Stokowski have to cram down the throats of reluctant audiences the most distinguished composers of this age?

Now, I am well aware of the interpretation that many critics put upon these facts. They simply indicate, such critics say, that all the arts have entered upon a decadent stage, and that the mass of the people, being still sound, instinctively protect themselves against the infection by shutting their eyes and ears.

Personally I am not prepared to accept this hasty and facile conclusion. It is really to convict ourselves along with the arts. For they are, after all, our own product, the expression of our own mentality and our own cultural status. And there are too many alternatives to this hypothesis The misunderstanding between creative artists and the *gros public* is a condition with which the student of history is only too familiar. It arises partly out of the natural want of taste of the ordinary man, and partly out of the laziness which leads him to prefer the familiar in the arts and to look with suspicion on everything new in thought and method. We know that nearly every original genius required at least a generation in which to make the public familiar with his idiom, and that accordingly there is a normal interval of at least a score of years between creation and appreciation. And this is not because the genius is an eccentric, speaking a different language from the public. It is often that he recognizes before them, and makes articulate, the language of their own hearts.

Still, it may be true that at the present time the misunderstanding between the public and the creative artist is more acute than usual. And in the case of the twentieth-century novel it is easy to distinguish the features that have temporarily alienated readers, even among the intellectual élite. In the first place, there is the extreme subjectivism so prominent both in the well-made novel and among the "modernists." Where the writers have been most interested in what their characters think, the average reader would rather be told what they do. Another unpopular feature of the later writers is the emphasis laid on abnormal types. Even when they have become reconciled to the tragic histories of Hardy, most readers are likely to be repelled by the psychopathic studies of Joyce, Frank, Lawrence, Faulkner. Insanity they will tolerate in Virginia Woolf because it is not too realistic; and all kinds of perversions in Aldous Huxley because he is so "intellectual." Mainly, however, in twentieth-century fiction, the reader has been baffled by an excess of the intellectual where it is not sufficiently formulated in good set terms. If you are to be intellectual, like Joyce, the average reader prefers that you should give him something tangible which he can carry off and file away with wise sayings of Fielding, Eliot, or Samuel Butler.

And then, finally, the very methods chosen by twentieth-century writers in order to make their narratives more dramatic, more vivid and intimate and real, often serve to make them difficult reading for the "tired business man," sitting down in his easy-chair for an evening's entertainment.

2

Well, it is true that in all the arts, as in the sciences, the specialist has in our day gone far ahead of the layman in precision and elaboration of method. It was possible for the educated reader not a scientist to make something out of the writings of Newton or of Darwin; where, without a specialized training in the higher mathematics, he must give up in despair all hopes of coming near an understanding of Einstein. But the educated man can, without too great difficulty, master the new technical refinements in the arts, and he will do so if he is once persuaded that it is worth his while. Even fiction he is willing to approach with the alert faculties of a student rather than the flabby passiveness of the tired business man, provided only that he has a strong expectation of getting something out of it.

The great Russian novelists were all read in their time with passionate interest, partly of course because they were men of genius, but partly also because they were felt to have something of prime importance to say concerning the spiritual life and the right approach to problems of social organization. For similar reasons Eliot, Meredith, and Zola were read with intense interest. And more recently Wells and Galsworthy have been widely read for what they had to say.

Of the earlier "modernists," the one who is most generally felt to have something to say is Lawrence. Many readers, to be sure, have thought that what he has to say is not altogether sound, that his social and sex philosophy is somewhat vitiated by the hectic and fevered strain of his own emotional make-up. But more and more, even conservatives are coming to recognize how much of significance there is in the one writer of genius who has made a special and honest study of sex psychology in the light of modern knowledge and speculation.

Of more recent novelists in English, the one who is most generally recognized as a genius is Joyce, by virtue both of originality and personal force. And I suppose he is the one most typical of a prevailing and significant attitude toward human nature and the efforts of the human spirit in our time. Which means, in effect, that he is the one who has the most to say.

But several circumstances militate against his being widely read. His most important work cannot be obtained in English-speaking countries without breaking the law. Moreover, his spirit is so corrosively critical that it seems to the average reader to leave nothing standing. It makes them feel as Pavel Petrovich felt, in "Fathers and Sons," when confronted with the "nihilism" of young Bazarov. In this Joyce is typical of the period through which we are going, a period of transition, of ruthless criticism and transvaluation of values. But this state of molting is not a comfortable one for those who are going through it, and readers are not inclined to be grateful to the man who makes them more conscious of their discomforts. Besides, this Joyce is so impersonal, so unwilling to give himself away, that few readers are capable of formulating the results of his criticism. That, again, is incidental to our present phase, which may be—who knows?—a mere by-product of an economic and political evolution in which we are so deeply involved that we cannot even make out its main lines.

That there is such a connection between our spiritual state and some profound metabolism in the social body, is strongly implied in all the novels of Dos Passos. And more and more, as he goes on, there grows palpable in his work something like a positive social idea. But in him, too, the nihilism runs strong, the corrosive criticism of old ideals, as it does in Joyce, in Butler, Dreiser, Lewis, Huxley, Hemingway, Faulkner. And the vast reading public misses in these men, not merely the romantic sentiment they are accustomed to in the novel, but something more fundamental, which for want of a better term we may call humaneness, and which is strongly felt in certain Continental writers like Knut Hamsun and Thomas Mann. What these writers in English have obtained by their ruthlessness is something significant and valuable, but they have paid a high price for it. They have certainly had something to say, but it has been mainly critical and destructive.

But in his later novels Dos Passos, while remaining the conscientious realist, has found the means, within the vehicle of the novel, for projecting a vision of that collectivist ideal which is his own guiding star. And this is bound to win him the attention of serious readers not capable of appreciating the subtleties of his art.

But coming back to Joyce, we are not done with the features which puzzle and repel his readers. His love of riddles, they feel, his literary virtuosity, have a tendency to run away with him. He is the classic example of that disposition among the modernists to pursue technique beyond the point where it can serve the ends of art. The whole trend is, in many ways, a continuation of the nineteenth-century movement of "art for art's sake."

Under the head of "art for art's sake" are often confused two quite distinct doctrines or tendencies, one of them altogether healthy and normal, another harboring the seeds of weakness and decadence. The first is the doctrine of artistic independence, which asserts the right of the artist to treat any subject that to him seems good, irrespective of conventional notions—most often reactionary—of what is suitable for artistic treatment. This doctrine has been the breath of life for all great work, the condition of progress in the arts.

But closely associated with this, in the nineteenth century, was a disposition of many writers to make an artificial distinction between art and life, and to divorce their work from the prime interests of men, turning the broad humane art of letters into a mere polishing of gems. This unhealthy side of the "art for art's sake" movement manifests itself whenever a writer, having little or nothing to say, lays all his emphasis on technique; or when, wishing to be "different," or actually bored with the normal, primary interests of men, he turns his back upon them, and finds his subjects on the remote fringes of life.

I will not assert that either of these cases is largely illustrated in the authors we have been considering. I will not imply that Virginia Woolf has little or nothing to say, when the truth is simply that she deals with elusive and imponderable but essential matters of psychology. I will not say that these twentieth-century writers have been wrong in giving so much attention to the subjective side of experience, or even in taking so much interest in abnormal types and those in which the connection between thought and action is largely broken. These are important aspects of human nature, worthy perhaps of being made a main subject of literary art through a period of one generation. Morbid psychology is, after all, a natural preoccupation of a scientific age. And already, I think, the serious reading public is coming to recognize the high interest and importance of this work.

3

Only, looking forward to probable developments in the coming generation, one anticipates, in writers as distinguished as those we have been considering, a movement away from this intense subjectivism, in favor of a closer connection between thought and action. I certainly do not expect serious novelists to abandon incontinently that psychological intimacy which has been the main fruit, and the *raison d'être,* of all this subjectivism. But they may well use with greater economy the devices for securing psychological intimacy, and bring the thought process to bear more directly upon the major actions and decisions which are the organizing principle of men's lives. That, as one surveys the whole course of literary history, is the normal state of things, as it is seen in Sophocles, in Shakspere, Goethe, Balzac, Hardy. That is one meaning of the movement described under the heading, "The Cult of the Simple." And the same trend is evident in writers with a more complicated technique, like Dos Passos.

Perhaps we may anticipate "a fresh insistence on the story, on plot," as Mr. Carruthers suggests in his acute, but somewhat peevish and dogmatic, essay entitled "Scheherazade: or The Future of the English Novel." But it will not be the plot of intrigue and surprise, or, as Mr. Carruthers describes it, "the old, arbitrary plot, glued to the surface of pasteboard figures." It was against this that the great French and Russian novelists all set their faces. It was this to which the well-made novel gave the *coup de grâce.* And among all varieties of fiction which marked the reaction against the well-made novel, there was none that showed the least disposition to bring back to life the old, arbitrary plot of intrigue and surprise. That seems to have been permanently abandoned to the writers of murder mysteries and historical romance.

Anything may happen in so eclectic a form as the novel. Whatever has been done in this form may be done again. It is natural that present-day writers should imitate the methods of admired masters in any period. It is open to any writer with the genius of Thackeray to employ the somewhat awkward and sprawling methods of that master and win our grateful plaudits. I have no doubt that examples could be found in contemporary fiction of every variety of technique employed throughout the two first centuries of the novel's existence.

Still, on the whole, fashions have changed, and in most cases it has proved unwise to try deliberately to revive the technical methods of our great-grandfathers. The neo-Victorianism of William De Morgan was pleasing in its time, but we still read Dickens rather than De Morgan; and not simply because Dickens was a genius, but also because with him the manner of Dickens was the real thing, instead of being a more or less antiquarian reconstruction. Mr. Priestley is a writer of talent, who has made a distinct effort to treat his material seriously; but one does not feel in him the artistic sincerity, let alone the sparkle, of the Victorian writers.

It is certain that writers of distinction will arise with more cheerful things to tell us of human nature than the majority of those who hold the stage to-day. On the whole, our race maintains considerable courage, good humor, and even gusto in the face of its undeniable limitations and distresses. Such is the instinctive reaction of healthy organisms to the challenge and invitation of life. And this spirit is bound to make itself felt sooner or later in first-rate literature. But that is something which cannot be forced without danger of sentimentalism and insincerity. For a long time now the tide has been running the other way, and there are no great signs of its turning yet. In any case, this is not our present subject. Our present subject is the form likely to be taken by fiction in the future, whatever its content and philosophical tone.

Much depends on the personal idiosyncrasy of future writers of genius who have something to say. But it is impossible to suppose that they can altogether escape the influence of either of the broad movements I have been tracing. The well-made novel, while it has been largely displaced, has continued to influence the later writers in several ways. Even when they proceed on formal principles the most opposite to those of the well-made novel, it has had the effect of making them decidedly form-conscious, and giving a greater finish and precision to whatever they do. It has tended to keep the writers themselves as much as possible out of the picture. It has made them more strongly conscious of the several units of composition, however conceived and arranged in relation to one another. Above all, it has made them aware of the artistic importance of the point of view, whether subjective or objective, whether narrowly limited or deliberately shifted for designed effects. This influence is strongly felt in writers as diverse as Conrad, Joyce, Virginia Woolf, Evelyn Scott, Dos Passos, Wilder, Hemingway, Faulkner. And the psychological intimacy so closely associated in the well-made novel with the limited point of view is felt in many others, like Lawrence, who do not seem to have been much concerned with the technique of the matter. So that in many ways the well-made novel has left a formal heritage which it will be difficult altogether to renounce.

Still less likely is it that the coming writers should be unaffected by the movement in favor of greater freedom and suppleness of narrative method, and a more imaginative treatment, which I have described under the headings of "Impressionism" and "Expressionism." If the writers of these groups have sometimes been carried away by their enthusiasm for new inventions, still the rationale of the new technique has, at every point, been clear enough. We cannot expect novelists to give up that wider social reference implied in the breadthwise cutting of the slice of life and return to the mere record of private lives governed by an individualistic system of ethics. From such varied experiments in form as those of Joyce, Virginia Woolf, Huxley, Frank, Wescott, Dos Passos, Evelyn Scott, it seems most likely that a tradition will be established which will have its followers in the time to come. And whether or not the form "takes," it is inevitable that future writers will be affected by the philosophical (the sociological) bias of which these experimental forms were the expression.

In general, the new writers have brought in use instruments too valuable to be thoughtlessly thrown aside. However much the genius of the future may see fit to modify, to adapt, the new technique, he will hardly abandon altogether such effective means of capturing, for taking off its guard, the elusive, protean thing that we call Life.

BIBLIOGRAPHICAL NOTE

In my first chapter I have mentioned several recent books of special interest in connection with technique—those of Lubbock, Grabo, Muir, Forster, and Edith Wharton. Other studies of the novel as an art form which are often suggestive on points of technique are "A Study of Prose Fiction," by Bliss Perry (1903); "A Study of the Novel," by Selden L. Whitcomb (1905); "The Technique of the Novel," by Charles F. Horne (1908); "Materials and Methods of Fiction," by Clayton Hamilton, with an introduction by Brander Matthews (1908; republished in slightly enlarged form as "A Manual of the Art of Fiction"); and "The Art of the Novelist," by Henry Burrowes Lathrop (1921). Here might also be mentioned "Scheherazade, or the Future of the English Novel," by John Carruthers (1928). "The English Novel, from the Earliest Days to the Death of Joseph Conrad" (1929), being from the hand of Ford Madox Ford, is of course both entertaining and suggestive.

Of general histories of the novel in English during the period covered by this study, the most important are "A Century of the English Novel," by Cornelius Weygandt (1925); "The American Novel," and "Contemporary American Novelists," both by Carl Van Doren (1921 and 1922 respectively). Mention should also be made of "The Advance of the English Novel," by William Lyon Phelps (1916); "Le Roman anglais de notre temps," by Abel Chevalley (1921; American edition, 1925); "Der englische Roman der neuesten Zeit," by W. F. Schirmer (1923); "The Modern English Novel," by Elizabeth A. Drew (1926); "Le Roman américain d'aujourd'hui," by Régis Michaud (1926; American edition, 1928); "Der englische Roman der neuesten Zeit und Gegenwart," by Ernst Vowinckel (1926). I should make particular acknowledgment of indebtedness to those indispensable handbooks by John Matthews

Manly and Edith Rickert, "Contemporary English Literature" (revised edition, 1928) and "Contemporary American Literature" (revised edition, 1929).

Among the more important historical studies of the English novel before the twentieth century are "The Development of the English Novel," by Wilbur L. Cross (1899); "The English Novel," by Sir Walter Raleigh (1894); and "The English Novel," by George Saintsbury (1913). More comprehensive and bringing the record down to the present is the excellent "History of the Novel in England," by Robert Morss Lovett and Helen Sard Hughes (1932). Special studies dealing with the origins of the novel are "The History of the Novel Previous to the Seventeenth Century," by F. M. Warren (1895); "The Rise of the Novel of Manners: a Study of English Prose Fiction 1600–1740," by C. E. Morgan (1911); "Geschichte der Romantheorie," by M. L. Wolff (1915); "Le Roman au temps de Shakespeare," and "Le Roman anglais du dix-huitième siècle," both by J. J. Jusserand (1887 and 1886 respectively).

There is a large number of books in print, both in England and America, with titles like these: "How to Write a Novel," "How to Write Saleable Fiction," etc., which may have been of service to young writers obliged to keep their eye on the common fiction market, but which are not worth mentioning in this study of the novel as an art form. Hardly more to the point are various German studies like "Die Theorie des Romans," by Georg Lukács (1920). This severely philosophic treatise soars as far above our subject—the art of novel-writing—as the commercial handbooks fall below it.

On the other hand, one can hardly overestimate the importance of Zola's "Le Roman expérimental" (1880), of James's prefaces in the New York edition of his novels and tales (1907–09), or of the essays on the novel by Maupassant, James, Stevenson, Eliot, Conrad, and Frank Norris, which have been conveniently brought together by Rollo Walter Brown in the volume entitled "The Writer's Art" (1924). Other books of a special reference which have much to yield to the historical student of technique are "The Eighteenth-Century Novel in Theory and Practice," by Charles Herbert Huffman (1920); "Dickens, Reade, and Collins, Sensation Novelists," by Walter

C. Phillips (1919); "Le Roman réaliste sous le Second Empire," by P. Martino (1913); "L'Esthétique des Goncourt," by Pierre Sabatier (1920); "Zola and His Time," by Matthew Josephson (1928); "The Later Realism, a Study of Characterization in the British Novel," by Walter L. Myers (1927); and "James Joyce's Ulysses," by Stuart Gilbert (1931). Here also I will mention my own monographs on "The Method of Henry James" (1918) and "The Technique of Thomas Hardy" (1922).

Since I deal hardly at all with the short story, I will give no list of books on that subject, mentioning only Henry Seidel Canby's "A Study of the Short Story" (1913), and, once again, Clayton Hamilton's "Manual of the Art of Fiction."

Special mention should be made of "The European Caravan, an Anthology of the New Spirit in European Literature" (Part I: France, Spain, England, and Ireland), edited by Samuel Putnam (1931); a book which contains considerable critical and historical matter along with the selections in verse and prose. While this book lays special emphasis on the underlying emotional and philosophical impulses of post-war literature, there is much incidental reference to resulting tendencies in form. And while it is largely confined to very recent left-wing writers, light is thrown on earlier, now classic writers, especially on the side of their philosophical import. This book will have a special bearing on the novelists discussed in Chapter XLII, and may be of help to persons wishing to forecast the future of the novel.

It would be only too easy to draw up an enormous list of books and articles dealing with the novel, or the English novel alone. I will content myself with calling attention to the more or less extensive bibliographies which are to be found in the above-mentioned works of Messrs. Cross, Horne, Myers, Perry, Van Doren ("The American Novel"), Whitcomb, and Weygandt, as well as in the following: "The Modern English Novel," by Wilbur L. Cross (1928), and "The Typical Forms of English Literature," by Alfred H. Upham (1917).

INDEX

Note: Arabic numerals refer to pages; roman numerals refer to chapters mainly devoted to the author or book named. In general page numbers are given under the title of the book where it is discussed or specifically referred to; otherwise, under the author's name.